1-30-75

THE COMMERCE
BETWEEN THE ROMAN EMPIRE
AND INDIA

THE COMMERCE
BETWEEN THE ROMAN EMPIRE
AND INDIA

by

E. H. WARMINGTON, M.A.

Sometime Scholar of Peterhouse,
Reader in Ancient History and
later Professor of Classics in
the University of London

LONDON · CURZON PRESS
NEW YORK · OCTAGON BOOKS

First published 1928
by Cambridge University Press

Second edition, revised and enlarged, 1974

Curzon Press Ltd · London and Dublin
and
Octagon Books · New York
A DIVISION OF FARRAR, STRAUS AND GIROUX INC.

ISBN
UK 0 7007 0037 4
US 0 374 98250 3

Library of Congress Catalog Card Number: 73-18790

Reproduced and printed by photolithography and bound in
Great Britain at The Pitman Press, Bath

TO

Dʀ W. H. D. ROUSE

THIS BOOK IS
DEDICATED

PREFACE

In this book I have attempted to give, from a western point of view, a history of the commerce between the Roman Empire and India from the triumph of Augustus to the death of Marcus Aurelius. The full story of its decline, of the oriental commerce of the Byzantine era, and its development into the commerce of the Middle Ages would form another volume and finds no place here. Various problems, too, which are incidental to Rome's commerce with the East, have been indicated rather than discussed and I hope to deal with them elsewhere. Readers will find that many items of Rome's trade with Africa and Arabia have been included; this was inevitable in view of the geographical position of India and the development of a special sea-traffic between that region and Roman Egypt. Some of my critics will question the wisdom of separating the Imperial age from the centuries which went before, but there are limits to a work which goes into any detail, and like Mr Charlesworth, I risk willingly the imputation that, in this book on one aspect of ancient commerce, I have given a description of which the beginning and the end are absent.

I wish to thank the Adjudicators for the Le Bas Prize of 1925, and in particular Professor Rapson, in return for valuable suggestions and indispensable criticisms, and the University for allowing me to publish beyond the time-limit. My thanks are due also to Mr L. Eaglesfield of Mill Hill, London, for constant clerical assistance, particularly in reading through the proof-sheets of the narrative, and I owe a special debt of gratitude to Miss E. Abbey of South Kensington for helping me in the translation of M. Khvostoff's monograph in Russian on the oriental trade of Graeco-Roman Egypt. Acknowledgements and thanks are due to W. de Gruyter and Co. of Berlin for permission to insert the illustration which faces page 143. Lastly, I thank the Cambridge University Press for its patience and care.

This book is based upon original sources, but I am much indebted to the work of others, especially for details upon subjects of which I cannot claim expert knowledge, and the extent of my indebtedness is shewn in the notes.

Two points about geography. I have used the expression "Indian Ocean" as including the Arabian Sea, and the expression "East Africa" means the African coast from Bab-el-Mandeb outwards.

E. H. WARMINGTON

Mill Hill, London
  January 1928

PREFACE TO THE SECOND EDITION

Since the first publication of this book in 1928 new discoveries have been made and more research has been carried out of which the main results are given in an Appendix. Opportunity has also been taken, in preparing this new edition, to make some minor alterations or corrections to the text of the first edition.

The original index is retained intact, and does not cover the new Appendix.

Mill Hill, London   E. H. WARMINGTON
   January 1974

CONTENTS

PART II

THE SUBSTANCE OF ROME'S COMMERCE WITH INDIA

SECTION A. THE OBJECTS OF IMPORTATION FROM INDIA

SECTION B. THE OBJECTS OF EXPORTATION TO INDIA AND THE "DRAIN" OF SPECIE THITHER

ILLUSTRATIONS

PART I

Impiger extremos curris mercator ad Indos.

HORACE, *Ep*. I. I. 45.

PART I

THE OPENING UP AND PROGRESS OF ROME'S COMMERCE WITH INDIA

INTRODUCTION

I. FOREWORD

THE first two centuries of the Roman Empire witnessed the establishment and development of a profitable commerce between two great regions of the earth, the Mediterranean countries and India. We need not wonder at this. In the first place, the century after Christ was an era of new discoveries and enterprises, for the western world, after ages of struggle, was united under the firm rule of Rome, and, in the enjoyment of lasting peace and prosperity, was ripe and ready for fresh developments in the intercourse of men; in the second place, the welding of the races of the West and of the near East into one well-governed whole brought into sharp relief the prominent geographical feature formed by Asia Minor, Palestine, Arabia, and the north-eastern corner of Africa. By using the near East as a base, merchants filled with the western characteristic of energetic discovery and the will and power to expand, backed by the governing power of Rome and the prestige of her great name, and helped by Roman capital, were readier to push eastwards by land and sea than they had been before. The moving force from first to last came from the West; the little-changing peoples of the East allowed the West to find them out. We have, then, on the one side India of the Orient, then, as now, a disjointed aggregate of countries but without the uniting force of British rule which she now has and, while open to commerce, content generally to remain within her borders and to engage in agriculture. On the other side we have Rome, also at first agricultural, but now risen after centuries of triumph to be mistress of a vast empire of peoples, with whom and through whom she conducted all her commerce. The peculiar attitude of Indians and Romans towards commerce caused them to meet each other rarely along any of the routes which linked them over long distances, and to conduct their affairs over unexplored seas and dangerous solitudes on land by means of intermediaries. These indispensable middlemen and carriers belonged, from geographical necessity, to the following: (a) Greeks, especially those of Alexandria and Egypt, Roman subjects who spread both east and west in enterprises conducted chiefly by sea; (b) Syrians, Jews, and other peoples of Asia Minor, Roman subjects who moved westwards and along land-routes eastwards; (c) Armenians and Caucasian tribes, Roman allies of very doubtful loyalty; (d) Arabians, non-Roman carriers upon desert-routes and oriental waters; (e) Axumites and Somali, non-Roman Arab-Africans who traded with the far East and the interior of Africa; (f) the Parthians, a great land-power, a rival of Rome, and controlling the great land-route to the far East. Of these, the non-Romans proved a difficult problem to Roman commerce through a succession of principates; the Parthians could place almost unsurmountable barriers in the way by land, and even on the sea, which is open to all, the Romans had to contest the right of control with Arabians and pirates.

If the vast expanse of Europe, Africa, and Asia be contemplated as a whole, it will be found that the long but narrow Mediterranean Sea and the extended curve of the Indian Ocean compress the tract formed by Asia Minor, Palestine, and Arabia, into what may be called a "waist" of land from which the coasts of Italy and India are roughly equidistant. The Mediterranean and Indian seas, thus brought close together, are brought closer still by the two western inlets of Indian waters—the Persian Gulf and the Red Sea, and by them the positions of Syria and Arabia between East and West are emphasised. Lastly, the Red Sea approaches the Mediterranean to within a very small distance at its northern end, especially by means of the Heroopolite Gulf, and this fact fixed as the main channel of Rome's trade with India the sea-route from Alexandria through the Red Sea to the Indian Ocean.

What we have called the "waist" of land received in some part of itself all the routes which connected India with the Mediterranean by land and sea, for the strip of land between the western coast of the Red Sea and the Nile must be included in the "waist." In these intermediate territories were found nearly all the receivers and carriers of Indian merchandise bound for the West; into these regions flocked merchants from the West bent upon oriental trade; within these regions were found nearly all those great cities or races which were made great by seizing the opportunities offered by the reception and carriage of oriental trade.

Beginning with Italy and the Mediterranean Sea, we will work our way eastwards and review the various trade-routes between Rome and India and the nature of the foreign races through which they passed at the time when Augustus made himself master of the Roman world.

II. TRAVEL BETWEEN ITALY AND THE NEAR EAST

Rome had received Asia Minor, Syria, and Egypt into her hands; her empire extended over the "waist" of Asia Minor so as to include all territories as far eastwards as the river Euphrates and the vague frontier separating Syria and Palestine from Arabia, but the arid tracts of the Arabian peninsula she did not control, while the uncouth tribes of the Caucasus mountains, surging between the Caspian and Black Seas, had felt but slightly the power of her military forces. The city itself, which had become the money-centre of the world through the speculative activities of Romans and through wars, had sent crowds of speculators to the near East and had received an extensive free population of Orientals; the old frugal austerity had long given way before the attractions of luxury, and wares of the far East were reaching Rome in some quantity at the end of the second century before Christ. Rome held the West as a unity, but India was not one whole. Central India with both coasts was under the sway of powerful Andhra kings; the north-west was chaotic, for Graeco-Bactrians and pastoral nomads (Sakas) from Central Asia were being driven southwards through Sind regions by the Yue(h)-chi, while Magadha kings ruled the north-east. Three strong Tamil kingdoms occupied the south of the peninsula. The Indians sent no ships farther westward than the Red Sea mouth, letting the Greeks come to them. Thus in dealing with the trade-routes, we start from the West(1).

Although Rome was the largest market for goods from the near and from the far East, the port used for landing the more precious and fragile wares in Italy was not Ostia, where the silting up of the Tiber caused danger and delay (2), but the safer one, Puteoli (Pozzuoli), close to fashionable Baiae, and more favoured for its proximity to the productive works of Campania than for its sheltered harbour, mole, pier, and large docks. Travellers, starting when the lamps were lit, could sail to Rome by night, but merchandise was sent thither along one hundred and fifty miles of road through Capua, Sinuessa, Minturnae, and Tarracina. Trade and travel between Puteoli and Syria and Alexandria were brisk and constant, and the place was a centre for transhipment to the provinces (3).

When the Empire began, one of three journeys was normally taken to the near East—(a) from Brundisium across the Adriatic, along the Via Egnatia, and across to Bithynia or Troas whence great routes to the far East could be reached at Sardis, Tarsos, Antioch, and other centres—a slow journey but available throughout the year; (b) a voyage from Italy to Ephesos by way of Corinth and Athens or round the Peloponnese (4) to Asia Minor and Syria, a route used in summer by sight-seers, leisured men of business, and by traders with Greece; (c) a voyage direct from Rome or Puteoli to Alexandria, where Indian wares destined for the West were concentrated after transport from the Red Sea and even from Antioch and were shipped again to Puteoli, especially from May to September when corn-ships sailed direct between Puteoli and Alexandria, direct voyages between Italy and Syria or Asia Minor being by far less favoured (5). About July strong N.W. winds forced westward-bound ships with cargoes and passengers to sail by night when calms prevailed, or to coast Syria and Asia Minor by means of local breezes (6), while between mid-November and mid-March any voyage at all was exceptional (7).

The firm establishment of Augustus in the principate brought peace and prosperity, and since much trade shifted from the near East to Rome, the Mediterranean Sea had become filled with merchants (8), and the fashionable world began to demand oriental luxuries on a scale unknown before, brought by Greeks, Syrians, Jews, and Arabians in Greek vessels, true Romans (resident not farther east than Asia Minor) helping them with moneyed capital when it was needed. The main channel for these luxuries through the Mediterranean was the sea-voyage from Alexandria to Puteoli, and so we naturally turn to look at the "province" of Egypt first and to consider the relations of that important territory with India.

CHAPTER I

The Trade-Routes between Rome and India

I. EGYPT AND THE SEA-ROUTE TO INDIA

THE great Nile river in a manner unites Egypt to that region of the world which we have called a "waist" of land, and, by way of the Red Sea, the Mediterranean and the Indian Ocean (which throughout this book includes the Arabian Sea of to-day) are placed geographically close to each other. Navigation in the Red Sea dates from very early times, and a definite but mostly indirect trade with India was established by the Ptolemies, under whom Alexandria became the inevitable entrepôt between East and West and a commercial meeting-place for the peoples of three continents, and when Augustus established himself as princeps of an united western world there were two permanent methods of travel between the Egyptian capital and Indian seas, one which avoided the Red Sea as much as possible, and one which braved that treacherous gulf throughout its length. Merchants who preferred the first method started from Iuliopolis on the canal which connected Alexandria with the Canobic arm of the Nile, and navigated that river southwards for about eleven days when winds were fair until the horseshoe-bend of the river was reached. In this region lay Caenepolis (Kenah) and Coptos (Keft) where roads struck out towards the Red Sea. From Caenepolis one track led N. and N.E. for six or seven days to Myos Hormos (Mussel-Harbour, now identified with Abu Scha'ar) while from Coptos another led S.E. for twelve days to Berenice upon the Umm-el-Ketef bay below Ras Benas. Coptos (1), reached through a short canal, was much frequented by Egyptians and Arabians with Indian and Arabian wares, and was in fact the starting-point of both these desert-routes,

for Coptos and Caenepolis were connected by road as well
as by river. Men travelled across the desert by camel or
caravan and generally at night, and the Romans, leaving
the tracks unpaved because of the camels, maintained
the Ptolemaic division of them into stages with fortified
supply-stations, cisterns (hydreumata), and armed guards;
the caravansaries were large and the hostels at Berenice
were considered good (2). The different statements made by
Agatharchides, Strabo, and Pliny shew that the use made
of the two ports varied at different periods. Both had been
established as havens by Ptolemy Philadelphos, but when
Agatharchides wrote in the time of Philometor (181–145),
only Myos Hormos was important, probably because the
Mons Porphyrites was close by the route and because
weather and shoals were a nuisance at Berenice. When
Strabo wrote under Augustus, Myos Hormos, where there
was a naval station, was still the chief port, but Berenice,
with its good landing-places, was rising. Lastly, when Pliny
wrote under Nero and Vespasian, Berenice had surpassed
the other, probably because a land-journey thither passed
near some emerald mines and avoided part of the Red Sea,
and it is possible that ships unloaded at Berenice but lay
in harbour at Myos Hormos (3), which retained, perhaps,
some importance as a receptacle of Arabian wares.

There were other desert-routes between the Nile and the
Red Sea, notably a track branching off from the Caenepolis—
Myos Hormos route at Arâs and leading to Philoteras,
probably at the mouth of the Wadi Guwesis; another
branching from the Coptos—Berenice route at Phoenicon
and leading eastwards to Leucos Limen (Albus Portus, Kosseir); and south of Thebes, a track from Redesiya on the
Nile (near Apollinopolis Magna, Edfu) joining the Coptos—
Berenice route at Phalacro (Dwêg); another from Ombos
joining that route at Apollonos (Wadi Gemal); and one,

beyond Roman influence, from Meroe to Ptolemais (4). Most of these had become unimportant when the Roman Empire began and in my judgment were used chiefly by people who were not in charge of loads of wares, but the route Coptos—Leucos Limen, provided with intervisible beacons as well as with stations, was used fully by loaded camels even in Roman times, and the route Redesiya—Berenice was also so trodden but less and less (5). Choice of route might vary according to a man's taste and to his home, to prevailing winds in the Red Sea, and to disturbances reported from time to time along the desert-roads.

If a man chose to risk the dangers of sea and pirates (6) he could use the ancient canal leaving the Pelusiac branch of the Nile at Phacusse (at least in the time of Augustus, though the point of departure has not been constant), and by taking a journey of seven days from Alexandria along the Wadi Toumilat and by way of the Bitter Lakes could reach the Heroopolite Gulf (Gulf of Suez) where the second Ptolemy, who cleared out the wide and deep canal-channel and added locks to prevent flooding from the Red Sea, had founded Arsinoë or Cleopatris (Ardscherud near Suez). Augustus probably cleared it out afresh, but the frequent south wind and the shoals at Arsinoë continued to deter many an intending voyager (7). We shall describe some important developments in the use of this route which served to connect Egypt with Aela(na) (Akaba), Petra, and distant Gerrha on the Persian Gulf, passing through irrigated country as far as the Gulf of Suez, but under Augustus and throughout the imperial period the route up the Nile to Coptos and then to Berenice and Myos Hormos was the chief passage for the trade with India. Strabo says that in times gone by very few vessels durst pass the Strait of Bab-el-Mandeb, but under Augustus and especially after the expedition to Arabia Eudaemon (Yemen) in 25 B.C.

Arabia and India became better known through frequent trading; one hundred and twenty ships (presumably Egyptian) left for the East every year, visiting India and the Somali in fleets which brought back precious freights to Alexandria—a city which controlled the trade, distributed cargoes to other regions, reaped double customs-dues, and attracted foreigners to a degree above all other marts. He emphasises the importance of Myos Hormos and Berenice in this traffic (8). The merchants who visited India, not yet knowing the best use of the monsoons, coasted all the way in small vessels, perhaps sometimes sailing across from Ras Fartak to the river Indus. In constant dread of the inhospitable and uncivilised Arabian coast and of the shoals in the Red Sea, they sailed under armed guards and with the help of professional guides down the middle of that long gulf or near its western side and called at Adulis (Zula, the present port being Massowa) chiefly for African wares, then on the east side at Muza (Mokha), and having taken in water at Ocelis (near Cella) near Capè Acila at the Strait of Bab-el-Mandeb (9) proceeded into the Indian Ocean and found Indians and Indian wares in African marts of the Somali, in Socotra Island, but above all at Arabia Eudaemon (Aden), a prosperous and wealthy meeting-place of Greeks, Arabians, and Indians. Farther along, in Hadramaut, Cane (Hisn Ghorab) and Moscha (Khor Reiri), both trading with India, invited a call (10). Leaving out most of the Persian Gulf, men coasted along until they reached Barbaricon on the Indus, where Indian, Tibetan, Persian, and Chinese goods could be obtained. Further sailing to the south brought them to the Gulf of Cambay and the Saka mart Barygaza (Broach) on the Nerbudda. Local marts along the coast of India could be visited under the supervision of Andhra rulers who controlled much of the western and eastern shores, but the chief goals were the three Tamil

States of South India—(*a*) the Chera Kingdom, controlling generally the sea-coast from Calicut to Cape Comorin, and possessing the famous pepper-marts, Muziris (Cranganore) and Nelcynda (Kottayam), though the latter may have passed already to (*b*) the Pandya Kingdom, occupying roughly the districts of Madura and Tinnevelly and bounded on the S. and S.E. by the north coast of the Gulf of Manaar to the Palk Strait—a kingdom famous for its pearls of Kolkai; (*c*) the Chola Kingdom stretching along the east side of India from the Vaigai, or at least the Valiyar to Nellore and the river Pennar, and famous for its muslins (11). Ceylon, sending its products to these Tamil peoples, was known to but not visited by Roman subjects who however, according to Strabo, were penetrating to the Ganges by sea in small numbers. He says that their visits to India and the Ganges were rare and hasty, and complains of the unscientific nature of their reports and, as a result, he relies much upon earlier Hellenistic writers, gives no details about the Indian peninsula, and ignores the tributaries of the Ganges (12). Possibly the Greeks were quite unacquainted yet with the proper use of the monsoons even for coasting and for sailing to the Indus, though some think otherwise (13); Roman subjects did not reside yet in India (14), nor did many Indians visit Alexandria, for Cleopatra gave audience to Ethiopians, Trogodytes, Hebrews, Arabs, Syrians, Medes and Parthians; no Indians are mentioned (15).

Through their geographical position and their ignorance of the monsoons, the Greeks of Augustan Egypt were hampered in their trade by the activities of intermediary races. In the first place, a great part of the Indian merchandise now reaching the Roman Empire was obtained by the Egyptians from Arabians. The southern area of Arabia contains the highland plateaux of Asir and Yemen, of which the latter chiefly concerns us. In temperate regions

with productive soil by the sea settled and prospered for
ages the Sabaeans in Yemen or Arabia Eudaemon; these in
the course of centuries, conquering the Minaeans of Jauf,
built up a prosperous and undisturbed trade with India,
their capital being Ma'rib (Mari(a)ba) and their chief mart
Arabia Eudaemon (Aden), named from the district, then
as now the only safe and shoal-free harbour between Suez
and India, and in ancient times a meeting-place of Ptolemaic
Greeks and Indians, particularly from the Indus. These
Sabaeans, together with the Gerrhaeans of the Persian
Gulf, grew immensely wealthy and were for a long time the
chief intermediaries of sea-trade between East and West,
checked only for a short period through the activities of
Ptolemies II and III (16). They made full use of the
sea and of desert-routes, and helped the Africans to exclude
Indians from the Red Sea and to keep secret from the
Greeks the use of the monsoons. About 115 B.C. the power
passed to the Himyarites or Homerites of the extreme
south-west of Arabia and the two came to form one people
under one king. Their importance in Rome's Indian trade
at the beginning of the Empire is shewn by the frequency
with which we find Indians and Arabians coupled together
in Augustan writers (17), and Roman knowledge, even of
the Sabaeans, in their time was vague. The kingdom of
Hadramaut (Chatramotitae), with the dependent Catabanes
and Gebbanitae, was an intermediary of less importance, but
passed oriental wares into a kingdom which, much nearer
Roman borders, created a barrier between the Romans
and direct trade with India, tapping steadily the trade
both of Egypt and of Syria. This barrier was formed by
the Nabataean Arabs of the Suez Peninsula and the N.W.
corner of Arabia, who extended their influence down the
Red Sea coast at least as far as Leuce Come (El Haura) and
to the north-east along the borders of Syria and Arabia even

to the Euphrates. Their very great wealth was due to their caravan trade with the Persian Gulf, with the Sabaeans and (through the Gebbanitae) with Hadramaut, and also to their bitumen traffic with Egypt, their geographical position giving them great advantages: thus their capital, Petra (Sela, and perhaps Rekem) in the Wadi Muza between the Dead Sea and the Aelanitic Gulf, with which it was connected, received wares from Leuce Come and passed them on to Rhinocolura (El Arish?) on the confines of Egypt and to Gaza ('Azzah, now Ghuzzeh) for distribution in the Mediterranean; at Petra too roads to Hebron and Jerusalem branched off from a track leading from Aelaṇa (Akaba) to Bostra, Damascus, Palmyra, and other Syrian centres; short tracks led across Sinai to Arsinoë or Pelusion; great routes ran from Petra to the Persian Gulf and to South Arabia—one through northern deserts to Forath and Charax (Mohammarah); another through Thalaba and Dumaetha to Gerrha (El Katif or perhaps Koweit), one through Leuce Come to Arabia Eudaemon and to Hadramaut, and another well inland to Hadramaut. All these routes carried Indian wares and Aelana received Chinese fabrics also, destined for Syria, but in Strabo's time it was the camel-traffic between Petra and Leuce Come (which was both a port and a station on a caravan-track) that had reached such large dimensions. Small wonder that the unfortunate tendency of the Nabataeans towards piracy on the Red Sea was giving way to more peaceful occupations (18). Almost the whole of their traffic was conducted without touching Egypt, which was thus perpetually a rival in commerce, but goods could be sent across the Peninsula of Sinai or across the Red Sea to Myos Hormos and Berenice in order to avoid a long journey by sea.

In the second place, some of the Arab-African peoples of

the marts of the Somali, and carrying on a traffic of very long standing with Indians of Cambay in Indian, African, and Arabian shipping centred at the Cape of Spices (Cape Guardafui), were beginning to unite themselves into an inland Axumite kingdom of Abyssinia, with Auxume or Axum as the future royal seat and Adulis in the Red Sea as the main port. With the Arabians and the now free Somali they held several trade secrets and perhaps persuaded the Indians not to go nearer to Egypt than Ocelis at Bab-el-Mandeb (19) even in the time of Augustus. King Iuba recorded a "Promunturium Indorum" on the Egyptian coast of the Red Sea, near the confines of Ethiopia; Pliny's sole mention of Barygaza, the chief centre of this commerce on the Indian side, is to say that some held it to be an Ethiopian town "on the sea-shore beyond," and the monolith at Axum is Buddhist in its inspiration (20). Hence arose that confusion between Ethiopia and India which caused writers, chiefly of a later age when Rome's trade had once more fallen into Axumite-Ethiopian control, constantly to locate India and Indians in the regions of south-east Arabia and the east coast of Africa (21), where so much Indian trade was centred.

By land, too, these Abyssinians controlled a route from the Red Sea across the Tigre highlands to Meroe and by the Atbara river to the Nile, which was then followed to the marts Elephantine and Syene, where the river became navigable with ease. Meroe had once been a centre of trade between the Red Sea and Libya, but the increasing use of the Red Sea by the newly-rising Axumites and the difficulties and expenses of a Nile voyage to Meroe from the Roman point of view caused this kingdom to decline; Nero's explorers found Meroe almost a solitude (22). The Axumites preferred more and more to meet the Greeks at Adulis, at Somali marts, and probably on the island of Socotra (Dioscorida) inhabited by a mixed population of Arabs, Indians, and Greeks under Arabian control, and visited by merchants going to and from India (23).

The veiled hostility of Parthia, the irruption of "Scythian" tribes into Central Asia, the great length and uncertainty of the land-routes, and the enormous expense incurred in buying wares from the desert-routes of Arabia—all those considerations influenced the Romans towards using so far as possible the route through the Red Sea, and the constant presence of the "Sabaean," Nabataean, and Axumite middle-men along that route impressed upon Augustus, for the sake of his empire's welfare and for the sake of his own interests in Egypt (part of his own domains), the necessity of taking steps to make the Roman trade with India easier and more profitable for state and people. With reference to Egypt itself, he cleared out the canals; maintained a military camp at Coptos and employed the soldiers in repairing the cisterns on the roads leading to Myos Hormos and to Berenice (24); established (so far as we can tell) a strategos as receiver (παραλήπτης) of the dues of the Red Sea (25) in the districts of Ombites, Philae, and Elephantine, doubtless in order to supervise the tax-farmers who were sent down to levy the dues of Myos Hormos and Berenice (26); reproduced a Ptolemaic system so that a strategos or the epistrategos of the Thebais, assisted by an Arabarches and a prae-fectus montis Berenicidis(-es), had military supervision over the routes from Coptos to the harbours and perhaps over the Red Sea as far as the Strait (27); maintained local or transit-dues, for instance at Coptos, Syene, Hermonthis, Fayum, Hermupolis, and Schedia near Alexandria; and levied road-dues on persons using the desert-routes (28).

Considerable efforts were made by Augustus in opposition to the powerful intermediaries of which we have spoken. The Himyarite-Sabaeans, prosperous and secretive, were the most substantial barriers to direct trade between Roman

territory and India along the sea-route, and against them
Augustus turned the force of Roman arms. In 25 B.C., influenced by reports of their wealth and, without a doubt,
desirous of controlling the traffic in oriental spices, aromatics, precious stones, and so on, of which many were
attributed to the peoples through whose hands they passed,
he sent out Aelius Gallus to explore southern Arabia and
Ethiopia and to subdue where he could not conciliate, but
the expedition, which crossed from Arsinoë or Cleopatris
to Leuce Come and was assisted dubiously by Nabataeans
and Jews, failed to injure permanently the Himyarite power,
failed perhaps to reach even Mari(a)ba the capital, and,
after crossing from Egra to Myos Hormos, returned through
Coptos to Alexandria. However, the Romans increased their
knowledge and made an impression upon the Sabaeans and
Himyarites, who put the head of Augustus on their coins (29).
Commercial schemes were renewed in connexion with the
journey entered upon by Gaius in 1 B.C. From what we
know of the work of Iuba and the investigations made for
Augustus by Isidore and apparently Dionysios, both of
Charax, and from Pliny's implication that there was a
Roman fleet in the Red Sea at this time, we can safely conclude that Augustus had planned a circumnavigation of
Arabia by two fleets, one starting from the Persian Gulf,
one from Egypt (30). With the death of Gaius the scheme
was abandoned but, as Augustan writers shew, Rome was
excited with the prospect of military glory in the East (31),
and the Red Sea fleet may have destroyed, dismantled, or
occupied Arabia Eudaemon at this time. The fate of this
mart is referred to by only one authority—the *Periplus of
the Erythraean Sea* of Nero's time, but the date, author,
and nature of the event are much disputed. But since the
author of the *Periplus* says plainly that not long before
his time "Caesar" subdued (κατεστρέψατο) the place, I have

no doubt that one of the earlier emperors must be held responsible, and the overthrow must have occurred before the Greeks fully discovered the use of the monsoons—for after that, military action was not needed (32). Of a Roman control over the Himyarites I can find no real evidence. By Nero's time Himyarite Muza inside the Red Sea had taken the place of Arabia Eudaemon, which however was destined to rise again as Adane.

Hadramaut was too far round the Arabian coast, and the dependent Catabanes and Gebbanitae were too far in the desert to come within the reach of Roman armed forces, but the activities of the Nabataeans were adequately controlled (33), their pirates on the Red Sea being chastised, probably with the approval of Petra, and there can be no doubt that the kingdom had become a client of Rome (34). Perhaps it was Augustus who instituted at Leuce Come a very high due of 25 per cent. (τετάρτη), which, I think, was a protective due levied by the Nabataeans for their own treasury at the command and under the military supervision of the Romans who wanted to drive trade to Egyptian ports. At any rate, Pliny states that goods from South Arabia passing through the Nabataean territory paid *Roman* dues first at Gaza and that the expenses of that route were enormous (35). The friendship of the Nabataeans with Rome was uncertain, and though Nabataeans came westwards to Rome and Puteoli, and Roman subjects frequented Petra, quarrels over lawsuits were frequent and the loyalty of the Arabs was unreliable (36).

In the case of the Ethiopian trade, which was not a brisk one except by sea, something was done by Augustus, but only in connexion with the kingdom of Meroe. Thus, in 29 B.C. Cornelius Gallus, after suppressing a revolt in the Thebais including Coptos and caused by the arrival of Roman tax-collectors, arranged that the region above the First Cataract

visit Antioch, there was the road from Ephesos through
Phrygia, Lycaonia, and Cappadocia to Melitene (Malatia),
near which the Euphrates was bridged at Domisa (45), and
another well-known route from Smyrna passed through
north Phrygia, Galatia, south Pontus, and Lesser Armenia to
Eriza through Satala, which was the goal of important roads
through the north part of Asia Minor also. Other important
crossings of the Euphrates were at Samosata and Zeugma
where the river was bridged to Apamea (Birejik) and soon
a legion and a customs-house were established there, for
it was a normal meeting-place for travellers going eastwards
(46). From here Mesopotamia was traversed south-eastwards
along the Euphrates or through the Arabes Scenitae to the
neighbourhood of Seleucia and Ctesiphon on the Tigris,
but in hot summers men often travelled from Melitene,
Samosata, and Zeugma through north Mesopotamia to
the region of Ninos (Nineveh) on the Tigris, whence they
reached the main route to the East either by turning south
to Seleucia or by proceeding east through old Arbela to
Ecbatana (47). All these routes avoided the Armenian
hills, but client kings held Melitene and Samosata.

But the great main route to the far East began at Antioch
in Syria (48). From here roads led to places on the Euphrates,
notably Thapsacos near Kal'at Dibse where, however, Arab
hordes were troublesome (49), and Zeugma, which became
the favourite meeting-place. The route then lay through
Anthemusias and then either roughly along the course of
the Bilecha to Nicephorion whence the left bank of the
Euphrates was followed all the way to Greek Seleucia
or else by a desert-road three days' distance from the
Euphrates but well supplied with resting-places and cisterns
and leading through the Arabes Scenitae who were friendly
and levied moderate dues. This road led to Parthian Ctesiphon, but the only disadvantage was Parthian raids which

centred often at Circesium (Buseira) (50). From Ctesiphon, frequented (51) by Roman subjects, the route lay eastward to the plateau of Iran which, consisting of the modern Persia, Afghanistan, and Baluchistan, was controlled by the ill-cultured, uneconomical, and loosely-ruled Parthians as far as the Hindu Kush range with its southern extension, the regions beyond being in the hands of tribes whose friendship was cultivated by both Rome and Parthia. The plateau is subject to extremes of cold and heat, and in the lowlands running waters are hardly known—hence the stations or "mansiones" into which the great land-route to China was divided in ancient times, though the problem of water-supply was not so great then as it is now, for after the melting of snows in Central Asia water is known to be valued at its own weight in silver. The plateau is approached normally by way of Mesopotamia so as to avoid the hills of Armenia, and the secret or open hostility between Rome and Parthia drove Roman subjects to using the Euphrates as far as possible. From the regions of Mesopotamia eastwards the geographical conditions of western Persia, Makran, and Baluchistan, which are riven by long lines of ridges and valleys more or less parallel to the southern coast, have caused travellers to follow not the shortest routes either to Afghan Turkestan with Badakshan (Bactria of the Greeks) or to India, but to take easier though longer ways through more favourable country. The Himalayan range to the north of India was in normal circumstances no serious obstacle to India's western trade, for the main passes were used only for trade with Central Asia along ancient routes about 18,000 feet in altitude leading from Punjab into East Turkestan; we are concerned therefore chiefly with the mountains of North-west India—the Hindu Kush, Suleiman, Safed Koh, and the western Kirdar groups, with the lower offshoots to the south—the Hala, Brahui, and

Pab mountains which separate India from Baluchistan. In these ranges lay the gates of India. The Hindu Kush mountains (Paropanisos, Caucasos (52)), which form a broad ridge jutting out westwards from the Himalayas for 500 miles and separate the river systems of Oxus and Indus, are pierced by many passes, some of them of great altitude, and all of them difficult, especially in their approaches, but successfully used by tribes, armies, pilgrims, and traders, in all ages. The Baroghil Passes are the chief ones which link high Asia to Chitral and Jellalabad. After the mountains bear away south-west from the Oxus, and overlook the deserts of Badakshan, there are more passes, in particular the Dorah group rising 15,000 feet and connecting the Oxus and Chitral basins. The Khawak group (12,000 feet) links Badakshan with Kabul across the Hindu Kush, while the Irak Pass links Balkh with Kabul across the Koh-i-Baba range. Of the Khyber, Kurram, Tochi, and Gomal Passes which connect Afghanistan with India, the Gomal now forms the chief entrance, but in ancient times the Khyber held the first place. There were three natural approaches to India from the West—(a) where the mountains of Afghanistan "become very narrow just north of the head of the Kabul river" where only the Hindu Kush separates the basins of the Oxus and the Indus; (b) 500 miles to the west and south-west, where the Afghan mountains end and an easy way round lies over 400 miles of plateau from Herat (Alexandria of the Arioi) to Kandahar (Alexandropolis) whence Kabul can be reached along the Helmund valley while south-east of Kandahar the way descended through the mountains into the Indus lowlands by the Bolan or the Mula Pass, entering opposite the Thar or Indian desert; (c) by way of barren Makran and then through the Mula or Mulla Pass or else near the coast of Baluchistan, "routes much frequented by Arab traders in the Middle Ages," but not favoured by the Greeks of Roman times even though the entrances into India are easy ones (53).

In Augustus' time merchants had not penetrated by land to India, but they had travelled over a good length of one route. From Greek Seleucia and its Parthian rival Ctesiphon (54) they went eastwards out of Assyria across the Zagros mountain (Jebel Tak) in Kurdistan into Media, past the rock of Behistun near Kermanshah, through Ecbatana (Hamadan, the summer residence of Parthian kings), and Rhagae (Kaleh Erij near Rhey or Rai near Teheran) to the Caspian Gates, forming the Teng-i-suluk Pass in the south-western spur of the Elburz range (55). The route then continued through Apamea and the old Hecatompylos, a Parthian centre (near Jah Jirm?), and its supplanter Apauarctica or Dara, probably near Meshed, to Antiochia Margiane (Merv), and here divided; two branches formed the great silk-routes to Central Asia and leaving the Hindu Kush on the south were not explored yet by Roman subjects; another branch turned south-wards towards India, this also being very little known as yet by the Romans, for Isidore gives few details between Merv and Alexandropolis (Kandahar) where his route ends (56). We may take it that Merv was the limit of Roman knowledge under Augustus, though the Romans had heard of the Sacae (Sakas) and of the Seres, that is the Chinese, meaning at present no more than the tribes of Central Asia (57). For details of routes east of Merv we have to rely upon Ptolemy who reveals the greater knowledge of the second century A.C. and upon Strabo and Pliny who rely upon Hellenistic writers. The silk-routes from Merv eastwards deserve our notice only because they had branches leading into India from the north. The route leading from Merv through Maracanda (Samarkand) crossed the Oxus and could tap its trade, and another route striking out from Merv reached Bactra (Balkh), a natural meeting-place of men, and led on through the Comedoi and the Sacae to the "Stone Tower" (that Tashkurgan which is in Sarikol, 12,000 feet above sea-level) where routes converged from India, the valley of the Oxus, and from Khotan, Yarkand, and Kashgar; here too the Chinese met the Parthians, Indians, and Kushans and later the Romans as well, and handed over their silk. From it the natural route for silk traders lay through the Yarkand valley to Daxata (Singanfu), capital of the Chinese, having been opened to western trade a little before the first century B.C. (58). By the sixth century A.C. the whole route was divided into about four hundred halting-places (59).

To reach India from Bactra terrifying defiles through the Hindu Kush or the Koh-i-Baba range had to be crossed, most of those within the Hindu Kush converging near Charikar, near which Alexander founded his "Alexandria under Caucasos." The normal crossing lay through the Irak or the Unai Pass over the Koh-i-Baba to Kabul (Ortospana, the Kabul river being called Cophen) and then south-east over the Khyber Pass to Peshawar; or the Ghorband valley could be crossed by the Shibar Pass, other crossings being of recent creation. From Kabul and the Khyber Pass the Indus, navigable to its mouths, was reached through Gandhara (Peshawar and Rawal Pindi), while through Taxila and Modura a route across Punjab reached Palibothra (Pataliputra, now Patna) on the Ganges, with a branch south at Modura through Ozene (Ujjain) to Barygaza (60). Thus was India linked with the silk-routes by roads leading north. But merchants who wished to deal with Indians only would turn southwards from the great route at Merv if not at Dara, and pass by an easy journey through Alexandria of the Arioi (Herat), Prophthasia or Phra

(Furrah, Farah?) in Drangiana (roughly Seistan) and then eastwards to Alexandropolis or Alexandria of "Arachosia" (Kandahar) in Afghanistan (61). By this means the western end of the Safed Koh mountains near Herat were the only heights to be crossed. From Kandahar one of three routes was taken. One went south-east and crossed the mountains into India by the Bolan Pass, or rather in a loop by the Mula Pass, but a more frequented one went north-east from Kandahar so as to join at Kabul (62) a branch from the silk-route after this had crossed the Hindu Kush, merchants probably desiring to reach at least the distant vicinity, so to speak, of the silk marts of Central Asia. A third way lay south from Kandahar through Rhambacia (near Bela in Las Bela) and then by road or by the river Purali to Oraea (in Sonmiani Bay) whence India could be reached by sea (63), or through low mountains.

Thus in ancient times two of the three natural approaches to India were in use. Were the route through central Persia and the approach to India through Makran at all important? A road from Babylon and Susa and another from Ecbatana on the silk-route met at the old Persepolis in Persis, whence a single road went through Carmania (the district Kerman) and Gedrosia, never very far from the Arabian Sea, through low mountains into the regions of the Indus. From Rhagae, too, on the silk-route a road went south-east through central Persia by way of Istachae or Isatichae (Yezd) to Carmana (the town Kerman): from here a branch joined the Persepolis—Indus route at Gulash-kird, but a more important one went through Neh to Prophthasia, and another from Gulashkird following the curves of the river Helmund to Kandahar and so to Kabul, or on to the Mula or the Bolan Pass farther south. Persepolis too was joined by road with Carmana and so with Kabul. The Romans of the Empire may have travelled (64) to Kabul by way of Persepolis and Carmana,

but there is no sure sign of the Makran route in the Peutinger Table and the Romans never knew much even about
Persepolis (after A.D. 200 Istakhr). I conclude then that
these routes were avoided by Roman subjects because
(a) although they had been trodden from prehistoric
times (65), Alexander first opened any up to western knowledge, and he and his followers became acquainted only
with the chief route as far as Merv and Samarkand, and
with the simplest way to India through Herat and Kandahar, and with the regions of Kabul and Bactra, while
the Seleucids and to a less extent the Parthians naturally
developed trade along routes which he had surveyed: but
his return from the Indus through the lonely desert wastes
of Makran was disastrous, and gave that route a bad
reputation; (b) the establishment of a real silk traffic on
the great silk-route just before or during the first century
B.C. drew merchants away from the use of other routes,
and any merchant of Parthia who wished to trade with
India, not the Chinese, would leave that silk-route at Merv
and take the Herat—Kandahar route; (c) the territory of
Baluchistan is in all truth forlorn and arid; (d) the Makran
route was too near the Persian Gulf which was connected
with India by a tolerably safe coasting route; (e) Persis
itself, in reality a vassal state of Parthia, tended to dis-
integrate and there were sometimes independent kings in
Carmana. Thus any variation from a well-provided route
through convenient north Parthian valleys was felt to be
not worth while, and therefore the routes through Persepolis and Carmana were of little importance, and the
Makran route of none at all, except perhaps to the kings of
Mesene and Characene in their trade with the Kushans
on the one side and with Roman Syria and Petra on the
other. Really wealthy towns rose and flourished for
centuries only on the well-provided silk-route to China
with its branch at Merv to India (66).

Besides these routes which we have described, there was a route along which Indian goods were sent to Russia and to the West, but which was not used in person by western merchants; it left Central Asia by the river Oxus (Amu Darya) and proceeded across or round the Caspian to the Black Sea. We do not know much about this route and its Indian trade, and it is doubtful whether any Greek saw the river Oxus except in the neighbourhood of Bactra, and this would mean that the volume of trade conducted down that river was not large in comparison with the trade along the routes which we have pointed out. Nevertheless, such commerce does, as I shall attempt to shew, provide one possible reason for the political negotiations carried on by Rome with Parthia over the possession of Armenia and for the relations existing between Rome and the tribes situated between the Euxine and Caspian Seas.

Strabo shews that in the time of Alexander the river Oxus was so easily navigable that wares of India were conducted down it to the Caspian Sea and then to the Euxine by other rivers—normally up the Cyrus (Kur) from its mouth into Albania, round the eastern part of the Caucasus chain to the sources of the Phasis (Rioni, Rion), and so to the Euxine Sea and the Mediterranean, or up the Araxes (Aras) valley from its mouth to the Armenian city Artaxata whence routes spread into the western parts of Asia Minor. The carriers were Medes, Armenians, Aorsi, and Siraces (67). Pompey learnt further details of this commerce; after a seven days' journey to the Iachrus (?) river which flows into the Oxus, people could be conveyed down the Oxus and across the Caspian to the Cyrus river, and Indian wares could be brought to Phasis (a town near the mouth of the river Phasis) in Colchis in not more than five days (68). The Phasis river and the Cyrus were connected by a paved road of four days' travel, and from the large fortress Sarapana (Scharapani) the river Phasis was navigable; after that a few days brought men to Amisos (Eski-samsun) and Sinope (Sinab) which was served by land-routes also. It seems that the Chinese found an established Oxus traffic at the end of the first century A.C. (69). Roman territory began with Colchis.

There can be no doubt therefore that the traffic existed during the opening centuries of the Roman Empire. The fact that the Oxus does not flow into the Caspian but into the Sea of Aral creates a problem which we shall not discuss here. In prehistoric times the Aral and the Caspian and much of what is now dry land may have been one large inland sea, and in historical times the Oxus may have had a branch leading into the Caspian, but it seems safer to conclude that after a journey down the river wares were carried by land to the Caspian and then across or round it (70).

There is no doubt too that not even the Greeks penetrated and thoroughly explored these regions, for Patrocles is the only one recorded as having sailed on the Caspian— Dioscurias, Phasis, and the Tauric Chersonese being the limit of eastward navigation even under the Roman Empire. Writers between Aristotle and Ptolemy were under the impression that the Caspian was connected with the "Ocean" to the north, and we find not only remarks about the bad conditions of navigation in the Caspian Sea, but constant allusions and references to the wild, uncouth, and inhospitable nature of Caspian and Caucasian regions and tribes (71). The shipwrecked "Indians" who were living as slaves among the Suevi or among the Boii were perhaps, as Lassen conjectured, victims of Caspian storms (72). We may compare the colony of Indians which existed in Armenia from 130 B.C. to about A.D. 300. These were descendants of fugitives rather than merchants, for the travels of Indians

westwards were few and far between (73). Neither Alexander
nor any Seleucid or Graeco-Bactrian monarch tried to
control this trade-route; nor did the Parthians, and we
cannot trace private activity even under the Roman
Empire and Ptolemy's lack of good knowledge is surprising.
Hence there is a tendency (74) to belittle the importance of
the route in ancient times. At any rate the Romans left
the trade in the hands of middlemen, perhaps in order to
avoid offending Parthia, contenting themselves, as we
shall see, with obtaining influence among the tribes.

We may take it, then, that in ancient times Indian
merchandise was sent out of India through ordinary channels to the silk-routes at Tashkurgan and at Bactra close
to the Oxus and that some of it was sent down the Oxus and
perhaps the Iaxartes through the nearly desert and low-
lying plain which includes Bokhara, Khiva, and Turkestan
proper, a region always infested by robbers except when
disciplined by a strong power, and in ancient times
peopled by wild and little-known tribes grouped under the
common name Scythae. Whether roads were used is uncertain, their absence from the Peutinger Table and other
sources being due perhaps to lack of exploration. As far
as the Caspian Sea the carriers must have been Indians,
Bactrians, Hyrcanians (of Tabaristan and Mazenderan),
Parthians, and Scythian tribes. Once upon the Caspian,
navigators had to reckon with the winds which generally
blow from the south-east between October and March,
and from the north and north-west between July and
September, with the extreme cold in case of the winter
season and with the ever present and most dangerous storms
which often forced carriers and merchants to skirt the
shores (75). If the wares were directed to the south-west
shore they were received by Armenians and by various
Caspian tribes controlling the ridge of the Caucasus

mountains stretching across the neck of land which divides
the Caspian from the Euxine, the Albanians occupying the
eastern end of the ridge, the Iberians the central portion,
and the Colchians the western end. The traffic along the
Cyrus, in spite of deposits of mud, had helped to make the
Albani and Iberi wealthy and prosperous tribes, while
in Colchian territory the river Phasis took its rise and,
receiving at Sarapana wares which came along the paved
road from the Cyrus, conveyed them to the town Phasis
by the Euxine Sea. From here the wares could be taken
across that sea or along the northern roads of Asia Minor
to the Bosporus, Hellespont, and Aegaean Sea, or spread
over Asia Minor, some taking routes towards the manufacturing towns of Syria. Towns like Trapezus, which held
relations with Alexandria, were made strong and wealthy,
perhaps to the detriment of older ones such as Sinope (76).

Instead of being taken up the Cyrus, wares could be sent
from the south-west shores of the Caspian up the Araxes
to Artaxata in Armenia and then spread over Asia Minor,
or they could be landed along the north-west shores of the
Caspian and taken over by the Aorsi who in their turn
passed them on to the Siraces north-east of the Euxine. The
Siraces probably passed them on to the Greek cities of the
regions of the Tauric Chersonese, and perhaps especially to
Panticapaeon Olbia and Tanais, a mart common to Asiatic
and European nomadic tribes on the Tanais or Don river.
Already we can trace the Khazars whose home was on the
spurs of the Caucasus and the shores of the Caspian. These
and the Barsileens with their capital on the Volga (Rha)
were destined to become the organisers of transit-trade
between the Euxine and the Caspian basins, but they do
not appear in history until after A.D. 190. Nevertheless, we
can trace the Barsileens in the "Royal Scyths," so called
"from their political superiority and commercial enterprise,"

well known to the Greek colonies of the Euxine as inhabitants dwelling north of Lake Maeotis. That they
controlled to a certain extent the oriental traffic between
the Caspian and the Euxine at the beginning of the Roman
imperial period is probable (77). From the Euxine westwards
the Mediterranean was doubtless used except perhaps in
winter when the Via Egnatia was favoured. That Indian
wares ever went from Byzantium to Italy by way of Serdica
(Sofia), Naissus (Nisch), Singidunum (Belgrade), Emona
(Laybach), and so to Aquileia is most improbable.

The question of traffic between India and the West by
way of the Persian Gulf would seem perhaps to find a place
in the description of the sea-route to India, but in reality
this channel between East and West was far removed from
Rome's idea of a sea-route thither; the broad neck or
waist of land formed by the Arabian peninsula has to be
crossed and that region is a desert one. Nevertheless it
was an important route at all times between Rome and
India in that in distance it was the shortest passage and
lay roughly midway between the Red Sea route and the
main overland route.

From the West the Persian Gulf, itself generally under
Arab or Parthian control, was and is approached either by
the Euphrates or by desert tracks; in the centuries preceding
the Roman Empire the merchants of Gerrha on the Arabian
side had controlled the passage of goods up the Euphrates
to Thapsacos and distributed them to all parts by land (78);
they had controlled traffic in spices across the desert to
Petra and so to the West; yet early in the imperial period
Charax Spasinu(-i) at the mouth of the Tigris, in spite of
the continuous deposits of silt, as a stronghold of the
Parthians eclipsed Gerrha; Charax was connected by road
with the silk-route at Seleucia; by river and road with
Palmyra (Tadmor) and Syria; and by a desert-route across

northern Arabia with Petra (79); the kings of Mesene and Characene, using Charax, Forath, Apologos and other harbours, set up trade with Kabul and Punjab by land and with the Indus and Broach by sea and embassies passed at times between Rome and Charax (80). Besides these marts, Ommana (in the bay of El Katan?) traded in precious woods from Broach in India (81). Merchants could travel to India by the Persian Gulf from the meeting-place at Zeugma or by going through Petra, and on their way from the East by land they could use the gulf in order to reach Egypt by sailing round Arabia (82).

Having traced and discussed every route (83) leading from the Roman Empire to the shores and gates of India, we must indicate here the chief routes used in India itself. When merchants entered India from the West they could descend the Indus and so avoid the Thar or they could use the Royal Road, built by the Maurya rulers across North India to the Ganges, marked off into stages and kept in good repair. It began at Peucelaotis (Pushkalavati, now Charsadda), reached by the Kabul valley, and went across the Indus, through Taxila (Shahderi), across the Hydaspes (Jhelum, Jihlam), the Hyphasis (Beas), the Hesydros (Sutlej), and the Iomanes (Jamna, Jumna), and apparently through Hastinapura to the Ganges. Then the road went by way of Rhodopha (Dabhai), Calinapaxa (Kanauj?), Prayaga near Allahabad and Palibothra (Patna) to the mouth of the Ganges probably at Tamluk (84). Thus the north of India was linked with Iran by a well-provided trade-route. Well beaten but to a Roman subject difficult tracks joined north and central India with the north-west coast. Roads from Pat(t)ala (Haiderabad in Sind) and Barygaza met at Ozene (Ujjain) and continued to Modura (Muttra) where the Royal Road was joined (85). The Andhra kingdoms were joined to the north and west by two ancient tracks starting one from Masulipatam, and one from Vinukonda, meeting near Haiderabad (not that in Sind) and continuing through Ter, Paithan, Dowlatabad, Chandore, Markinda, to Kalyana and by a difficult way over the Western Ghats to Broach (86). The caravan and the river-boat were the chief means of transport (87). North and North-west India had been subjected to various upheavals after the death of Alexander, and when Augustus established the principate the Yue(h)-chi, a tribe allied to Tibetans or Mongolians, who had been driven westwards about 195 by the Huns, had occupied Bactria and had spread south to the Upper Indus, were a settled race about to be dominated by one of their own tribes (Kushan) under Kadphises, while in Baluchistan and Kandahar Sakas and Parthians were being welded together, a process completed by the accession of Gondophares early in the first century A.C. (88). Men could hope therefore that the land-routes between East and West, outside Roman control, were nevertheless destined to be made safe for mercantile activity (89). In South India, local traffic went chiefly by sea.

We have seen how Augustus took vigorous steps towards establishing a prosperous sea-trade between Egypt and India. With reference to the land-routes, as results of the activities of Lucullus and Pompey peace was brought to Asia Minor, the Euphrates became the boundary of Roman territories, the Mediterranean was cleared of pirates, the Nabataeans were pacified, new towns flourished along trade-routes, the Arabs of Mesopotamia were made friendly, the Albanians and Iberians were chastised, Armenia was not hostile and the Romans gained fresh knowledge of the Indian trade brought along the great land-routes and across the Caspian, and were introduced to new Indian products; Pompey had wished to reach the "Erythraean Sea." After 53 Armenia became an ally of Parthia (90).

Julius Caesar meditated the subjection of Parthia followed by an expedition through Hyrcania to the Caspian and the Caucasus mountains and by the conquest of Scythia, and planned to improve the conditions of Ostia and the Tiber, and to cut through the isthmus of Corinth (91), but he died too soon. Armenia was won again and lost. Augustus, as emperor, was able to take steps which caused a great increase of trade with the East along the normal land-routes. He wisely left Syria unchanged, but a resident agent was apparently established at Palmyra; round Damascus robbers were put down and the roads protected (92), while the route from Antioch and Zeugma along the Euphrates became a model of good repair safety and Roman peace (93). Geographers like Strabo, and compilers of knowledge like Isidore of Charax and Iuba of Mauretania, were surely encouraged by Augustus: large maps were to be seen in Rome, and Horace's references to the East seem to reflect this. Surveys were carried out—notably along the silk-route at least as far as Merv; the Commentarii of Agrippa (and perhaps those of Dionysios of Charax) embodied (94) a survey of the whole Empire, and the spirit of Augustus is shewn by the fact that he left at his death a "breviarium totius imperii" (95).

Discovery of the Caspian trade by Pompey and Roman efforts to develop it seem to be the ultimate cause of the constant rivalry between Rome and Parthia over Armenia. Above all, Rome wished to be free of intermediaries or at least to have them friendly. As we shall see, along the cheaper sea-route Rome was ultimately successful. The land-routes through Parthia she could never control; but the Caucasian tribes—Albani, Iberi, Colchi, and other wild peoples—could be won over. Now south of these tribes lay Armenia, itself receiving large quantities of Indian merchandise from the Parthians as well as from the Caspian regions; Armenia is a continuation of the Iranian plateau and through its long valleys ran roads bringing eastern trade to Asia Minor—especially to ultimately Roman centres such as Comana Pontica, Mazaca (Caesarea), Comana in Cappadocia, and others. The Caucasians would be influenced in favour of the power who gave Armenia her king. Eastern commerce, therefore, besides frontier defence and the productiveness of the land, was a motive for establishing influence in Armenia (96). Augustus must have taken into his considerations the Caspian trade with India, but the result of Roman efforts made in Caucasian regions becomes manifest only in the reigns of his successors. Agrippa, in his survey of the Empire, included much information about Caspian tribes; the Albani and Iberi and other tribes sent friendly embassies to Rome; in the case of Armenia Augustus secured recognition of his overlordship in 20 B.C. but the land remained in an unsettled state (97). As a general rule we may take it that whereas along the Tigris and the branching road which connected Artaxata with both Hamadan and Rhagae on the silk-route the Parthians completely controlled the oriental commerce of Armenia, they had no control over the relations of that country with Caspian and Caucasian tribes except indirectly.

Such were the oriental trade-routes when the Roman Empire began. The next chapter will describe firstly the development of Rome's eastern commerce into an active traffic by sea with India, chiefly through epoch-making progress in the use of monsoon winds by Greek shipowners of Roman Egypt; and secondly the immediate effects of these developments on the life of the Empire.

CHAPTER II

Early Developments: The Discovery of
the Monsoons: Results

T H E clash of arms in Asia (1) during the preceding century,
the union of the western world under the authority of one
man in the person of Julius Caesar and again in the person
of Augustus, diplomatic activities between Rome and Parthia, the frequent meetings of Greeks and Indians in the
newly-established sea-trade, the expedition of Gallus,—all
are events which perhaps led to the first Indian embassies
sent to Rome. Hitherto such official communications had
been rare between East and West, and on the side of the
Indians confined to the Maurya empire of the north. Seleucos
Nicator sent Megasthenes near the end of the fourth century
to Chandragupta, and Deimachos to Vindusara, son and
successor of Chandragupta, and these two Greeks resided
for some years at Pataliputra in Bengal; Vindusara's
great son Asoka sent missionaries and ambassadors to Antiochos II of Syria, Ptolemy II of Egypt, Antigonos Gonatas
of Macedonia, Magas of Cyrene, and Alexander II of
Epiros (2). But no Indian embassy reached the Romans until
Augustus had become princeps; then, however, as confused
but striking evidence shews, embassies came to him from
several Indian states, for Augustus himself says that Indian
embassies came "frequently" (3). Nicolaos of Damascus met
at Antioch in Syria three members of an Indian embassy
sent by a sovran of six hundred kings, named Poros or
Pandion, with a letter granting to Augustus free passage
through Indian territory and assistance where reasonable,
and with gifts of a boy born armless (seen by Strabo),
snakes, and a large bird (perhaps a monal pheasant, perhaps

merely an Indian jungle-fowl). They were accompanied by a gymnosophist called Zarmanos or Zarmanos Chegas (a chief?), who had come from Bargosa (Broach) and committed himself to the flames at Athens, a fact confirmed by Dio Cassius and Plutarch (4). Dio Cassius, who perhaps implies that this embassy came twice, adds tigers as gifts, but Florus, who mentions alliance sought by Scythians, Sarmatians and Seres as well as Indians, makes the gifts much finer —precious stones, pearls, and elephants—and the journey very long. Horace (who also seems to add Seres), Suetonius, Victor, and Orosius speak of Scythian and Indian ambassadors, Victor adding Bactrians also, while Orosius, here perhaps trustworthy, brings them to Augustus at Tarraco in Spain (5). It would seem that at this time the Romans became familiar with, but scorned, Indian trousers (6). In these accounts there is much mixture of names, dates, localities, presents, and so on and in the embassies themselves, and I think several different embassies can be traced in two different ways. Thus the evidence of dates points to an embassy received by Augustus in Spain in 26 or in 25 B.C.; he certainly received one at Samos in 21—an embassy referred to by Horace writing in 17 B.C.; and again Augustus exhibited a tiger (in 13 or 11) and a python, and, as we know he lost no time in exhibiting such curiosities (7), we may deduce an embassy between 14 and 11. Again, the evidence given above reveals, I think, four (8):—

(a) From North-west India, where the regions of the Hydaspes and Acesines and other rivers near the Indus formed the original sphere of Puru potentates, each known as Poros to the Greeks; where there was much unsettlement of Graeco-Bactrian and other chiefs by the Yue(h)-chi, so that one might boast of his rule over many; this embassy brought snakes, a monal, and tigers—animals characteristic of North India, and a letter written in Greek—a language long spoken in Punjab.

(b) From Broach on the Nerbudda, not far south of the Indus districts, including the Buddhist monk Zarmanos. Both (a) and (b) perhaps came together by land or the Persian Gulf to Antioch on diplomatic business connected with the land-route Herat—Kandahar—Indus—Royal Road—Ganges and its branch south-east to Ujjain and Broach, and with the coasting voyage from Egypt to North-west India.

(c) From the South Indian Chera Kingdom (sometimes confused with the Seres or Chinese, because of the soft "ch" and the appellation Seri given to the Cheras by the Ceylonese), whence came pepper, and where at some time a temple was built to Augustus at Muziris (Cranganore), perhaps by way of thanks to that emperor. Hence the alleged "Seres" as ambassadors, unless they were Bactrians (Kushans).

(d) From the Pandya Kingdom, famous for its pearls, and ruled by kings entitled by the Greeks Pandion. Both (c) and (d) brought typically Tamil products, precious stones and pearls, and elephants perhaps from the breeding-grounds of Ceylon. Probably the Chola Kingdom also sent an embassy. Thus we have two groups of embassies, some apparently coming by land or the Persian Gulf, the long journey including perhaps the time spent in Augustus' suite and the return to India, and the deaths being due to the unac-. customed climate. All may have been planned as commercial embassies by Alexandrian or Syrian Greeks in order to cut out if possible the Arabians, as Priaulx suggests. He reduces the embassies to one, but I would eliminate only the Chinese —though even this is perhaps unnecessary (9). At any rate, the outstanding fact is the communication between Indians and the ruler of the Roman world, and though we cannot judge how much the new relations advanced the trade between India and Rome, we can at least say that a really active traffic commenced with Augustus' reign (10), and that the visits of these embassies were some of the few occasions on which true Romans and Indians met each other face to face, for Greeks, Syrians, Jews, and Arabians did most of the trading, "Roman," as it appears in western and in Indian literature, meaning so often a Roman subject of the provinces (11). True Romans visited Egypt not often, Arabia and the Euphrates seldom, the Caspian and India never. At the beginning of the Empire hardly anyone of any race knew the trade-routes between East and West throughout their length, for in the only half-developed traffic the land-routes were not yet fully explored for or by western merchants, and sea-voyages to India were not yet made by Greeks with the full use of the monsoons. But the western world was at peace under a strong government; on the Red Sea the Arabian pirates were chastised and the more peaceful Arabians partly deprived of their monopoly, and even Palmyra was not entirely left alone. Moreover, with the coming of peace and prosperity rose a real demand for oriental luxuries in the West which stimulated activity along the trade-routes to India, and our next task is to consider the extent of this trade so far as we can estimate it for the earlier emperors in order to contrast it with the result of the full discovery of the monsoons during the reign of Claudius, and of progress made later on.

When we examine the volume of trade between Rome and India, even at its real beginning under Augustus, we are confronted at once with a phenomenon which has always been characteristic of commerce between Europe and India. From the very start the Roman Empire was unable to counterbalance the inflow of Indian products by a return of imperial products, with the result that the Romans sent out coined money which never returned to them, not even in the form of Indian money. Full lists of the imports and exports of this trade will be given when we have sketched

a fuller development of it; for the time of Augustus and
Tiberius it will be sufficient to shew how even then Roman
money was apparently pouring into India in order partly
to pay for an already large quantity of Indian merchandise.
Importation of Roman wares we cannot yet trace.

Discoveries of coins are regulated by chance, and though
they indicate commerce, do not afford conclusive evidence
of its extent at any given period. But the large numbers of
Roman coins found in India (12) and representing a commerce
lasting for several centuries lead us to certain very definite
conclusions. Hardly any authenticated Ptolemaic or Seleucid
coins have turned up in India, and of Roman Republican
coins only a few have been found, all in North-west India—
in Kohat, the Hazara district of Punjab, and at Manikyala
—the result of early coasting voyages during the last years
of the Republic (13). But of emperors down to Nero very large
numbers of gold coins and silver coins have been found in
the Tamil States, and of these a phenomenally large number
have stamps of Augustus and Tiberius; those of Augustus
occur (14) in all three Tamil Kingdoms, sometimes in large
numbers, and of these at least some came in his reign.

With Augustus, then, the trade really commenced, for the
coins confirm what we know from other evidence; perhaps,
too, had begun the systematic exportation to India of coin
in bulk to become the basis of exchange there; at any rate,
of Augustus' coins a type shewing Gaius and Lucius, his
adopted sons, has turned up in numbers in India, and these
coins are nearly always plated. Ernst therefore thinks
that they were struck especially for trade with South
India, where the natives could not as yet distinguish good
Roman coins from bad. If this be true the deception cannot have been successful for any length of time. It may
be that the sending out of these coins was in some way
part of the commercial scheme which included the circum-

navigation of Arabia and the eastern mission of Gaius in 1 B.C. (15). In North India the coins of the early reigns are very few—the twelve of Augustus from Hazara being the largest number for one reign (16).

Augustus was unable to check the luxurious tastes of his wealthier subjects, nor does such a reformation ever come about through legislation merely; moreover Augustus, himself not luxurious, aided commerce all he could and gave Rome the beginnings of an imperial court, and the atmosphere of a court did not tend towards simple living. Contemporary literature shews that at the beginning of the Empire much merchandise of Indian origin was being paid for—thus we find Indian lions, tigers, rhinoceroses, elephants, and serpents already brought for exhibition, though rarely; Indian parrots kept as pets; Indian ivory and tortoiseshell employed for all kinds of ornaments; oriental pearls and Chinese silk worn by women; again, Celsus and Scribonius Largus reveal the use of Indian plant-products in Graeco-Roman medicine, but the evidence of ordinary writers is a better test of trade. We find aromatic spices and juices, such as Indian pepper, spikenard, cinnamon (Indian and Chinese), costus, and cardamom in common use, mostly coming by land or through the Arabians, as the epithets shew, and in medicine, besides these, Indian ginger, bdellium-myrrh, raisin-barberry, sugar, and aloes; again, we find gingelly-oil as a food, indigo as a paint, cotton used for clothing, ebony for furniture, rice as a cereal, and citrons, peaches, and apricots (17), as table-fruits or medicines. Again, Augustan literature, Pliny's accounts, and extant collections shew the already wide use of Indian precious stones—diamond, onyx, sardonyx, agate, sard, carnelian, crystal, amethyst, opal, beryl, sapphire, ruby, turquoise, garnet, and others. Poets like Tibullus and Propertius shew how fashionable was the wearing of gems by women, and Suetonius and Pliny how abnormal were the extravagant tastes of Gaius and Nero among emperors. Full details of all these Indian products are given later with others as part of a complete survey, but even at the beginning of the Empire the traffic, mainly through intermediaries, was brisk; before that time we have very few references to Indian products in Roman literature, and passages in Cicero's speeches against Verres revealing the trade between Sicily and Asia, Syria, and Alexandria, and the luxurious side of Sicilian life, do not shew any abundance of wares peculiarly Indian (18). Pompey's campaigns introduced the Romans to new Indian wares from the land-routes; much larger quantities came to their notice on the downfall of Cleopatra, who rejoiced in Indian products (19), and with the battle of Actium began Rome's most luxurious period.

The Emperor Tiberius pursued a careful and successful financial policy, and expressed his anxiety at the great increase of oriental trade. He censured the wearing of silk by both sexes and checked its use by men, but his greatest anxiety was the extravagant tastes of ladies not only in dress but in jewels and precious stones—tastes which, he said, were sending Roman money (20) away to foreign and to unfriendly peoples. This ominous complaint seems to be confirmed by discoveries made of coins in India, for those of Tiberius are extraordinarily numerous, sometimes predominating over those of other reigns in single hoards, and they include both gold and silver. The remarkable instances are finds made at Pollachi, Vellalur, and Karur—all in the Coimbatore district (21). The total number of known coins of Tiberius found in the south and west of India is 1007 as against the 453 of Augustus, and large numbers of both these reigns have occurred together. In all they come to more than half the total number of identified Roman

coins found in South India (22). Some were found in the
Hazara district, and some ultimately reached Ceylon and
even the Kistna district well up the east coast of India.
Many were very fresh and new. The comparative scarcity of
coins struck under Gaius and Claudius perhaps indicates
that the remonstrances of Tiberius took effect, but a discussion of this is given later. Tiberius wished to alter, not
to check the trade; he was tempted to make the Nabataean
kingdom into a province, and he did abolish the clientships
of Commagene and Cappadocia; a watch was kept upon
Palmyra; after a short struggle with Parthia, a Roman
candidate ascended the throne of Armenia, and the Albani
and Iberi gave their help (23). Under Gaius (37–41) Commagene was restored to a native prince, and the Parthians
seized Armenia. Gaius himself was addicted to astonishing
luxuries and wasteful fooleries and tried to increase his
revenue by new import-dues at Italian harbours and at
Rome. His own consumption of oriental luxuries, especially
pearls and unguents, was beyond the ordinary, and he
revived the wearing of silk at least by the emperor (24).

The reign of Claudius is interesting because of the full
discovery of the monsoons made in his reign, as we shall describe, but we can give only an outline of the developments,
owing to the lack of interest in commerce shewn by
ancient writers. In order to revive the corn-trade, Claudius
constructed the Portus Romanus, a new haven above
Ostia, connected by a channel with the Tiber and provided
with a lighthouse; this development had an adverse effect
upon Puteoli, which however received from Claudius the
benefit of a fire brigade (25). Particular attention was paid
to the Bosporan kingdom on the north-east shores of the
Euxine—where kings for more than three centuries struck
the only non-imperial gold. Relations were established
with the Dandaridae near the Hypanis (Kuban), the

Siraces, and the Aorsi, and the Romans penetrated to within three days of the river Tanais (Don). Complete control was not kept over two of the important Euphrates crossings—Melitene and Samosata—but at Zeugma, for the protection of the customs-station, a legionary camp was established (26). There was much trouble in Parthia, reaching even the Bactrian plain, and Armenia was seized by Vologeses I, so that the land-routes were disturbed. Seleucia gave much trouble to Parthia, and Palmyra seems to have drawn closer her bonds with Rome (27).

The general tendency of these events must have encouraged the use of the sea-route to India from Egypt, and in the reign of Claudius the secret of the monsoons was revealed finally to a western power. That the full use of these winds was unknown to the Romans until the reign of Claudius is shewn by two remarkable pieces of evidence. Diodoros tells how one Iambulos, after an adventurous time in the spice trade of the Somali coasts, was eventually taken by winds to an island now supposed to have been Ceylon; after years spent there he visited Palibothra and returned by land. The story is full of fable, but the one fact seems to be that the man was drifted to Indian regions by a monsoon wind (28). Much more truth is revealed in the account given by Pliny of a freedman of Annius Plocamus, who in the reign of Claudius had farmed the collection of the Red Sea dues (29). The freedman, while sailing round Arabia, was carried helplessly by winds until a fortnight later he reached Hippuros, somewhere in Ceylon, where he was entertained by the king, who much admired the constant weight of the Roman denarii, and sent back to Claudius (obviously for commercial reasons) four ambassadors led by Rachias (a Raja). Here again we have a man who did not know the use of monsoon winds in order to reach Ceylon. The information brought back by the castaway contained much that was not true; and we may doubt whether the "Seres," with whom Ceylon traded, were the Chinese or merely the Chera Tamils; but we need not, at least, as does Ferguson, deny that Ceylon was meant. Vincent dates the embassy in 41, Priaulx between 44 and 47, suggesting that the fall of Messalina caused it to pass without much notice (30). For reasons which will appear later, I also would place the event before 50 (see pp. 46-7).

Soon afterwards, the discovery of the proper use of the monsoons was made, perhaps partly as a result of reports given by the embassy and by Plocamus' freedman, and of the chance talk of Indian and Arabian merchants in Indian seas but chiefly through enterprising Greeks. Of the two passages which tell us of this development the one in the *Periplus* implies that one HIPPALOS discovered the use of the south-west monsoon for voyages direct from African and Arabian regions to the Indus, Barygaza, and the Malabar coast, and that all these voyages were suggested and made by him about the same time. But the passage in Pliny shews (31) that the discovery was made in successive stages, developing in a natural manner from voyages to North-west India to voyages to Malabar, and his words shew that we must either put Hippalos in an early period, as Chwostow does, and, assuming that he merely discovered a direct voyage to the mouths of the Indus, assign the further developments to others than Hippalos; or we must give him the credit of one of the later developments. We can hardly credit him with the testing of all the voyages indicated. Having observed that neither the *Periplus* nor Pliny shews precisely what voyages Hippalos made or planned; that neither gives us a date for him; that the fame of Hippalos rested on the use of the south-west monsoon only, for the outward voyages; and that the use of the name Hippalos for the south-west monsoon does not

indicate what voyage caused the wind to receive his name (32),
I propose the following stages in the discovery of the use
of the south-west monsoon by Egyptian Greeks:—

Stage I. From the time of Alexander and Nearchos'
voyage to the time of Tiberius' reign they set sail from
Arabia Eudaemon and came in small vessels, and following
round all the gulfs coasted along Arabia, perhaps even to
Ras Musandan, or perhaps only as far as Ras el Had and
then along the Asiatic coasts of Carmania and Gedrosia
to the Indus and southwards, returning the same way
(Pliny, VI. 100; *Peripl.* 57; so also in Strabo).

Stage II. Between the reign of Tiberius and the end
of Gaius' reign (A.D. 40–41), men started to coast from
Arabia Eudaemon, or its ruins, or from Cane, until, after
Ras Fartak (Syagros), the Arabian coast receded, whereupon they sailed across the sea to Patala on the Indus.
This may be taken as part of Hippalos' discovery, though
the author of the *Periplus* in speaking of this voyage, ending
in his day at Barbaricon, mentions not Hippalos but the
"Indian Etesian winds" and merely remarks that it was
more direct and quick but more dangerous than coasting
(Pliny, *l.c.*; *Peripl.* 39).

Stage III. Between roughly A.D. 41 and 50 (the "secuta
aetas" of Pliny, which lasted "diu"), men not desiring to
take only the voyage to the Indus began coasting or sailing
from the ruins of Arabia Eudaemon or from Cane as far
as Ras Fartak as before, and then taking a "shorter and
safer" voyage across, so as to strike the Indian coast at
Sigerus (Melizigara in the *Periplus*, Melizegyris in Ptolemy,
either Jaigarh or Rajapur) whence they could proceed
north or south at will. Even this stage was probably un-
attempted before Claudius' reign, but it surely came
about soon after 41, and I would put the first attempt
in 42 (Pliny, VI. 101). Presumably men started to sail direct

to Barygaza also during this time, returning the same
way, and calling, if they wished, at Socotra o Moscha
(*Peripl.* 31, 32). (See p. 79.)

Stage IV. About A.D. 50 men desiring to visit the Tamils
only or preferably became convinced that after leaving
Ocelis, the ruins of Arabia Eudaemon, Cane, or Cape
Guardafui, in July, they could by throwing the ship's head
off the wind with a constant pull on the rudder and a shift
of the yard (thus sailing in an arc of a circle) go across
to Malabar marts in forty days (*Peripl.* 57; Pliny, VI. 101).
We might think that *this* was Hippalos' discovery through
combining a knowledge of winds and Indian geography
with steering a vessel; if so, he would be the "mercator"
who at last in Pliny's own time found this still shorter way
than before, so that India was "brought near by lust for
gain" (Pliny, VI. 101 ff. and 96). For by others than the
author of the *Periplus*, Hippalos is a name given to a sea
and to a promontory, both near Cape Guardafui, and only
when he has told of Muziris and Nelcynda does that author
mention Hippalos, and only in connexion with a voyage
to those marts. Then at once he says the whole voyage
thither used to be done by coasting in small vessels until
Hippalos discovered how to cross the ocean...but from
that time onwards men sailed from Cane or the Cape of
Spices to Malabar (this is the voyage at once attributed
to Hippalos). The author of the *Periplus* might mean that
the voyages which he describes next, namely those taken
to Barygaza and the Indus from Ras Fartak with the
monsoon blowing straight behind, were begun before
Hippalos' time, though he appears at first sight to credit
Hippalos with the whole development. But Hippalos simply
"observed the placing of the ports and the shape of the
sea," and appears to me only to have realised in theory
the southern extension of India and the *possibility* of using

for crossing to various points a wind which only his successors durst fully to use in practice by successive stages, as set out above, and he seems to have used the neighbourhood of Cape Guardafui as a starting-point for observation and calculation (33). The return voyage from Malabar was made in the same way, but by tracing a southern curve, and men called at Socotra if they wished (34); the *Periplus*, written about A.D. 60 or later, shews that in Indian seas Hippalos was a respected memory and, as I shall shew, Nero's reign (54–68) saw the effects of his discovery. The freedman of Annius Plocamus knew nothing of the last stage though his adventure may have given the Greeks some hints; Pliny, writing his sixth book after A.D. 51, says that only after the last development did a regular use of the south-west monsoon take place "every year," and that only of late had reliable information of the whole voyage direct from Egypt to Muziris and Nelcynda come through (35). He shews, too, that Muziris now became the nearest or the first mart in India, and direct voyages thither and back became the regular proceeding, especially for pepper-merchants, and such voyages easily caused some of these to forget the fact of the southern projection of the Indian peninsula. In the Roman world Hippalos' memory had soon faded; in Pliny Hippalos is only the name of the south-west monsoon and of an African promontory and in Ptolemy and the *Itinerarium Alexandri* the name of a sea, yet this man had helped to unravel a secret held perhaps for ages by Arabians and Indians, the Greeks knowing only that the winds existed (36).

Putting therefore Hippalos in Tiberius' early days we make him the pioneer and perhaps give him the credit of the initial voyage direct to the Indus. If we do this and date him in A.D. 47 as does Vincent, or in 45 as does Schoff (37), we ignore the stages given by Pliny or must compress them into too short a time. With better reason, Kornemann and Chwostow suggest that Hippalos lived in the first century B.C.; that the next development as recorded by Pliny (the voyage from Ras Fartak across to Sigerus) took place under Augustus, and that the final achievement (the voyage from Ocelis to Muziris, of course not attempted by Hippalos but through his efforts) came about shortly before Pliny wrote (38). Chwostow puts this final development near the end of Claudius' reign and accounts for progress made in relations with the East under Augustus not to development in the use of monsoons but to the consolidation of the Mediterranean and of Egypt under stable rule (39). Pliny's record of a journey taken from Egypt to Nelcynda in a pepper-ship presents probably the greatest achievement made up to his time. Such a ship sailed from Berenice about mid-summer and, leaving out Muza, halted preferably at Ocelis whence, if the wind Hippalos blew, Muziris in the Chera Kingdom could be reached in forty days, but the reported presence of pirates at Nitrias made Bacare (Porakad) in the land of the "Neacyndi" a better place. The return voyage commenced in December or at the latest the first week in January, when the north-east monsoon (which by a slip Pliny calls Volturnus) carried ships to the Red Sea so as to catch a south-east or east wind at the Strait (40). This account is in harmony with the remarks of the author of the *Periplus*, though Pliny's notice contains some mistakes, and the statements of both authors fit in with the conditions of the monsoons to-day, for they blow with greatest force and regularity between the east coast of Africa and North India. When the sun is in the southern hemisphere a north-east wind blows over the sea, and when the sun is in the northern hemisphere, a south-west wind blows; when the sun passes the equator, the winds are irregular, varying between calms and storm-gales. The north-east monsoon blows from

November to March, and with most regularity and force in January, especially between Socotra and Bombay, while the south-west monsoon blows from the end of April to the middle of October, or at least from May to September inclusive. On the sea they are moderate winds, but in the Bay of Bengal their force is irregular (41). After Hippalos' discovery the Greek mariners became so well acquainted with these conditions that they chose the end of the old year or the beginning of the new (when the north-east wind blew most regularly and strongly) as the time of their return voyage. To an Egyptian Greek it was of course in the middle of the year. Sometimes on the return journey ships missed their course, as Eudoxos' did, and one Diogenes who was returning from India, when he approached Cape Guardafui, was blown by an adverse wind southwards for twenty-five days to the Cape of Rhapta on the African coast (42). Pliny wishes us to believe that on one occasion Eudoxos, evidently returning from India, was blown round Africa to Spain, and at last reached Gades (43). The winds of the Red Sea itself influenced the periods at which voyages were taken. In the northern part north and north-west winds predominate all the year, and this fact, together with the awkward breezes of the Gulfs of Suez and Akaba, helps to account for the late development of the Canal route to Suez and the still later development of Aelana as a port; for the return journey might be retarded if they were used. From June to August a north-west wind blows down the whole of the Red Sea, and hence the voyages to India commenced about July. In the southern part and out as far as Aden the normal conditions are alternate north and south winds, but there is a tendency towards east and south-east winds, especially in the winter, and these wafted on their way up the Red Sea the ships returning by north-east monsoon from India (44). (See also Appendix p. 83.)

We can estimate roughly the time taken by the voyage to India and back with the help of the monsoons, but we cannot be precise in estimating the voyage between Puteoli and Alexandria, for it varied not only according to the season of the year but also according to conditions of weather or war which affected the choice of route; thus we have news travelling to Egypt in 27 days in summer and as many as 67 in winter; in spring it could take longer than 52 days to reach the Fayum; in summer it could reach Elephantine in 57 days (45). Transport by river or camel was not capable of being hurried; a good pack-camel with an ordinary load of 400 lb. will go from 20 to 25 miles a day, requiring water every third or fourth day except in winter, when the animal will not require water for 25 days or more. Now Pliny says that men usually sailed from Berenice about mid-summer (July, says the *Periplus*) after a journey of about 24 days from Alexandria; this means that a would-be traveller from Italy to India took a corn-ship from Puteoli to Alexandria at the beginning of May when direct sailings commenced under summer conditions, which made possible an average voyage of about 20 days from Puteoli to Alexandria. From this reckoning and from Pliny's authentic figures we obtain the following results, bearing in mind the fact that a ship sailed by night as well as by day (νυχθήμερος δρόμος) whenever possible (46).

(A) *From Italy to India* (47)

	Days
Puteoli or Ostia—Alexandria (with average winds) ...	20
Alexandria—Coptos (up Nile by boat with wind) ...	12
Coptos—Berenice (by camel)	12
[Coptos—Myos Hormos (by camel)	7]
Berenice (mid-summer)—Ocelis or Cane (evidently with delays)	30
Ocelis—Muziris with monsoon (perhaps with delays) ...	40
Total (with favourable winds and no long delays) ...	114
	(about 16 weeks)

Six months would be a fairly constant average.

It is possible that the slower speed of ships in the Red Sea and Indian Ocean as compared with the rates of speed in the Mediterranean was due not only to delays in ports but to the abnormal bulk of the ships and quantity of the loads.

(B) *From India to Italy*

For the return journey we have no figures (48) and no recorded example of transmission of news, but we can perhaps calculate that as far as Alexandria the return took about the same time—thus: from Muziris, which was left during the month of December or early in January, the journey to Alexandria by way of Berenice and Coptos and down the Nile took about 94 days (49) so that Alexandria was reached before the end of March. Now although by that time summer navigation in the Mediterranean had begun, and the north-west Etesian winds were not due to blow until July, nevertheless the corn-ships were not sailing direct between Alexandria and Italy. Therefore the merchant or passenger, if he did not take any other ship sailing direct to Italy, thus completing his return journey in about seventeen weeks, spent a month in Alexandria until the direct sailing of corn-ships began in May. Or he might take a coasting voyage from Alexandria to Syria and Asia Minor in a vessel calling at ports on the way, leaving Crete on the right, and rounding Cape Malea so as to reach Italy in 70 days; such a voyage is pointed out by Lucian (50). But this partly coasting voyage took more than six weeks longer than the direct, so that a quicker alternative would be taken if possible. At any rate, Pliny is right in saying that under suitable conditions people could go to India and return within one year, and, as he states, India had been "brought near" by gain. The full use of the monsoons partly remedied, but in the Indian Ocean only, the chief lack of early navigators, the lack of the mariners' compass which caused coasting to be the rule, and that is why Hippalos inaugurated such a vast increase in Rome's oriental sea-trade. Direct and independent traffic with India was very fully developed by voyages from Egypt, or from any Arabian or East African mart across the ocean to towns on the west coast of India from the Indus to Cranganore and the east coast too could be reached more quickly. But as we shall see, the Axumites and Arabians were not quite eliminated as middlemen.

Coins of Claudius have been found in India and possibly in Ceylon, though the point is doubtful. Under Nero the effects of the new discoveries were fully felt and the traffic increased greatly and flourished to the death of Marcus Aurelius. It so happens that our evidence for studying the effects of the monsoons is particularly plentiful through the work of Pliny, who dedicated his Natural History in A.D. 77, and the anonymous writer of the *Periplus of the Erythraean Sea*, which is a merchants' practical guide-book for Indian seas, giving details of harbours, marts, anchorages, tides, prevailing winds, local tribes and rulers, exports, imports, and so on, compiled after several years' travel between the accession of Nero and A.D. 100 by a merchant, apparently of Berenice. Since the author held Hippalos vividly in his memory, unlike Pliny, and while attending to great increase in trade, knew, it seems, nothing of the fire of 64 and of the chaos of 69 (though this is at best inconclusive) and indicates only a restricted trade in the Persian Gulf controlled by the Parthians, who were in a state of war with Rome after A.D. 58, I adhere to Schoff's former dating of the *Periplus* in about A.D. 60 though the question must remain unsolved (51). From the evidence of this guide-book, of Pliny, and of other sources, both western and eastern, we can learn something definite about Roman trade in Indian seas as it developed after Hippalos' discovery.

Merchants could leave Egypt at Arsinoë (52), but did so normally at Myos Hormos or Berenice about July, and could obtain Indian wares at the ἐμπόρια νόμιμα or ἔνθεσμα (legal marts where foreign trade was allowed and dues levied) of the newly-rising Axumites and of the Somali or of the Arabians. Thus they could visit the somewhat unruly Red Sea port Adulis (Zula, though Massowa is now the port), apparently a joint mart of the Egyptians and the Axumites controlled from a place ultimately called Auxume (Axum), royal seat of the Axumites, situated eight days' travel inland through Coloe, and ruled by the honest, cultured, but miserly Zoscales (Za Hakale) who could not quell the local chieftains of Somali marts outside the Red Sea:—of Avalites (Zeila), Malao (Berbera), Mundus (Bandar Hais); Mosyllon (at Ras Hantara?), at the Neiloptolemaeon (the Tokwina?), the Market of Spices (Olok) near the Cape of Spices (Ras Asir, Cape Guardafui) and Tabae Cape (Ras Chenarif?), Pano (Ras Binna?), and Opone (Ras Hafun)—at all of which Indians and products of North-west India could be found (53). Beyond Opone the trading was controlled by Muza (Mokha) with its Red Sea port Masala (54), but this rising mart, now trading with India, was ignored by Roman traders in Indian wares; if they wished to find these in Arabian ports, they went straight from Egypt out of the Red Sea to the ruins of Arabia Eudaemon, now rising again under King Charibael (Karib'il) who ruled from Saphar over Sabaites and Homerites as one people, and possessed a vassal in Cholaebos of Muza and Saue, and was in communication with Rome through embassies (55); or they visited Dioscorida Insula (Socotra island), peopled by Greek, Arab, and Indian merchants, garrisoned by Arabians, and ruled by King Eleazos (Ili-azzu) of Sabbatha in Arabia; it received Indian wares, but Roman subjects used it chiefly as a place of call on the way back from India (56). Farther afield the Indian trade of Cane and Moscha of Hadramaut under Eleazos could be used, though after Hippalos' discovery Cane was usually passed by and Moscha was frequented more by voyagers who arrived late in the season from India and wintered there. The Gulf of Oman and the Persian Gulf were not popular, both coasts of these being controlled by Parthia (57), which was hostile to Rome after 58, and was pressing down upon Arabian trade, but Omana (by which was meant the Arabian coast from Ras Hasik and much of the southern shore of the gulf) was well known. The chief marts were Apologos (the old Obollah) and Ommana (in the Bay of El Katan?) conducting reciprocal traffic with Broach; Charax Spasinu, a Parthian stronghold in diplomatic communication with Rome; and also Kalhat (Acila in Pliny, near Sur), a port in the Gulf of Oman used for embarkation for India. As Pliny shews, Roman trade with the Persian Gulf had corrected false ideas about the position of Ommana and the importance of certain marts, though Mela's account still shews much distortion of the gulf (58).

Indians and Indian trade could still be found therefore on the way to India. By mutual arrangement the Arabians and Somali excluded Indian ships from the Red Sea—at least we find that they did not allow them nearer the west than Ocelis (59), and if this is so the supposed differential customs-dues against Arabian and African vessels in Egyptian ports were either a cause or an effect of it. But the Romans and Axumites were entering the traffic as new powers on equal terms and sooner or later Indians were bound to frequent Adulis and Alexandria. The Greeks sailed direct to India and depended less and less upon the trade at Arabian ports, using generally for watering purposes Ocelis near Cella at the Strait of Bab-el-Mandeb, which was regarded as the best place of call for voyagers to and from India, and then sailing straight across to India (60). The author of the *Periplus* describes for us the extent of this traffic as he knew it in his time. The mouths of the river Indus or Sinthos could be reached by direct sailings with the south-west monsoon blowing straight behind. On the middle stream of its seven mouths lay Barbaricon, perhaps surviving to this day as Bahardipur, where ships unloaded their cargoes to be carried by river to Minnagara, the metropolis of the Scythians; these Scythians were Saka people unseated by the Yueh-chi under pressure from the Huns, and hence we find the name Minnagara ("city of the invaders") given to several towns during the Saka and Yueh-chi epochs, that one on the Indus being probably Bahmanabád near the ancient foundation Patala (Haiderabad); it was ruled by Parthian (Pahlava) princes constantly expelling each other—that is to say, it was taken and lost by the Indo-Parthian (Saka) remnants of the line of Maues, who, once subject to Parthia and centred in Kabul, were already pushed south by the Yueh-chi—the "war-like Bactrians" of the *Periplus*. The Egyptians, who left Egypt about July, brought presents for the king and imperial products for exchange with Indian, Parthian, and Chinese products (61).

The north-west districts of India, called Ariace by the *Periplus*, Larice by Ptolemy, and including especially the part round the Gulf of Cambay—Cutch, Kathiawar, and Gujarat—were a great centre of trade and production controlled by Saka princes from another Minnagara (near Chitor?). Roman subjects noted and avoided the dangerous sand-banks of the Rann of Cutch (Gulf Eirinon) and the violent waters of the Gulf of Cutch (Gulf Barace) and made for the great mart of the district—Barygaza (62) (from the Prakrit Bharukacha, a corruption of Bhrigu kachha? the modern Broach) in the Gulf of Cambay at the

mouth of the river Nammados (Nerbudda) down which
inland goods were brought. Behind this whole region lay
the warlike Bactrians (Yueh-chi) now under the direct rule
of a Kushan monarch, namely Kadphises I, not known by
name to the author of the *Periplus*, while from the direction
of the sea the mouth of the Nerbudda was difficult to find
and its entrance dangerous because of shoals, and the
number of visiting ships made necessary a regular pilot-
service consisting of men in the service of the king who
directed them to meet strangers along the coast of Kathiawar (Syrastrene), and to guide them to the river and tow
the ships up it to Barygaza, from which the departure too
was perilous by river against an in-coming tide. But in spite
of all this, to Barygaza were directed large quantities of
Indian and Chinese products, some of which were sent
from China and Central Asia through Kabul and Poclais
(Pushkalavati, to-day Charsadda on the Suwat), so as to
join other supplies at the great centres Minnagara and
Ozene (Ujjain), and some in carts along difficult roads from
Paethana (Paithan) about twenty days' travel south of
Barygaza, and from Tagara (Ter, Thair—or perhaps Col-
hapur or Nagram) ten days further away; lastly, Barygaza
apparently received by way of Tagara wares brought by
an old Andhra route across India from the east coast. The
Egyptian Greeks, leaving Egypt in July, brought, together
with costly presents for King Nambanos (Nahapana), quantities of Roman merchandise, but a balance of gold and
silver had to be brought as well and this coin was exchanged for Indian money with advantage (63).

Sailing southwards, merchants could put in (but not for
trade) at various local marts (τοπικά), among them Suppara
(Sopara, the old Sovira near Bombay) and more often
Calliena (Kalyana) which at one time under Saraganos
(the Andhra king Arishta-Satakarni) had been a legal

mart, but in the time of the *Periplus* was much restricted under its ruler Sandanes, and Greek merchants who landed at Calliena for commerce took a risk of being sent under guard to Barygaza. The causes of this apparently were that this port was not ἔνθεσμον or νόμιμον and not that Sandanes was an Andhra King Sundara whose port Calliena was obstructed by Saka ships from Barygaza, as some would have it, but an intruded Saka chief Chandaka sent down by the king of Barygaza; this chief sent all ships that put in at the town Calliena to Barygaza, where alone official and taxed trading was allowed (64). Some of the localities had Greek names, such as Byzantion (Vizadrog?), Island of the Aegidioi (Goa?), Chersonesos (Karwar Point), but there is no reason to think with Lassen and others that any one of them was the site of a Greek settlement. The coast as far as Damirice (the west coast of the Tamils) was much infested by pirates as it was even in much later times, though it is possible that not pirates but the strong dynasty of the Andhrabhritya, which ruled over parts of the Deccan and the district and coast of Konkan, are represented by Ptolemy's ἄνδρες πειραταί, and legend makes St Thomas land in India at a royal city Andrapolis. Leuce Island (Nitrias in Pliny, Nitra in Ptolemy) was apparently Pigeon Island —much infested by pirates, according to Pliny—and robbers must have been active at the first two marts of Damirice, namely Naura (Cannanore?) and Tyndis (Ponnani?), for about these the *Periplus* has little to say: yet Tyndis lay on the navigable river Ponnani which would bring down the pepper of the Anaimalai hills and the beryls of Coimbatore. As far as we can tell, the pirates of South Konkan and Canara were Tamils of the Satiya Kingdom, not much frequented by the Greeks for commerce (65).

But with the three chief Tamil States of South India —namely the Kerala or Chera, the Pandya, and the Chola

Kingdoms, the Romans were conducting a very active commerce. The Chera Kingdom was the one within easiest reach of western merchants and afforded them as a staple article pepper in unlimited quantities; in the *Periplus* the country is called Cerobothra, that is Cheraputra or Keralaputra, at one time extending from Cape Comorin to Karwar Point, but now the northern end was lost and the southern part (south Travancore) had passed into the hands of the Pandya rulers so that Kerala corresponded closely with the districts of Malabar, Cochin, and the north part of Travancore. Its most northern market-town was Tyndis, but its chief mart was the most well-known of all the coast-towns of India, namely Muchiri, residence of the ruler of Kodungalur or Kranganur, called by the Greeks Muziris and represented to-day not by Mangalore but by Cranganore on the river Periyar. The place was crowded with Greek and Arabian vessels; the Greeks brought imperial products in large ships and exchanged them for Indian, but much money had to be brought as well to make up the balance and to create a basis for exchange in India. Men paying a first visit traded silently with the Chera folk, as Pliny shews, but already, according to the Peutinger Table, a temple had been built at Muziris in honour of Augustus, though I feel doubtful about the two Roman cohorts alleged to have been stationed there. A Tamil poem speaks of the thriving Muchiri whither the fine large ships of the Yavana (Greeks) come bearing gold, making the water white with foam, and return laden with pepper, the Chera king giving rare products of the sea and mountains. As Lucian shews, the importance of the place lasted during the second century. Fifty miles to the south by sea and river lay another very important mart called Nelcynda represented not by Nileswara, as some have thought, but by the modern Kottayam in the backwaters behind Cochin. It was approached by stretches of water full of shoals and blocked channels, and vessels paying a visit unloaded and reloaded their vessels about twelve miles away at Bacare or Barcare, the modern Porakad. At this time Nelcynda belonged to the Pandya Kingdom which would be jealous of the control exercised by Cheras over the pepper trade and of their possession of Porakad where ended a route through the pass of Achenkoil and forming the chief highway for goods brought across South India to the west coast, and we may conclude from Pliny that Greeks visiting only Nelcynda for pepper were told by the Pandyas that Muziris was not rich in merchandise. In Cochin too, or Malabar, a colony of Jews seems to have settled during the first century; they, possibly, sent out the Jewish families which migrated later to the districts between Lü Shan and Tcheng-tu in China. Kottayam has one of the oldest Syrian Christian churches in India. When the *Periplus* was written, Greek merchants were not visiting Carura, the residence of Chera kings, also called Vanji and to-day represented by Parur or Paravur, but leaving Egypt about July were content to deal simply with Muziris and Nelcynda, the trade of both places being of the same class (66).

The Pandya Kingdom occupied generally the districts of Tinnevelly and Madura with part of Travancore, but in the time of the *Periplus* it extended beyond the Ghats so as to include more of Travancore. Just as the Chera Kingdom was famous for its pepper, so the Pandya Kingdom was famous for its pearls, obtained chiefly in the Gulf of Manaar from fisheries sheltered from the dangerous cyclones of the Bay of Bengal and worked by condemned criminals from Colchoi (Korkai, now Kolkai at the mouth of the sacred river Tamraparni). They were subject to control from the inland capital Modura, which was not yet visited frequently by the Greek merchants. It is probable that the author of the *Periplus* did not go farther south than Nelcynda or perhaps the Red Bluffs, for his information becomes more scanty, even very inaccurate and his statements are founded on hearsay reports of other merchants. He mentions besides the Pyrrhos mountain (the Red Bluffs), Balita, Cape Comorin the southern extremity of the Indian peninsula (Comari), and Colchoi, but we miss the personal note which is a characteristic of the former parts of his narrative; yet it cannot have been long before Roman subjects resided in the Pandya Kingdom just as they did in the Chera region. Powerful Yavana and dumb Mlecchas (that is, barbarians) in complete armour formed bodyguards to Tamil rulers, and it has been definitely stated, on the authority of Tamil poems once more, that "Roman" soldiers enlisted in the service of Pandya and other kings; for instance, in the reign of Pandya Aryappadai-Kadantha-Nedunj-Cheliyan the gates of the fort Madura (a great city with streets appropriated to special trades) were guarded by Roman soldiers with drawn swords; another poem, in which is described a Tamil king's tent on the battle-field, speaks of it as guarded by powerful and stern-looking Yavana, while dumb Mlecchas, in complete armour and using gestures, watched in the antechamber all night. Likewise the poet Nakkirar exhorts a Pandya prince to drink in peace the cool and fragrant wine brought by the Yavana in their good ships (or bottles = skins?) (67). From the very beginning of the Roman Empire the Pandya people had probably taken the leading part in encouraging the Romans to come and trade, for they had sent, as we have seen, an embassy to Augustus.

Prosperous as the Chera and Pandya Kingdoms were at this time, the largest, richest, and most flourishing Tamil State was the Chola Kingdom, of which the coast is called Aegialos by the *Periplus*, stretching roughly from the Pennar river and Nellore to Pudukottai and the Valiyar or the Varshalai, or perhaps even the Vaigai river

on the south. Its capital Argaru (Uraiyur, destroyed
in the seventh century), now part of Trichinopoly, was
famed for its muslins and perhaps for its own pearl-fisheries
in the Palk Strait, but its greatest emporium was Kaviripaddinam or Pukar, Puhar (the Camara of the *Periplus*, on
the river Chabari or Chaberis of Ptolemy), a busy place
on the east coast at the mouth of the northern branch of
the Kaveri or Cauvery river. We learn a great deal about
it from Tamil literature, and since town and harbour
are now buried beneath the sand near Tranquebar, the
accounts which we have are all the more interesting. The
river could take heavily laden ships without forcing them
to slacken sail, and these ships brought wares of all kinds
to the platforms and warehouses of the town; merchants
and artizans had their own streets, and the place was particularly favoured by Greeks who soon resided near the
warehouses and exposed attractive wares for sale; the magnificent palace of the Chola king had been built partly with
the help of Greek carpenters, who appear to have been a
class of worker in particular demand in India at this time.
Thus long before the Empire began Eudoxos had taken artizans with him when he set out for India; again, according
to the later tradition accepted in the fourth century, St
Thomas was induced to go to India because he met an
Indian merchant who had been sent by Gudnaphar (reign-
ing in A.D. 45) to fetch him a skilful carpenter; it is true
that older tradition makes St Thomas the evangelist not of
India, but of Parthia, and does not make him suffer martyr-
dom at all. But since Gudnaphar (or Gundaphar) of the
Acta Thomae is the Gondophernes of Indo-Parthian coins,
both legends (?) come from the same origin, and reflect
travel to North-west India. Lastly, an inscription of Rhodes
tells us of one Amphilochos whose renown in his art reached
furthest Indus. If this is not mere boasting, and if India

is not Ethiopia, he may have been an architect who visited India (68).

Along the coasts of the Chola Kingdom lighthouses were placed for the use of merchants, and one wonders whether the idea was taken from the Greeks resident in the kingdom, or from the famous lighthouse at Alexandria when the Pandyan embassy visited the Roman Empire in the time of Augustus. Of the three important Chola marts given by the *Periplus*—Camara, which we have described, Poduce (Pondicherry not Pulicat), and Sopatma—the last-named, called Sopaddinam (Madras?) in Tamil poems (see p. 393), was furnished with one of these lighthouses. All three marts traded with the regions of the Ganges and the Malay Peninsula, with the coast of Malabar, and with Ceylon, in large ships of their own, and a Tamil poem shews that the far-famed Saliyur (Selur, Salur, Delur in Ptolemy), opposite the north end of Ceylon, was a similar mart, ever crowded with ships which had crossed the dangerous ocean and from which costly wares were landed. The *Periplus* shews that the Greeks imported into the kingdom more merchandise of their own than they did elsewhere, but the author had not been beyond Cape Comorin himself, and so is content to give a general statement (69).

Of Ceylon the author knew little except that pearls, precious stones, muslins, and tortoiseshell came from there; he gives its name Palaesimundu, and says that the northern part was a day's distance from the coast of India, but enumerates no ports or marts, and exaggerates the size of the island tenfold, and makes it almost touch the Azanian district of the east coast of Africa, but he is not so ill-informed as Pomponius Mela, who not only exaggerates the size of Ceylon in a similar manner, but is also uncertain whether it was an island or the eastern end of the supposed great southern Continent. As I shall shew, Greek merchants were generally content to find the products of Ceylon in the marts of the west coast of India, without visiting the island itself (70). Few coins have been found there for certain dating before Nero, and even after him only about a dozen dating before the end of the second century.

Of the eastern coast of India beyond the limits of the Chola Kingdom the *Periplus* has only a short summary without records of ports and cities, but it draws attention to the region of Masalia (Masulipatam), famed for its muslins (and probably as the trade-centre of Andhra kings), and of Dosarene (Orissa), famed for its ivory (71). From the Chola Kingdom northwards Andhra kings (72) controlled the coast and the marts, and Roman trade did not flourish yet so far east, though we need not doubt that the wealth and literary activity of at least the nearer Tamil States at this time were due to their traffic with the Roman Empire, as well as the Arabians, Burma, Malay, and regions beyond. In regions included in the ancient Chera, Pandya, and Chola Kingdoms have been found large numbers of Roman coins struck chiefly by emperors down to Nero, and after the death of that emperor the traffic on Rome's part was not confined so closely to the Tamils, but was spread more evenly along Indian coasts in general, and was conducted more by barter than with money, resulting in a decrease in the numbers of coins found in southern districts representing emperors subsequent to Nero.

The last notices of importance given by the *Periplus* are concerned with the regions of the Ganges and beyond; the author applies this name (73) to the districts of Bengal, to the river itself (particularly the Hughli estuary) and to a mart which is probably the modern Tamluk (74); and in these regions there was a considerable trade in Chinese and Himalayan cinnamon-leaf, Chinese silk, and articles of local produce; the Malay Peninsula, regarded as an

island, was known to send the finest of all tortoiseshell
in the Indian seas, while to the north lay the land of This,
that is, the great unexplored states of China, of which
a great city was Thinae, that is, so far as we can tell,
Nanking; the country produced silk sent to the West
partly by land, partly through India and the Indian Ocean,
and cinnamon-leaf; but few Chinese merchants ever came
from there; instead the Besatae once a year brought
cinnamon-leaf and sold it by silent barter at a spot (near
Gangtok?) situated on the confines of their own homes in
the Himalayas and the regions ruled by the Chinese (75).
We shall deal with this trade and its importance
later on.

This thriving commercial activity in Indian seas as revealed by the *Periplus* was of course in existence to a certain
extent before the discovery of the best way in which to use
the winds of the Indian Ocean, but the account was written
at a time when the effects of the discovery were beginning
to manifest themselves to their fullest extent. Certain
general considerations of the available evidence will illustrate the far-reaching effects of Hippalos' discovery on
Rome's traffic with India.

Considerable improvements had been made in the shipping of the Indians, who had from time immemorial been
active along their own coasts and had traded with Malay,
East Africa, and the Persian Gulf (76), but in their voyaging
they were always restricted by their own attitude towards
crossing the sea, and by the Arabians. In Alexander's time
Nearchos was struck only by the river-traffic of the Indians,
not their voyages to the Persian Gulf; later on, Agatharchides shews that although Indians visited the Sabaeans,
these controlled the trading; and when the Greeks used
the monsoons fully and the Axumites arose in Africa, the
Indians were still victims of trade rivalries, and only the

North-west Sakas took regular voyages. Thus Barygaza sent large ships to the Persian Gulf—but with Parthian, not Arabian permission; North-west India traded in its own ships with North-east Africa, freely to Cape Guardafui, and then, in conjunction with Greeks and Arabs, with Somali ports—but only with Axumite and Arabian sanction. The Arabians were still masters of much of the trade (77), and the Indians did not trade in the Red Sea beyond Ocelis except in so far as the Axumites apparently allowed them to use Adulis (78); but around their own coasts they were unrestricted, and the kings controlled their own shipping. Thus the Indians of north-western districts, with Barygaza as the chief port, sent large timber-ships to Apologos and Ommana, and other ships to the marts of the Somali and even to Adulis, and well-manned boats (trappaga and cotymba) went up the the coast, piloted foreign ships to the mouth of the Nerbudda, and towed them up the river to Barygaza, whereas at the Indus mouths ships unloaded at Barbaricon on to river-vessels (79). The Tamils of the south did not sail across to the west, but instead supplied foreign ships in Cochin backwaters and at Bacare from large boats, each hollowed out of a single tree, though the Greeks often sailed themselves up to Nelcynda (80). The older rush-built vessels of Ceylonese traffic had been supplanted (before the Greeks fully used the monsoons) by vessels with a capacity of about 33 tons and provided with prows at either end chiefly for use in the narrow channels, and the time taken by voyages to and from the Ganges had been much reduced (81). But the largest and most extensive Indian shipping was that of the Coromandel coast, controlled chiefly by the Chola Kingdom. Thus Camara, Poduce, and Sopatma were frequented by ships which coasted to Malabar marts; by others (sangara), very large, made of single logs bound together, apparently double canoes either Malay in origin or corresponding with the "jangar" of Malabar to-day; and by very large ships in which men sailed to the Ganges and to Malay (the name of the ships —colandia—being either Sanskrit or Malay in origin) resembling probably the Burmese "laung-zát" or the Chinese junks. It was for their use that the lighthouses were built on the Chola coast (82). Farther north, as we know from native coins, the Andhras and the Pallavas built two-masted ships, and still farther away the shipping of Bengal seems to have been active and important (83). Sometimes Indian ships had three masts. From Philostratos we may judge that small coasting passenger-ships could be used along all Indian coasts (84).

We may conclude then that the discovery of the monsoons by the Romans caused the southern Indians to improve their local shipping, but did not make them extend the reach of their westward voyages across the seas beyond the regions which their north-west peoples had been in the habit of visiting, namely the Persian Gulf and Africa. It was typical of the western and of the eastern mind that the possession of a boon like the monsoons sent Greeks pouring over the seas to India, but did not stir up Indians to come westwards with equal energy, though as we shall see they did visit Alexandria more frequently than before.

On their side, the Egyptian Greeks were sending specially large ships to the coast of Malabar to fetch the pepper and cinnamon-leaf, and there was also a need felt for greater ships than ever at Mosyllon for the trade in cinnamon-bark, and we need not doubt that the need was supplied by wealthy Roman capitalists who were willing not only to buy the goods of export and import, but to provide ships of sufficient size and equip them with armed detachments, and there is reason to believe that some Indian or Arabian states at one time not only forbade the appearance of

foreign warships near the shores of India, but went so far
as to allow each merchant to send only one commercial ship
to India (85), and that this tendency towards restriction,
besides the consideration of efficiency against shocks from
wave and weather, of speed, and of the bulk of cargoes, made
Egyptian merchants increase the dimensions of their ships,
fitting them out (as a Chinese record apparently states) with
seven sails for travel across the Indian Ocean. At any rate,
those which were sent to Muziris were much admired by
the Tamils—they were large and fine and lashed the sea
into foam (86). The great increase in trade in the Indian
Ocean seems to have reacted even upon Roman shipping
in the Mediterranean. St Paul was wrecked on an Alexandrian ship which carried a cargo and many passengers,
and after the wreck another Alexandrian ship took all the
castaways aboard in addition to their own freights; Josephus
travelled to Rome in a ship with six hundred passengers,
and most of the references to large ships, such as these
must have been, occur after Hippalos' discovery, and later
in the time of Lucian we hear of an enormous ship 180 feet
long, 45 feet wide, 44 feet deep, with a crew like an army,
passengers of both sexes, and corn sufficient to supply
Attica for one year; it brought a large annual profit to its
Egyptian-Greek owner (87). Even in the Mediterranean
Sea the cargo-boats were Greek, not Roman, and averaged
from two hundred to three hundred tons, like the Salem
vessels which traded in the far East (88). According to writers
of the period, the Mediterranean Sea was crowded with
merchant-men long before the full discovery of the monsoons; after that event it thronged as the land (89).

What we have said above makes clear that the use of these
winds resulted at once in residence of Roman subjects in
India in considerable numbers. An Egyptian papyrus of the
latter part of the first century A.C. gives us a letter of

a woman called Ἰνδική to a friend or relation of her own
sex; she was perhaps the Indian wife of a Greek merchant
who had resided in India, but I prefer to see in her
a daughter who, born to an Egyptian Greek while he was
resident with his wife in India, was called Ἰνδική in
memory of that event (90). The tariff list of Coptos shews
that men took their wives with them on voyages from
harbours of the Red Sea. The travellers to the East were
others than true Romans. Catullus, Propertius, and Horace
had in times gone by suggested that Romans *might* go to
India, but we cannot prove that they ever did (91), and to
the Indians Rome and Roman meant Alexandria and
Alexandrians, and Roman subjects were called Yavana
(Ἰάϝονες, Ἴωνες). Thus the Yavana soldiers and bodyguards
in the service of Tamil kings, the temple of Augustus at
Muziris, and the colony of Jews in Malabar and of
Yavana at Kaviripaddinam, all point to residence but not
of true Romans; the Egyptian of the inland district
Arsinoë, registered on a census-list of Vespasian's reign
as absent in India, may have been such a resident.
A convenient way of merely visiting India was to go on
a pepper-ship as a passenger, and from such a person Pliny
seems to have obtained his account of a voyage to Nelcynda from Egypt (92). But even this class of traveller to
India from Europe must have consisted almost completely
of Greeks. Such towns on the Arabian, African, Persian,
or Indian coasts as have European names always shew
them in a Greek form, but it is a mistake to suppose
that places like Byzantion on the Indian coast were Greek
settlements or factories (93), for distortion of Indian names
accounts for these apparent settlements of Roman subjects.
We are justified only in saying that Rome's trade was
conducted by Greek, Syrian, and Jewish merchants, in
many cases resident in India, soon after and perhaps even

before the time of Pliny. As we shall see, during the second century the habit of residing in India had become a widely spread one, revealing itself very clearly in the geographical work of Ptolemy.

The thriving commerce which resulted from Hippalos' discovery is reflected in the increase of geographical knowledge revealed in writers of the first century A.C. The general outline of the Red Sea is, as we naturally expect, fairly accurate as represented by Mela and Ptolemy, but in Mela there is much greater distortion of the Persian Gulf than there is in Ptolemy, and Pliny shews that in spite of the survey and description of Iuba and of Isidore, it was not until later that mistaken ideas about the localities in the Persian Gulf were put right. Iuba thought that the Atlantic Ocean began at the promontory of Mosyllon, though Strabo could write about the coast as far as Cape Guardafui: Mela again shews knowledge of the configuration of Africa only as far as this point and does not establish the southward bend and extension of either Africa or India (94): but the author of the *Periplus* shews a knowledge extending to the Zanzibar channel and a realisation of the southern extension of both Africa and India to distances not grasped by any of his predecessors. With regard to India, the ideas of Mela are vague and imperfect; he gives the usual tales of earlier Greek writers, and has only short accounts merely of the Indus and the Ganges, with a promontory Colis or Collis between the two, forming the angle where the coast by turning from the eastern to the southern sea formed the south-eastern angle of Asia; no southern extension of India is realised at all, and the whole extent of the coasts could be covered by a voyage of sixty days and nights (95). Pliny is hopeless; for the interior of the Indus and Ganges regions he relies upon writers of the time of Alexander and his successors, and gives particular details of the Calingae of Bengal and Orissa, nearest the mouth of the Ganges; the Prasii with their capital at Palibothra are still very powerful in India. He supposed that the east coast went north and south and does not indicate the southward bend of the whole peninsula: he gives recognised voyages taken in his time, yet, in describing the geography of the peninsula, does not use the details so obtained. Of North-west India he knows little, makes no mention of Barygaza except in a passage not describing India at all, and when he states that according to some the place was the only town of Ethiopia "beyond, on the shore," the sole interest of this remark is the way in which it reveals the importance of the trade carried on by North-western Indians with the east coast of Africa, as we described from the *Periplus*. So too, in his description of Arabia, Pliny gives a long list of places on the coast, but they come from Iuba; in that account Pliny makes no mention of Muza, Cane, and Syagros—names which he does include in his account of voyages taken to India in his age! In a word, with few exceptions Pliny gives us the knowledge of India such as it was to the time of Augustus (96). The author of the *Periplus*, as we have seen, knew the west coast of India very well, as far as Nelcynda at least: but beyond that he relies upon others with the result that he carries the west coast of India wrongly beyond Cape Comorin to Colchoi and Cape Calimere, a mistake not corrected until we come to Ptolemy. We may excuse the exaggeration of the size of Ceylon as indicated by the *Periplus*; the Greeks always knew more of the products of Ceylon (which they obtained in the marts of Malabar and also the other Tamil States) than they did of its size.

Beyond the limits of the Chola Kingdom, the east coast of India and the regions of the Ganges were not yet frequently visited by Roman subjects, though, as we saw from Strabo, visits were occasionally made to the Ganges even in his time; but beyond that no exploration had been made by sea, for Poseidonios thought that Gaul lay opposite to India on the east (97). However, when Mela wrote, the Malay Peninsula (Chryse) began to come, at least by report, within the view of Roman subjects, and to the author of the *Periplus* (who, as we saw, knew something of the trade in the regions of the Ganges) was a real country, but he regarded it, as Mela had done, as an island east of the Ganges and south of the Chinese empire, sending excellent tortoiseshell (98). Josephus regarded Malay as belonging to India (99), Pliny as a headland; later one Alexander reached China by the sea-route, as we shall describe below.

With regard to the Chinese, the Augustan poets had used the name Seres in a vague way and usually with a general reference to the peoples of Central Asia and the far East. But now we find that Mela and Pliny make endeavours to assign more accurately the position of the Seres, and this name comes to refer, apparently, to China in its northern aspect. For example, Mela, proceeding in his description from south to north, describes the most remote parts of Asia as occupied by Indians, Seres, and Scythians, just as we might refer vaguely in a general way to Eastern Asia consisting of the Indies, China and Tatary, and he also says that the Seres were in the far east of Asia. Later in Roman literature Seres are the northern, Sinae the southern Chinese—in other words, the Seres were the Chinese as approached by the overland route, and the Sinae were the Chinese as approached by the southern sea-route; in this latter aspect the Chinese word Ts'in first appears in Greek literature where the *Periplus* calls China the land of This, and in Ptolemy the Sinae and Serice are distinct. The Chinese as Seres approached by the land-routes were known centuries before they were known as Sinae—except to the Arabians, for when Isaiah refers to the Sinim (100), he surely reflects Arabian knowledge; it was the discovery of the monsoons which brought the notice of the Sinae to Roman subjects; this was the real name for the Chin or Ts'in dynasty ending in 209 B.C., but the passing of silk along the land-routes from the Chinese had perhaps caused them to be called Seres after their name for silk (*ssi*, Korean *soi*, *sir*). As we shall see, during the second century Roman knowledge of the furthest East increased, and is reflected in the geography of Ptolemy, who shews the advance of men's knowledge not only south to Mozambique and to the inner parts of Africa beyond the Sahara and even to the beginnings of the Nile, but also east to China both by land and by sea, retaining, however, certain geographical errors of old standing and not corrected by the reports of merchants.

The remarkable intercourse by sea so clearly revealed by the *Periplus* as existing between India and the east coast of Africa is perhaps a striking proof of the secret kept with regard to the monsoons, first by the Arabians keeping tributary the Somali, and then by free Somali and the Axumite kingdom as well as it slowly rose to power in Africa, for the Axumites on their part did not wish to let the Romans into the secret, which thus became a possession of three races—Indian, Arabian, Axumite. That secret was discovered, but another one closely connected with it —namely, the secret of oriental cinnamon, was never revealed; the Romans found out that this plant did not grow in Arabia; but they never went beyond the idea that cinnamon was not produced in regions farther east than Africa. Nevertheless they were now free to trade directly with India, and they did so without opposition. Ultimately, in the age of her decline, Rome at last let slip her advantages and conducted her oriental trade once more through the

Axumites, but for the present such a relapse was far ahead. It is curious that the secret was kept, for we find that the distances over which Roman merchants travelled by sea in the first and second centuries A.C. were sometimes very large, one voyage sometimes covering some thousands of miles. The following table gives rough figures of distances which a western trader in oriental goods might be called upon to travel in the course of business.

					miles
From	Puteoli	to Alexandria direct—about			1100
,,	Ostia	,,	,,	,,	,,	1220
,,	Massilia	,,	,,	via Straits of Messina	,,	1400
,,	Tingis	,, Alexandria direct—about			1900
,,	Arsinoë	,, Arabia Eud. direct	,,		1300
,,	Arabia Eud.	,, Barbaricon	,,	,,	1470
,,	Arabia Eud.	,, Barygaza	,,	,,	1700
,,	Arsinoë	,, Barygaza	,,	,,	3000
,,	Myos Hormos	,, Barygaza	,,	,,	2820
,,	Berenice	,, Barygaza	,,	,,	2760
,,	Euphrates Mouth	,, Barbaricon	,,	,,	1400
,,	Euphrates Mouth	,, Barygaza	,,	,,	1850
,,	Bab-el-Mandeb	,, Cranganore	,,	,,	2000
,,	Arabia Eud.	,, Ceylon	,,	,,	2100
,,	Barygaza	,, Ceylon	,,	,,	1000
,,	Ceylon	,, Ganges	,,	,,	1200–1250
,,	Chola Kingdom	,, Ganges	,,	,,	700—800
,,	Ceylon	,, Lower Burma	,,	,,	1230
,,	Ceylon	,, Sumatra not taken di-		about 1345
,,	Malacca	,, Hanoi rect yet		,, 1300

It is hardly conceivable that during the Roman Empire a merchant ever travelled over so great a distance as from Britain to India. The distance from London to Bombay is 6260 miles by sea, and over 6000 miles from Southampton. I do not believe that men ever made voyages (with or without numerous delays on the way) longer than from the coast of Spain or of Gaul to India and back. In times previous to the imperial period Eudoxos had attempted to sail from Spain to India by the unknown Cape route, but was never heard of again, and when Pliny speaks, on the authority of Caelius Antipater, of a man who had sailed from Spain to Ethiopia for the sake of commerce, we must accept the story as true only for a voyage by way of Egypt. He mentions Nepos as the authority for a successful voyage of Eudoxos from the Red Sea to Gades round Africa and for the story of Indians who were caught by storms and were driven round the north of Asia to the Baltic! Seneca, writing at a time when the effects of Hippalos' discovery were making themselves felt, says that a voyage from Spain to India with a favourable wind was a matter of a very few days, and later Lucian says that in two Olympiads a man could sail from the Pillars of Heracles to India and back again three times, with leisure to explore tribes by the way. That is, a man could spend one year and four months between Spain and India on a journey deliberately delayed on all suitable occasions (101). Now Seneca and Lucian do not refer to imaginary voyages taken round the Cape of Good Hope but reflect, in my judgment, actual voyages then taken by way of Alexandria and the Red Sea by merchants intending to carry to India the lead and other metals of Spain and Britain, the coarse clothing of Spain and northern Gaul, and the coral of Gaul—all of which were, as I shall shew, articles of great importance in Rome's trade with India. In spite of the size of the canal leading from the Nile to Arsinoë, it is probable that such long voyages were made with a change of sea-vessel in Egypt, for the ships used in Indian seas (102) were especially large, and a lower speed of travel was attained in the Red Sea and Indian Ocean than in the Mediterranean, so that the journey from Berenice to Muziris took seventy days (103).

From what we said above, it is clear that the activities of Indians by sea after the discovery of the monsoons by a western power did not increase to any very large extent, except in the matter of local navigation round their own coasts, and we may be sure that they increased the size of the ships in which they sent cinnamon-bark to the east coast of Africa. But as soon as the Roman Empire began, and embassies had been sent by Indian states to the Mediterranean, possibilities of much greater trade than they had carried on with the Ptolemies chiefly through the Arabians filled the minds of a certain type of Indian; thus the aspirations of Indian merchants about the beginning of the first century A.C. are given in the *Milinda* as follows: "a shipowner who has become wealthy by constantly levying freight in some seaport town will be able to traverse the high seas and go to Vanga or Takkola or China or Sovira or Surat or Alexandria or the Coromandel coast or further India or to any other place where ships congregate" (104). The rest of our information on this point comes from writers living subsequent to the discovery of the monsoons, yet even now we find that the Indians found certain difficulties in the way of visiting Egypt. Dion Chrysostom implies (105) that Indians, Arabians, Babylonians, and others found it a difficult matter to set foot in Egypt, and in the case of the Indians himself gives what was one of the reasons for this—the mercantile class of Indians was not held in repute and was censured by the rest of their countrymen (106). Another reason was the partial exclusion from the Red Sea of Indians by Arabians even after the discovery of the monsoons by a western power, as is clear from the *Periplus*. A third reason was, if Mommsen's conjecture is true, the imposition by the Romans of differential customs-dues at Egyptian ports against Indian and Arabian vessels of transport possibly

before, not I think after the full discovery of the
monsoons; Mommsen makes his deduction from the *Periplus*, where we read of reciprocal intercourse between non-
Roman Africa, and Arabia and India; between Persia and
India; and between India and Arabia (107); yet there is no
sign that the merchants of these regions, engaged in
a fully active trade, came to Berenice or Myos Hormos
—not even the merchants of Muza, by far the most active
of Arabian marts at this time. This theory is supported by
the remark of Dion Chrysostom, but absence of *Indians*
is attributable to exclusion *by Arabians*. Nevertheless
the discovery of the monsoons did let many Indians into
Alexandria; for the long-standing agreement between the
Arabians and Indians by which the Indians were excluded
from the Red Sea was bound to fail when the Axumites
arose in Africa and allowed Indians to use Adulis and to
reach Egypt by land, and when a western power became
master of the Red Sea, used fully the monsoons in the
Indian Ocean, sent merchants in large numbers to India
and cancelled restrictions against Indians.

Dion Chrysostom, who was in Alexandria when Vespasian
had just been proclaimed emperor, speaks of the commercial activity of that city, and not only of Jewish, Greek,
Egyptian, Italian, Syrian, Cilician, Ethiopian, Arabian,
and Persian, but also of Bactrian, Scythian, and Indian
merchants whom he saw there attending the spectacles with
the Alexandrians (108). Again, after speaking of the marvels
of India, he adds that his statements were not false, for
some of those who had come from India had already as-
serted them to be facts, and a few Indians did come (says
Dion) in pursuit of trade, though they were not in high
repute among their countrymen (109), just as Brahmans of
high caste to-day suffer heavy penalties if they cross the
sea; and again he says that in times gone by one rarely

heard of the Red Sea or of the Indian Ocean, whereas now
Alexandria was full of merchandise and men from every
nation (110). Furthermore, we can trace an Indian on his
journey between Alexandria and India, for in an inscription of the temple at Redesiya near Apollinopolis Magna
at the end of a route from Berenice to the Nile is the name
of an Indian who halted there to worship at the shrine of
the Greek god Pan, according to a widely accepted reading,
the name Σόφων being taken to represent the Sanskrit Sub-
hanu (111). The Indians whom Dion Chrysostom saw in Egypt
may have given him the information which he gives about
Indian epic poetry—the first notice which we have of it;
Dion reports that Homer was, men said, sung among the
Indians, translated into their own language (112), and this
seems to allude to certain incidents of the Mahabharata,
of course not concerning Troy at all (113). We might note also
that the fables of Babrius and of Phaedrus (and Phaedrus
at least belongs to the earlier half of the first century A.C.)
contain Jataka stories known in India in the fourth century
B.C., while the book *Aesop's Fables* put together by Planudes
at Constantinople in the fourteenth century A.C. has Jataka
stories also. These of course reached Rome along various
channels.

After the discovery of the monsoons the presence of
Indians in Alexandria was more or less continuous, but
that many ever reached Rome itself in search of business is
very doubtful. It is true that the Romans sometimes employed Hindus to teach their elephants, and perhaps came
across Indian fortune-tellers in Rome, but these appear to
have been slaves; it is true also that Indians visited Rome
as members of an embassy; but these came on special occasions; they did not appear in Rome as they did in Alexandria
—for Martial enumerates the men of various races that
witnessed Domitian's exhibitions; of the oriental peoples

we find that Egyptians, Arabians, Ethiopians, and Sabaeans are mentioned, but not Indians, even in the sense of Ethiopians. Had Indians or Chinese really been there, Martial would never have denied himself the ecstasy of paying Domitian yet another compliment. When the same poet includes Indians and Arabians among the lovers of Cloelia, he surely presents us with fictions of his own imagination (114). Thus, though true Romans and Italians preferred to confine their travels to the Mediterranean and the provinces of the Empire, and Indians still to a large extent kept themselves to their Indian seas, Alexandria did become a point of personal contact between the two. For the rest, Greeks, Syrians, Jews, Axumites, Somali and Arabs remained wholly or partly the middlemen and traffickers between India and Rome throughout the sea-routes; Greeks, Syrians, Jews, and in some cases Arabians dwelt in India and in Italy as residents, and all along the sea-routes these same peoples were the carriers of the merchandise (115). Again, along the overland routes no discovery was made like the one made by Hippalos along the sea-route, but we know that Apollonios went to North India by the main land-route and returned from the Indus to the Persian Gulf by sea (116), and at the end of the first century and during the second century Indians and Chinese, as we shall see, visited Syria and Asia Minor, and private merchants of the West broke through the barriers of intermediaries to Central Asia and perhaps beyond; but even this development, which came in the second century, was brought about by Greeks, not Romans.

As we proceed farther west in contemplating the general results of Hippalos' discovery, we find that the effects on the life of the Roman Empire were considerable. One important result was the temporary increase of deliberate exportation of Roman coin to India in order to assist Roman trade, and the extent and probable result of this will be indicated later. It is certain that the system was regularly established before the death of Tiberius, but I think we may go farther than this and so far as to say that the development of Rome's trade after the discovery of Hippalos affected the silver coinage of the Alexandrian mint, which was intended primarily for local circulation. Tiberius restored the issuing of tetradrachms struck by that mint, but not to any great extent, yet in the second year of Claudius the mint suddenly became more active, and this activity reached its height in the twelfth year of Nero's reign, for in that single year so many silver coins were struck at Alexandria that they formed about $\frac{1}{10}$ of the Egyptian silver currency for more than a century (117) and some of them reached South India. I believe that this was due directly to Hippalos' discovery and the rapid developments which followed it, and to the increased bustle of Egyptian trade with the Red Sea which resulted, and I think it most likely that the increased activity of the Alexandrian mint in the second year of Claudius' reign enables us to suggest that an advance was made in the use of the monsoons in 41 or 42; again, we find that in 65 Poppaea Sabina died and Nero consumed an enormous quantity of oriental spices, apparently cinnamon and casia, at her death, and his luxury was in all respect notorious and abnormal; here, again, the great output of coinage in Egypt (where the emperors possessed spice- and unguent-manufactories), in the twelfth year of his reign, fits in.

This remark brings us to the next point, and that is that the wide use now made of the monsoons in the Indian Ocean opened up larger sources of articles of luxury, and caused the consumption of such products of commerce to be increased largely in the Roman Empire and above all in Rome itself. Tiberius complained of the ominous tendency, and Philon was by no means easy in his mind about certain forms of expense, while the Emperor Gaius passed all previous limits in reckless extravagance. But it is only after the full discovery of the monsoons that we get constant lamentations upon the subject of luxury, particularly as a fault of women who rejoiced in their Chinese silks and other expensive dresses and in their Indian pearls and precious stones, and St Paul and Christian writers generally, with Petronius, Seneca, and above all Pliny, voice the universal complaints of the moralists against all forms of extravagance. There can be no doubt that there was a more plentiful satisfaction of the demand in Rome for objects and products of the East that minister to luxury. Romans and Indians dwelt far from each other, yet on the one hand India with its manifold supplies of precious stones, perfumes and spices (all of which we shall consider later) contributed a very large proportion towards satisfying the luxurious inclinations of a Rome which had lost most of its ancient morality, and helped to increase certain tendencies which led to the downfall of the western Roman Empire, while she remained unchanged, though at the same time the prosperity of all alike who engaged in traffic between East and West was inevitably very great. The discovery of the full use of the monsoons brought an immense increase in Indian commerce generally and in Roman importation of Indian goods, which stimulated a yet further demand in oriental articles of luxury—as Pliny says, India had been brought near by gain (118). Nero's court set an example, especially during the ascendency of Poppaea Sabina, who, together with Otho, must have taught Nero many secrets in the art of luxury. Pliny in referring (119) to the enormous quantity of oriental spices used at her death takes occasion to complain of the large amount of specie drained annually by the East from the Empire Nero himself was accustomed to adorn shoes, beds, chambers, and so on with oriental pearls; most of his palace was decked out with gems, mother-of-pearl, and ivory, and he distributed precious stones among the people. The richer classes in general shewed a similar prodigality; Otho deliberately invited Nero to his house in order to shew him that he was not to be surpassed by the Roman Emperor in the use of fragrant essences which he caused to flow like water from gold and silver pipes, a system introduced by Nero also in his palace. Perfume-scented footsteps were nothing—a private citizen would anoint his bathroom—but we must look ahead to Elagabalus before we can find a man who wore garments wholly made of silk and took baths in Indian spikenard, and slaughtered parrots as food for men and beasts. Extravagant feasts were frequent; for one dish, says Pliny, India provided food, and in a humorous passage of Petronius a man has been sent by Trimalchio to India with a letter, in order to fetch mushroom-spore, and other passages in the same writer reveal a lavish use of ointments. All this is reflected in the statement that a need was felt at Mosyllon for larger ships in order to deal with the trade in cinnamon, and in the fact that large ships were being sent to the Malabar coast in order to carry away the vast quantities of pepper and cinnamon-leaf destined for the Roman Empire. We shall see that in A.D. 92 "horrea piperataria" were erected in Rome itself for pepper and other spices.

For the increase of display in other ways we may refer to a passage in Seneca who indulges in an outburst against the prevailing luxury of men and women; he complains about the use of most costly tortoiseshell, tables and precious woods bought at huge prices, crystal and agate vessels, pearls of enormous value lavishly displayed, and extremely costly clothes of silk which involved traffic with races not yet known to personal commerce. The whole is in effect a denunciation, as we shall see, of costly display of Indian and Chinese luxuries, though the wealthy Seneca himself possessed five hundred tables embellished with ivory legs. Petronius speaks more playfully of luxurious and vulgar display of costly Indian pearls, emeralds, crystals, rubies, and muslins by women, and the fact that "gems" of glass paste, common early in the first part of the first century, were more rarely used in the second half, I take to be due to the great influx of real precious stones from India after Hippalos' discovery and its developments(120).

Such were the general results of the discovery made by Hippalos and the developments which followed rapidly on that discovery, as far as I can judge from the evidence and I do not think that I have exaggerated. Rome's trade with India underwent two remarkable and sudden developments, of which the first took place as soon as the Roman Empire began with the establishment of Augustus in the principate; the peaceful prosperity which was thus brought to the world, the prestige of the Roman name, and the interest taken by Augustus himself, caused what may be called a sudden beginning of Roman trade with India along all possible routes. The second development came about in the reign of Claudius when some bold merchant found out the method of reaching Malabar with the monsoon, the results of which were made manifest in the reigns of Nero and his successors.

The best illustration of these results could be presented by a survey of the articles of merchandise which the Romans imported from India during the latter part of the first century A.C., hardly a single certain addition being made after that until the Arabian era. But since I have devoted the several chapters of Part II to a consideration of these importations and followed them up by a review of the imperial products which the Romans sent in return, and by a consideration of the exportation of Roman specie which was adopted in order to make up the balance of trade, I must refer the reader to that survey for full details and merely state here that from the *Periplus* and Pliny, from ordinary writers, from archaeological survivals and in particular collections of ancient gems, and from oriental sources we can obtain full records for the period represented by the reigns of Nero and Vespasian. To give details here from the *Periplus* and from Pliny would place in a false light the extent of trade at both earlier and later periods when similar sources are wanting.

APPENDIX

St Thomas and Voyages to India

EVEN if we cast aside as unhistorical every allegation of fact in the stories about St Thomas, we must at least admit that they reflect voyages habitually taken to India during the most prosperous period of the Roman Empire. Thus the story which brings the Saint to Gondophares is an echo either of land-journeys taken through Parthia towards India, or of voyages taken to the Indus by using the monsoon, as begun in what we described as Stage II. Again, the tradition which makes him land at Andrapolis is, I think, a reminiscence of voyages taken with the monsoon to some point on the west coast of India under Andhra control, perhaps to the Sigerus of Stage III. Again, the South Indian tradition which makes St Thomas land close to Cranganore recalls voyages of the final stage; and lastly, when that same tradition brings him overland from Malabar to the Chola coast, we have an echo of inland penetration of Greek merchants, possibly to Madura, Argaru, and so on, as appears from discoveries of coins, from Tamil poems, and from details in Ptolemy's *Geography* (see *J.R.A.S.* 1924, Far Eastern Section, 215 ff.; *id.* 1917, 241; Philipps, *Ind. Antiqu.* 1903, 1 ff., 145 ff.).

CHAPTER III

The Commerce from the Reign of Nero to the Death of Marcus Aurelius

IT is uncertain how far Nero or his ministers such as Burrus and Seneca (who was a diligent money maker of the old type, and wrote a book about India) deliberately fostered commerce along all possible routes. Such a policy was followed by Roman emperors generally during the first two centuries of the Empire, and in any case we cannot agree with Schur and others in carrying the Roman protectorate over the Himyarites, Hadramaut and Socotra (1). Nevertheless oriental trade may have influenced Nero in sending a mission to Meroe, now declining and apparently harassed by Axumites, and towards the sources of the Nile, and also in his projects of the invasion of Ethiópia, from which region the Axumites were perhaps causing trouble on their trade-route to the Nile, and of cutting through the isthmus of Corinth. He united the populations of Puteoli and he received special honours in Egypt which was peaceful except for increasing disputes between Greeks and Jews in Alexandria (2).

The prestige of Rome among tribes situated on the trade-route between East and West by way of the Caspian Sea, was such that Corbulo in his first campaign against Parthia was assisted by the Iberians and the Moschi from the sources of the river Phasis, and the Hyrcanians soon came in, with whom Corbulo seems to have had peculiar relations, since in order to ensure the safety of their envoys he had them escorted to a port on the Persian Gulf whence doubtless they reached home by going to the Indus mouth and through the dominion of Sakas and Kushans, in touch with Rome and probably receiving suitable gifts (3). Besides annexing Tyras and Polemon's kingdom, Nero contem-

plated an expedition against the Alans north of the
Caucasus, because of their plundering raids into Media
and Armenia, and probably it was his intention to oc-
cupy the "Caucasian Gates" (often wrongly called
"Caspian")—that is, the Darial Pass between Tiflis and
Vladikavkaz; the Aorsi, who as we saw from Strabo,
shared in Indian trade, had taken this name Alani, and
appear as Alanorsoi in Ptolemy (4).

Rome's hands were further strengthened on the eastern
frontiers by Vespasian (69–79); a hostile Parthia and
a doubtful Armenia affected in a general way the commerce
along the old main lines of communication by land between
East and West, but the Armenian settlement under Nero's
reign lasted for many years, so that the Flavians and the
Arsacids were at peace. A Roman garrison was placed at
Harmozica in Iberia itself, and the districts of the Upper
Euphrates were ·strengthened. Thus Commagene became
a province once more, legions were placed probably at
Samosata and Melitene, a road was soon paved (by
Domitian) Samosata—Melitene—Satala—Trapezus, an-
other Satala—Elegia, and another through Pontus by way
of the Lycos valley (5).

Developments of a more directly commercial kind took
place on the borders of Syria, for we find a strange jugglery
going on as a result of the Indian trade which concentrated
there. On the Tigris Seleucia represented the Roman,
Ctesiphon the Parthian interest, and when Seleucia re-
volted from Parthia (6), Vardanes tried to put Ctesiphon in
its place, and after 50, Vologeses I (A.D. 51–78) founded
Vologesocerta (Balashkert) in order to drain Seleucia,
perhaps with some success; between 78 and 108 Pacorus increased Ctesiphon (7). Vologesias (Arabian Ullaish), another
foundation of Vologeses, near Hira on the Euphrates, was
soon like Charax and Apologos in constant touch with

Palmyra by caravan, and with that desert mart the Romans now commenced close relations. For as Pliny says, Palmyra, situated between two large empires, Roman and Parthian, was the constant anxiety of both. An Egyptian, we find, was resident there; a phyle appears named after Claudius, and Corbulo sent to a freedman there named Barbaros a letter in connexion with the tolls of the city, which were levied locally but under the general supervision of Rome (8). We shall speak farther of Palmyra and its Indian trade later. This trade rivalry between the Romans and the Parthians with special reference to the Persian Gulf route from India to Syria is reflected in the similarity which exists between the Roman coinage of Cappadocia and Syria and the coinage of Parthian Babylonia, for the coinage of Cappadocia and Syria varies from the ordinary imperial currency according to the standards which held good in the neighbouring Parthian territory (9). There is an interesting passage in the Han Annals of China, based partly on a report made by the ambassador Kan Ying in A.D. 97, describing Roman Antioch, and the commerce of Syria. That province (Ta-ts'in) was full of merchandise and traded by sea with Parthia (An-hsi) and India (T'ien-chu), with tenfold profit, and the people were honest and had no double prices and were only prevented from trading with China by the Parthians who desired to retain control of the silk trade. Again, according to the Liang-shu, the Indians carried on trade with Parthia and Ta-ts'in (used often as applying to the Roman Empire in general), and as the Chin-shu perhaps implies, the Parthians and Indians came themselves to Syria, and it seems that sailors on the Parthian frontier acted as employés of Syrian ship-owners in the carriage of Chinese and doubtless Indian wares to Syria for Roman marts. We have here striking evidence of the Indian trade of Rome as conducted by way of the

Persian Gulf in the period of peace which followed the settlement of the Armenian question by Nero and preceding the Parthian war of Trajan (10). The routes to the Euphrates and even beyond were felt to be secure:—

> Tu rapidum Euphraten et regia Bactra sacrasque
> antiquae Babylonis opes et Zeugma, Latinae
> pacis iter (*scil.* narrabis).
>
> (Stat. *S.* III. 2. 136–8, to Maecius.)

In Syria, says the Nestorian inscription of Hsi-an-fu, robberies were unknown and the people enjoyed peace and happiness(11); in Mesopotamia beasts rather than men were to be feared, and hence men formed caravan-companies of one hundred, or relied on military equipment (12). It devolved upon the governor of Syria to defend the Euphrates frontier against marauders, and Mommsen thinks that the district of Sura and even Circesium was guarded for Rome by Palmyra (13). We may take it then that the great increase of trade between Egypt and India after the discovery made by Hippalos stimulated the Syrians in particular towards increasing Rome's Persian Gulf traffic as well, and that in general Rome sought to improve the conditions along all land-routes, especially with a view to eliminating Parthian middlemen.

In Central Asia, the reassertion of Chinese authority over Turkestan by Kwang Vouti between A.D. 25 and 28 led to the aggressive policy of Mingti, and to the conquests of General Pan Chao who defeated the Kushan Kanishka near Kashgar, reaffirmed Chinese authority over all Central Asia, and reached the Caspian, sending an ambassador to Syria in 97. The submission of Khotan and Kashgar in 73 opened up and made safe the route running south of the central desert to Bactra, and by 94 the route north of the desert through Samarkand to Merv was opened up by further conquests (14), so that the way lay ready for

the enterprise of Greek merchants such as Maes Titianus,
though the internal troubles of Parthia especially after the
death of Vologeses I made matters very uncertain.

Already in Nero's time Pomponius Mela knew of the silent
trade of the Himalayas, a mode of transacting business
which was perhaps the rule at Tashkurgan where normally
the Chinese met the western merchants (15); and one of the
few real facts which emerge from the stock-in-trade stories
out of which Philostratos (floruit c. 230) composed Books
II and III of his Life of Apollonios of Tyana is a journey
taken by a Greek from Aegae in Cilicia through Mesopotamia to the Hindu Kush, Kabul river, Indus river, Taxila,
and the Hyphasis, and back by way of the Indus mouth and
the Persian Gulf, at some time between the accession of
Nero and the death of Domitian (16).

Two events of this period might have dealt serious blows
at Rome's oriental trade; one was the great fire of A.D. 64,
but however disastrous that event may have appeared to
a merchant arriving by way of the Tiber, as it did to St
John as shewn in the eighteenth chapter of the book of
Revelation, the destruction was only local in its effect,
and did not touch Puteoli the chief Italian port for oriental
wares; moreover Nero remedied the damage swiftly and
in such a way that Rome became more splendid than before. India supplied all the Empire, not Rome only. The
other event was the chaos of A.D. 69, but here again
Vespasian did not use to the detriment of Rome the opportunity given him when he was proclaimed emperor at
Alexandria. Both in 64 and in 69 there was perhaps a
slight depression of trade, but Egypt, wholly untouched
by the first disaster was only slightly disturbed by the
second.

The reign of Vespasian brought fresh peace, prosperity,
replenishment of the State treasury, a less extravagant
court, and a less extravagant commerce, but we cannot

maintain with Sewell that the Indian traffic grew less, or that the upper classes desisted from their extravagant tastes. Pliny bewails the luxury of the age, and does not indicate that Vespasian changed what Pliny thought were contemporary evils. Both Vespasian and Titus wore silk at Rome in their triumph over the Jews (17), Titus dissipated the funds accumulated by his father, and Domitian in his turn was equally lavish and waged expensive wars. Nerva did his best to relieve the burdens of the treasuries and made the mistake of confining his interests too much to Italy, but the provinces generally remained in peaceful prosperity; the well-being of Syria is revealed by the Han Annals, as we saw just now. The best evidence we have of Indian commerce carried on unchecked in the age between the death of Nero and the death of Domitian is revealed by Martial and Statius, who refer constantly to Indian wares of all kinds. Of the animal world we hear of Domitian's tigers, Indian ivory (this Indian kind ever growing more frequent), tortoiseshell, and above all pearls which are mentioned again and again by Martial especially, and by Statius (18). Quintilian too, who seldom mentions luxury or commerce, speaks of pearls, and shews that silk, which Martial shews was still characteristic of wealthy households, was being used as a material in the Roman toga (19). The Indian parrots were still favourite pets, kept in sumptuous cages and honoured at death by memorial odes of which Statius gives us one.

Among plant-products of the far East we have frequent references to cinnamon and casia by Martial—(the costlier shoots only by Statius, who reflects the society of richer men than Martial), to amomum, nards, and above all to pepper, which continued to be an article of general use, but still sometimes fetched high prices. In 92 Domitian constructed in Rome warehouses for spices (horrea piperataria, so called from the chief spice pepper)—buildings of which

remains have come to light, and I take farther in connexion
with this the construction by the same emperor in 95 of a
new and shorter road from Rome to Puteoli (the port for
eastern cargoes) by a branch leaving the Appian way at
Sinuessa, and called the Domitiana (20). These facts alone
are sufficient to prove that there was no decline in the
traffic in oriental spices and unguents. But, besides this,
famous manufacturers of and dealers in unguents appear,
above all a man named Cosmus (21), who was well known
even in Nero's time and gave his name to an unguent and
to a kind of jar, and another named Niceros who was
apparently a dealer in cinnamon especially (22). Even
Domitian wrote a book *de capillorum cura* (23). So great was
the use of aromatics at funerals that the death of any living
thing tended to call forth from the poets reference to Indian
and Arabian perfumes. With the remark that we cannot
be certain that by "sindon" Martial means fine cotton
muslins, we pass on to the mineral products of Indian
origin.

That the supply of these in Rome was still plentiful is
quite clear from Martial and Statius whose references are
generally to Indian stones and reveal that the tastes of the
wealthy were just the same as they were under Nero. Most
prominent were the crystal and myrrhine vessels used for
drinking the finest wines; they were often classed together
and were both a sign of wealth and extravagance. Of ring-
stones the Indian sardonyxes still held the highest place, and
these together with emeralds, diamonds and "jaspers" were
worn on one finger: these with emeralds, silk, and spikenard were demanded by mistresses of their lovers; these
with all kinds of precious wares were sold in the Saepta;
decoration too of goblets, bedsteads, and so on, was still
more frequent than it had been before.

Considerable activity was taking place on the eastern
frontiers of the Empire, and Domitian paid particular

attention to the roads in the north part of Asia Minor (24).
The crossing at Zeugma had become very familiar, and
although the regions round the Caspian Sea were still
regarded as inhospitable, nevertheless considerable interest was being taken in that region of the world (25)
from which the Alans were causing trouble at least
to the Parthians. The continued prosperity of the sea-
route is shewn by the importance of the arrival of the
Egyptian corn-fleet at Puteoli bringing Indian wares on
board (26).

Thus, without using the *Periplus* and Pliny to fill in the
details for us, we can shew the constant activity of
Rome's commerce with the East even from writers who
have no special occasion to mention India or Indian
articles.

Trajan is sometimes regarded as a second Augustus in
Roman history, and he may be said to have been a second
Augustus in Roman commerce. His aggressive policy was
certainly due partly to his soldierly nature, but we shall
see that like many other soldiers of Rome in days gone by
he conducted his campaigns with a view to helping Rome's
commerce. We see a tendency to abolish client kingdoms
in the eastern parts of the Empire and to increase Roman
prestige in those regions, and although Trajan's policy was
not imitated in all respects by his successors, nevertheless
of the examples of annexation that took place during his
reign, the only one of which the object was entirely commercial was maintained by subsequent rulers; if he really
had dreams of boundless conquest in the East they were only
temporarily and partly realised (27). I wish to shew here
that we can trace activities on the part of Trajan with reference to all the routes between Rome and India, and that
we must not apply to him that hideous term "militarist"
without qualification; and I consider that he planned to
link with each other Egypt and Nabataean Arabia;

Nabataean Arabia and Syria; Syria and the Persian Gulf; Syria and the Upper Euphrates; the Upper Euphrates and the Black Sea; and to foster oriental trade with all these regions.

Already in A.D. 100 or thereabouts steps were begun to link up the eastern boundaries of the Empire commercially and otherwise by the reduction of frontier districts to a common level. Cappadocia with Armenia Minor and Pontus were placed under one governor whose authority extended from Trapezus on the Black Sea and along the Upper Euphrates frontier to the northern borders of Syria, and, further to the South, the kingdom of Herod Agrippa II (who died about A.D. 100) was incorporated with Syria and the region of Damascus became strictly Syrian(28). Soon after, Trajan determined to do away with the client kingdom of the Nabataeans, and in 106, perhaps on the extinction of the native line in King Dabel, their territories were broken up and the greater part of them formed into a Roman province often called Arabia Petraea, that is, Arabia belonging to Petra the chief town(29). Hellenism now spread more easily among the people, and inscriptions in the native tongue cease after 106 and Greek ones begin; splendid buildings arose, but a portion of the profits which hitherto were reaped by the Nabataeans was diverted to Palmyra, which rose rapidly and silently during the second century, and it is only after the destruction of that city that we find Petra described once more as full of merchandise in plenty(30). Leuce Come ceases to be mentioned in records dating after the beginning of the second century unless we identify it with Auara in Ptolemy's *Geography*; but Aela or Aelana becomes an important haven, superseding Leuce Come (perhaps because this was destroyed by the Axumites) and an excellent road was constructed from the boundaries of Syria through Philadelphia in Palestine and Petra to the Red Sea itself, ending at Aelana(31), and at

Bostra was instituted a legionary camp which controlled Hauran; Bostra soon became a city of commercial as well as military importance, for its position made it a favoured eastern mart for the Syrian desert, Arabia, and Parthia; the remains of a Roman road leading from Bostra to the Persian Gulf tell their own tale, while on the western side the chief routes leaving Bostra led north-north-west to Damascus, south-west to Judaea. Greek coins appear under Antoninus Pius, and colonial rights were bestowed by Alexander Severus. Garrisoned forts secured the road from Damascus to Palmyra (32).

These various changes inevitably affected the relations between the Roman and the Parthian Empires, but of course other reasons besides produced the war against Parthia which caused Trajan to leave Rome in A.D. 113 (33). He now determined to treat Armenia as he had treated the Nabataeans. In the first stage Samosata was lost and recovered, and at Satala Trajan met kings of Colchis and of other Caucasian peoples such as the Iberians, Albanians, and Apsilians, and bestowed special honours upon the kings of other northern tribes called the Heniochi and the Machelones, thereby increasing the prestige of Rome along the northern trade-route to the East; Armenia became a Roman province and the Caucasian tribes stood in the same relations with Rome as Armenia had before (A.D. 114). Melitene was raised to the rank of a great city (34).

Meanwhile Media was invaded by the Moor Lusius, who crossed the Araxes, and Parthia was further embarrassed by civil strife; hence without difficulty Mesopotamia was organised as a Roman province, Nisibis was made a permanent Roman fortress, and Trajan retired to Antioch (A.D. 115) (35). A fleet was now built on the Euphrates, Adiabene was conquered and according to Eutropius converted into the province of Assyria, and after the fall of Babylon and of Ctesiphon the Parthian capital (36) Trajan with fifty ships descended the Tigris to Charax Spasinu in the territory of the King of Mesene, which was now made tributary to Rome instead of to Parthia, and put in order the ferry- or harbour-dues of horse- and camel-traffic of the Euphrates and the Tigris (37). Since the customs frontier of Syria was not well defined, control now established over the traffic existing between the great commercial towns of the Tigris and the Euphrates was a substantial gain to the Roman Empire (38).

Trajan's next scheme was one which had been suggested at the imperial court for some time owing to past dealings with Parthia and the reputed wealth and new accessibility of India through the discovery of the monsoons. According to the words of Statius, Babylon Bactria India Arabia and the Chinese were awaiting conquest by Domitian; Martial says Rome could present Trajan to the Chinese, the Parthians, and others, and Plutarch was of the opinion that, given leaders such as Pompey and Caesar acting conjointly, India could not have resisted 70,000 Roman troops (39). With such ideas as this already in his mind (we may suppose) Trajan's ambitions were thoroughly aroused by his introduction to the marts and traffic of the Persian Gulf, especially when he found (as he must have found) that Mesene and Characene were in direct trade with the Kushans and India a few hundred miles away, and he turned his eyes towards Indian seas and India. He interviewed the pilots of the Persian Gulf and people who had visited India, and when he saw a ship bound for India, remarked that if he were young he would sail to India himself (40). He was forced to return by the revolt of northern Mesopotamia, in the suppression of which towns were burnt down. Parthia was granted a king by Trajan and the Kushan Huvishka put RIOM on coins.

Thus ended a strange episode in Trajan's life. Now Dio

Cassius says that after his return to Rome in 106, he had received many embassies from barbarian courts and especially from the Indians, to whom he exhibited shows and granted seats among the Senators. This may have been the spark that fired Trajan's ambition. One of these embassies may have come from a Kushan ruler (41) who would be Kanishka (perhaps seeking help against the Indians or the Chinese, perhaps with commercial objects), for it is certain that Kanishka bears in his inscription at Ara the title "Caesar," and a rock inscription at Manikyala reveals that the Kushans now divided the day into hours according to the Roman system. Roman and Christian influence has been traced in Indian sculptures of Gandhara, Benares, Mathura, and Amaravati, but the supposed resemblances between the sculptures of Trajan's column and the bas-reliefs of Amaravati, and the supposed parallel development of bust-portraiture in Roman stone and on Kushan coins (42), appear to me to be mere speculation. Relations between Rome and the Kushans had always been friendly, and the actual presence of the Roman Emperor himself in the East, victor on the Danube and on the Euphrates, must have increased the fame of the western power. The Kushans found the Romans, though more remote, yet more advantageous friends than the uncommercial Parthians, while Trajan on his side knew well that by his wars he had for a time closed to Romans the silk-route through Parthia. The general results of Trajan's visit to the East are reflected in the rise of Palmyra, in the occurrence of three gold coins (of Domitian, Trajan, and Sabina) together with coins of Kadphises II, Kanishka, Huvishka at Jellalabad, and above all in the detailed information of North-west India contained in Ptolemy.

A severe and disastrous rebellion of Jews in Egypt probably influenced Trajan's policy with reference to

the sea-route to India. The old canal leading to Arsinoë
was cleared out by Trajan, who constructed another
(Τραιανὸς ποταμός) between the Nile and the Gulf of Suez,
starting at the fortress of "Babylon" (Baboul), which was
now rebuilt, and ending at Clysma where as Ptolemy shews
a permanent garrison was established. The importance of
these improvements of Trajan is revealed by the fact
that papyri record the keeping clean of this canal during
the fourth and fifth centuries, and by reference to the use
of Clysma as a port in Lucian, Antoninus Martyr, Epi-
phanius, and so on; the canal lay near the military centre
of Egypt and would be used more and more as robbers and
nomads began to infest the Thebaid. In Lucian a boy sails
from Clysma to India on a cargo-boat.

Trajan is said to have established a Roman fleet upon
the Red Sea. Both Eutropius and Jerome (who appear
to me to refer to the Persian Gulf) say that this was
for the purpose of laying waste the "boundaries of
India," and Kennedy connects the temple at Muziris
with a sea-expedition sent by Trajan. Now I do not
say that such a thing is impossible, especially since pirates
were a nuisance off the Indian coast, and the Indian embassy received by Trajan may have been connected with
some such trouble, but I prefer to confine Rome's military
activities within the Strait of Bab-el-Mandeb, and to deduce hostility on the part of Trajan towards Arabian
pirates in the Persian Gulf(43).

I think that the clearing of the old canal (100 feet wide,
receiving the largest merchant-ships), and the construction
of a new one with a military post at each end, are to be
connected if not with a "Red Sea" fleet at least with
the new province of Arabia, and that Trajan had two
objects in view:—(i) to re-open an old commercial passage
to the Red Sea and the Indian Ocean; in order to do this

the voyage down the Red Sea must be made safe from pirates; hence the φρούριον at Clysma which could be used as a base, the object of any fleet which Trajan put upon oriental waters being exaggerated through the Indian trade and the reputation of Trajan. (ii) Just as he linked Gaul with the Black Sea (men said) by his roads, the Black Sea with Syria, Syria with Petra, so he sought to join the new Arabian province with Egypt. Alexandria and Nabataea had not been easy of access to one another through Pelusion and Rhinocolura, but there was an easy way from Clysma and Arsinoë across the Sinai peninsula, and, granted that pirates were not active, round that peninsula to Aelana (44).

Finally, in Italy Trajan excavated a large basin called the Portus Traiani (now Lago Trajano) and surrounded with quays, connected it with the port of Claudius, enlarged the artificial channel leading to the Tiber, continuing it to the sea, and took measures to ensure regular sailings. A new city grew up called Portus, or Portus Urbis, or Portus Romae, which not only caused the decline of Ostia (in spite of constant efforts to prevent it) but had an adverse effect upon Puteoli, so that in 174 a Tyrian agency reported to their head office at Tyre that they had experienced much loss of trade while their "statio" at Rome flourished. Perhaps the spread of nard-manufacture to Rome, as indicated by Galen, represents a part of this decline. But Puteoli was not supplanted; merchants always got a better return cargo there than they did at Rome (45).

Thus the apologists for Trajan have a good case. Writers in both ancient and modern times have misunderstood his mixed motives in dealing with problems affecting the eastern boundaries of the Roman Empire, and see little other than military ambition. His real mistake lay in trying to deal with the great land-routes as he did with the remainder—by force, namely against Parthia; he tried it

W C   7 last and ultimately the scheme failed though other routes were improved. Hadrian was wiser and looked to Egypt and Palmyra, and his more peaceful attitude created a better impression. On the whole, we may go so far as to say that the period extending from the accession of Trajan to a time shortly preceding the death of Marcus Aurelius was the period of Rome's most widely spread, if not her most intense, commercial intercourse with India and China. The gold coins of this reign and Hadrian's with one of the elder Faustina found at Nellore (some of Trajan's being very fresh and new), and one of Trajan's found inland at Athiral, indicate extensive trade up the east coast of India (46).

Hadrian, acting upon his own ideas which differed much from those of Trajan, seems to have paid careful attention to Rome's eastern trade, inaugurating an era of peace and prosperity which lasted for nearly fifty years; commerce flourished and probably reached the highest point attained in ancient times, though we can trace only indications of it. Hadrian visited all parts of the Empire, one journey (129–134) being confined to the eastern provinces. His first important act was to surrender the three new eastern acquisitions, Armenia, Mesopotamia, Assyria. We will not discuss here the various criticisms passed upon this abnegation of Trajan's policy (47), but simply put forward the following suggestions. During the peaceful. administration of Hadrian and Pius the commercial relations between the Roman marts on the eastern limits of Syria and the towns on the Euphrates seem to have been especially lively and to the north of Armenia Roman prestige and activities continued to increase; Hadrian paid particular attention to these northern regions, to Palmyra, and to Petra, and we may surmise that he was influenced by the following considerations: (a) If Rome could secure control over Arabian routes from such marts as Charax, Vologesias, and Apologos to Palmyra and Petra, there was no need to retain Mesopotamia (48). (b) If Rome could secure influence in the Euxine and Caspian regions, there was no need to hold Armenia as a province. (c) A peaceful Parthia was the best security for a share in the overland route. If these were really the ideas of Hadrian, we shall find them justified by their results. Doubtless during his reign Maes Titianus was able to send his agents along the land-route through Parthia to Central Asia, unless indeed they went by sea to the Kushan dominions and worked from there. At any rate, we read that Hadrian was on good terms with the Parthians, Mesopotamians, Albanians, and Iberians and received messengers of friendship from Indian and Bactrian kings—the last being Kushan (49). There was no question of resigning the new province of Arabia Petraea, which was visited by Hadrian, who bestowed favours upon Petra, went on to the Euphrates (123), and returned westwards by way of Pontus and the Euxine (50).

Most particular attention was paid to the commerce between Syria and the Persian Gulf. Having bestowed favours upon Damascus, Hadrian turned his attention to Palmyra; this city, which long before attracted the greed of Antonius, had risen slowly from comparative obscurity (for Strabo and Mela make no mention of it) to a state of importance which caused it to be an object of care to both Rome and Parthia, being free but closely watched and permitted to develop on the lines of a Greek municipality of the Roman Empire. It was destined to rise in any case, and reaped advantage from the action of Trajan in regard to Petra; at first the prosperity of the new Arabian province and of Palmyra went on parallel with each other, but Petra had Egypt as competitor, and the position of Palmyra was such that trade flowed irresistibly towards her; when Appian

wrote, her carriage of Indian wares to the Romans after
receiving them from Parthians and Arabians was specially
noticed (51). The source of her wealth was her caravan
trade in Indian, Chinese, and other wares controlled
by apparently permanent ἀρχέμποροι and conducted by
organised and protected caravan-services across the desert
from Vologesias, Forath (Basrah = Ferath Maisan), and
Charax Spasinu (Mohammarah) (52), through Palmyra to
Antioch, Epiphania, Arados, Laodicea, Damascus, and so
on, and the profits obtained by merchants and the town
itself from this carriage-trade were sufficient to raise a
city of few local industries to a position of brilliant prosperity, as the remains of the place shew. After his visit in
A.D. 130 Hadrian granted special favours to Palmyra, and
in 137 the dues were revised and a new tariff was pro-
mulgated cancelling the old system of taxation "by custom"
and having for its object the prevention of disputes
between collectors and merchants; the collecting was
done by the town, but all dues valued at more than one
denarius were to be paid in Roman coin and the modius
was to be the measure of quantity. The list shews that the
bulk of the trade consisted in the carriage of sweet oils—
the Syrian and Assyrian (that is, Indian Parthian and
Arabian) unguents of Roman poets (53). The Palmyrenes
erected buildings in honour of Hadrian, but the rank of
colony and *ius Italicum* granted by Rome belong to a
later reign (54). The town was destined to rival Rome herself,
and her great rise in prosperity between 130 and 273 was
doubtless partly due to the fact that merchants realised
that Palmyra lay upon the shortest route between Rome
and India, and was placed between the Parthian and
Roman Empires, and now that the caravans were properly
protected, the desert-roads lost one of their disadvantages,
and merchants tended to deal along a well protected route

and to leave routes such as the one which led from Gerrha to Petra. Stuffs destined for Syrian marts would be attracted towards a short desert-route, and were brought by Arab and Indian (55) (not Palmyrene) ships to the Persian Gulf and the Euphrates, where at given places the Palmyrene caravan-men took over the consignments. Hadrian may be said to have given a new turn to oriental commerce not wholly to the advantage of Egypt (where, be it noted, he was heartily disliked), and later on Palmyra became dangerous—and in a crisis hesitated whether she would side with the Sassanids or with Rome.

There is evidence that Rome obtained a paramount influence at this time over the northern trade from the East to the Black Sea. The Iberians troubled Media, the Alans Armenia and Cappadocia; both were dealt with by Rome and Parthia (56). By Hadrian's orders Arrian carried out a tour of inspection round the Euxine Sea, and from a report we learn that there were garrisons at Hyssu Limen (at the mouth of the Sourmun), at Apsaros (Gonieh?), Phasis, and Dioscurias (gradually replaced by Sebastopolis) and of course there was one at Harmozica (since Vespasian's time), and all these places tended to become "canabae." Kings were given where required, and dilatory tribes reminded of their duties. The Euxine became a Roman lake scoured by warships when necessary. Imperial subjects frequently visited Phasis above all and doubtless Dioscurias where many interpreters of languages were employed, but the Caspian Sea was rarely reached (57). Here also Hadrian may have been moved partly by ideas of frontier defence, but in so remote a district northern and oriental commerce must have been the chief consideration.

Hadrian visited Egypt twice, and, perhaps startled by a raid made upon loaded camels in the Thebais (58), and desirous of tapping the resources of the Mons Porphyrites and of shortening the journey between the Nile and the Red Sea, founded a new city called Antinoë or Antinoöpolis north of Tell el-Amarna, and in order to divert traffic from the ports into it, constructed a road through level country to Berenice (by way of Myos Hormos and then along the coast), provided with stations, guards, and cisterns. Completed in 137, it is not mentioned subsequently and at any rate does not seem to have diverted much of the traffic from the regular Coptos—Berenice road (59). Coptos retained its ancient importance, and from it was still controlled a transport-service (60). In the Red Sea, it is possible that the Romans left the necessary repression of pirates to the Axumites—for in the inscription of Adulis (2nd cent. A.C.?) the Ethiopian king claims to have made war from Leuce Come (which now disappears in literature) to the land of the Sabaean king (61). Hadrian and the Alexandrians (62) did not like each other—possibly because Hadrian had shewn such favour to Palmyra, but, as we have seen, he cannot be charged with an undue predisposition towards any important centre of commerce. Egypt, Petra, Palmyra, Damascus, the Euxine, all received their share of attention from him, the Empire was at peace, and commerce flourished. We may conclude that the wealthy indulged their tastes, for Hadrian himself had a large and most valuable collection of gems under the care of his "a dactyliotheca Caesaris," and the highest point in the art of gem-engraving is reached between Nero and Marcus Aurelius. Hadrian could dedicate very costly objects—even an Indian serpent—and distributed aromatics among the people; moreover the usual array of Indian things appears in Juvenal (63).

The result of Hadrian's policy was the peaceful rule of Antoninus Pius, marred by only one serious war. The Scythians were kept back from Olbia, the Alans from

Armenia, and the Lazi of Colchis requested the Romans to grant them a king; Palmyra continued to rise, Bostra was hellenised, Egypt was generally peaceful, and it was a happy age. The "justice" of Pius was such that Indians, Bactrians, and Hyrcanians sought his friendship, perhaps really as a result of the enterprises of men like Maes and Alexander—we have no further details (64). That Pius forbade luxury at his court is no evidence of any change in the manners of men and women.

With Marcus Aurelius we see the beginnings of a decline in the vitality and resources of the Empire, which was devastated by a dreadful plague contracted by the army in the East. There were fearful wars on the Euphrates and Danube; migratory movements of tribes surging in regions north of the Empire caused the Marcomanni and other peoples to press down upon Roman territory for thirteen years, and this was only a beginning. In order to pay his expenses Marcus Aurelius had to sell the gem-collection of Hadrian, the imperial Indian crystals and agates, and the partly silk wardrobe of the Empress. The results of this are reflected in the falling off in the finds of coins in India dating from his reign, and the best period of the glyptic art of Rome terminates with Commodus, while Christianity influenced many people against the wearing of gems and the cutting of pagan subjects upon them. After the death of Caracalla Roman commerce by sea was reduced to a very low ebb and perhaps ceased altogether. Even at the end of Marcus' reign the issue of gold stopped and much of the silver currency was called in for re-issue in a farther debased form, and after Caracalla coins in South India cease for a long time (65).

Yet under Marcus Aurelius the Empire may be regarded as still prosperous. In Egypt the increase of trade which followed the discovery of the monsoons had caused the rate

of interest to drop to ten or twelve per cent., and the coinage
was good and plentiful at least to A.D. 170. But in the reign
of Antoninus Pius complaints about taxation began and
under Aurelius the Bucolic War made matters worse.
Under Commodus the supply of Egyptian corn to Rome
had to be supplemented by an African corn-fleet, and the
standard of the coinage was lowered (66). Disputes between
collectors customs-informers (delatores) and merchants
caused Marcus Aurelius between 176 and 180 to issue
a rescript laying down certain rules and giving a list of the
chief imports from Arabia, East Africa, and India subject to
the "vectigal Maris Rubri" on entry into Egypt (67). Palmyra
seems to have remained free from every misfortune, but
a Parthian war brought the devastation of Syria and the
destruction of Seleucia and Ctesiphon and the closing of the
overland route to Roman subjects, though at the same time
the Romans won freedom from Parthian aggression for
many years. The destruction of Seleucia almost extinguished
Greek culture east of the Euphrates, and the kings of Mesene put Aramaic legends on their coins, but otherwise the
oriental traffic was not much harmed, and men in stations
of life not connected with commerce had had the intensity
of this trade thrust upon their notice. Thus we have in
Aristeides an exaggerated statement of the vast quantities of Indian and Arabian merchandise to be seen in Rome;
Pausanias learnt of the extensive barter going on between
Greeks and Indians in India; Xenophon the Ephesian could
speak of the merchants who passed through Coptos on the
way to Ethiopia and India (68); in Lucian (who shews the
interest of the Syrian in oriental trade) we have echoes of
land-journeys to Babylon and Bactria, Roman troops led
across the Indus, mention of Muziris (in a way shewing
how much quicker the sea-route was), a journey from Greece
by south Asia Minor to Seleucia, and from Parthia to Egypt

by way of Babylonia and the Arabian desert; we have also a journey to Coptos, and to India from Clysma, and even a suggestion of travels from Spain to India (69). On the other side we have a possibility of Bactrians and even Chinese being known in Asia Minor (reading Σῆρας not Σύρας? though Lucian is only joking and the names Indopatres, *var. lect.* Indopates, and Heramithres suggest Syrians—in which case Indopates is one who had walked in India); in an epigram Lucian apostrophises an Indian perhaps with more than mere rhetorical wit, and in the *De Syria Dea* we see the wealth of Syria through varied associations beyond the Euphrates. People sent to India and the Hyperboreans for their curiosities, treasures, and delicacies, and a man might wish to fly with wings from Greece to India in a day. Even the Euxine trade is not without an echo (70). At this period Appian was impressed by the Indian transit-trade of Palmyra, Plutarch by the possibility of the conquest of India (71). In ordinary writers too Indian products appear as usual. Thus we have Indian tortoiseshell, ivory, muslins, silks, spices, pearls, stones (sardonyxes, sards, "emeralds," sapphires and so on) and peacocks in Lucian; parrots and other strange creatures and a true knowledge of silk in Pausanias and Pollux; special mention of pearls, Indian white cotton muslins, and parrots in Arrian who, like his friends, had seen many of these birds; he likewise notices the bringing of Indian wares in general into the Roman Empire in his time; we read too of the extravagances in oriental wares of Verus, Commodus, and later on of Elagabalus who surpassed all in his extravagance in Indian beasts, parrots, precious stones, spices, and silk, and writers like Clemens, Cyprian and Tertullian lament the luxury of women in their time.

The evidence of technical writers is also valuable. To give a list of the Indian plants mentioned by Galen in his

voluminous writings would only make a repetition of the
list which will come in detail later. But we must notice
that although Indian medicine as a whole did not spread
west until the time of the Arabian conquests, Galen mentions Indian prescriptions and perhaps an Indian physician,
and we can at least use his works to prove that all the
Indian plant-products continued to play their part in Rome's
Indian trade in much the same proportion as in the latter
part of the 1st century A.C. The work of Apicius (written
in the 3rd century but based on earlier material) shews us,
as we shall see, to what extent Indian spices, aromatics,
and so on were used as table-foods, and he appears to describe one Indian recipe for the kitchen (72).

Such evidence as this is good enough as far as it goes,
but it is not to be compared with that which is given by
Ptolemy's geography. From the point of view of the student
of Rome's commerce of the second century, since Ptolemy's
work is above all considerations geographical, wherever
he departs from his general custom of giving mere lists of
names, and mentions other particulars, for instance with
reference to an article of commerce dealt in at any particular locality, there we are justified in assuming an important peculiarity of the trade of Rome's merchants during
that century when Ptolemy was writing; bearing in mind
that many important details are omitted by the geographer
who was not writing a mercantile treatise for the use of
merchants, and that even in the geography we see the
astronomer rather than the geographer. It just happens
that Ptolemy's descriptions of Indian seas possess a quality
not very prominent in the rest of his work—in describing
Indian seas Ptolemy relied above all upon the *recent* accounts
of merchants, some of them contemporary. The most remarkable characteristics are these:—

(a) In dealing with Indian seas, where any fresh discovery

has been made in India or beyond in recent times, he adds it to his descriptions—often it is a notice of some commercial product, rarely it is characteristics of races. But in his survey of the western world additions about commercial articles do not occur.

(b) Throughout all the coasts of Indian seas *not* subject to Rome, Ptolemy designates among the coast-towns and villages a certain number, each called ἐμπόριον, and diligently enumerates each foreign capital and royal seat (μητρόπολις, βασίλειον). But in his survey of the West (mostly included in the Roman Empire) he does not trouble to point out "emporia" as such at all (73).

(c) His use of the word ἐμπόριον is restricted. A general comparison between the Arabian, East African, and Indian coast-towns designated by the *Periplus* as ἐμπόριον or ὅρμος with or without the epithet νόμιμον, -ος or ἔνθεσμον, -ος, or the like, and the oriental coast-towns designated by Ptolemy as ἐμπόρια (he never adds any epithet) shews that with few exceptions, due to local alterations in political or commercial status, Ptolemy designates as ἐμπόρια only those sea-coast marts which the *Periplus* had called νόμιμα or ἔνθεσμα; thus by the single word ἐμπόριον Ptolemy means a νόμιμον ἐμπόριον— a legal mart where foreign trade was officially allowed and taxed. But no Egyptian port is called ἐμπόριον by Ptolemy; hence I conclude that in the geographer's descriptions of Indian seas (in other words, as soon as he describes *non*-Roman but well-known territory) ἐμπόριον means an authorised sea-coast (not inland) mart in the Orient where *non*-Roman dues were levied by *non*-Roman authorities; these were facts naturally noticed by Roman subjects, and the rule applies throughout the oriental coasts described by both the *Periplus* and by Ptolemy, being especially clear in the case of the Arabian and west Indian shores, and it applies also surely to regions explored since the *Periplus* was written.

(d) In dealing with regions of the East, Ptolemy tells us in his prefaces that he relies upon the testimony written and oral of merchants and voyagers, and he cites examples. In dealing with the West, however, he cites none such and in dealing with the North one only—on the length of Ireland (74). But from Marinos he reports that Diogenes sailed beyond Aromata, Dioscoros to Cape Prason, Theophilos as far as Rhapta; Ptolemy talked, it seems, with merchants who had visited Simylla, Malay, and regions beyond, one Alexander having reached even Chinese waters. Likewise his extraordinarily copious account of Ceylon and its products comes from such a merchant or merchants, while for the great land-route to China the particular authority is Maes Titianus as referred to by Marinos of Tyre (75). Put shortly, Ptolemy's accounts of the far East come chiefly from παραδόσεις, ἱστορίαι, and ὁδοιπορίαι (itineraries), including works like the παράπλους τῆς Ἰνδικῆς of Androsthenes mentioned by Athenaeos (76), works often studied at first hand by Ptolemy.

The reason for this double character of Ptolemy's work is due partly to the fact that he deals with a Roman and with a non-Roman but well-known world, partly to the fact that Ptolemy as an Egyptian Greek took a natural interest in the trade of the Roman Empire by sea with the far East, and at Alexandria met many oriental traders. The result is that while in his description of the West Ptolemy (as he admits) relies almost entirely on the Syrian Marinos, in the East he uses this authority much less except for the land-route—for Marinos as a Syrian had a natural bent for the West and the land-route to the East. For Indian seas the sources used by Ptolemy were often reports (77) of merchants as is revealed every time he mentions an "emporium" and some commercial product, often, it seems, not relying upon Marinos; and here indeed we seem to see the mercantile instinct in Ptolemy, who emphasises his reliance upon the direct reports of traders, a class which Marinos, it seems, distrusted; he seems to imply too that his informants about the districts of India and of remote regions beyond Malay were not only Greeks who had visited and resided in those regions but Indians who were visiting Alexandria and could talk some sort of Greek (78). They affirmed that outward voyages beyond India went in an eastern, return voyages in a western direction—and if Ptolemy himself had trusted these simple statements instead of a preconceived system of geography, he would never have made the coast bend south so as to cause the Chinese coast to face westwards and Cattigara (Hanoi? or Canton?) to fall by calculation in Borneo. Likewise, had he merely accepted the statements of even ordinary merchants and not superimposed the system of Marinos, he would not have given the coast of India from the Indus to the Ganges a great excess of longitude and denied in his scheme the southern peninsula formed by India.

Yet many merchants, now using the monsoon wind to reach often a given mart and no other, would fail to realise this geographical fact, and so spread false reports. The author of the *Periplus* made no mistake here because he coasted the Indian seas as far as Cochin backwaters. But at any rate Ptolemy has given us much more than an arm-chair reproduction of a previous compiler; he has given almost a first-hand report, in a word, contemporary.

What we have said surely proves that of set purpose Ptolemy adds to his descriptions of Indian regions information not contained in previous geographers of the first century and in handbooks such as that written by the author of the *Periplus* and others used for instance very sparingly by Pliny. So it is in just these Indian regions that Ptolemy relies above all upon traders, and that is why I lay so much stress upon his evidence, especially where it includes the mention of emporia, capitals, and royal seats. Of set purpose too Ptolemy interjects, so to speak, some new facts recently established about certain articles of oriental commerce (in *all* cases Indian): why otherwise should we be told suddenly of the diamond in one place, the beryl in another, and so on? Almost always the information is such as is not found in earlier writers—of pepper, for instance, Ptolemy says nothing—all knew its source. Similarly with the sudden wealth of description when we come to Ceylon. Descriptions of climate, produce, and inhabitants are exceptional in Ptolemy, and where introduced must have been introduced for a particular reason, and novelty can be the only reason in Ptolemy's work.

Let us review Ptolemy's account of Indian regions, and its peculiarities and various points of significance will be revealed. The identification of places is often very doubtful, and I have almost confined myself to the localities important in the matter of trade.

In the first place, Ptolemy gives remarkably accurate details of Saka and Kushan districts in North and North-west India; the seven mouths of the Indus are noticed; Patala still existed, and also Barbaricon as Barbara, but the established mart was Monoglosson (79). Inland Ptolemy has marked a long list of various rivers, tributaries and divarications of the Indus and of cities on both sides of the river, along its course, and on islands in the Delta, while in the extreme north of India are given eighteen cities of the then Kushan Κασπιραῖοι of Kashmir including "Modura of the Gods" (Mathura, Muttra) and the metropolis Eragassa (80) and also other regions (81) of the north-west. The descriptions given of the districts watered by the rivers are copious but the geographer's reliance upon itineraries of merchants to the exclusion of survey-records of Alexander's time has caused great confusion. The sources were doubtless partly merchants who had come overland by way of Kabul, Bolan Pass, and Mula Pass, but surely the Persian Gulf approach is also indicated, a great increase of trade along that route being due, we may surmise, to (a) the policy of Trajan which we described and the establishment of Kushan rule in Mathura, Punjab, and Kashmir; (b) Hadrian's peaceful policy following upon an increase in the prestige of the Roman name; (c) the rise of Palmyra with its active trade with the Persian Gulf. The good knowledge shewn by Ptolemy of all regions connected with the Ganges also may be due to the same causes, but in spite of the statement of Ptolemy (on the authority of those who had learnt from experience) that the periods of voyages made east of Cape Comorin were neither fixed nor regular (82), it seems natural to assume that knowledge of the Ganges regions was obtained rather from men who had sailed round India to the mouths and made explorations from there. His account of the Ganges is meagre when compared with that of the Indus districts; for instance, he gives three affluents compared with the seventeen noted by Megasthenes, according to Arrian. The reason is clear—Megasthenes had been officially sent to Patna and had resided there; ordinary merchants of the Roman Empire did not do so in inland regions so far afield, and Roman coins dating previous to the third and fourth centuries A.C. have not turned up in Bengal. Nevertheless the statement about the voyages and the tolerably good descriptions of the divarications of the Ganges into its mouths shew that these merchants were at least visiting those districts under Magadha kings (83).

Tracing Ptolemy's description from the north-west southwards, we find that Semyla (or Simylla) was no longer a mere local (τοπικόν) mart but a legal emporium together with the city Barygaza, having become a place of trade in the latter part of the first century. Simylla therefore had grown in importance since the time of the *Periplus*, and the mutual visits of Greeks and Indians to and from that place as indicated by Ptolemy reflect the rise of the place, perhaps as a result of the cotton-trade. With this rise we may connect the discovery made of coins at Darphal, representing apparently emperors from Antoninus Pius to Geta, and the enumeration by Ptolemy of nine inland cities ruled by a king Tiastanes, a Kshatrapa-Saka ruler of the line of Chastana, who had his royal seat at Ozene (Ujjain) and was doubtless visited by the Greek merchants (84), and of another group of seven cities including the Tagara and Paethana of the *Periplus*, Baethana in Ptolemy being the royal seat of King [Siri]ptolemaeos (that is, the Andhra Sri-Pulomavit or Pulumayi II, A.D. 138–170), successor to Baleocuros (Vilivayakura II) who ruled at Hippocura (Nasik?) (85). Inscriptions of Nasik shew that Ramanakas, who may have been Romanakas, that is to say, Roman subjects, dedicated caves there; and Yavanas are recorded at Kalyana. The Greek merchants must have visited the kings and gone well inland beyond the neighbourhood of the Sardonyx Mountain (the district of Rajpipla) and to towns including Cosa where they obtained diamonds (86). Explorations into the interior eastwards and southwards had revealed yet more inland peoples and their cities as far as the Ganges. The Indians now called a Greek (Yavana, Yona, Yonaka) "Roman" (Romanaka); Alexandria, too, appears not only as Yavanapura but also as Romakapura and even Alasando, while the Chinese apparently began to call that city Ch'ih-san. Roman influence in art occurs in Aurangabad, Bagh, and Ajanta (87).

Konkan is called by Ptolemy the district of the "Pirates"

and included Byzantion, Chersonesos, Armagara, one emporium Nitraeae or Nitra (Leuce in the *Periplus*,—Pigeon Island, Nitran) and two inland towns Olochoira and the metropolis Musopallis (Miraj?). Here again an increase of knowledge is shewn above all predecessors. When the *Periplus* was written pirates were apparently feared along the whole coast from Kalyana to the river Ponnani, and, when Pliny wrote, these pirates, basing themselves on Nitra away to the north, infested even a part of the Malabar coast not far from Muziris; but in Ptolemy's time they do not seem to have extended their depredations regularly at least so far south, though we cannot be sure of this, and it is a fact that, until the British took efficient action in the nineteenth century, the northern parts of Malabar, Canara, and South Konkan were infested by pirates from very early times. The presence of an inland metropolis and an established mart close to the sea-coast points either to consolidation during the second century of an organised pirate-state between the Western Ghats and the sea, or to conquest perhaps by the Andhra Pulumayi (88).

Ptolemy gives much fuller detail about the three Tamil States in the south, and we find that in the Chera Kingdom "Muzeris" was now the only authorised mart, "Melcynda" and Bacare having ceased to be such, and Tyndis ranking as a coast-town. Of the fourteen inland towns now known to the Greeks, Punnata (Seringapatam? or near Kittur on the river Kabbani) was known to produce beryls. The *Periplus* shews that about A.D. 60 the status of Muziris and Nelcynda varied, and both the author of that book and Pliny state that Nelcynda belonged to the Pandya Kingdom, Pliny adding that Modura was the royal Pandya capital. But, when Ptolemy wrote, Nelcynda and Bacare had ceased to be legal marts. The reason for this must be, in my opinion, either unauthorised activities of the Aioi

WC   8

(that is, local "Ay" chiefs of the Pothiya hills) in whose
territory Nelcynda was, or to recovery of that place by the
Cheras who prevented all places from being legal marts
except Muziris. Carura (once called Vanji and Karuvur
or Karuvai, now Parur near Cranganore) was known to
Ptolemy as the royal seat of the Chera kings. There is
nothing in Ptolemy shewing which Tamil Kingdom controlled Coimbatore with its beryl-mines. Tamil tradition
puts the meeting-place of all three kingdoms near the
modern Karur or Karuvur in Coimbatore, and we must
suppose that the mines were free to all the Tamils or were
a source of contests between them. The nearest way from the
mines to the Malabar coast lay through the Chera country
and it is true that the frontiers of that region sometimes
extended eastwards beyond the Ghats to Mysore, Coimbatore, and Salem, yet tradition reveals the Cheras as
generally a peaceful folk; again, the mines were within
short distance of Pandyan Modura; they were also near
the confines of the Cholas who controlled surely those of
the Salem districts between whom and the Pandyas Tamil
tradition records disputes. Yet the Coimbatore district was
never a political entity and we only know that it passed
into Chola hands before A.D. 900.

We are tempted to conjecture that by agreement the
Cheras monopolised pepper, the Pandyas pearls, the Cholas
beryls and fine muslins. Though Ptolemy does not clearly
separate the three kingdoms, he appears to give the Pandyas
a restricted area. Obviously in their kingdom were two
places marked as emporia by Ptolemy—Elancoros or Elan-
con (Quilon = Kulam, not the old Malankara near Cranganore) and Colchoi with its pearl-fishery; there was a
metropolis in Cottiara (Kotaur, Kotar, Kottaru) and
a coast-town Comaria on Cape Comorin, while inland there
were a number of places including Modura the seat of the
Pandya kings (89). But Aioi held both Quilon and Kotaur.

In his account of the east coast of India beyond Cape Comorin and Cape Calligicon (Cape Calimere) Ptolemy reveals the extensive though irregular travels made by Roman Greeks and the decline of the Chola Kingdom, the name of which (Soras, Choras, Cholas) is hidden in his Soreitae, Soringoi, and Sorae, with a capital apparently at Arcot, and in his king Sornas (the name is obviously the racial title) whose palace was at Orthura. This place seems to have been in reality the inland capital Uraiyur, the name of which (Argaru) was transferred by Ptolemy to a coast-town and included in the Pandya territory. Schoff has pointed out the power of the Pandyas and the decline of the Cholas (perhaps already harassed by Pallavas) during the Roman imperial period (90), and I think this is reflected in Ptolemy—for the Cholas were partly nomad according to him and it is clear that the Pandyas, by seizing the coast-land originally controlled by Uraiyur, and by seizing the Argaric Gulf (Palk Strait), completed their control of the pearl trade, monopolising the fisheries of the Palk Strait as well as those of Manaar. Other Chola marts recorded by Ptolemy are Nicama (Negapatam); places seized by Pandyas, such as Salur (the Tamil mart Saliyur); Chaberis (Camara in the *Periplus*), Subura or Saburas (Cuddalore?), Poduce (Pondicherry not Pulicat), Melange (Kistnapatam), and Manaliarpha (near the mouth of a river still called Manara); and in the Andhra districts men visited in the district of Maesolia (of Masulipatam, called Masalia by merchants of the first century) Contacossyla (Kondapalle?) and Alosygni (Koringa?) near which place ships bound for the Malay Peninsula left the coast, perhaps at the mouth of the modern Baroua. Not far inland near the mouth of the Tyna (Pennar river) lay Malanga (Allur?) the royal seat of Barsaronax, and many other cities were known, particularly Pitura or Pityndra, the metropolis of the Maesoloi—probably near Bezwada.

It is uncertain whether the river Maesolos is the Kistna or the Godavari, so that one of these rivers was left uncharted by the Greeks. The evidence seems to me to favour identification with the Kistna. Frequent visits of Roman subjects to these districts, and beyond, seem to be reflected in the discovery at Gudivada, twenty miles north-west of Masulipatam, of a lead coin shewing a double-masted and large-ruddered Greek or Roman ship; in the reputed existence at Vaisali near Patna of a ruined stupa with the name Kesarîya, and by the presence of the name Caesar elsewhere, as, for instance, in the Mahabharata and in the annals of Orissa (91). This evidence however appears doubtful, and Roman coins near Nellore, at Bezwada, and in the Kistna district, and the coin of Trajan found inland at Athiral reflect better the travels and explorations which provided Ptolemy with his information on regions well up the east side of India.

Altogether Ptolemy enumerates nearly forty inland places of the Tamil Kingdoms, with their royal seats and their kings (92), and he gives plenty of detail about the Andhras. The chief towns and tribes of the Tamils especially are given with remarkable accuracy and far from believing that a decline of trade took place after the reign of Nero I am convinced that the trade was more prosperous than ever, Roman subjects being resident in all three Tamil States. This is confirmed by the description which Ptolemy gives of Ceylon, by the fact that distances between places situated between Cape Comorin and Malay are given in stadia, and by various other signs. It is noteworthy that the version of the legend of St Thomas originating among the Syrian Christians of Malabar makes St Thomas cross India by land from near Cranganore to the Chola Kingdom and then go farther eastwards still.

In the Ganges Gulf many places are enumerated by

Ptolemy but only Palura and Tilogrammon are designated as cities and no emporia are marked at all, while the greater part of the coast beyond the Kistna district is left undescribed, and the reason for this appears in the *Periplus*, where it is shewn that ships sailing beyond Maesolia left the shore and sailed straight to the ports of Orissa.

The mention of a river Adamas, perhaps the Suvarnare-kha or the Sank branch of the Brahmani river, which provided diamonds in the period of Mogul greatness, and of the Sabarae (towards the Ganges, perhaps in the district of Sambhalpur) among whom the diamond (not steel?) was found in great abundance gives us one of the motives for Greek exploration so far afield: the exportation of mala-bathrum, nard, muslins, and silk, and pearls from the Ganges, provided perhaps another reason (93). The mouths of the Ganges are described accurately for the first time and they were controlled by the Gangaridae whose king had his royal seat at Gange (Tamluk?), and the great town of Palibothra (Patna) on the Ganges was still a royal seat, according to Ptolemy. He gives a long list of tributaries and branches of that river and a list of nineteen cities belonging to four races dwelling east of the Gymnosophists and round the Ganges (94). There is a tendency towards repetition, and as we said, this detail is due to voyages taken round Cape Comorin to the Ganges, and not to inland explorations. Dionysios Periegetes, who wrote perhaps under Hadrian, says that he is neither merchant nor sea-farer, and does not go through the Indian Ocean to the Ganges like many men who stake their lives for great wealth (95).

We must now deal with the altogether exceptional account which Ptolemy gives of Ceylon, called Palaesimundu, but in his time Salice (96). Besides the extraordinary wealth of geographical detail, the geographer, contrary to his usual custom, gives a list of what were supposed to be the products of the island—rice, ginger, honey (sugar), beryl, sapphire, mines of gold and silver and other metals, tigers, and elephants—the breeding grounds of the last-named being placed correctly to the south-east of the Malaea mountain-group (including especially Adam's Peak?). Of the list of alleged products only the tiger seems to be quite incorrect, but it probably enumerates merely some articles met with in Ceylon in the course of trade. Anything coming from Malay and beyond, from Bengal, the Coromandel coast, and so on, through the Gulf of Manaar or round the south of Ceylon (unlikely at this era) might be taken as "from Ceylon" by the Greeks on the Malabar coast. In his account Ptolemy gives a very full list of its geographical features, the general shape being described with fair accuracy, but at the same time a preconceived system of measurement makes him exaggerate the size of the island to fourteen times its real area; we have seen how the peninsular character of India is ignored, Cape Comorin being only four degrees south of Barygaza, and there is further distortion of regions beyond the Ganges. On the coasts of Ceylon the geographer places at least twelve cities together with two emporia Moduton (Kokelay?) and Taracori (Manaar); the peoples of the island are named together with six inland cities including the royal seat Anurogrammon (Anuradhapura) and a metropolis Maagrammon (Mahayangana or Mahawelligam, or modern Bintenna). Good transliterations of place-names into Greek are everywhere, as is the case with the other Indian regions. In all, Ptolemy enumerates in Ceylon two coastal marts, eighteen cities, fourteen races, eight capes, two bays, six rivers, two mountain ranges, and five ports, while its general outline and its position with reference to the Indian peninsula are given with a tolerable degree of accuracy.

The island is included in the twelfth segment of the Tabula Peutingeriana.

The peculiar character of this description shews that merchants of the Roman Empire had rarely visited Ceylon, being content to obtain its products in the Tamil and especially Malabar marts—a habit encouraged, of course, by the Tamils; Strabo (97) shews that of old time Ceylon sent ivory, tortoiseshell, and other wares in quantities to the Indian markets where merchants like the author of the *Periplus* found them. In Vespasian's time Pliny knew no more than what was told by the small party that was wafted by accident to the island during Claudius' reign, and the resulting embassy from Ceylon does not seem to have opened up direct commerce—perhaps it was merely to confirm with Rome an arrangement with the Tamils. There is strong evidence too in the strange work of Dionysios Periegetes, who wrote apparently before the reign of Trajan, certainly, I think, before the death of Hadrian, before the time of Ptolemy the geographer. Dionysios mentions the voyages made to the Ganges for the sake of gain (98) and has a tolerably clear idea (based however only on chance meetings and verbal reports) of the boundaries of Indian territories, and extols poetically the products (chiefly precious stones) of India; yet of Taprobane he merely says that it is the mother of elephants and its waters are infested with huge sea-beasts; the old fables are not dispelled because the island was not being regularly visited (99). In short, in the first and second centuries A.C. Greek subjects of Rome passed round the Indian peninsula again and again without going round this mysterious island of Ceylon, preferring to brave the dangers of the straits between. But the description given by Ptolemy shews that, shortly before he wrote, certain merchants had traded direct with Ceylon itself, and had

coasted round the whole of the island and so Ptolemy gives
his account as an attractive novelty to his readers, the
discovery, one might say, of a new land reputed to be
something of El Dorado. It was natural that western
merchants should ultimately include Ceylon within the
range of their activities; and we conclude from Ptolemy
alone that this had recently come about. He indicates
expressly that sailings beyond the Cape were not very
regular, and it is possible that even in his time and afterwards the bulk of the produce of Ceylon reached the Greeks
by way of Tamil (and especially Malabar) marts in Indian
vessels. Still, we may conclude perhaps from Ptolemy's
description that Ceylon was beginning to foreshadow its
future position as the centre of trade in Indian seas. This
tendency took shape only after the era of Ptolemy when
direct Roman trade with India languished and ceased and
when Rome's trade with Ceylon itself ceased to be direct.
We find the tendency revealed in its maturity in Cosmas
Indicopleustes, from whom it is clear that by the sixth
century A.C. Ceylon had become the centre of the Indian
sea-trade. During the first two centuries the Tamils who
held the north part of Ceylon must have discouraged or
forbidden trading between Greeks and Ceylon so that they
could control Ceylon's trade, and we know that the Pandya
and Chola Kingdoms were constantly involved in quarrels
with Ceylon, due partly perhaps to the pearl-fisheries which
came between, these being controlled usually by the
Pandyan power, and Palladius shews that on enquiry at
Muziris Greek merchants were told that the Sinhalese
channel was dangerous, which was and is in fact true (100).

The history of Roman coins discovered in Ceylon is
instructive, and the peculiarities shewn by these discoveries
have not, in my judgment, been sufficiently accounted
for, and an attempt is made to do this in the following

survey. With about twenty certain exceptions, all the Roman coins found in Ceylon date from the third century A.C. and end with Heraclius and his son; the finds consist of numbers of small and comparatively valueless coins of copper, with a very small number struck in the more precious metals, and the mint-abbreviations shew issues of Carthage, Treviri, Antioch, Narbonensis, Constantinople, Rome, and other cities. They have been found at most of the ports and in regions covering the greater part of Ceylon, the largest finds being in the islets of Balapitiya (dating from Constantinus I to Honorius), in the Colombo districts (dating to Honorius) and at Sigiriya (about 1700 chiefly of the fourth century, mostly of one type apparently imported and circulated, and others dating from Licinius II to Honorius). Very few are found after Arcadius and Honorius. For fuller details the reader is referred to "Ceylon Coins and Currency" by H. W. Codrington, and to the article by J. Still in the *Journal of the Royal Asiatic Society* (Ceylon Branch), vol. XIX, 1907—from which this information has been taken. Discoveries still continue, and a friend has lent to me lately four coins of base metal recently found on the site of an old town at Jaffna at the northern end of Ceylon; of the coins two are Ceylonese, but one is a coin of Licinius I and the other a barbarous imitation of a Roman coin struck between A.D. 330 and 340. I wish to dwell upon the following peculiarities which I think can be explained in the light of evidence set forth at various points in these pages.

(i) The finds include very few examples dating from a time previous to the full discovery of the monsoons in Claudius' reign, alleged coins of Claudius being of doubtful identification and authenticity. This is quite in agreement with what we should expect, for, as we have shewn, until that discovery was made, there was little chance of Greek ships visiting Ceylon under the Empire except by accident, and only two such visits are recorded, that of Annius' freedman, and that of Iambulos, and the visit of the last-named at least is very doubtful and both of them maybe went to Sumatra with which, through reports made by the Tamils who traded with Sumatra or Java, Ceylon was confused.

(ii) From the time of the full discovery of the monsoons in Claudius' reign to the beginning of the third century about a dozen coins have been found, one of Nero, three of Vespasian, two of Trajan, five of Hadrian and a few of the Antonines; most of them were struck not at Rome, but at Alexandria, being debased tetradrachms, and turned up in the district of Kurunegala. J. Still offers explanations which may be part of the truth—the Greeks may have conducted their trade chiefly by barter since the natives were unused to coined currency, and we shall shew how Vespasian (?) checked the exportation of silver, and again, the precious metals may have been melted down ultimately for ornaments or for dedication. But in my opinion the chief reason for the scarcity in Ceylon of coins of the first two centuries A.C. as opposed to the abundance of them in the near-by South India during the same period is the fact which I have maintained above—namely that the Greeks were content to find (and the *Periplus* says they *did* find) the products of Ceylon, above all pearls and precious stones, especially sapphires, not in the island but in west Indian ports and Pandya and Chola marts, whither they imported money, while Ceylon cinnamon was got in East Africa. Evidently Roman denarii did not pour into Ceylon, and it is possible that the Tamils, when they received a few debased tetradrachms of the Alexandrian mint, passed them on when they could to Ceylon so as to get rid of them— when a ruler of Ceylon saw Romans and good Roman money he was surprised; Pliny shews that Roman subjects found silent trading between Cheras (Seres) and Ceylonese in Chera backwaters, and that the reports which he gives about Ceylon from Roman merchants were hearsay reports. But even without this evidence Ptolemy's detailed description of the island bears on it all the marks of having been given by the author as a new and interesting account provided in his own day; it is different from all his other notices.

(iii) Ptolemy gives a mainly accurate but meagre list of some of the island's products, which shews that even in his time the Greeks were not trading extensively and directly with Ceylon but were still content to pass by without paying a visit. But for Ptolemy's notice we would conclude that scarcity of coins of the second century was due simply to a return to trade by barter; Roman coins of the third century are also rare in Ceylon.

(iv) The Roman coins in Ceylon became abundant only during the fourth and fifth centuries, and the worn state of many of them and the predominance of one type suggest that the object was circulation. I notice that coins of Arcadius and Honorius are the most frequent and occur in nearly every find which contains clearly identified coins. The following are the main considerations: (*a*) The abundance of coins is due partly to revival of western energy through Axumite Himyarite and Persian middlemen after the foundation of the Byzantine Empire, partly to the gradual shifting of the focus of trade from the Malabar coasts southwards to Ceylon, which appears as the main focus of sea-trade in Indian seas by the sixth century A.C., and we may agree with Chwostow that the "Roman" coins were brought by the middlemen. (*b*) The frequency of the coins of Arcadius and Honorius in Ceylon and in South India as well is due, I think, to the fresh demand for pearls, spices, and precious stones (notably sapphires of Ceylon) created by the barbarians who harassed and invaded the Western Empire; Arcadius, emperor of the East, would assist his western "colleague." The revival of trade may be due to the embassies of Indians, Serendivi (Ceylonese) and the Maldive people to Julian. (c) After the emperors Arcadius and Honorius the finds in Ceylon cease, and since at Naimana in S. Ceylon, as also in the Madura district of South India, have been found hundreds of coins of the fourth and fifth centuries of rough workmanship, minted in Ceylon and South India but imitating in size and appearance contemporary "Roman" issues, we may conclude that the middlemen (notably Axumites) deemed the quantity of currency sufficient (especially when the Indians of the south departed from their custom and imitated western currency), and ceased to import. The evidence seems to contradict the idea of a Roman colony holding on in Modura. I feel that in spite of the uncertainty inherent in even general conclusions drawn from finds of coins, the deductions shewn above may be accepted as reasonable (101).

The friend who lent me the four coins mentioned above says that when discovered by the natives ancient coins are passed into circulation again. It is strange that Roman coins of base metal, being of small value, should be found in Indian regions at all, but this fact can be explained not by the existence of Roman commercial settlements of long standing so much as the extensive use of barter and the reversion to the native materials of currency after the retirement of the Romans. The sudden and temporary burst of direct trade with Ceylon, which we deduced from the detailed account in Ptolemy, occurred perhaps in the reign of Hadrian or Antoninus Pius, for a good many coins struck by Pius, Marcus Aurelius and Commodus seem to have been

found in Ceylon, but most of them have been lost (102).
Again, this burst of direct trade may have been brought
about by a final development in the use of the monsoons so
as to sail direct to Ceylon from the Red Sea, for near
Ceylon merchants had counted as many as thirteen hundred
and seventy-eight islands forming a crowd, and these are,
of course, not the Laccadive but the Maldive islets which
might be passed and visited on a voyage from the West to
Ceylon. Ptolemy names as many as he can, nineteen (103).
There are to-day seventeen "atolls" and innumerable islets.
The Laccadive group can hardly be said to be near Ceylon,
but direct voyages to the Malabar coast must have made
them also known to the Greeks.

In the second chapter of Book VII Ptolemy commences
his description of India beyond the Ganges, and he is in
reality our only authority in this matter. One general motive
probably influenced enterprising Greek merchants both in
their travels into Central Asia and in their voyages to unknown lands east of India—I mean the desire to trade
directly with the distant Chinese from whom came the
much-prized silk, the land-traffic in which was subject to
much interruption. Besides this there was the tortoiseshell
brought from beyond the Malay Peninsula—the finest
known; there were reputed mines of silver and mines or
washings of gold, and the precious stones of Burma (104).
By the time Josephus wrote at least one merchant had
reached perhaps the Malay Peninsula, called Chrÿse or
Chryse Chersonesos, with particular reference to the Irawadi delta (105), and by the time of Ptolemy merchants
had resided in these regions and had brought back reports
upon which the geographer based his account of the Malay
Peninsula and other remote regions (visited by merchants
after the time of Marinos) as far as a port of the "Sinae"
called Cattigara, which has been identified with Canton,

with Hanoi or Kiau-chi in the gulf and district of Tongking
in Cochin China, in which region one copper coin of Maximinus I (A.D. 235–8) has been found, and with some other
localities, while calculation from Ptolemy brings it into
Borneo (106). Perhaps Hanoi, which was already Chinese
when Ptolemy wrote, is right. The most well known of
these daring navigators was one Alexander who had sailed
beyond the Malay Peninsula (probably with three years'
supplies on board, for Chinese records say this was the rule
for the few men who sailed to China) and had found himself in communication with the Chinese at Cattigara. He
wrote an account of his voyage which was used by Marinos
of Tyre in his description of voyages taken round Cape
Comorin into seas round the mouths of the Ganges and to
the Malay Peninsula (107), of which the western part was
now visited with some frequency, being reached in either
of two ways; men sailed from the town Curula near
Karikal in the Chola Kingdom to the town Palura (Gan-
jam?), then across to Sada (the old Ezata? possibly Thade,
north of Sandoway, on a river and not far from the coast),
the first port in this voyage on the east side of the Gangetic
Gulf, then to Temala (Cape Negrais) and then to the Malay
regions. This may be taken as a new stage in the use of
the irregular monsoons in the Bay of Bengal; but soon
a further advance in navigation was made, for as an alternative to the voyages to Sada men bore away from the
Indian coast at a point (ἀφετήριον) not far from the mart
Alosygni (Koringa?) in the district of Masulipatam, and
this voyage was taken apparently direct across the Bay of
Bengal. Beyond Malay the voyage taken by Alexander
lasted twenty days to Zabae (near the southern end of
Cochin China?), a few more days bringing him to Cattigara (108). Alexander almost deserves to be called a second
Hippalos, although he was of course wrong (unless the

mistake is only Ptolemy's) in making the coast turn south after the Malay Peninsula and fortunately Ptolemy used better sources than did Marinos who does not seem to have known the Gulf of Siam: but it is to be regretted that Ptolemy himself adapted all sources to a preconceived notion that makes him turn the coast southwards after that gulf, so that the Chinese face west. This shews how Ptolemy obtained more commercial data than Marinos without gaining further accuracy in geography. We have his results. His account of further India is much greater than any given before, the marts and numerous rivers being obtained obviously from the reports of traders, but there is at the same time much confusion (109). Immediately east of the Ganges on what was supposed mistakenly to be the coast of the Cirrhadeoi in the Gangetic Gulf was one emporium Baracura, perhaps near Ramu, about 68 miles south-east of Chittagong; next to them was the "Silver? Country" (Lower Burma, Arakan, and part of Pegu) (110), with five places called cities and two emporia Berabonna (Gwa? or Sandoway) and Besynga (Bassein) (111). In Chryse (which comprehended Malay and the Irawadi delta) there were also two emporia Tacola (Rangoon?) and Sabana (Satung, Thatung), one city, and a number of mountains and rivers (112). The Sabaracos Gulf is the Straits of Malacca from their portals to the Gulf of Martaban, while the Perimulic Gulf is the Gulf of Siam, and the Great Gulf is the Chinese sea beyond. A country of the "Brigands"? (Λησταί) in South Siam and Kambodia had one emporium called Thipinobastae (Bungpasoi near Bangkok) and one city Zabae, and two other places, while in the Great Gulf were several towns each known as a metropolis but none called an emporium (113). It is to be noted that the Malays of the peninsula and the archipelago have been famous for their piracy. Besides the regions here indicated we have an account of more places, inland mountains, and peoples, roughly indicated east of the Ganges and north of Burma including the flat-faced Saësadae or Besadae and the district of Cirrhadia where merchants reported that the best malabathrum grew (114). Few details are certain, but above the "Silver Country" lay the "Golden Country" (Burma) with numbers of supposed silver and gold mines, tigers and elephants, and ugly inhabitants (115). In the interior of the region of the Ganges and eastwards more than thirty places were reported including Randamarta (Rangamati, now called Udepur) which produced much nard, if the reading be correct, and to the south-east Tosale and Tugma, each a metropolis, with Triglypton as a royal seat, capital of Arakan (116). Merchants brought back stories of bearded cocks, white "crows," and parrots. It looks as though the existence of an excellent kind of nard was a motive for Greek enterprise in these regions.

On direct voyages men at last saw Nicobar, Nias, Sibiru, and Nassau Is. and Iabadiu, which Ptolemy says means barley, and the name is of course Java Dvipa, that is, Island of millet, to-day Java. Ptolemy says that it contained much gold and that its metropolis was called "Argyre." It is thought that this description is not one of Java but of Sumatra; the presence of gold indicates Sumatra, and the capital at the western end of Ptolemy's Iabadiu would be in Acheen in Sumatra. A similar mixture of ideas seems to occur in Ptolemy's Ceylon, which partakes of the characteristics of Sumatra. Thus Sumatra may have been visited by Greek voyagers, yet it is clear that their voyages beyond the Malay Peninsula must have been very few in number; we have only to think of the apparent lack of knowledge of the Straits of Malacca, the very few islands mentioned of those which compose the great Archipelagos, and the fact that Sumatra (which is nearer than Java) has no separate identity (117). India clearly remained an important intermediary between the West and China, the carriers between Malacca and Malabar being the large ships (colandia) of Malay and Coromandel, rarely Greek or even Chinese vessels, and the Greeks used India on their way to China as is shewn by the Indian wares which (as Chinese records shew) they brought to China from time to time. Malay was less important than Sumatra and the archipelago beyond—from regions beyond Malay perhaps came the spices which even Megasthenes of the third century B.C. says came to the Ganges from the "southern parts" of India.

The Chinese in their southern aspect as visited by sea were called the Sinae, bounded on the north by the Seres (the Chinese in their northern aspect, as visited by land-routes), on the east and south by unknown *land*, and on the west by "India beyond the Ganges" and by the "Great Gulf." Two cities and various river mouths are enumerated along this gulf, and then there is a gap in Ptolemy's text. Round the Gulf of the Sinae dwelt the fish-eating "Ethiopians," and here was situated Cattigara, ὅρμος Σινῶν. Ptolemy then names various peoples, and four inland cities, concluding with Thinae the metropolis (Nanking?) (118). Ptolemy's configuration of the coast beyond the Great Gulf is utterly wrong; Cattigara is made to face west and is a port of an unknown land (with coast running north and south) joined to Africa and enclosing the Indian Ocean on the south side. This mistake is due to recognised notions followed by Ptolemy without question; Cosmas of the sixth century is the writer who first knew that men had to sail round the Malay Peninsula and then turn northwards if they were bound for China. Yet among the travellers of even the second century were some perhaps who had ideas more correct than Ptolemy—at least this I deduce from the statement by Pausanias that China was an island in the innermost (meaning surely the easternmost) recess of the Erythraean Sea, a term which means very much more than merely the Red Sea (119). May he not reflect the discovery by merchants that China was not only approached by sea from the west but was bounded by sea on the east and south? The supposed Northern Ocean would complete the growing idea that China was an island. Chinese annals fill in this meagre picture of Roman activity in the far East. They state that in October, A.D. 166, Antun (Marcus Aurelius) sent "ambassadors" by sea; from the frontier of Annam (perhaps having landed at Hanoi) they brought to the Chinese emperor Huan-ti Indian articles obtained on their way; from that time, the annals say, dates the direct intercourse of Ta-ts'in (Syria, or the Roman Empire in general) with China, and moreover later Chinese records continue to mention the Roman Empire and its honest traders. The visit of 166, magnified by the Chinese into an "embassy" with "tribute," but not mentioned by Roman writers, was doubtless private enterprise on the part perhaps of Syrians, who, disturbed by the destruction of Seleucia, spread of plague, and the closing of trade with Parthia, used the Roman name to persuade the Chinese to send all their silk to the Roman Empire by sea (120). At any rate we know (from these Chinese records) that the "Syrians" had been thwarted continually by the Parthians in their desire to open sea-trade with China, and it looks as though Kan Ying was deliberately deterred from coming farther westwards in 97 by the Parthians—he was discouraged by nothing else than the stories of terrible sea-voyages told him by sailors on the Parthian frontier. We know too that much more correct ideas about Chinese silk reached the Romans, as Pausanias and Pollux shew (121). Chinese records shew that it was the Parthian king who sent Syrian (?) jugglers and musicians to China, but it was the Roman Empire which sent the embassy of 166; it was a Syrian (?) merchant who in 226 having reached Cochin China by sea was presented to the Chinese emperor and was accompanied on his return journey by a Chinese official who died on the way; it was at least a Roman, and probably an Egyptian "embassy" that in 284 gave the Emperor of China 30,000 rolls of thin aghal-wood (122). We read that to Siam, Kambodia (?), Annam, and Tongking merchants from Ta-ts'in came often, but those lands sent very few men westwards. Soon the Chinese sent their own ships to the Persian Gulf and Mesopotamia, but this took place only after the Romans had retired altogether from the Indian Ocean (123).

We have now traced Rome's activity in the far East along the sea-route to the furthest limits of its development. We have seen how during the first century Roman subjects became resident in India, and by the end of that century the word denarius and perhaps traces of Roman law and procedure had become part of Indian commercial life; were Roman subjects continually resident in India during the second century also? The words of Ptolemy alone lead us to believe that. Clemens of Alexandria gives information about Indian worship, about the Brahmans, and about a Buddhist stupa which could have been obtained only by residents in India. About A.D. 180 Pantaenos is said to have discovered in India Christian Jews from the Persian Gulf; one of the traditions which make Bartholomew and Thomas go to India shews a good knowledge of the state of affairs likely to be found by a permanent resident. Jews trading with the mouth of the Indus established a trading colony in Afghanistan in the first century (124). The destruction of Jerusalem, the troubles in Alexandria, and the fate of Seleucia and Ctesiphon would help this tendency in Jews to settle in

India. More striking evidence is provided by a papyrus of
the second century A.C., which gives us a kind of contemporary (surely not Ptolemaic) farce wherein a Greek lady
is stranded on a coast bordering on the Indian Ocean; the
king of the country addresses his followers as Indian chiefs;
they dance a Seric (Chera?) step and use their own barbarian
language. The foreign words that occur point if anything
to a Canarese dialect (according to a tentative identification put forward by Hultzsch, rejected by Barnett) learnt
by a Greek resident somewhere on the coast of India between Karwar and Mangalore (125). We must not suppose
that Syrians took no part in these developments; this is
clear from architecture of Gandhara, and we may add
here the occurrence of gems in India executed by Indians
during the first two centuries A.D. but shewing a Roman
influence spreading from Asia Minor and also an inscription of Tanjore which mentions an ornament executed after
the fashion of the "Jonakas" (Greeks) (126).

We are not much concerned with the non-Indian coasts
of Indian seas except so far as they illustrate intensity
of trade. Ptolemy gives copious lists of cities, villages, and
peoples (with royal seats and capitals) in the interior of
Arabia, but in such a way as to shew that Greek exploration then was not extensive (127). The four legal marts were
Muza, Ocelis, Cane, and Ἀραβίας ἐμπόριον on the site of
Arabia Eudaemon now rising again; of Arabian ports in
the Persian Gulf, only Ommana was a legal mart, perhaps
because Trajan had made Characene tributary to Rome,
and the influence was perhaps not entirely renounced by
Hadrian. Similarly, in East Africa Adulis had ceased to
be a non-Roman mart when Ptolemy wrote: outside the
Strait, however, marts of the Somali had become legal emporia, which means that the Axumites had subdued the
local chiefs of the first century (128). Exclusion of Indian

vessels from the Red Sea apparently had ended, while the Axumites now held no port inside the Strait. Ptolemy makes it clear that Greeks had penetrated deep into the interior of Africa and down the east coast as far as Cape Delgado, probably in search of ivory, African supplies of which were failing even in Pliny's time (129).

During the second century the Greeks had made progress along the great land-routes: in order to cut out Parthian middlemen and to trace Indian, Chinese, and other oriental products to their true sources, Maes Titianus, a Macedonian and a merchant by hereditary profession, early in this century sent his agents to explore a land-route to China; they found the Chinese at the Stone Tower, that is, Tashkurgan. Dionysios alludes to travels to Hyrcania and the Hindu Kush, and maybe the Greeks soon reached Loh-yang (Sera, new Han metropolis), but the agents of Maes had only *heard* of the stormy seven months' journey thither from Tashkurgan, by way of the Casioi (Kashgar), and they learnt too that Thinae had not any walls of brass. The Seres (130), says Ptolemy, were bounded on the west by "Scythia beyond Imaos" and on the east and north by unknown land; a few particulars of mountains and rivers are added, with lists of different peoples and of fifteen cities, ending with Sera Metropolis. However great may be the mistaken ideas held by Ptolemy with reference to the vast tracts of Sarmatia and the Seres, and however obvious the fact that he gives his notices of the Chinese with a precision not justified by his knowledge, it is clear that a great advance in knowledge had been made. "Ptolemy is the first to have anything like a clear idea of the north and south dividing mountain range of Central Asia (the Pamirs and Tian Shan) which he called Imaos," placing it too far eastwards. The names used by Ptolemy suggest that his information came from the Brahmans who knew little of China, and especially the people of Kashmir (in a wide sense), whom the Greeks knew well. The land of the Hyperboreans is a western counterpart of the earthly paradise of Kashmirian mythology (131). Normally the Indians, Parthians, Romans, Chinese, and Scythians met at Tashkurgan, but the discoveries of Sir Aurel Stein in Central Asia shew that from the second century onwards Roman subjects traded personally in the regions of Lop Nor and Miran. At Lop Nor Coptic and Byzantine influence was noted; at Miran paintings were found shewing Christian, Egyptian, Greek, and definitely Roman influence in shape, feature, attitude, and technique. Syrian influence seems to have been prominent, and in the name Tita, the name of a painter, Sir Aurel Stein sees the name Titus; compare Agisala, Kanishka's overseer of works, and carpenters we spoke of. Even a bale of silk was discovered (132). Along this route Christianity spread not only to Kashgar but even to Kambaluk (Peking) and Singanfu—a Syrian mission is known to have existed in China in the seventh century A.C.; in the eighth a strong wave of western influence appears in the architecture of Kashmir. Nevertheless the bulk of the trade along these land-routes was always conducted by the Parthians and Persian Sassanids, and exchange by barter and by uncoined metal was perhaps the normal rule. Thus a collection of coins found in Central Asia and now in the Indian Museum at Calcutta contains one silver coin of Alexander, a forgery or copy of a silver coin of Antiochos, two Bactrian coins, one Indo-Scythian, one silver coin of Antoninus Pius, nineteen Parthian and twelve Sassanian coins, and a copper one of Constantius II. Near Singanfu (133) have been found a few Roman coins dating from Tiberius to Aurelian. The strong policy of general Pan Chao between A.D. 47 and 94 made Central Asia a more tranquil region than it had been before.

Thus from about the end of the first century onwards private merchants from the Roman Empire penetrated beyond the sphere of Parthian influence, but this was a regular thing only when Rome and Parthia were at peace with each other and Parthia was not disturbed within herself, and when the Chinese kept order in Central Asia. The relations between Rome and Parthia and the internal state of Parthia were unstable, and when Ptolemy wrote Chinese authority in Central Asia was uncertain, and though in Lucian we have echoes of the travels of Roman subjects to Babylon Bactria and India, Pausanias in wide travels met no one who had seen even Susa or Babylon. Later on too the Persian Sassanids kept the land-routes for themselves, and the activities of the White Huns were a further drawback. Yet the details of the routes to India (as well as to Central Asia) given by Ptolemy and the Peutinger Table and the discoveries of Sir Aurel Stein prove the far-reaching activities of Roman subjects by land in spite of all, and there was no reason why they should not reach Central Asia by way of the Persian Gulf and the Indus, even when the Kushan power had declined in North-west India.

We do not find that Roman subjects even in the second century attained a direct control over the Oxus—Caspian route. Ptolemy's accounts (134) of Bactriana, Sogdiana, the Oxus, the Iaxartes, Hyrcania, the Iberi, and the Albani do not shew any exceptional advance in the knowledge of these regions except in two important points. He shews some knowledge of the relations between the Tanais or Don and the Rha or Volga, the latter of which he correctly describes as flowing into the Caspian Sea; and he rightly recognises that the "Northern Ocean" was nowhere near the Caspian which thus appears once again as an inland sea. But he makes the longer axis of that sea lie east and west so that the Aral and the Caspian were one stretch of water (135), and in some ways his knowledge was inferior to that of Strabo who relied upon special authorities. The conclusion is that but for isolated exceptions these regions remained unexplored under the Roman Empire, and the oriental trade there was conducted by Scythian and Caucasian tribes, the Romans being content to maintain as far as possible good relations with them and complete control of the Euxine. This tends to shew that the oriental and Siberian trade of this route was not important as the oriental trade of other routes was; had it been so, we should be able to trace Roman connexions with these regions in far greater detail.

THE DECLINE

The reign of Marcus Aurelius marks the turning-point in the general well-being of the Roman world, and from this time on we see the decline and breaking up of the Western Empire (a collapse reflected in its oriental commerce) and a shifting of stable authority to the near East without a corresponding revival of trade with the far East, but the oriental commerce of the Byzantine Empire forms a story by itself and can find no place here. During the third century, in spite of the withdrawal of Kushan power to within the Indus valley and Afghanistan, Palmyra (136) reached an extraordinary degree of prosperity, but the Roman Empire as a whole suffered a steady economic and political decline, and emperors were many, most of them dying a violent death. Egypt shared in the troubles and was unable to protect the desert-routes, and after the cruel treatment of Alexandria by Caracalla, direct sea-trade between the Roman Empire and India almost ceased to exist, enterprises like those of Scythianos and Firmus (who laid his hopes of protection apparently on Palmyra) being noted because they had become so rare (137), and discoveries of coins in India become very few for reigns succeeding that of Aurelius, and cease altogether between Caracalla and Constantius II with the exceptions of mostly isolated discoveries in the north of India, reflecting, if anything, the activity of Palmyra. We must not forget however that barter now became a general system of trade, and Roman subjects could go to India under the protection of the Axumites, for along the sea-route across the Indian Ocean control of the traffic passed once more into the hands of foreigners—the Arabians and still more the Axumites, who took the place of the Egyptian Greeks and became the middlemen for the Indian sea-trade with Egypt. The oriental luxuries of Commodus (138) and the astonishing excesses of Elagabalus (139) (who received an Indian embassy) and the commercial efforts of Alexander Severus (140) may have reacted in different ways towards a revival, but the chief gainer was perhaps Palmyra, which received honours and privileges from Rome (141), and after the death of Alexander Severus, civil disturbances, Alamanni Goths and Franks, and economic decline warred against commerce. The Parthian Empire became strong and imbued with a commercial spirit under the Persian Sassanids and completely controlled the Persian Gulf, the land-routes, and the silk trade (142). Only in the north of India (which could be reached by land) have Roman coins turned up, especially in Bengal, representing reigns from Gordian to Constantine (143), and India, though much written about (for example by Aelian, Philostratos, Clemens, and others), begins to fade away into a land of fancy and fable, and more often than not by India and Indians nothing more is meant than Ethiopia and the Axumites, sometimes even South Arabia, and so far as we can tell direct trade with India by Roman subjects took place almost entirely with the north by way of Palmyra and along the silk-route to China, as finds of coins and the discoveries made by Sir Aurel Stein seem to indicate (144).

In the latter part of the century Palmyra, which in its great but unstable strength had broken loose from Roman control, and by means of the Blemmyes controlled even Coptos, was destroyed by Aurelian (145); the town had played its part in the history of the world's commerce and had made the Persian Gulf a focus of trade coming from the far East, for we find that in the ages following on the destruction of Palmyra, Indian and Chinese, besides Arab and Persian ships, sailed up the Euphrates as far as Hira, and Indians and Chinese for about two centuries frequented a great fair at Batnae near that river (146).

Along the sea-route Trajan's canal was kept in repair and Clysma, Aela(na), and Berenice were still important havens, but they were eclipsed by Adulis which rose to great importance as an Axumite (not Roman) port for setting sail for East Africa and India; it was much frequented by "Romans" and Arabians. The economic, political, and religious troubles of Egypt were too great to allow a recovery of prosperity, and we find that while the Blemmyes harry Upper Egypt, the Axumites and Himyarites control the trade by sea, and the Sassanids by land, and through their hands passed the silk, pearls, aromatics, and precious stones which continued to be mentioned by "Roman" writers and which were doubtless in growing demand among the barbarians.

At his triumph in 274 Aurelian received ambassadors from the Blemmyes, Axumites, Arabia Eudaemon, Persia, Iberians, Saracens, Bactrians, India, and China; Probus drove the Blemmyes out of Egypt (147); and the hopeful reign of Carus was followed soon afterwards by the reforms of Diocletian; the hands of the Romans were much strengthened in Caucasian, Armenian, and Mesopotamian regions, and

on the site of Palmyra a new town began to rise. But the
economic evils of the age were too strong; Egypt under
Diocletian suffered more than ever, and Romans no longer
taking any real interest in a sea-trade to India; intermediaries controlled it all and it was immaterial who these were.
The abdication of Diocletian in 305 was followed by inde-
scribable confusion and civil war until in 324 Constantine
united the whole Empire under his rule. A new era commenced and Constantinople rose on a site well-placed for
trade coming from the East, (a) by way of the Persian Gulf
and the Euphrates; (b) by the overland routes; (c) by the
Caspian and the Euxine. There was a revival of commerce
with the East, as the evidence of literature, of coins, and of
archaeology shews (148), but the activities of Byzantine
subjects in the new development cannot be compared with
those of the first two centuries of the truly Roman Empire,
for the middlemen still remain supreme. Roman coins re-
appear in South India as well as in the north from Constantius onwards, increasing in the course of the fourth and
fifth centuries (149), and Constantine received an Indian embassy in the last year of his life (150), while Julian (aggressive in the East, like Trajan before him) received embassies
from various oriental peoples, including Indian tribes, the
Maldive people, and the Ceylonese (Serendivi) (151), of whom
the last-named were becoming the centre of Hindu trade
in Indian seas. Nevertheless the Axumites and to a less
extent the Himyarites remained the intermediaries of the
Byzantine and Roman sea-trade with India, the general
revival causing "Roman" treaties with the Axumites and
with the Himyarites, and Adane is called a "Roman mart,"
while "Romans" could sail to India from Adulis in Axumite
vessels. Aela, Clysma, and especially Berenice (152) revived
in importance, but the so-called trade with the "Indians"
was in reality trade with the Ethiopians, and even under

Justinian in the sixth century Byzantine subjects visited not India so much as Arabia and the Axumite realm (particularly Adulis), and the ignorance now shewn about India was truly prodigious. Still, in the latter part of the fourth century the sea-trade was encouraged by disturbances upon the land-routes and the loss of "Roman" influence in the regions of the Caspian and the Persian Gulf. The "Roman" world was now weighed down by general misery, high taxes, tyrannous exactions, riots, insurrections, civil war, and above all, barbarian raids. In 476 the Western Empire was extinguished, but the Eastern Empire, more stable, solid, and wealthy, and placed nearer to the far East, had a better chance, and among its subjects the demand for oriental luxuries was large. The barbarians too in the West fell victims to the allurements of oriental products, as is shewn for instance by the inclusion of four thousand silk robes and three thousand pounds of pepper in the demands made by Alaric upon Rome in 408. As a result in North and South India have been found gold coins of the Theodosii, Marcian, Leo I, Zeno, Anastasius I, Justinus I, and many copper coins of Arcadius, Honorius, and others, in South India and Ceylon (153). This is strange when we consider the dreadful chaos of the West, the constant troubles of Egypt, and the hesitation of the Himyarites and of the Axumites to help the Byzantines whenever such action might involve them in a quarrel with Persia, and Chwostow is probably right in thinking that the Roman coins were brought by intermediaries.

Something like the conditions indicated here continued until the Arabians, by conquering Syria, Egypt, and Persia during the seventh century, established in oriental commerce a new era of which the period covered by this section on the "Decline" was as it were a prelude.

PART II

Rerum autem ipsarum maximum est pretium in mari nascentium margaritis, extra tellurem crystallis, intra adamanti, smaragdis, gemmis, myrrhinis; e terra vero exeuntibus in cocco, lasere, in fronde nardo, Sericis vestibus, in arbore citro, in frutice cinnamo, casia, amomo, arboris aut fruticis suco in sucino, opobalsamo, murra, ture, in radicibus costo; ex eis quae spirare convenit, animalibus in terra maximum dentibus elephantorum, in mari testudinum cortici; in tergore pellibus quas Seres inficiunt...non praetereundum est auro, circa quod omnes mortales insaniunt, decumum vix esse in pretio locum, argento vero, quo aurum emitur, paene vicensimum.

PLINY, *N.H.* XXXVII, 204.

SILVER DISH FOUND AT LAMPSACOS

SILVER DISH

Found at Lampsacos

(*Jahrbuch des Kaiserlich Deutschen Archäologischen Instituts*, Band xv, 1900, p. 203.)

ON this dish, which was found at Lampsacos, a Greek worker in silver has given an artistic representation of India as a woman surrounded by mammals and birds which were supposed to be typical of that region, and has reflected in his art a current error about the far East, namely the confusion of East African regions with India. The inclusion of the East African Guinea-fowl certainly proves that the dish is not Graeco-Indian work, and probably shews that it was carved not by a Greek of Alexandria, whether merchant or not, but rather by an Asiatic Greek who had seen or heard something of the Indian trade brought along the land-routes. The figure is typically Asiatic and sits upon a typically Indian chair resting on ivory tusks as on legs. The addition of mammals and birds reflects, I think, the only part of Rome's Indian commerce which, during the Roman Empire, remained a land-trade, namely the traffic in living Indian animals and birds—a traffic which might impress itself upon a Greek of Asia Minor who was probably not a merchant but was at any rate an artist. The mammals represented on the dish are as follows:—on each side of the chair stands a hanuman monkey, each distinguished by the long hind limbs and tail in spite of slight misrepresentation of the face; there is a collar round the neck of each; underneath the chair two keepers hold in check with ropes two unmarked carnivorous animals, the one on the right distinguishable as a leopard, the one on the left as a tiger. Two birds are shewn; on the left of the figure of India stands an Alexandrine parrakeet, carelessly done, but the large bill fixes the species, while on the right stands an African Guinea-fowl, which is not only mistakenly added among Indian things, but is furnished with a head unlike that of a Guinea-fowl. The dish would be work of the first or second century of the Roman Empire.

PREFACE TO PART II

THE following complete survey of the articles of merchandise imported by Rome from India serves better than anything else to give us a correct idea of the extent of Rome's commerce with India during the first and second centuries of the Empire, and as already pointed out, forms a vivid picture of the results of Hippalos' discovery and its developments, for nearly all the wares are traceable in sources belonging to the latter part of the first century A.C. and hardly any new articles were brought into the commerce until the supremacy of the Arabians. I have dealt first with animals and animal-products; then with plant and mineral products, which the Romans imported from India and from farther East. After these the articles of exportation to the far East from the Roman Empire have been described, and the question of the exportation of Roman money to India discussed in some detail.

In dealing with the importations from India the plant-products have not been classified scientifically because a different arrangement produces a more intelligible account. On the other hand, the minerals and the animals and animal-products are best arranged in some sort of scientific order and that method is adopted here. With a few exceptions the classification of animals is the one now generally accepted, while that of minerals is based largely upon Dana's *System of Mineralogy*, 6th edition, 1892, but I have departed from it in one or two instances.

PART II

THE SUBSTANCE OF ROME'S COMMERCE WITH INDIA

SECTION A
THE OBJECTS OF IMPORTATION FROM INDIA

CHAPTER I
Animals and Animal-Products

THE class of human beings and animals comes naturally at the head of any list of the products of nature, though it formed on the whole a minor and mainly indirect part of Rome's commerce with India, except where the traffic was not in living animals, but animal-products.

That Indian slaves reached Rome, at least through the Arabian slave trade, need not be doubted, for slave women of India seem to have come in times gone by into the hands of Ptolemy Philadelphos, who obtaining them doubtless from the Sabaeans exhibited them in his procession, and the *Periplus* says that a few female slaves were sent from India to Socotra, and there is no reason for not supposing that some were passed on to the Roman Empire by the Arabs or the Greeks who were resident in that island. But the vague way in which the epithet Indian is misapplied by many writers to the regions of the Red Sea and of East Africa makes it impossible to treat all our references to "Indian" slaves as though they reveal the true source. The Indian eunuchs, for instance, which are included in the Digest-list of oriental products subject to the "vectigal Maris Rubri" on entry into Egypt, manifestly include Ethiopians of the same type. Doubtful too must remain the dusky and sun-burnt "Indian" attendants which are mentioned by Tibullus; the Indian trainers of elephants (though we must suppose that with Indian elephants came Hindu trainers); the female "Indian" fortune-tellers apparently referred to by Juvenal; and such instances as the "Indian" cook of the Emperor Justinian, and the fashionable prostitutes, upon whom, according to our extant tariff-list of Coptos, such a heavy due was levied. On whole, the commerce in slaves between India and the West was, as we shall see, mainly concerned with exportation of them from West to East rather than the reverse(1).

When we come to deal with the animals and animal-products imported to the Roman Empire from the far East, we can speak with greater certainty, but we are met by a peculiar phenomenon which shews that the traffic in eastern mammals, birds, and so on continued to remain an indirect one; for the author of the *Periplus*, writing when the numbers of direct sailings by Greeks to and from Indian coasts were rising to an unprecedented height, speaks of the animal life of the Deccan (Dachinabades), yet nowhere mentions the exportation of any animal by sea from any Indian port (2). Again, the lions and leopards included in the Digest-list are surely African; for the list contains no mention of Asiatic or Indian animals such as the one-horned rhinoceros, the tiger, and the Indian parrots (3). I would conclude from this that the importation of animals and birds from the far East was exceptional and was conducted along the land-routes, even in the case of the regularly imported parrots, which are not mentioned by the *Periplus* or by the Digest-list, while Diodoros calls them Syrian, which shews that they came by land or by the Persian Gulf (4). Transport of animals by sea was disadvantageous from the point of view of space, sanitation, and real or imaginary dangers of sea-sickness; in spite of the existence of trapper-villages in India, hunting and trapping were despised callings there (5), and the animals after entry into the Roman Empire had to pay a poll-tax, as well as customs-dues on entry at the frontiers, unless the importers were senatorial givers of shows (6). Importation of animals therefore was felt by the Greeks to be not worth while, though the Indians of old transported living animals by sea to the Persian Gulf and to Africa and China and were probably responsible for sending Ptolemy II his peacock and parrots. With the exception of parrots and monkeys Indian animals were imported by the Romans for exhibition, and the land-routes only were used, even after Hippalos' discovery, so that this traffic was really traffic with Parthia (7).

Among the apes and monkeys, in particular the long-tailed kinds called cercopitheci imported from Africa and Ethiopia to become pets, especially of fashionable ladies, were included probably hanuman, Madras, Malabar, and Nilghiri langurs of India; for Arrian, in declining to speak of Indian parrots and of the size and gracefulness of Indian monkeys or of the ways in which they were hunted, seems to be influenced by more than a mere desire of omitting what earlier writers had written, and on a silver dish found at Lampsacos is represented India as a woman surrounded by a parrot, a guinea-fowl, a tiger, a leopard, and hanuman monkeys (8); though the guinea-fowl was certainly African, the others were Indian. So, also, with the larger cats such as lions and leopards imported from Africa to Rome for exhibitions and beast-baitings came Asiatic and even Indian lions and leopards. The lions exhibited by Sulla and Pompey may have included the Indian lion, so that Catullus, who at any rate knew that the animal was found in India, may have seen one in Rome, while Aelian at a later date says that black-maned lions were found in India. Pliny too distinguishes lions with and lions without manes, and a maneless lion used to be found commonly in Gujarat and other regions of India (9). Likewise ounces and caracals (lynces) may have entered indirectly into Rome's traffic with Indian regions by being brought through Parthia.

Of the Indian and Hyrcanian tiger, which comes next to the lion in the animal kingdom, we can be quite certain. It is true that the name τίγρις was applied loosely to animals such as jackals, and that Pliny's description of the tiger is not accurate, but other writers distinctly describe the real tiger, and all doubt is dispelled by the occurrence of the tiger on mosaics and modelled tigers' heads in jewelry, and on engraved gems, and so on (10). The animal was rarely brought to Rome; one had been presented to Athens by Seleucos, but Varro thought that the animal could not be captured alive. A tiger was first exhibited at Rome in a cage or den by Augustus when the theatre of Marcellus was dedicated in 13? B.C., and the four specimens exhibited by Claudius created perhaps a great impression, for on a mosaic found near the Arch of Gallienus are represented four tigers devouring their prey. A passage in Petronius appears to indicate that a tiger was carried about in a gilded cage, probably in Nero's reign, and gorged with the blood of human victims; Seneca probably saw these tigers, for he knew their striped appearance well, and their presence may have prompted Pomponius Mela to give his somewhat detailed reference to Hyrcanian tigers. The Romans noted the swiftness of their spring. Several more were exhibited by Domitian, and if we may so judge from Martial, some of them came from India—perhaps from their typical home in Bengal; Silius the poet seems to have seen them, since he too refers to the striped bodies of tigers. As many as ten were got by Gordian and killed by Philippus with many lions, elephants, and rhinoceros, and it is to be noted that in a great find of coins made in Bengal there were several of Gordian's time, though this may be accidental (11). Greek merchants in the course of the second century A.C. seem to have met with tigers in Ceylon and in the region round the Gulf of Siam, but it is certain that these animals did not form a regular part of Rome's Indian trade either by land or sea; indeed it is probable that the example exhibited by Augustus and even those exhibited by Claudius were gifts made by Indian ambassadors (12).

The Romans may have supplemented their breeds of dogs by occasional importations of Indian and Tibetan hounds, these last being the famous "ants" which dug up the Tibetan gold! According to Herodotos, the Persians of his time caused the supplies of four large villages in the plains round Babylon to be appropriated for the feeding of Indian hounds; Ctesias also notices the Indian hounds of the Persians, and similar dogs were shewn in the procession of Ptolemy Philadelphos. We also have a papyrus of the third century B.C. on which are two separate epitaph-poems written for Zenon in honour of his Indian hunting-hound Tauron, which had given its life in saving its master in a fight with a wild boar (13). But when all is said, it is probably safer to conclude that by "Indian" is meant an established domestic breed introduced to Europe centuries before the Roman Empire began, and valued because of its large size (14).

The remaining mammals which entered into Rome's eastern trade all belong to the varied and useful order of ungulate or hoofed animals, but, as we shall see, it was not the animals themselves so much as the products of a few of them which were of any real importance in trade.

It was natural that the Indian humped cattle (*Bos Indicus*) used for draught, burden, and riding should spread westwards by land and we find that it was brought in large numbers so as to form part of the domestic cattle of Persia,

Syria, and Africa. Thus we find representations of it in Assyrian and later art, and Indian cattle were displayed in Ptolemy's procession, but there is no specific evidence that they ever reached Rome (15). The Yak (*Bos* or *Poephagus grunniens*), which is the common cattle of the Tatars, is well described by Aelian under the name "poephagos," and may have found its way westward occasionally, with the help of man, while the Buffalo (*Bos, Bubalus bubalis*), with the wild Buffalo (*Bubalus arni*) which was known to the Greeks after Alexander's conquests as the "wild bull of Arachosia," was not brought to Italy, as far as we can tell, until late in the fourth century A.C. (16). The "Indian camel" seen by Pausanias and described by him as coloured like a leopard was a giraffe (known to the Romans as "camelopardalis"), but by "Indian" he must have meant African, for, although the giraffe lived in India and in Europe in late tertiary times, it has been confined for ages to Africa. African also was the Indian one seen by Cassianus Bassus at Antioch in the sixth century A.C., like the "Indian" specimens sent to Anastasius I in 496 (17). Likewise the horse named Ἰνδός in a late inscription was an African one, we may presume, for by the sixth century A.C. horses were an export not from India to Persia, but from Persia to Ceylon, though the fine wild horses of Tatary, for example the dziggetai, may have been brought westwards in ancient times like all other animals which can be used for domestic and public purposes. Bactria was famous for its horses (18).

The two other types of mammals with which we have to deal are the large thick-skinned ungulates—the Rhinoceroses and the Elephants. Of the rhinoceroses, the Romans were acquainted both with the two-horned kinds, nearly all African, and the one-horned kinds, which are Indian. According to the description of Dio Cassius, the rhinoceros exhibited by Augustus and killed to celebrate his victory over Cleopatra possessed only one horn; so had the specimen seen by Strabo. Both therefore belonged to the Indian species. We find also that Pompey exhibited a one-horned rhinoceros and Pliny says that this kind was not an un-usual sight in Rome. They were most frequently seen, we need have no doubt, in the Asiatic part of the Empire, and the Hou-han-shu (Dynastic History) states that they were met with (doubtless in captivity) in the district of Chaldaea or Babylonia (T'iao-chih). Those exhibited by Domitian were chiefly African kinds, as shewn by the image stamped upon some of his coins, but the one-horned type is the one generally appearing on engraved gems and on tesserae until his reign. The so-called unicorn is an imaginary creation arising from a confusion of the Indian rhinoceros with the Indian wild ass and with some species of antelope (19).

The Indian elephant, which was used frequently in war after Alexander's conquests, was first introduced to the Romans when Pyrrhos transported some from Epiros to Italy in 281 B.C. Whether the Carthaginians used them together with the African species, and employed Indian mahouts to train both kinds, I am not certain. But it is to be noticed that Hasdrubal at Panormos in 251 used ele-phants driven by "Indians"; so did Hannibal and Hasdrubal during the second Punic War with Rome; and at the battle of Raphia Ptolemy's Libyan beasts could not stand against the Indian troop of Antiochos. Again, centuries later than this, it is true, Cosmas shews that elephants destined for use in war were bred chiefly in Ceylon, and that the Ethiopians did not know how to train the beasts at all. The Greeks and Romans always thought wrongly that Ceylon and India produced larger elephants than Africa, but it may be that Polybios, inaccurate as he is in matters of geography, when he said Indian, meant Indian and not Ethiopian. Arrian and Dionysios Periegetes shew that the statement of Cosmas about the war-elephants of Ceylon applied to earlier times as well, and we know that Apamea was once a great breeding-centre for Asiatic elephants. But on the one hand the Ptolemies naturally found the procuring of African elephants a much cheaper business, and on the other hand the Romans did not adopt the custom of using elephants in war, so that, as Lucretius distinctly points out, Indian elephants were very rarely seen in Rome. It is interesting to note that the white albino variety of elephant, a favourite beast of Indian princes, and not uncommon now in Burma and Siam, is mentioned in folk-lore of Kashmir, was known to Megasthenes and was a special attraction at Rome in the time of Augustus, who had large numbers of elephants killed. Generally, however, under the Empire elephants were used not for exhibitions but, as literature, coins, and gems shew quite clearly, for drawing ceremonial cars of the emperors, and occasionally for heavy loads [20].

Grace and beauty of plumage formed the motive for importation to the West of the very few birds which the Romans obtained from the far East. First among these come the several species of parrots, of which one at least was a favourite cage-bird among the wealthy, and they formed the only branch of the Animal Kingdom which entered as a regular item into Rome's traffic with India. The evidence of ancient classical writers and of extant mosaics, gems, tesserae and so on reveals three species at least, and possibly more, all of them coming from India, and Aelian had heard of three different Indian species. Descriptions given by ancient writers shew that the birds most frequently imported were the Ring-necked Parrakeet (*Psittacus torquatus = Palaeornis torquata*) and the Alexandrine Parrakeet (*P. Nepalensis*). Both are green; the male "Ringed-necked" has a purple collar, while the

"Alexandrine" is a larger bird, with a very large bill, and (in the male) a broad pink neck-ring. The first-named is the species most frequently engraved upon classical gem-stones, sometimes with unmistakable detail (21). It is found in India Ceylon and Indo-Burmese regions as far as Cochin China, and in Africa, but the Romans did not discover the African birds until the explorers sent by Nero to Ethiopia brought some back, and India remained the chief source throughout the Empire. Representations of the Alexandrine species of North and Central India are not uncommon (22). So far as I can tell, several extant gems are engraved with a figure of the little Rosy Parrakeet (*P. Rosa*), green with pinkish-purple head, and found (23) in North-east India and so east to Burma and Cochin China, and other gems shew *P. Alexandri = eupatria*, a native of Ceylon (24). Again, since Ctesias (long before the era of the Roman Empire) describes what is clearly a male example of the beautiful Blossom-headed Parrakeet (*P. cyanocephalus*), we ought perhaps to include this species also among the Roman cage-birds, although we have no Roman descriptions of it; the bird is native to many parts of India and Ceylon (25). Lastly, during the second century A.C. Roman subjects discovered white cockatoos in regions of Arakan; they had been unknown before, and must have been brought to Burmese regions from the Indian archipelago (26).

Parrots were known, then, since the times of Ctesias and Aristotle and a regular trade in them, begun by the Hellenistic Greeks, was developed by the Romans, among whom they were favourite pets of adults and children, particularly of the higher classes of Rome. They were taught to speak single phrases, and in the time of Augustus were kept in wicker cages, but by the time of Martial and Statius in cages of ivory or of tortoiseshell adorned with ivory and provided with silver wires—a pretty picture of Roman

luxury ministered to by the far East. The representations
on gems shew that they were kept in pairs and fed upon
cherries (27) and both Ovid and Statius wrote a poem on
the death of a pet parrot. Sometimes they were carried
about in public even as macaws are to-day, and with other
birds were displayed at exhibitions and probably as adorn-
ments to the forum on occasions of spectacles. Supplies
increased during the second century, for Pausanias speaks
of parrots and other τέρατα brought from India, and Arrian
declines to describe the birds, while Elagabalus obtained
such large supplies that he could create table delicacies
out of the heads of parrots, and feed his lions and other
animals upon them. Much earlier than this the name of the
parrot had been given to a green eye-salve. As the Roman
Empire declined, the demand for these Indian birds became
small and references to them in literature become rare
during several centuries, but they still appear on gem-
stones and so on (28). We have one memorial inscription.

I have no intention to assert positively that parrots were
not brought by the sea-route through Egypt (especially
as sailors' pets) but I believe as a general rule they were
not. For since they do not appear in the Digest-list of articles
of commerce subject to duty on entry into Egypt, the conclusion is that they did not come by way of Egypt; and
since they do not appear in the *Periplus* either, the conclusion is that they did not come either by way of Egypt
or by way of the Persian Gulf; on the other hand, Diodoros
attributes the birds to Syria, which can only mean that at
least until the beginning of the Roman Empire the birds
were brought along the land-route ending at Antioch, and
it looks as though the same thing was done by the imperial
Romans. Moreover, in Greek and Roman graves in South
Russia have been found parrots represented on various
objects of art, and vases occur painted and fashioned in

the form of a parrot; a natural deduction is that the birds were brought also by way of Oxus and the Caspian or through Armenia to the Black Sea, and were valued as pets even in remote places (29).

The remaining examples of birds imported from the far East all belong to the Order Gallinae which for ages have provided birds for food, ornament, and sport. The various Pheasants of the far East were perhaps no more than an occasional gift from an Indian embassy, but the Common Pheasant which was a great favourite among the Romans was brought continually from Caspian regions beyond the river Phasis and from Parthia, so that other oriental birds from farther East may often have come with them along the silk-route through Parthia and by other oriental highways especially the Oxus and the Caspian to Rome. Among these we may include perhaps the Ring-necked Pheasant (*Phasianus torquatus*) which had its origin in China but is nevertheless a variety of the Common Pheasant (30). Likewise the gorgeous Golden Pheasant (*Chrysolophus pictus*), which inhabits in a wild state southern and western China and eastern Tibet, but is easily domesticated, was a striking product of the overland silk-route from China to the Roman Empire, for at his "secular games" in A.D. 47 Claudius exhibited in the comitium what he claimed to be a "Phoenix," generally supposed to appear in Egypt once every five hundred years and I feel convinced that the bird was really a golden pheasant, for this appears to be the bird described by Pliny as the phoenix, which he states to be as big as an eagle (the pheasant is of course smaller, but it has a long tail) and decorated with brilliant golden plumage round the neck, the throat having "a crest" and the head a tuft of feathers; so far, at least, Pliny might be describing a cock golden pheasant, and Herodotos also says that the plumage is partly red, partly golden; this consideration is not altered

by the fact that the prototype of the fabulous phoenix as
an astronomical symbol is generally admitted to have been
the Egyptian bird "benu," apparently the Purple Heron (31).
We are tempted to connect the phoenix's nest, built of casia,
cinnamon, frankincense, or myrrh, and the attribution of
the bird (by Lucian, the Physiologus, and so on) to India,
with some creature coming from the far East by the sea-
route, but such a connexion is unfortunately impossible.
At any rate, golden pheasants imported after the reign of
Claudius were not called phoenixes (for the exhibit of
Claudius was regarded as an imposture at the time), and
so receive no attention (32).

The original of the Barnyard Fowl is the Indian Jungle-
Fowl (*Gallus banciva*), but the domesticated form spread
westwards at a very early date; yet the dwarf fowls of Pliny
may have been unknown until the Roman imperial era; they
seem to have been highly prized bantam fowls, originally
imported from the far East, perhaps from Japan (33).
Whether the magnificent peacock, which, having spread
westwards from India through the Persians in ages gone
by, was now bred extensively on Roman estates, was still
an article of commerce with India is uncertain, but it is to
be noticed that Lucian writing in the second century A.C.
expresses the desire of a man for "Indian" peacocks (34).
The τέρατα brought back from India with Indian parrots
were doubtless gorgeous Indian birds of different kinds.

The only other living animals which we can name as
brought from India are snakes. India produced the Cobra-
di-Capello (*Naia tripudians*), known to the Greeks and
Romans as "aspis," and other members of this Order,
but the only clear records of importations of serpents refer
to large pythons of India, Ceylon, Burma, the Nicobars,
Malay and its archipelago, and Indo-China, namely *P.
molurus* of India and Ceylon, and *P. reticulatus*, the com-

monest species in Indo-China and the Malay islands. Thus an Indian embassy which came to Augustus presented a small python and other snakes and Augustus exhibited in the comitium one fifty cubits long, while Strabo saw in Egypt a serpent nine feet long and brought from India; Hadrian too is reported to have obtained a serpent from India (35). These examples shew how even in curiosities there must have been a not altogether negligible traffic between Rome and India.

The importation of animal-products by Rome from the far East consisted partly of useful substances provided by certain mammals of which we have mentioned most already, and by several lower forms of animal-life which we have not yet touched upon. The traffic in animal-products stood upon a footing entirely different from the trade in the living animals, and was conducted by the Greeks and Romans as far as possible by direct communication along the sea-route, but as we shall see, not entirely so.

The traffic in oriental hides and furs was probably one of greater importance than the available evidence suggests. The *Periplus* says that "Chinese" hides or furs were exported from Barbaricon on the river Indus, and Pliny says that iron made by the "Chinese" was sent by them with their tissues and skins to Rome, and that dyed skins obtained from the "Chinese" were the most valuable of the coverings furnished by animals. Again, amongst agricultural products exported from North-west India to East Africa we find κανυάκαι, perhaps rough skins with fur left on, or perhaps heavy woollen coats, and woollen clothes could be obtained in Kaviripaddinam. All these seem to be included under the heading "Capilli Indici" in the Digest-list to which we have referred already. Now Pliny's reference to "Chinese" iron, tissues, and skins is now taken to refer in reality to products obtained not from the Chinese but from the "Chera" Kingdom in South India, so frequently visited by Greek merchants from the reign of Claudius onwards, but the "Seric" skins exported from Barbaricon on the Indus we may take it were partly Chinese furs brought with silk and diverted to the Indus, partly Tibetan furs (especially of martens and ounces or snow-leopards which we may identify with the skins of the gold-digging "ants" seen by Nearchos, for instance), and partly raw furs from regions even north of Tibet, brought by caravans to Indian seas and destined for ordinary wear and for purposes of luxury in the West (36). We may go farther and conclude that, besides these, good Parthian and Babylonian hides came westwards not only by land-routes but by way of the Indus, as did several kinds of Persian stones and plants, as we shall see; for Babylonian and Parthian hides appear in the Digest-list, and this means that they came either from the Persian Gulf round Arabia or direct from the Indus to the Red Sea and Egypt. Even to-day it is very easy to get various skins from Tibet and Turkestan at the towns of the Indus and yet difficult to get them elsewhere in the East. Naturally, however, much of this trade must have been carried on by Rome through the Parthians who added hides from their own territories, and Caesarea in Cappadocia was a well-known centre for them. The "negotiatores Parthicarii" seem to have had special connexion with Parthian peltry, and a "praetor Parthicarius" had jurisdiction over them. In ancient India special trapper-villages existed for the supplying of pelts and so on, but the hunting and trapping of animals was not regarded as an honourable calling, and generally we find that the supplies of skins came from the northern districts. The Mahabharata in the Sabha Parva speaks of presents brought to Yudhisthira from the Saka, Tukhara, and Kanka tribes, and they include clothes of the goat and sheep wool, skins of martens and weasels, besides

silk and fine muslins, and, in the Ramayana, Sita receives
woollen stuffs, furs, fine silks, precious stones, and so on.
The wool would be native (probably Kashmir wool) while
the furs may have come with silk from distant regions of
Asia. We may be quite sure that among those sent westwards by the Indians were fine skins of lions, tigers, and
leopards. But when Pliny says that lycium was sent to Rome
in the skins of rhinoceroses and camels by Indians, he indicates no more than a native method of packing for the
purpose of exportation (37).

The remaining mammal-products with which we have to
deal were furnished by the Ungulate Order which comprises
animals of such varied outward aspect. The "butyron"
(Sanskrit *bhutari*), which the *Periplus* says was exported
from Ariace and from Barygaza to East Africa, was a
preparation of oil from butter, called by the Indians "ghi,"
and by us "clarified butter." On the African coast, which
produced little oil, it was naturally in demand, but it
probably entered into western medicine like ordinary
butter. It is still sent from India to Africa by Indian
traders to-day and is prepared by the Indians chiefly from
the milk of humped cattle (*Bos Indicus*) and in certain
districts from the buffalo, while in the north the Tibetan
yak is available (38). The yak, too, may have provided for
exportation to the West in ancient times not only horns
like that which Ptolemy Philadelphos received from India,
but also tails of long silky white hair, referred to by Aelian
and by Cosmas, and called to-day Chowri(e)s and used all
over the East to drive away flies and to create currents of
air. They are articles of taste and luxury and may have
provided some of the Roman fly-flaps or fly-whisks, and
formed perhaps a part of the "Capilli Indici" mentioned in
the Digest-list (39).

Again, for fine texture and softness no Asiatic wool has

been found to equal the *pashm* or *pushm* wool of the shawl-goat of Kashmir, Bhutan, Tibet, and the northern face of the Himalayas, and this wool, from which are made the famous Kashmir shawls, is a valuable article of trade between Tibet and the lower plains of India. We know that Aurelian received a red-dyed short woolly pallium as a present from a Persian king, and there is no reason why the fine raw wool should not have been exported westwards by way of the Indus or Broach. I suggest that what has been a settled opinion for a long time is a correct one, that the material called, apparently, "Marococorum lana" in the Digest-list was raw wool of the shawl-goat sent from North-west Indian ports to Egypt to be worked up there or in Syria or in the looms of private households generally. The Muztagh on the northern side of Kashmir is called the range of the Karakoram or Korakoram (Black Mountain) from which we get some such word as Ma(c)rococorum; again, this wool of the Digest-list was important enough to be included in a tariff-list for import-duty in Egypt during the second century A.C., after Trajan had fostered, as we have seen, closer relations with the Kushan monarchy, which included Kashmir—a district of which, together with the north-western regions of India, Ptolemy shews a remarkably detailed knowledge. When the author of the *Periplus* wrote, inland districts of those regions had not been explored by Roman subjects, and no wool appears among the exports given by him, so that it is possible that for some time the Arabians kept it a secret in their hands (40). Their own broad-tailed sheep were known to the Greeks, but only the fat tail was useful, the body being covered by coarse hair instead of wool; the Arabians therefore would be much tempted to pass on to the West as "Arabian" the finer fleeces from the higher regions of Asia. Dirksen thinks that in the Digest passage (which is exceedingly corrupt)

the wool is named from a trade-route, or that the name is
a collective one for all oriental wool which the East provided in ancient times. The wool was probably not sent
dyed, for the lac-dye and wool would fetch higher prices
if sold separately and from the western point of view
there were in Egypt imperial manufactories not only of
wool, but of dyeing, and there were also the dye-works of
Syria; moreover the red-dyed wool astonished Aurelian
and his successors as a thing of novelty, and the dye and
the wool would have to compete with imperial products.
The high value of this shawl-goat wool in ancient times is
shewn by the fact that when the Sassanid Hormisdas
(Hormizd) II (302–310) married the daughter of the king
of Kabul, the bride's trousseau excited great admiration
as a wonderful product of the looms of Kashmir, and
it is probable that the practice of sending the wool
westwards commenced only during the second century
A.C. (41).

We can speak with greater certainty in the case of the
Musk Deer (*Moschus moschiferus*) the male of which
produces the famous odour which is very highly valued in
the East and is more persistent and penetrating than any
other odour. It was known to Cosmas in the sixth century
A.C., as a product obtained, as we should expect, in the
Indus district, and it is difficult to believe that so important
an ingredient in perfumes to-day was not imported to the
West through Persia or from the Indus or from Broach
before the time of Cosmas, though it was only established
in trade during the Arabian epoch. The musk deer inhabits
the Himalayas above the height of 8000 feet, from Gilgit
eastwards, extending to Tibet, North-western China, and
Siberia, and the musk (from the Sanskrit *mushka*, that is,
the scrotum) is known to-day in three kinds, the most
valued coming from China, a less valued from Assam or

Nepal, and the least valued from Central Asia. With it at the Indus mouth the Romans found beaver-musk of N. Asia (42).

So far we have been dealing with animal-products which on the whole formed a part of Rome's trade with North-west India and with regions north of that country; but the next items bring us to part of Rome's trade with India and Africa alike. The hides, teeth, and horns of rhino-ceroses probably formed articles of this trade with both regions. Horns were exported from Adulis, the depôt of the Axumite kingdom, but these were the product of the African species. Pliny says that lycium was sent by the Indians in the skins of rhinoceroses and camels, but the more important were the horns, out of which the Romans made oil flasks called "gutti," and vessels made out of the horns of Indian rhinoceroses and the so-called "unicorns" (which, as we have said, were the same animals) have always been esteemed for their supposed medical properties, and for the alleged property of rendering harmless any poison drunk out of them (43). We find that the Romans brought rhinoceros-horns to China apparently from India in A.D. 166 (44).

We now come to one of the most important of the articles which formed Rome's eastern trade—namely ivory, which has been used for ornament and for decoration from the earliest times, and, except when fossil ivory was used, the supply in historical times came from Africa and India, being tusks of the African and the Indian elephant respectively. Down to the end of the epoch before Christ Africa had been a natural source for supplies of the best ivory, but the early rise of the Babylonian and Persian civilisations across the land-routes between India and the West had created a more extensive trade in Indian than in African ivory, until Ptolemy II obtained large quantities of the African. It has been said that the usual derivation of the

Greek word for elephant and its ivory (ἐλέφας, Latin *ebur*)
is etymology at its wildest, and yet the explanation is
probably correct that the word represents the Sanskrit
ibha (elephant) with the Semitic definite article prefixed.
We are told distinctly that the Greeks at the height of
their culture used Indian as well as Ethiopian ivory for
the exposed parts of the body in statues, and we have
"Indian" ivory mentioned frequently (45) as soon as the
Roman Empire begins. That the Roman commerce in ivory
was enormous is shewn by the large number of uses to
which it was put—the references in ancient writers being
very common and the surviving articles in ivory endless.
In literature alone we find it used for statues, chairs, beds,
sceptres, hilts, scabbards, chariots, carriages, tablets, book-
covers, table-legs, doors, flutes, lyres, combs, brooches, pins,
scrapers, boxes, bird-cages, floors, and so on, and extant
examples in their multitudes would add to an already remarkable list, covering as they do the whole epoch of
ancient history. It is no wonder that Lucian makes a man's
riches consist of gold, raiment, slaves, and ivory. Ivory is
white, durable, hard, and yet easy to work, and the Romans
used it at first in temples and for the insignia of the higher
magistrates, but the growth of luxury brought with it im-
moderate display, particularly in the covering of whole
articles of furniture and in the use of ivory in luxurious
couches, table-legs, and beds (46). Indian supplies came
of course partly by the land-routes, but the sea-route received much also, and as the epithet Assyrian shews, the
Persian Gulf too (47), and when the author of the *Periplus*
wrote his book after the discovery and use of the monsoons,
the traffic along the great sea-route was well developed.
In his time the main centre of the trade in African ivory
was Adulis, the trade-depôt of the Axumites, but the material
was also sent from Barygaza, Muziris, and Nelcynda on

the western coast of India, and Dosarene (Orissa) on the
eastern—the last-named region producing the best Indian
ivory. So far as we can judge from the remarks of
the *Periplus*, the supply of African ivory was more important in the time of Nero than the Indian supply, but
we can trace, I think, a curious development. We have seen
how large the trade in ivory must have become, and there
is evidence that from the time of Tiberius the demand
increased. Men like Gaius, Nero, and Seneca were extremely
lavish in their use of ivory; Gaius provided his horse with
an ivory stable; Nero used ivory profusely in his palace;
Seneca possessed five hundred tripod-tables with ivory legs.
Such extravagance as this seems to have produced a state of
affairs which caused Pliny to say that the supply of good
ivories was failing, with the exception of those which were
being brought from India, and Pliny's remarks seem to be
founded upon fact; to the depletion of the supply from
Africa and the increase in the demand for Indian ivory we
may attribute the gradual increase of references to ivory
definitely called Indian from the beginning of the Roman
Empire, and to the same cause we may ascribe the exploration which took place farther southward into Africa and
down the East African coast as far as Cape Delgado (a fact
manifest from Ptolemy writing at a later date)—the motive
was demand for more ivory. In the fourth century the
dearth of African elephants was a source of complaints. One
wonders if Seneca was at all interested in the ivory trade;
we know that he possessed hundreds of ivory-legged tables;
he also wrote a book on India, and the exploration to the
south of Egypt carried out in Nero's reign may have been
proposed by Seneca as a possible method of reaching fresh
supplies of ivory (48). Literary references to ivory increase
in writers of the latter part of the first century, so that the
profusion must have become greater still (49). Another

curious development reveals itself by the sixth century A.C., when African ivory was again supplanting the Indian. Cosmas says that the ivory of the small tusks of Ceylonese elephants was not being used in commerce, and this is largely true of Ceylon elephants to-day; again, he says that the ivory obtained from the fine tusks of Ethiopian elephants was being exported even to India, and this also is done to-day (50). It is probable therefore that when the African elephant-hunts of the Ptolemies declined, the demand for Indian ivory increased, and no serious efforts were made by the Romans to exploit more completely by exploration the African supplies until the end of the first century; then further explorations in and round Africa resulted in renewed plenty in African supplies, which, as Rome's direct trade with India declined during the third century, again took the precedence of supplies from more distant India; this tendency was helped by the fact that the Indian elephants never produce such a large quantity of ivory as the African. To-day the African elephant is in danger of extinction—so great is the European demand for ivory, and it is possible that for the same reason the Indian species will be likely to follow the same fate in course of time (51), though at present it holds its own.

We cannot tell whether the Romans obtained from Indian coasts any ambergris of the sperm-whale, but in the Arabian period later traffic in the best greyish kind was centred, according to Symeon Seth, at "Silachetum" in India. All the ambergris of ancient times must have come from the Atlantic Ocean or the coasts of Indian seas (52).

We need not doubt, however, that a special oriental preparation of the flesh of lizards (called by the Greeks saurae and scincoi) formed a part of Roman medicine. The scincoi inhabited Gaetulia, Egypt, Red Sea coasts, Arabia, and India, and great saurae, of which the flesh was eaten

and the melted fat used instead of olive-oil, were found in
Socotra. Of these the Arabian and larger Indian "scincoi,"
said to be land-crocodiles, were sent to the Roman Empire
salted. This must mean that the Romans imported an Indian
and Arabian preparation of the flesh of typical skinks
(genus *Scincus*) which range from Northern Africa through
Arabia and Persia to Sind, yielding medicine and food to-
day; and a similar preparation from the very large lizard
Varanus niloticus of Africa (often more than 5 feet long)
and from the still larger *V. salvator* of India and beyond,
providing odorous flesh for food (53).

Most of the remaining animal-products with which we
have to deal formed a very important part of Rome's Indian
trade, being materials much in demand among the wealthy
and luxurious for purposes of decoration and personal
adornment—namely tortoiseshell, pearls, silk, and lac.

Tortoiseshell could be obtained by the Romans from several
Turtles belonging to coasts of Indian seas, but the chief
kind valued by them was the tortoiseshell of modern commerce also, obtained from the Hawk's Bill (or Tortoiseshell)
Turtle (*Chelonia imbricata*) which is found in the Indian
waters widely and was apparently attributed to Ceylon even
before the imperial period, but was traced to the Malay
Peninsula during the first century A.C. after the discovery
of the monsoons. The best must have come chiefly from the
Eastern archipelago especially between the east coast of
Celebes and New Guinea. This fine and durable material
came into general use early in the first century, since
references to it (often with the epithet "Indian" added) are
frequent (54) from the beginning of the Empire and the
price rose to a considerable figure from the time of Tiberius.
In the West it was put to various uses but it was sought
above all by wealthy Romans to provide a veneer for
their rich furniture, in particular for decorating bedsteads

made of solid ivory; the flesh was not eaten by western peoples in ancient times. The trade, which was conducted naturally along the sea-route, increased greatly after Hippalos' discovery, as is shewn by the increase of references in classical writers from the time of Nero onwards, and the *Periplus* reveals the nature of the traffic. That guide-book shews that the best of all tortoiseshell known was sent from the Malay Peninsula (Chryse) by way of Muziris and Nelcynda to find a market, much shell being known to come from Ceylon also; these supplies, together with some more from the islands off the west coast of India, reached the Greeks at the marts of Damirice (55).

As we descend to lower forms of animal life we reach one of the staple articles of trade between Rome and India, namely the pearl. In ancient times as now there were no fisheries of the true pearl in European waters, all references to British pearls, for example, indicating merely pearls from the River-Mussel (*Unio margaritifer*); the Romans, therefore, in order to obtain the true pearl from the Pearl-Mussel (*Meleagrina margaritifera*), turned to the far East; just as is the case to-day, the Romans could obtain inferior pearls from the Red Sea, and pearls of very best quality from the Persian Gulf (Bahrein Islands), but their most abundant supplies (their famous lapilli Indici) came from India. The chief locality for these was the Gulf of Manaar, with the result that Ceylon is constantly mentioned as a source for pearls not only in Buddhist and other Indian literature, but in Greek and Roman writers from Megasthenes onwards; the *Periplus* and Pliny shew that the fisheries (worked by condemned criminals) were centred at Kolkai in the Pandyan Kingdom, controlled from Modura, whither, as Pliny shews, the Pandyas had removed their capital from Kolkai, while the pearls sold at Argaru and Kaviripaddinam in the Chola Kingdom came obviously from the Palk Strait. The large supplies obtained from these sources and, still under Pandyan control, from Ceylon, together with inferior sorts from the Ganges, were found by the Greek merchants at Muziris and Nelcynda where particularly fine ones could be obtained. At the same time large quantities of inferior pearls were brought from the Persian Gulf to Barygaza to find a market there. The conditions of the Indian pearl trade are very similar to-day. The chief fisheries are in the Gulf of Manaar, on banks situated roughly from six to eight miles off the western shore of India and from sixteen to twenty miles off the northern part of the west coast of Ceylon, extending many miles north and south, "the Tinnevelly fishery being on the Madras side of the Strait, near Tuticorin"; moreover pearls are obtained also in the Tambalagam Bay near Trincomalee, inferior pearls come from the Ganges, and many of the best specimens from the Persian Gulf are sold in Bombay as "Bombay Pearls." The remarks of Pliny, confirmed by extant jewelry, shew that among the Greeks of the flourishing period of Greek history pearls were not highly favoured; Pliny shews that, introduced to Rome during the Jugurthine war and made popular by the large quantities brought back to Italy by Pompey, pearls became common at the fall of the Republic when Augustus brought back the treasures of the Ptolemies. Before that emperor died, the Romans learnt from Isidore of Charax full details of the Persian Gulf pearls and their high value, and in due course the already extensive trade in Indian pearls was raised to an enormous height by the discovery of the full use of the monsoons and by the demands of Greek and Roman girls and ladies for this typically feminine adornment. Earlier, in the time of Cicero, when pearls were scarce, one valued at eight thousand pounds in modern money was taken from the ear of Caecilia Metella and deliberately swallowed by the son of Aesopus that he might have the satisfaction of swallowing a huge sum of money at a draught; but soon the wearing of pearls by women was frequently referred to by Greek and Roman writers; already we have visions of Roman matrons appearing in public covered with pearls, and expensive dedications of pearls were made, even when they were valued at millions of sesterces. As Androsthenes shews, they were being paid for mostly in gold.

Beginning with the Jewish philosopher Philon of Alexandria and St Paul we find moralists lamenting the wearing of pearls by women and girls, while Pliny becomes almost incoherent with wrath in his contemplation of this form of luxury, which he said reached the extreme of expenditure and necessitated travel in Indian seas over large distances and in torrid climes, and perils undergone amidst wild beasts—presumably sharks. It is not enough, he says, that Romans should live upon dangers (oysters)...they must needs wear them. It is in connexion with pearls that he speaks, with a gust of anger against feminine luxury, of the wealth drained by India and the Chinese (?) from the Roman Empire. He grieves that people should love the sound of clashing pearls (the "crotalia" worn in ear-rings), should wear them on their shoes, and walk upon them. Even the poorer classes desired them, since the pearl was as good as a "gentleman-usher" (*lictor*) to a woman in public. Indeed the references to pearls worn by women, especially in writers subsequent to Nero, are very common; for instance, again and again do Martial and Statius mention the oriental "lapilli," their high value, their dearness to the hearts of women; the frivolous Gellia lavishes all her affection upon them; the adultress glitters with them; the coquette in silk and rings wears pearls in her ears; Issa is more precious than Indian pearls. Extant papyri reveal pearls enumerated in dowries of young brides; Pliny saw Lollia Paulina, wife of Gaius, covered head, neck, ears, and fingers, with strings of pearls and emeralds, the produce of spoliation but not of trade, placed alternately to the value of 40,000,000 sesterces. The craving was not confined to the one sex, a fact lamented by Quintilian; emperors like Nero possessed large quantities of pearls; he adorned shoes, beds, bed-chambers, actors' wands and actors' masks with them, swallowed them in drink and scattered them among the people; he consecrated in the Capitol his first beard, decorated with the most valuable pearls. Normally this kind of luxury took two forms—the pearls were either worn in necklaces up to three rows, often together with emeralds as is shewn by the example of Lollia Paulina, by a passage in Tertullian, and by an inscription found in Spain; or else pear-shaped specimens ("elenchi") were worn by ladies who suspended them from their finger-rings or from their ears in such a way as to rattle together in movement ("crotalia"). The necklaces could be obtained in India, as Indian literature reveals, but the work was done mostly in the West by "diatretarii," a name given in particular, as Godefroy (J.) shews, to drillers of holes in pearls. Sometimes unguents were stored in the shells with pearls still attached. The traffic was so extensive that there were corporations of "margaritarii," and "officinae margaritariorum" near the "tabernae argentariae" in the Forum; the pearls were sold in the Saepta and along the Sacra Via, and also (as the Notitia of the fourth century shews) in a "porticus margaritaria." Special keepers of pearls and pearl-studded jewelry appear as "ad margarita," and "margaritarii" (pearl dealers) spread all over the Empire. Instances of smuggling were perhaps common, for we have a mock case of a woman who smuggled four hundred large pearls in her bosom and a papyrus records a runaway slave who had made off with ten pearls in his possession. The Romans followed the Indian valuation and placed the pearl after the diamond, but they seem to have paid a higher price for the largest and best pearls (called "uniones") than they did for any other article of jewelry. Their extreme value caused the name "Margarita" to be used as a term of endearment applied to dear children good slaves and pet dogs. The largest pearl known to the Romans weighed more than half an ounce. The account given above illustrates the peculiar importance of the pearl in the oriental commerce of the Romans, and it is possible that no other article of that trade formed such a large part of it. In the New Testament we have the pearl of great price and each of the gates of the Heavenly Jerusalem is made of one pearl. " Small is the pearl, but Queen among jewels" are the words of St Gregory. As Pliny says, the pearl being durable descended from heir to heir, and we find the virtuous Calpurnia, in the time of Maximinus, in the possession of "uniones Cleopatrani," that is, pearls which had once belonged to Cleopatra—but the demand for fresh supplies in the West probably never declined (56). As we shall see Rome paid for her Indian pearls partly with amber, copper, lead, and perhaps coral, beside coined money, from the first century A.C. onwards.

It was natural that the Romans should use mother-of-pearl to a certain extent in decoration; for instance, Nero decorated parts of his palace with this material and here and there examples occur in extant collections of antique gems and jewelry. Nero at least must have obtained his supplies from merchants trading with the far East, for the most valuable species of mother-of-pearl "oyster" is not found west of the Malay archipelago, and the best shells of the Persian Gulf are sold in Bombay as Bombay shell; for ordinary purposes, however, mother-of-pearl could be obtained from the Red Sea (57).

From meagre pieces of scattered evidence I think we may deduce that there was a trade carried on by Rome with India in products of molluscs other than the pearl-mussels. (i) It is to be noticed that the word "conchylia" was applied to several kinds of molluscs (the so-called shell-"fish"), but in particular to oysters, and Pliny says that some conchylia came from Indian seas; again, on the authority of Androsthenes, Athenaeos mentions together with χοιρίναι (cowries?), molluscs and particularly oysters of the Indian Ocean. Again, Seneca speaks of "*conchylia ultimi maris ex ignoto litore,*" and if this was written after A.D. 43 when the south of England became a province, he refers perhaps to oysters of the Indian Ocean, brought I suppose in tanks to the West; but if he was writing before 43, he refers to British oysters of Rutupiae (Richborough, Kent) and other places. Again, at a later date Tertullian, who claims to speak from experience, having just mentioned pearls, says "but whatever it is that ambition fishes up from the British or the Indian seas, it is a kind of conch not more pleasing in savour than... even the giant mussel." This evidence points at least to edible molluscs, but when we find that Pliny speaks of oysters and conchylia found at two places near the Indus, confusing at the same time, I think, localities in the Ganges regions, and that Philostratos speaks of very large cockles, mussels, and oysters, and a white pearl-producing shell from an island near the mouth of the Indus—then we are probably right in pointing to the oyster-beds of Karachi which are still important for local use, and to the now unimportant beds of the Ganges (58). The coasts of Madras and Bombay also produce good edible oysters. (ii) In the *Periplus* there is a corrupt passage which has been taken to mean that in the Chola Kingdom was spun and sold a silky thread called πιν(ν)ικόν obtained from the pinna-mollusc, such thread being still so spun into a fabric at

Taranto in Italy. The point is, however, quite uncertain, since the sole source is a corrupt passage, and πιν(ν)ικόν elsewhere in the *Periplus* means pearl. We can gather from the text of the *Periplus* that the product of a certain mollusc called πίν(ν)α (a name certainly used for pearl, for instance in papyri) collected (συλλεγόμενον) along the coasts of the Chola Kingdom was sent inland and sold (or is it worked up?) at one place only, Argaru, that is, Uraiyur, the old capital of the Chola Kingdom. If the πιν(ν)ικόν so collected (from the sea) and sold in the capital only was pearls, then these pearls came from the fisheries of the Palk Strait, north of Adam's Bridge, belonging in ancient times to the Chola Kingdom, whereas the fisheries of the Gulf of Manaar belonged to the Pandyan Kingdom and were controlled from Modura. Sometimes I am inclined to think that the author of the *Periplus* does describe a material obtained from the byssus-thread of a species of pinna-mollusc, for he goes on to say (if we read γὰρ, not καὶ) "for from there are exported muslins called Argareitides." But it must be admitted that the textile industry of Trichinopoly and Tanjore, famous from early times, was not based on a product of a sea-mollusc, so that the author may have added his statement about the muslins of Argaru independently of his notice about the pinna-product; if we take πιν(ν)ικόν to mean the thread here, then the Argaritic muslins were fabrics made of pinna-thread (59). (iii) Dioscurides has an extraordinary account of what he calls "onyx-shell," the lid of a mollusc, similar to the lid of the purple-mollusc, found in the nard-bearing "lakes" of India, which results in the lid being aromatic since the animals feed upon the nard! The Red Sea and Babylonia each sent another kind, apparently bearing a similar odour. Now since the purple-mollusc is not a bivalve, but a gastropod, the "lid" which Dioscurides mentions can only mean the operculum (nail) closing the shell, and I have found on British shores many pretty examples of these. But it is possible that there is a confusion with a much larger shell—perhaps some species of scallop-bivalves of which either of the two shells can be called the lid—the smaller flat valve, or the larger convex valve. Both valves are in some species often very large, and I have collected specimens of a beautiful mottled colour, and others banded with shades of brown, which might well earn the name onyx-shell. Any sweet odour noticeable in the Roman shells might be due (if they were the shells of gastropods) to the fact that they had contained some unguent, or (if they were bivalves) to some special treatment at the hands of Arabians. It is possible that the "onyx" of four denarii in weight, mentioned in conjunction with the aromatic gum bdellium (which came from regions not far distant from those which produced the Indian spikenard) by a papyrus of the third century, is applicable to odorous imported shell. On the whole, the accounts of Paulus Aegineta, Avicenna, and Rhazes point to the gastropod Wing-Snail (*Strombus lentiginosus*); the "lid" would be the well-known odorous operculum of this *Strombus* (60), but it is noticeable that *S. gigas* of the West Indies is used for cameos. Thus there was a small commerce in oriental shells from north-western districts of India.

(iv) From South India too we find that conch-shells or chank-shells were being exported at Marallo (Mantotte?) during the sixth century A.C. The sacred chank (a gastropod, *Turbinella rapa*) of the Gulf of Manaar still provides vessels, ornaments, musical instruments, and so on, and we learn that of old chank-cutters worked in Korkai and in Kaviripaddinam. Salang I. produced many κόγχοι (61).

Throughout the era of the Roman Empire, and with ever increasing importance, Chinese silk was the staple article of commerce along the land-route through Parthia and regions north of India to China, but it entered into Rome's Indian trade as well. In earlier ages western races had used Coan "silk" spun by a European moth, but during the first century A.C. this material was supplanted by the true silk of China, taken from the cocoons spun by the mulberry-fed caterpillar of the true Silk-Moth (*Bombyx mori*), though the Romans for a long time thought that the material was produced by trees. The d'mesheq (Arabic dimaks, Greek μέταξα, English damask) of Amos may be Chinese silk; the Romans noticed the silken flags of the Parthians, and Caesar was reported to have possessed silken curtains, but the introduction of silk to Rome in quantities began only in the reign of Augustus and may be traced to Marcus Antonius who communicated with Bactrians. Both Roman and Chinese history records that silk was worth its weight in gold; at any rate the price was very high, but wealthy women, and men too, constantly wore silk to the disgust of moralists, though clothing made wholly of silk was rare until Elagabalus set the example, the material normally being woven into linen or woollen fabrics after importation. Wholly silk cloth was perhaps pulled to pieces for this purpose (62). The name, but no more, of the Chinese (Seres) became familiar to the Romans, and references to the true silk used for clothing, pillows, cushions, and so on, begin in Augustan writers (63).

Soon after the Empire began a tendency grew up to send silk to the Roman Empire without passing through Parthia. Discoveries of silk in tombs in south Russia indicate use of the Oxus route, while discoveries of silks at Achmim (Panopolis) in Egypt worked into linen and wool indicate the use of the sea-route (64). Woven silk destined to be dyed for wear, and unwoven silk destined to be worked up in Egypt, Syria, and Galilee could be sent conveniently by way of the Persian Gulf or the Red Sea, and this cheaper route

avoiding Parthia would be encouraged by the Romans.
Literary evidence confirms this use of Indian routes; thus
Propertius calls the "bombyx" (silk-worm) Arabius where-
by he seems to shew that knowledge of an animal-spun
silk from the far East was suggesting itself to western
merchants. Even if we reject this, the system was incon-
testably established after Hippalos' discovery, with India
and the Kushans as the intermediaries, the Kushans taking
a great share in it if Rome and Parthia warred (65).

When the *Periplus* was written, silk yarn was exported
from Barbaricon on the Indus probably in exchange for
frankincense, while the more valuable silk cloth, besides
raw silk and silk yarn, was sent to Barygaza by way of
Bactria and also to Muziris, Nelcynda, and other marts of
Malabar by way of the Ganges and presumably down the
east coast of India—silk sellers frequented Kaviripaddinam in the Chola Kingdom. Hence silken fabrics, yarn,
and thread appear in the Digest-list (66). Evidently the
system was a permanent one welcome to Egyptian Greeks
and Syrians and provides the chief reason for the adoption
by the Kushans of a currency assimilated to that of Rome,
who encouraged such developments for the purpose of
eliminating the Parthians and the expensive land-route,
and we ultimately hear of Indian silks besides Chinese,
Parthian, and Median robes (67). But the Indians became
intermediaries in two ways—for though part of the silk sent
by them to the Romans was diverted from the land-route
for that purpose, part of it was the result of India's own
trade in Chinese silk. Thus the mouth of the Indus may
well have received silk purposely diverted from Central
Asia; the Gulf of Cambay may have received its silk in the
same way and by ordinary trade between India and China;
but geographical considerations make it probable that the
silk of the Ganges had come from China by sea or through

Yunnan or Assam (down the Brahmaputra) to the Bay of
Bengal (68) only as trade between India and China. Some
hold that the Chinese silk, coming from Singanfu, was
diverted at Lanchowfu so as to come through Lhasa,
the Chumbi vale and Sikkim, or through the Arun valley
and Nepal, to the Ganges; or along the Upper Brahmaputra
to the source of the Sutlej; or through Gartok to the Upper
Indus. But with the exception of the Lanchowfu—Lhasa—
Sikkim road these routes were exposed to wild tribes as
the Tibetan were to great cold—hence the exportation of
silk from the Ganges, where we find a native gold coin, the
κάλτις, was current. Native Indian silk spun by native moths
may have reached Rome with the better kind, and silks of
all kinds were esteemed by Indian men and women as much
as by the Romans (69).

As the first century progressed, Rome's commerce in silk
continued to increase; according to Mela all men knew the
Seres through their commerce, and we have evidence of
silk-dealers in Berytos, Naples, Tibur, and Rome; nard and
silk were the most costly things gathered "from trees," and
chaplets made from one or the other formed the choicest
gifts (70). Early in the second century Maes Titianus and his
agents traced silk beyond the Parthian barrier at least
as far as Central Asia, while Alexander reached Cattigara
(Hanoi?) along the sea-route beyond India; such enterprises as these and the Roman "embassy" which reached
China in A.D. 166 revealed to Greeks like Pausanias and
Pollux the true nature of Chinese silk as a product of an
insect (71). In the third century and in the Byzantine era,
the silk traffic with the Persians took on an entirely new
aspect, but I will only mention the traces of Roman civilisation left along the silk-routes, the failure of the Axumites
to forestall in Justinian's interests the Persians in the sea-
trade in silk, the opening of a new silk-route round

the north of the Caspian and the secret introduction of living eggs of the silk-moth to Byzantium in Justinian's reign (72).

The last animal-product which we have to consider is the red substance obtained from the lac-insect (*Tachardia Lacca*), native to and almost confined to India, Pegu, Siam and Assam; the insect yields two products: lac-dye taken from the bodies of the females, and lac-resin (shellac) prepared in thin pieces from the swarms of larvae as they adhere to various trees. Both substances were brought to the West in ancient times, but rarely, our evidence tending to shew that such importations consisted generally of lac-dyed cottons. Ctesias records that to the Persian king in his time fine fabrics were sent dyed with a colour obtained by the Indians from very red beetles, and we may be sure that the Romans did obtain such fabrics from the Parthians. Yet when (according to the account of Vopiscus) the Persian king presented to Aurelian a short, woolly, "purple" pallium (clearly a Kashmirian shawl dyed with lac) obtained from the inner parts of India, it was such an extraordinary occurrence that not only Aurelian himself, but also Probus and Diocletian made efforts to obtain a similar "purple" but were unsuccessful. Nevertheless the Romans appear to have obtained sometimes the dye separately, for Vopiscus goes on to say that "Indian Sandyx" was supposed to produce such a colour if suitably treated, and we know that sandyx was a kind of vermilion-red; again, lac-dye may have come together with σανδαραχή (red sulphide of arsenic) from Persia and Carmania by way of the Indus—mixed with an equal amount of ruddle it produced the colour sandyx; again, the "purple" given in the Digest-list seems to refer to some such colour as lac; again, the "cancamum" which was imported from the East and which is identified below with Indian copal, is wrongly called a dye by Pliny, who seems to be confusing the substance with lac; moreover the author of the *Periplus* states definitely that lac-dye (λάκκος, Sanskrit *raksha*, later *laksha*, Prakrit *lakkha*) was being exported from Ariace to the East African coast, where Greek merchants must have found it often. It was either used separately or united with the murex as an element in the Tyrian purple for dyeing cloth. But if the emperors whom we mentioned just now not only did not know the dye but also failed to obtain it, we are forced to conclude that it was due either to decline in Rome's sea-trade with India or to absorption of the supplies by the eastern part of the Empire. With regard to shellac, on a papyrus containing an inventory of household furniture (A.D. 103–117) is mentioned the item σκούτλια ξύλινα λελακκωμένα δύο, which may have been not simply deep-hollowed dishes, but wooden platters covered with shellac, manufactured perhaps in India, and Pliny in his account of amber seems to refer several times to lac or shellac (73). But of both substances the Romans knew very little, and even the Arabians of a later age did not shew a very wide acquaintance. In the Roman Empire the dye would have to compete with the imperial purple.

CHAPTER II

Plant-Products

WITH the exception of a few cases which we have described above, plant-products obtained from India were of greater importance and utility than animals and animal-products. Our records for the era of the Roman Empire shew that these plant-products were used first and foremost to satisfy the demands of luxury in different ways, but besides this they were employed for useful purposes as well, very frequently in drugs and medicines, and much less frequently for food and for other ordinary demands of life. But to whatever use an Indian product was put, it received the reprobation of the moralists of the time, because of the high price nearly always paid for it as a result of its carriage over long distances, the burden of customs-dues and other exactions, and the profit expected and obtained by merchants after their hazardous adventure.

In the following survey the plant-products which entered into Rome's Indian trade are not arranged according to scientific classification, but are grouped roughly according to their nature from the point of view of the ordinary consumer and according to the uses to which they were put. The most important of such groups contains, as will be seen, plants which are aromatics and spices and the carriage of these together with fragrant gums and resins and other commerce by Arabians across their peninsula had already lasted for ages, so that, with the addition of further land-trade across Parthia and of the sea-trade commenced by the Ptolemies, the traffic in aromatics, spices, and other plant-products was fairly extensive when the Roman Empire began, and the Romans already knew that India produced many odorous and medicinal plants and roots and plants yielding a variety of colours (1); and

the traffic increased to a wonderful extent after the full
discovery of the monsoons in the reign of Claudius.

Early in the imperial era pepper (Tamil *pippali*) became a staple article of Rome's sea-trade with India.
Apparently the Romans first had it in quantities after
their conquests in Asia Minor and Syria, and to a greater
extent after the annexation of Egypt. Rome itself soon
provided the greatest market for it, and the whole of
their pepper traffic was conducted along the sea-route
through Alexandria. Frequent references begin in Augustan
writers [2], but they increase greatly in writers who lived
subsequent to the discovery of the monsoons, an event
which firmly established pepper as a staple article of the
sea-trade and almost removed it from the class of luxuries
by reducing the price considerably. The spice came from
Malabar and Travancore and consisted chiefly of the common Black Pepper which, when the *Periplus* was written,
was exported in vast quantities from Muziris and Nelcynda,
being brought down from Nelcynda to Bacare in large boats,
while doubtless the port of Tyndis, receiving supplies down
the river Ponnani, sent them on to swell the quantities
gathered into Muziris and carried away by Greeks in
especially large ships brought for the purpose; Tamil
literature tells how the Greeks carried away very large
sacks of pepper giving apparently gold in exchange—and
Roman money was deliberately imported into Muziris and
Nelcynda. References are made frequently to "white
pepper," which was and still is a less pungent but more
tasty preparation of the black (*P. nigrum*). Originally obtained through the Phoenicians and Carthaginians (as
Persian, Syrian, or Libyan), the spice was bought by the
Romans direct in south Malabar (Cottonara, that is Kuddanadu, the country round Kottayam and Quilon) after
the discovery of the full use of the monsoons, and in such

quantities as to supply almost the whole of the West. Even
before that discovery very large ships carrying passengers
and Egyptian goods generally included a consignment of
pepper from India, while afterwards the spice probably
formed more than half the cargo of many a west-bound
Roman ship. The consignments included another kind
called Long Pepper exported from Barygaza and used, as
ancient writers shew, chiefly in medicine; this was obtained
from the fruit-spikes of *Piper longum*, native to various
parts of India, Ceylon, Malay, and so on, and perhaps
P. officinarum of the Indian archipelago. It was more expensive than the ordinary kind (3).

Pepper became part of the everyday life of every respect-
able household in Rome, since its chief use was as a
culinary spice—only a few old people, it was said, were
unable to taste pepper and other eastern fruits in their
food. In consequence the spice appears in almost every
recipe given by Apicius in his ten books and seems to have
been more important than salt or sugar is in the cookery-
books of to-day (4). But besides this both species of pepper
were used in all kinds of medicines and drugs, as Pliny,
Galen, Celsus, Scribonius, and other writers who deal with
medicines, constantly shew, and pepper is generally the
only Indian spice which appears in medical recipes pre-
served on papyri (5). Its use as a medicine dates from the
time of Hippocrates to whom it was the "Indian remedy,"
and the constant mention of it in Graeco-Roman medicine,
particularly in connexion with agues and fevers, has led
Dr Jones to the conclusion that it was used as an antidote
against the ever present malaria in the Roman Empire (6).
We need not wonder that attempts were made to introduce
the cultivation of pepper to the West, and in Petronius the
wealthy Trimalchio grows his own pepper, but Pliny says
that when planted in Italy it lost its flavour. The trade

therefore continued without abatement for centuries and in 408 Alaric demanded from Rome as part of his terms three thousand pounds of pepper. Vast profits came to all who dealt in this chief of Indian spices, and hence Juvenal says that a man would be willing to load his ship with pepper and set sail even in bad weather, and Persius says that avarice invites a man to get up and "be the first to take the fresh-bought pepper from the camel's back"; the Greeks have brought effeminate philosophy to Rome—together with pepper and other merchandise. Abundance of pepper after full discovery of the monsoons is revealed even by ordinary writers like Persius and Martial, who had no special reason to mention it at all. Men like Pliny, of course, regarded it with infinite disgust, but in general we find that the moralists were reconciled to the constant presence of the pungent pepper, of which in Pliny's time the black fetched four denarii a pound, the white seven, and the long fifteen (7). We can trace roughly its progress from India to Roman meal-tables. It was brought ground, or as unground "caunia" by Indians from inland trading houses on buffaloes to Muziris and Nelcynda, packed in huge sacks, loaded upon barges or boats, taken in them from Nelcynda down to Bacare, reloaded upon large Greek vessels, paid for by the Greeks in gold, carried by the monsoon wind to Berenice, on camel to Coptos, down the Nile to Alexandria, across the Mediterranean to Puteoli and Rome, stored (after A.D. 92) in special spice warehouses (called *horrea piperataria* because of the principal spice stored in them) near the Sacra Via, ground (if not already crushed) in pepper-mills (*molae piperatariae*), or mortars, sold in paper packets in the Vicus unguentarius, and brought to the table in dishes (πιπέραντες) or pots (*piperatoria*) of which an example in silver has been found at Chaource and Cahors and others

less choice at Arles-Trinquetaille, Saintes, Saint-Maur-de-
Glanfeuil in France, at Pompeii and Corfinium in Italy,
and at Murmuro in Sicily (8).

From pepper we pass naturally to ginger (gingiber or
zinziber, ζιγγίβερι, Sanskrit *siñgavera*, Tamil *inchiver*, the
Zingiber officinale of to-day) which, although coming from
the far East, was obtained by the Romans through Arabian
intermediaries, who succeeded in keeping the secret even
after the Greeks fully used the monsoons. This is manifest,
I think, from our authorities. Dioscurides, who was well
acquainted with ginger, says that it was produced chiefly
in Trogodytica and Arabia, and describes the uses of it in
those regions, adding also that a great deal was sent to
Italy in jars; Pliny ascribes the spice to the same regions
and gives its price—six denarii a pound; and the *Periplus*
makes no mention of it at all—it does not appear among
the exports by sea described by the author as coming from
India to Egypt or elsewhere. Only during the second century, or at least after Pliny wrote, did the Greek merchants
find out that the spice came from the far East, for Ptolemy
gives it as a product of Ceylon in a manner suggesting that
it was a fresh piece of information, and at the same time it
appears in the Digest-list. Dioscurides says that ginger was
much used in Italy for food, especially with dried fish, and
like pepper it was a good digestive, but its use as a food is
best illustrated by the references in the recipes of Apicius,
and as a medicine by the isolated references in Celsus and
Scribonius of the early half of the first century A.C. and
the references in Galen at a later date (9).

To the same Order as ginger (Zingiberaceae) belongs (as
far as we can tell from the inaccurate knowledge of the
Romans) the important spice amomum or cardamomum,
named according to the shape of its seeds. Amomum and
cardamomum were produce of the Cardamoms of to-day

(*Elettaria cardamomum*) found in Travancore, Malabar, and especially in the highlands overlooking the districts of Madura, Tinnevelly and Dindigul. Costly amomum yielded by the seed-capsules was used by the Romans in medicines and in perfumes (especially funereal) and it appears to me that it was brought almost entirely by the land-routes; for it is not mentioned anywhere in the *Periplus,* and it is called by various epithets revealing the routes which were used or places where ointments were prepared; thus Sallust attributes it to the land of the Gordueni in Armenia; Pliny says that the plant grew in Armenia, Media and Pontus, and Dioscurides adds Commagene and the Bosporus; Gallus or Virgil in the *Ciris* calls it Tyrian, Galen Babylonian, Statius Assyrian, while the epithet Syrian certainly indicates no more than the preparation in Syria of unguents containing amomum. From these statements the only sea-route which suggests itself is that from the west coast of India to the Persian Gulf. It must be noticed that Pliny says that the plant lost its strength when grown anywhere outside India, and his remark occurs in a passage which seems to imply travel by sea, but the text is corrupt. Perhaps the plant was considered perishable if brought by sea and so came by the land-routes only, or it may be that the Arabians kept the sea-traffic in their hands, for Pliny's "cardamomum" is Arabian and Median. That the spice did come by sea in the second century is proved by its inclusion in the Digest-list. Pliny shews the importance of the spice by his description of the different qualities, of which the best sort fetched sixty denarii, and when crumbled forty-nine denarii a pound, and poets such as Statius and Juvenal attest the frequent use of amomum at the funerals of well-to-do people; the four oblong kinds (cardamomum-seeds) cost never more than three denarii a pound (10).

Next to the secret of the monsoons, the strangest example

of secrets kept by the Arabians Somali and Axumites is that of Indian and Chinese cinnamon. This spice, much prized by the Romans as a perfume, as an incense, as a condiment, and as a medicine, was and is produced from several species of laurel native to China, Tibet, Burma, Ceylon and India, but the parts of the raw plant were known by different names: (a) Casia (Hebrew *Kezia*) was to the Romans the wood split lengthwise and the bark and root rolled up into small pipes (in Hebrew *Kheneh*), and this was often called "cinnamomon" or "cinnamomum"; (b) Cinnamon proper, probably the tender shoots and flower-tips and very delicate bark reserved, as Galen shews, for emperors and wealthy classes (11), and distributed on solemn occasions; (c) Cinnamon-leaf, obtained from certain varieties of cinnamon growing in China, the Himalayas, and the Malabar Mountains, and called by the Greeks and Romans malabathrum (a hellenised form of the Sanskrit *tamala-patra*). Now this leaf the Romans knew was a product of the far East, obtainable in India, but they never knew that it was cinnamon-leaf, though they used it in large quantities for making unguents; on the other hand, "casia" (the bark root and wood of cinnamon) and the "cinnamo-mum" (the tender shoots) were obtained throughout the period of Greek and Roman history partly through the Arabians, but later, when the Axumites had become a power, almost entirely from the coast-marts of Somali. Thus Herodotos says casia came from Arabia; Agatharchides, from the Sabaeans; Strabo, from the "cinnamon-country"; the *Periplus*, from Somaliland (the same as the "cinnamon-country"); Pliny, from Ethiopia; a papyrus, from Trogo-dytica—and so on. But in these regions and in that of the "Market of Spices" of the *Periplus* (the modern Olok) which Strabo says produces cinnamon and "false casia," there is no trace of cinnamon having grown at all. Hence it has been concluded that the true cinnamon of the Egyptians, Hebrews, Greeks, and Romans (the more expensive cinnamon-shoots and the cheaper casia-bark) reached the Mediterranean from countries no nearer than Burma or Ceylon, perhaps from China itself; that in passing through middlemen's hands it was falsely attributed to the regions and peoples of southern Arabia and East Africa, and then to the people of East Africa mostly, a mistake made easier because even after Hippalos' discovery Indian ships were not allowed by Arabians to pass Ocelis into the Red Sea, but by an understanding with the Arabians dating from very ancient times Indian ships could and did trade freely with the Somali coast; that the real commercial article was the casia (for the *Periplus* always uses this word, not cinnamon); that all produce of cinnamon, except the leaf, called malabathrum, was brought from the far East to the Somali coast in particular, and was then sometimes mixed with bark from the laurel-groves mentioned, for instance, by the *Periplus* (hence the frequent mention in other writers of ψευδοκιννάμωμον and ψευδοκασία, but not ψευδομαλάβαθρον); that it was thence passed on to Arabia and to Egypt and to Syria; that even after direct trade with India was established and the Romans found that at least Arabia was not the true source of cinnamon, the fact that India had traded for many centuries with Somaliland but not with the Red Sea and still did so, was even then strong enough to cause the Romans to think that cinnamon-bark and cinnamon-shoots were products of Somaliland, whereas they knew that malabathrum came from India and yet did not know that it was cinnamon-leaf; this point is especially strange and it was once thought that by malabathrum the Romans meant betel-leaf (of *Chavica betle*, not the betel-nut of *Areca catechu*), which may indeed have been an article of ancient commerce. Of Ceylonese cinnamon, now so famous, we can only surmise that though the Romans knew nothing of it, it must have entered into the cinnamon-trade of their middlemen (12). This strange secret of the Arabians and then the Africans as well is the most remarkable one of all. At the beginning of the Roman Empire cinnamon is constantly attributed to the Sabaeans or to their country, Arabia Felix, but there are signs that here and there Greek merchants of the past had found a leakage and obtained an inkling of the truth; the evidence is in Strabo (13). I find that although the Arabians and East Africans duly appear as the sources of cinnamon, nevertheless in one place Strabo says that according to some the greater part of casia is brought from India, and in another passage he says that South India, like Arabia and Ethiopia, produces cinnamon; in one passage the epithet "Indian" given to the cinnamon-country (East Africa) must be a very late addition to Strabo's text.

The curious fact that even after the discovery of the full use of the monsoons by Greeks, the Arabians and Axumites tightened up the secret with success, is revealed I think by the *Periplus*, Dioscurides, Pliny and Galen, who give us full accounts of cinnamon and reveal the enormous but natural increase in the traffic of that spice after Hippalos' time (14). Not even the author of the *Periplus* knew that malabathrum was the leaves of cinnamon, but we have a tolerably clear picture of the traffic in this part of the plants. Probably most leaves of Chinese cinnamons came to India by way of Yunnan and Burma, but from notices in the *Periplus*, Pomponius Mela, Ptolemy and Pseudo-Callisthenes we may conclude that some came from Singanfu by way of Chumbi, and in silent trade was handed over to the Besatae (Sesatae, Saēsatae), an active, uncivilised, but peaceful Tibeto-Burman tribe noted for their short stature, broad body, large head, broad face, fair complexion, and straight uncut hair, and dwelling in Sikkim. These Besatae then added the Chinese product to much larger supplies of leaves gathered from *Cinnamomum tamala* of the Himalayas, and once every year took them in large packs to a fair near the modern Gangtok in south Sikkim and left them on mats; whereupon the leaves were silently taken up by another tribe, which, as Ptolemy seems to shew, the Greeks of the second century discovered to be the flat-nosed savage Cirrhadae or Cirrhadeoi of Cirrhadia, a Bhota tribe allied to the Besatae and represented by the Kirata to-day, living in Morung or Morang, south-west of Sikkim. These Cirrhadae then prepared the leaves into balls of three roughly standard sizes and brought them into India, sending much towards the mouths of the Ganges for shipment at Tamluk with silk, pearls, nard and muslins in Indian ships to the western marts of India (15), and much direct across India to Muziris and Nelcynda for exportation. In these marts the Greeks obtained the leaves, sending large ships for that purpose and for carrying away the local pepper (16). The Indian gold coin called κάλτις and current in the regions of the Ganges must have been struck to assist a traffic in costly silks, pearls, nard, cinnamon-leaf and muslins in places where no Roman currency was created of any sort. In the Roman Empire the cinnamon-leaves as raw product generally fetched 60 denarii a pound, but as much as 300 or 400 denarii could be obtained for one pound of the manufactured oil. Malabathrum was frequently used to flavour wines and foods such as oyster-sauce and (like the bark) was valued in medicines and as a protection for clothes against moth-caterpillars. The leaves were generally imported in bulk and the oil produced by manufacture in the Roman Empire, and that is why Pliny (like Horace) attributes malabathrum to Syria, adding that Egypt produced more of it. This was natural in so much as the sea-route was in his time the most important one, and much

malabathrum oil produced in Egypt from raw stuff imported
from India was made and sold by the imperial authority
by special rights (inherited from the Ptolemaic system of
monopoly) often let out to private persons. When Pliny
says farther that the Indian kind was more highly esteemed
he shews that when the oil was sold under a name derived
from the ultimate source (India) of the raw ingredient, and
not from its trade-route, it fetched a higher price (17).

Any leaves which the Romans obtained from plants
growing in southern India must have come from the species
Cinnamomum iners and perhaps *C. zeylanicum* of Ceylon,
while the superior leaves obtained from the Himalayas were
produced by *C. tamala*, which ranges from the Indus to
Burma, and from Chinese cinnamon of which the leaves were
brought to the Besatae (as we saw) and through Yunnan.
Dioscurides and Pliny describe malabathrum vaguely as a
rootless surface-plant of Indian swamps, neither knowing
it was cinnamon; Dioscurides points out that some confused
the leaves with nard-leaves, and as far as we can tell both
plants were sent as rolled balls, one lb. of large leaves fetching
forty denarii, smaller leaves sixty, the smallest seventy-five.
Of later writers not even Galen knew the true nature of
malabathrum, for the "cinnamon" of the Caucasos in
Philostratos must reflect trade in the bark by land (18).

The very best bark must have come to the Romans from
the Chinese as it does to-day; in Persian records cinnamon
is always called "Chinese bark" and from the third century
onwards it was brought to the Persian Gulf by the Chinese
themselves. The inferior bark must have come from Malabar. Three hundred denarii were paid for the best, ten for
the very woody, five for the worst, and the oil mixed with
other aromatics fetched from thirty-five to three hundred
denarii, while special preparations from the flowers and
shoots reached fifteen hundred denarii! All were used in

medicines, unguents, wines, and in incenses for funerals.
The *Periplus* shews (19) that the greatest quantity of all was
obtained at Opone (Ras Hafun), and very large quantities
at Mosyllon (Ras Hantara) where a need for larger ships
was felt for the trade; six kinds were obtained in the
Market of Spices (Olok); a certain amount at Mundus
(Bandar Hais), and hard (woody) stuff at Malao (Berbera)
—all in north-east and east African markets. From Dioscurides and Galen, who nowhere mention India in connexion
with cinnamon, we get a good idea of the trade in the
different kinds of bark, and there is no sign, as Schoff
thinks, that the Axumites were revealing the secret in
Pliny's time; keeping it still, they profited from the great
demand on the part of Roman women and druggists who
learnt only to distinguish between various qualities. Apparently Nero consumed at Poppaea's death more than a
year's supply of cinnamon and casia, and, when Galen
wrote, the demand being unabated, raw supplies were
brought from Somali in cases up to $4\frac{1}{2}$ cubits long. The
Periplus says nothing about the flower-shoots of cinnamon,
but Dioscurides gives distinctive details. When Apuleius
spoke of Indian cinnamon (20), he meant no more than
African, and it is only when India had disappeared beyond
the Roman horizon that we find the plant attributed to
India constantly, but then only East Africa was meant.

But most curious of all is Pliny's account of the cinnamon
trade—an account which is vague and mysterious just as
the Arabians and their offshoot the Somali meant such
accounts to be and is a monument of the commercial lies
told to the western merchants before Hippalos' discovery.
Pliny says that the Ethiopians and Trogodytes carried on
a traffic in cinnamon with their neighbours across vast
tracts of sea in boats without rudders, oars, or sails, and
after sailing with a S.E. wind during the winter, reached

Ocilia (Ocelis). Merchants were reported to be hard put to it to return even in the fifth year, and many were said to die during the voyage. In return, traders took back with them vessels of copper and glass, clothing, and jewellery. *Ergo negotiatio illa feminarum maxime fide constat*, adds Pliny. This half true, half fabulous story indicates surely that the East Africans and the Arabians by concerted action allowed or caused false stories to grow up; the large tracts of sea are the Indian Ocean, but the alleged nature of the boats used and the S.E. wind would give the Greeks the impression that the voyages were not taken over the open sea at all. The traffic indicated is the long-established sea-trade between India and the East African coast. The "S.E." wind used in winter was the north-east monsoon, bringing voyagers from India to East Africa, Arabia, and the Red Sea(21). Again, the journey taken by the cinnamon traders (to and from India) would not or at least need not take even as much as one year, unless they went as far as China; the Arabians chose to exaggerate the voyages into several years' length, and to add a death-roll; all this tended to discourage Greek traders. Lastly, the articles taken back were, as we shall see, typical of the exports sent to the far East by the Roman Empire. Thus the advice of the Arabians to Greeks coming to Ocelis was —you need not even go to Africa for your cinnamon; a longer journey is futile and dangerous; if you hand over the necessary money and western products, you can receive your cinnamon here at Ocelis, which is a well-watered locality, and your first place of call.

A little farther on Pliny has another passage instructive in its very vagueness. With reference to a kind of cinnamon in his time much in favour, he says that the King of the Arabians called Gebbanitae, whose capital was Thomna, once had the sole right of control, regulating sales by edict;

the price of the juice had been as much as one thousand denarii, and even fifteen hundred denarii a pound, through the burning of the plantations at the hands of wild men, whether by malicious act of those in power, or by mere chance, it was not certain. Some of Pliny's authorities accounted for such a disaster by the explanation that the south winds blew so strongly as to kindle the plantations. Here we have two points to note—firstly, strict control of cinnamon trade by an Arabian ruler, and secondly a false explanation to account for a failure in supplies by alleging a local cause instead of a real one, which might be for instance some disastrous storm experienced during the voyage from Indian regions. But a truthful explanation such as this could not be given to western merchants without revealing the true source of cinnamon. The Arabians would be capable, we may be sure, of holding back supplies and accounting for the lack by giving some false but plausible explanation merely with the object of inducing the Greeks to pay a still higher price than was usual for a spice in great demand among the wealthy. Bengalese, Coromandel, Malabar, and North-west Indian shipping must have brought most of it from China and India to the Arabians frequenting the marts of West India or East Africa. Thus the completeness with which the Arabians Indians and Africans kept the secret of the true source of cinnamon from the times when Greeks had not even begun to sail to India direct, through the period of Rome's most flourishing direct trade with India, and so on to the era when Rome let that direct sea-trade slip back into the hands of Arabians and Africans, is made especially clear. Some Greeks of Hellenistic and perhaps later times knew that casia was an Indian spice, but it is manifest that after Hippalos' discovery the secret was tightened up by the Arabians with a truly astonishing and exceptional success; we have only to compare the *Periplus* and the descriptions of Dioscurides Pliny and Galen after complete discovery of the monsoons with comparatively meagre accounts of previous writers in order to realise this. Yet that there was a vast increase in the cinnamon traffic after the discovery is sufficiently proved; it was due to the increase of voyages taken to the East African coast. As in the case of pepper, trade by Rome in cinnamon-shoots and bark was carried on almost entirely by sea; if it was conducted by land at all, the Parthians, who certainly traded in Chinese cinnamon, must have kept the secret well on their part. The trade in the leaf was also carried on by sea, but the leaf-oil was well known in Persia. The quantity of cinnamon and pepper which passed through Alexandria must have been enormous, as it consisted of supplies for almost the whole of the Roman Empire, including perhaps large consignments of cinnamon for manufacture into unguents and perfumes in Syrian towns, and although it is not safe to speak definitely with reference to the corrupt passages in the Digest-list (which gives five kinds of cinnamon, including malabathrum), that list appears to mention Turian casia which we must suppose was a sort introduced or first prepared by a member of the *gens Turia* of Rome. If efforts were really made to grow the plant in the West, the only results were odourless plants of no use (22).

More highly prized than cinnamon in ancient times, but now of no importance, was the oil of the true Spikenard (*Nardostachys jatamansi*, a perennial native of the Himalayas—Sanskrit *nalada*), which held the first place in ointments and was one of the most costly of all plant-products, regularly kept in alabaster boxes, and used as other odours were, as an ingredient in drugs and in cookery. The Romans imported two parts of the plant—the root-stock clothed with fibrous leaf-remains, something like a bearded ear of wheat, whence it was called ναρδόσταχυς, nardistachys or spica, and the larger leaves which were called folia; Pliny says that the larger leaves were worth forty denarii a pound, smaller leaves sixty, the smallest seventy-five, and as we have stated this appears to apply equally to cinnamon-leaves. He also states that the genuine spikenard-oil contained costus (for which, see below), amomum and other elements besides Indian nard, but adulteration and therefore variations in price were very frequent. The price of the nard-spikes was often one hundred denarii a pound, and sometimes more than three hundred denarii (about £10) a litra as shewn by the box of spikenard with which Mary anointed the feet and head of Jesus; Horace too promised to return a cadus of wine (about three dozen modern bottles full) for a small onyx box of spikenard. As we should expect, the sea-route formed a natural passage for nards during the most flourishing period of the Roman Empire. The *Periplus* gives three kinds which were sent through Poclais and exported from Barygaza; one kind (*Caspapyrene*) came apparently from districts near the modern Attock, another from the Hindu Kush, and a third from the Kabul valley, and these are undoubtedly true nards; spike and leaves appear in the Digest-list, and Strabo definitely attributes nard to South Arabia and Ethiopia as well as to South India, and this indicates the sea-route again. But there can be little doubt that the land-routes were very widely used, at least at the beginning of the Roman Empire; thus we find that nard is called Assyrian and Achaemenian (that is, Persian) by Horace, Syrian by Meleager, Tibullus, Dioscurides, and so on, and these are examples of a product taking its name not from its land of produce but from countries through which it passed and in which it was in fact obtained from intermediaries. Spikenard may have been grown in Syria, but Dioscurides gives that epithet to nard merely, as he shews, because one side of the "mountain" (Hindu Kush and Himalayas) on which it grew looked towards Syria, and one is led to suspect that like the nard of Tarsos and the nard of Commagene the Syrian nard was, if not the product of some valerian, then surely Himalayan nard made into ointment chiefly in Laodicea in Syria (23). There is also another point to notice, and that is that as far as we can tell the Greeks and Romans included under the name "nardos" oils obtained from oil-yielding species of *Andropogon* and *Cymbopogon*, that is lemon-grasses and ginger-grasses of India. The *Periplus* mentions a "nard" exported from Barbaricon on the Indus (not "folium pentasphaerum" nor "folium barbaricum" as given in the Digest); again, nard from the Ganges, shipped, according to the *Periplus*, to Muziris and Nelcynda, where the Greeks obtained it, appears to have been that inferior sort to which Pliny says the name Ozaenitis was given because of its fetid odour, (though in reality I believe this name applied to a plant coming from the inland town Ozene (Ujjain, Ougein), which was a centre of supply for Barygaza) and even in Augustan times Gratius called the Ganges "nardifer." These "nards" may have been produced from (*a*) the root of *Cymbopogon schoenanthus*, a ginger-grass native to western Punjab, Bengal, and other regions of India, and also to Baluchistan and Persia; (*b*) *C. jwarancusa*, which skirts the bases of north-western mountains of India and is common in the upper regions of the Ganges, the Jumna, and other districts, spreading also farther south; (*c*) *Andropogon muricatus*, a still more fragrant plant much used in Bengal to-day; (*d*) other varieties common in the Courtallum hills and in the Indian peninsula generally. In this class of fragrant plants we may include the "Indorum gramen" and the "Indorum seges," and also the "sweet cane" and the "schoenos" of the Greeks. The Hebrews knew of a rich aromatic reed "from a far country" and the Κάλαμος ἀρωματικός appears in medical writers from Hippocrates onwards. Theophrastos describes a species of calamos and a species of schoenos together, and his naming of the source beyond Libanos is due to the trade-routes which carried the plant. Dioscurides shews that by his time the aromatic reed or cane, which he describes just after "schoenos" or "schinos," was known to grow in India alone, though Pliny ascribes it to Arabia and Syria as well. The attribution of "schoenos" also to Libya, Arabia, and Nabataea shews through whose hands the product had been known to pass on its way from India (24). The second species of ginger-grass which we mentioned above is called in Arabic "izkhir" (cp. σχοῖνος, σχῖνος). The genus can be used generally to provide perfumes, medicines, and astringents in ointments. Oil from all of these plants, but especially the true spike-nard, was in much demand throughout the period of the Roman Empire as "nard," especially among the rich ladies of Rome itself, and in spite of the high price, a regular custom prevailed of anointing guests at banquets with the oil, and in expensive recipes, too, we find nard-leaf (folium) used with cinnamon-leaf in oyster-sauce, and both nard-leaf and nard-spike in a sauce for roasted venison, and lemon-grass also appears in preparations of this sort. In drug-lists of some writers the spike is the most frequent of all the Indian remedies mentioned. The demand must have been constant, especially among Rome's rich women, as Galen says, and when during the second century the Greeks discovered a plentiful supply at Randamarta (Rangamati) beyond the Ganges, the geographer Ptolemy thought fit to mention the fact (25).

Another of the most expensive plant-products was the root of costus(m) (from the Sanskrit kushtha), that is, of *Saussurea Lappa*, native to the lofty slopes of the vale of Kashmir, and especially the basins of the Chenab and the Jhelum, still being used for scenting shawls. In several respects the trade resembled the trade in nard; for the small pieces of costus (sometimes called simply radix) were used in unguents and perfumes, in medicines, in seasoning of food and wine, in sacrifices, and also, as Columella says, in the preservation of fruits, and the geographical habitat of the plant caused the trade-routes used to be similar to the case of spikenard. Thus Pliny, with a remark upon the pungent taste and pleasant smell of costus, says that the two kinds of costus were found on the island Patale at an entrance to the Indus, and the *Periplus* says that the costus was exported from Barbaricon on the Indus and from Barygaza as well; it was included in the Digest-list, and one kind is called Arabian by Dioscurides. But in writers living before Hippalos' discovery of the monsoons we find epithets which shew that the land-routes were being used, for although Ovid calls costus Indian, Horace calls it Achaemenian, and Propertius calls it Assyrian. Again, just as in the case of spikenard, Dioscurides gives, besides an Indian kind, a Syrian kind, and here again we are to understand ointment made by Syrians from imported raw costus. In Pliny's time the normal price paid was $5\frac{1}{2}$ denarii a pound. It is one of the Indian aromatics very frequently occurring in drug-lists (26), but as a perfume it does not seem to have been nearly so much in favour as nards.

It appears that some of the aromatics which we have described above were employed by the Indians in manufacturing special articles of luxury before exportation to the West; for Pliny indicates a development in the manufacture of chaplets from the simple arrangement of the foliage of the laurel and other trees to more durable articles of horn or thin metal, and, in the case of chaplets used for honouring the gods or for decorating tombs, wreaths of roses or of plaited and embroidered materials, until in Pliny's own time there was a demand for chaplets imported from India or even beyond, made generally of nard-leaves or of silk in many colours, soaked in unguent. It has been suggested that the Sweet Clover or Melilot exported from Egypt to Barygaza in Nero's time was intended for the manufacture of chaplets in India which would be exported to Rome, and early Buddhist literature shews that in India garland-making was deemed an honourable profession, and was included among the trades possessing an "elder" or head of a kind of guild, while a Tamil poem states that in Kaviripaddinam, a place much frequented by Greeks, dwelt makers of flower-garlands. In a temple of Livia a man dedicated the unadorned root of a large cinnamon-tree placed on a golden dish, but as time went on and Indian trade increased, even those who had no reputation for extravagance increased the value of such offerings. Vespasian, economical as he was, was the first to dedicate crowns of cinnamon set in gold filigree (27).

Three other aromatics must be dealt with here. It is possible that the "cinnamon" called Syrian "comacum," the product of a nut and valued at 40 asses a pound, was a preparation from nutmeg reaching Syria by land or by the Persian Gulf from the Moluccas, and the Byzantines knew a small aromatic Indian nut (28). Again, the caryophyllon (Sanskrit kaduaphala, katukaphala) of Pliny, imported from India for the sake of its smell, was not the nutmeg, since Pliny's notice points to *Myrtus caryophyllata* of Ceylon; but it is manifest from the clear description of Paulus Aegineta that the name was given ultimately to the dried unexpanded flower-buds of *Caryophyllus aromaticus,* or *Eugenia caryophyllata*, called to-day Cloves, and coming chiefly from the Moluccas. Since these aromatics did not come within notice of the author of the *Periplus* and, even when it occurs in a version of the Digest-list, caryophyllum is one of the nards, we may take it that there was no great demand at all until the voyages beyond India indicated by the geography of Ptolemy brought the Greeks into more extensive contact with the East, but in the period of Rome's decline and of the early Byzantine Empire references to cloves reveal that it was becoming known. Cloves formed part of the rent paid by Egyptian estates to churches in Rome during the fourth century A.C. and Cosmas shews that in the sixth century this aromatic was well known to come from further India by way of Ceylon to the marts of the west coast of India (29).

The sources from which the ancient world obtained its most valued oriental gum-resins were the regions of South Arabia and East Africa, which produced the famous frank-incense and myrrh. But supplies of these gum-resins were supplemented by an influx from India during the early imperial period; for Indian incense appears in one version of the Digest-list, and Dioscurides distinctly describes an Indian frankincense, yellowish and livid, moulded into a round shape by stirring; this when dry was called Sy-agrian, and since at Syagros frankincense was stored, we may deduce that the Arabians had something to do not only with its carriage but with its manufacture also. To-day a good kind of frankincense is sent from Somali to Bombay for re-exportation to Europe and to China and in a similar way perhaps the resin reached the Roman world from India. When the author of the *Periplus* wrote, frankincense was being imported into Barbaricon on the Indus, and this was perhaps for exchanging with silk. On the other hand, there are native Indian kinds of incense: the incense which, as a Tamil poem tells us, was sold in Kaviripaddinam of the Chola Kingdom, where Roman subjects were resident, was perhaps produced from the two varieties of *Boswellia thurifera* called *glabra* and *serrata* respectively, plants indigenous to the mountainous regions of Central India and the Coromandel coast, not however producing to-day any of the incense-resin of commerce (30). Likewise, the true Myrrh (*Balsamodendron myrrha*), which came from Arabia and East Africa, was often adulterated with inferior kinds of gum-resin belonging to the same genus of plants. One of these was known as an Indian kind of murra, easily distinguished from and inferior to the true myrrh, and this we may identify with *B. pubescens* of Sind and Baluchistan, exported doubtless from the Indus and from Broach together with a much more important kind called by the Greeks and Romans "bdellium." This was an aromatic gum produced from *Balsamodendron Mukul* growing in North India, Baluchistan, and also in Arabia and East Africa. It was in ancient times Indian or Arian "thorn" of hills between the Hindu Kush and the Indian Ocean, and thus we find that it was obtained at Barbaricon on the Indus and at Barygaza whither it was brought from the interior for exportation, that there was a "Scythian" kind, and that the best of all came from Bactria; the *Periplus* says that on the coast-lands of Gedrosia (Makran) was found nothing but bdellium. But even in ancient times the plant seems to have spread to Media, Babylonia, and Arabia. The gum was adulterated in various ways and was used in certain medicines, and, mixed with wine, in sacrifices, and in other adulterated compounds; when pure its average price was three denarii a pound (31).

There is another Indian resin which seems to have been called κάγκαμον by the ancient Greek merchants, and is now identified with the gum exuded from *Vateria Indica*, and known as Indian Copal, or Malabar tallow, or white dammar, found in the forests extending from Canara to Travancore. It has never been well known in western

commerce, and the Romans obtained it only through intermediaries. Thus the author of the *Periplus*, without mention-
ing India, says that it was sent to the east coast of Africa
and thence to Arabia; Dioscurides calls it an Arabian wood,
while Pliny says that it came, from the neighbourhood of
the country which provided cinnamon, by way of the
Trogodytici. The first mention made of it occurs after the
full discovery of the monsoons, and while Pliny wrongly
calls it a dye, Dioscurides says that it was an incense used
in fumigating clothes and a remedy for various diseases,
particularly tooth-ache(32).

The trade in several other gum-resins shews peculiar
features. One of these was Aloes, attributed partly to
Arabia, Asia, and Andros by Dioscurides, and partly to
Asia by Pliny; but both writers shew that the greatest
part of the supplies was supposed to come from India to
which medical writers such as Scribonius and Galen sometimes attribute the gum aloes. Now the *Periplus* speaks of
no other aloes than that which was exported from Cane
under King Eleazos, and yet that kind of aloes which is the
dried cathartic juice so much favoured in medicines is
obtained from *Aloe Perryi*, almost confined to Socotra,
which is nowhere mentioned in connexion with it, the juice
of *A. hepatica* of South Arabia being less favoured. The
explanation of the epithet "Indian" seems to me to be that
the trade in both species was controlled by and from Cane
which certainly traded with India and perhaps sent thither
much aloes which was then exported again in a prepared
form. Aloes is sent to Bombay to-day. Moreover the plants
may have been introduced early to India. Galen obtained
from the camel's back "Indian aloes" and "Indian lycium"
(for which see below) which had come by way of Palestine
to Phoenicia(33).

Another gum-resin was that which we call "Dragon's

Blood," a reddish exudation from species of *Dracaena*. The Greeks and Romans applied to it a name κιννάβαρι also used by them in describing thick red earths (including red sulphide of mercury, our Cinnabar), often adding, however, the epithet Ἰνδικόν when the expensive plant-product was meant. Merchants used this name and epithet in referring to drops and juice used in medicine, dyes, and paints, and gathered from *Dracaena Cinnabari* of Socotra, *D. Schizantha* of Somaliland (Order Dracaeneae) and *Calamus Draco* (False Dragon's Blood, Order Palmaceae) of Sumatra, Penang, and above all Borneo—*D. Cinnabari* taking the first place. The epithet Indian may be accounted for by the inclusion of the Calamus and by possible re-exportation from India of the Socotrine and Somali products. Possibly the Indians who dwelt in Socotra and those who traded with Africa tended to add more and more the product of the Calamus which did ultimately supersede the Dragon's Blood of Socotra (34). The name κιννάβαρι is connected with the Hindu "shangarf" (Cinnabar) and the curious story which Pliny gives of the origin of the name as used for red earths came from the Indians (35).

Besides these, there was Laser or Asafetida, a medicinal "gum-resin obtained principally from the root of *Ferula fetida*" growing in Persia and Afghanistan, Herat and Kandahar being the present centres of the trade; Galbanum (Hebrew helbenah), a medicinal gum from *F. galbaniflua*, native to Persia; Sarcocolla, a gum from the Persian *Penaea Sarcocolla*; and also that kind of Mastic which Pliny by mistake calls a "spina" and mentions as Arabian and Indian, being probably the product of two trees *Pistacia Khinjuk* and *P. Cabulica*, growing throughout the regions of Sind, Baluchistan, and Kabul. A natural route westwards for all these, especially when Rome and Parthia were at war, would be by way of the Indus through Saka (or Kushan) territory, and though none is mentioned by the *Periplus*, asafetida, galbanum and sarcocolla (36) appear in some versions of the Digest-list. Moreover, it is possible, I think, that the kings of the "Frankincense country" (Hadramaut) from the west of Cane to as far as Ras Hasik and the Kuria Muria islands, ruling Cane, Syagros, and Socotra from Sabbatha inland, tried to monopolise the traffic in all the gum-resins by trade with the Indus and Broach (37).

Loads of gum-resins from India were clearly incidental additions to the famous Arabian and African supplies, but non-resinous juices and oils from Indian plants, used variously as colours, foods, and medicines, played a more important part. Of colours there were three which the Romans obtained from two genera of Indian plants. The Indigo of to-day, produced from *Indigofera tinctoria* and other species and by the time of the *Periplus* exported from Barbaricon on the Indus, had become known to the Romans soon after the Empire began, when India was known to produce plants yielding various colours; for Vitruvius indicates that its introduction to Rome was a recent event; in his day the scantiness of supply caused the wide use of a substitute prepared from woad, and Pliny says that the importation of indigo was a recent development—a curious fact in face of the acknowledged use of it by the ancient Egyptians and the long-standing dye traffic of the Arabians across their desert-routes. After the discovery of the monsoons indigo was an important material in Roman painting and a less important dye and medicine. When broken small it produced a black colour used by painters in "light and shade" work, and when mixed with water a beautiful purplish-blue, but it could be adulterated in various ways. The price of the black was seven denarii a pound, and the price of the blue twenty. There is no need to assume that Ἰνδικὸν μέλαν of the *Periplus* and the atramentum Indicum of Pliny (who confesses his ignorance of what the substance Indicum was) was Chinese Black coming by way of India, for both the black and the blue were produced by the Indian Indigo. Pliny bewails the decadence of painting in his time with particular reference to the walls of rooms and the use of Indian material, but since neither Chinese Black nor Indigo could be used for frescoes, the colour-basis of blues on surviving wall-paintings of ancient times is always found to be oxide of copper. The Scythian blue of Pliny, the κύανος of Theophrastos, is sulphate of copper: still, we hear of ἰνδικοπλάσται(38).

More important than indigo because of its suitability for more varied uses was the juice called "lycium" used by the Romans to provide a yellowish dye, an astringent for the eyes, and for sores, wounds, and so on, and a cosmetic for the face. It was produced from the roots stem and berries of several species of Raisin Barberry growing for the most part high up among the Himalayas, and hence we find that it was exported from Barbaricon on the Indus and from Barygaza, being sent, according to Pliny, by the Indians in the skins of camels and rhinoceroses, and it appears in the Digest-list. Much of this was obtained probably from *Berberis Sinensis* of China, *B. Wallichiana* of Nepal, *B. floribunda* of North India, *B. asiatica* chiefly of Nepal, and *B. aristata* chiefly of North India but extending southwards, but the bulk must have come from the *Berberis Lycium* of Nepal, forming the best kind of "Indian" lycium; the preparation of the juice in Lycia caused one kind to be called "Pataric" and the general importance of the juice (which is called rhuzot or houzis to-day) in the period of the Roman Empire is shewn by the numerous lycium pots which have been found in the ruins of Herculaneum and Pompeii. Dioscurides and Scribonius indicate that the trade had been conducted partly along the land-routes, but it is clear that after the monsoons were discovered the sea-route carried the supplies destined for consumption in the Roman Empire (39).

Gingelly (*Sesamum Indicum*), to-day the chief oil plant of India, seems to have been a part of early Indian trade, for its oil and seeds were well known to the Greeks of the fifth century B.C. and perhaps before, and the plant was introduced into Egypt where it became of considerable importance during the period of the Ptolemies, and its cultivation is described by Columella. Now the *Periplus* says that the oil, produced in large quantities in the region of Ariace, was exported from Barygaza to the east coast of Africa and to Moscha (Khor Reiri) in Arabia, and thus some of this, together with Egyptian produce, may have reached Rome from India, to be used for food, medicines, and cosmetics, and in Egypt itself, local supplies, as a papyrus shews, sometimes ran short. But it must be admitted that although Sesame (Semitic *semsem*) took the place of olive-oil among the Arabians, still it is perhaps safer to conclude that it did not enter largely into Rome's Indian trade (40).

The difficulty of decision is greater still in the case of the "Indian or Assyrian poppy-juices" (*opia*) which were, if we may accept the reading "opia" in a corrupt passage of the Digest-list, subject to the Red Sea due in Egypt. So far as we can tell, the facts are these: there are about forty species of the true poppies, mostly native to Central and South Europe and to temperate Asia; of these the Opium Poppy (*Papaver somniferum*) was originally indigenous to Southern Europe and Western Asia and from the first to the twelfth century the only opium known to commerce was that of Asia Minor, its introduction to India being connected apparently with the spread of Islam. In Theophrastos is indicated a narcotic drug obtained from poppy-juice; in Dioscurides we find the name ὀπός applied to the more potent juice of the seed-capsules only. In a word, under the Roman Empire opium was a medicinal product of the West and of the near East, not of the far East. To-day an excellent "vegetable oil is obtained by pressure from the minute seeds," and is used in painting, salads, soap-making, varnish-making, and as a lamp-oil, by western nations; in the Ganges valley of India and in other opium-regions the oil is used for food and for other domestic purposes by the poor, poppy-oil cakes being especially beneficial; and in Egypt when mosquitoes and fleas cause trouble the natives often chew poppy-seed in order to induce sleep. Whatever kind of poppy-oil is meant in the Digest passage, it is difficult to see why Indian kinds (mentioned nowhere else in classical literature) should be so important as to appear in a western duty-list, and it is to be noted that the wording of the passage, if "vel Assyria" is correct, gives Assyrian as an alternative appellation of the same juices. Is it possible that we have here poppy-juices of Asia Minor exported to the Persian Gulf to be sent to India, but purchased by kings of Hadramaut and Cane, diverted by them to the Red Sea, and sold to Egyptian Greeks as superior "Indian" juices at the high price usually paid for Indian products (41)?

Another interesting problem is presented by the ancient trade in Rhubarb—that is, not the vegetable leaf-stalk but the vegetable drug, which is apparently included in the ῥῆον or ῥᾶ of, for instance, Dioscurides, who describes it as a root brought from beyond the Bosporus. The evidence (which does not come from ancient classical writers) shews that the ancient commerce in rhubarb-drug, which was not fully established until the Arabian epoch, presents some analogy to that in silk. The drug is produced in the four northern provinces of China proper and in regions extending to the frontier of Tibet, in Mongolian districts, and in the western provinces of Sze-chuen. Now in ancient writers it is called Rha ponticum and by the middle of the sixth century A.C. Rha or Rheu barbarum. The native name for the river Volga was Rha, and this alone, together with the epithet ponticum, is sufficient to shew that the drug came by way of silk-routes to the Caspian and the Euxine; moreover after the fourteenth century A.C. rhubarb came by way of Bokhara, Persia, and the Caspian to Syria and Asia Minor, reaching Europe from the ports of Aleppo and Smyrna, being called under those conditions "Turkey rhubarb," and after the middle of the seventeenth century the drug came by way of Moscow and ultimately became known as "Russian rhubarb." But how are we to account for the name rha barbarum? An alternative route would be by way of Kabul or even the Yunnan Valley to the Indus and the Barbaricon of the *Periplus*, which, I notice, appears as Βάρβαρα in one reading of Ptolemy's text, and it is a fact that in the fourteenth century rhubarb came to Europe by way of the Indus and the Persian Gulf and by way of the Red Sea and Alexandria, and ancient Arab writers quote ῥῆον as the Greek synonym for their rhawund (rhubarb plant) of which they describe various kinds such as the "Indian," "Turkish," "Chinese," and rhubarb "from Khorasan." Vincent holds therefore that the name Rha being already established in European speech, the Rha obtained at the Indus mouth received the name barbarum whence comes "rhubarb" of modern speech. We cannot compare "folium barbaricum" of the Digest-list—meaning a nard? obtained at Somali marts (42). Maybe the Romans obtained it with silk and used it in medicines, and the price was probably high, as it was in the Middle Ages.

The traffic in Sugar, which is so important to-day, was quite unimportant in ancient times except so far as sugar was used in medicine, for in the sweetening of foods it never took the place of honey, though it has been proposed that the shekar, shukur, shuker of Hebrew writings, described as a strong drink and always in connexion with some wine, was a sugar-sweetened drink. It does not appear to have been used at all in Rome until Hippalos' discovery opened a new era in Rome's sea-trade with India; Varro was merely aware of its sweetness, and Strabo knew it only as honey obtained from trees in India and without the aid of bees (43), and no further knowledge appears in the earlier medical writers who from the time of Theophrastos included sugar in their medical recipes. Down to the discovery of the monsoons the Greeks knew it vaguely as a sweet "honey" without any specific name; even after that event it is only medical writers who know anything about it; thus Seneca says it was a kind of honey found upon reeds and either exuded therefrom or dropped as dew from heaven, but Dioscurides is the first to use the name σάκχαρον from the Sanskrit sarkara, Prakrit sakkhari, and describes it as a kind of congealed honey found in India and Arabia Eudaemon, which means, of course, that much of it passed through the hands of the Homerites, and he describes also powdered sugar, likening it to salt; both he and Pliny describe it as brittle to the teeth, and Pliny mentions lumps as large as a hazel-nut. In the *Periplus*, sugar (σάκχαρι) appears as an export from Barygaza to East Africa and Arabia, whence of course it reached Rome, but other writers shew that sugar obtained direct from India was regarded as the best. The sum total of Roman knowledge was now reached; the Romans never found out, so far as we can tell, that the juice was extracted from the plant by art, and never used it for sweetening table-foods. Solinus (relying on Pliny) merely notes its honey-sweetness, Alexander and Oribasios rely upon Dioscurides and Galen, and Isidore goes back to

Varro, and Paulus Aegineta gives us the recommendation by Archigenes (of the first century A.C.) of a remedy: "Indian salt," colourless and like common salt in texture, but sweet as honey, pieces to be taken about the size of a lentil or bean. We can be at least certain that the saccharum of the Romans was not the bamboo-"tabaschir," as some have thought, but ordinary cane-sugar, and that it was used by them in medicine. Sugar is grown to-day in India, Burma, Assam, South China, and so on (44).

Only two products of the far East were widely used for making clothing and other woven fabrics. One of these, Chinese silk, we have dealt with already. The other was Indian Cotton, which was of greater importance than ordinary Roman literature would lead us to suppose. The Greeks and Romans did use *Gossypium arboreum* which they grew in Egypt, but the material obtained from the seed-fibres of *G. herbaceum* native in India completely eclipsed the other, for from the *G. arboreum* of both India and Africa is produced only a soft and silky cotton used for padding pillows and so on, while the Indian species produces not only material for padding but also material for weaving cloths; these cotton cloths first came under the notice of the Greeks through Alexander's conquests and the plant spread to Persia at an early date; the Hebrews, too, seem to have been acquainted with muslins, and the Romans seem to have had cotton at their disposal after their Asiatic wars, but the transfer of the name carbasus (from karpasa, the Sanskrit name of the cotton plant) to fine linens shews how little the material was used by the Romans at least until the reign of Nero. Virgil and others seem to refer to true cotton, but our difficulty is increased through the use of the words sindon and byssus (besides carbasus) not only for cotton but also for fine linen, and we cannot tell when cotton is meant, for there was evidently some confusion except

among men who had technical knowledge. After the
discovery of the monsoons, however, importations of Indian
cotton increased continually and became quite an important
part of oriental commerce, and in spite of the fact that the
plant now grew in Egypt, Tylos, Arabia, Cilicia, Palestine
and possibly in Greece, the finer sorts of muslins from India
were highly valued in the Roman Empire, and the increase
of discoveries in cotton-growing districts of India of coins
issued by emperors subsequent to Nero seems to reflect a
great increase in demand. The author of the *Periplus* states
that of cotton cloth the best broad sort (called μοναχή) and
a coarser cotton (called σαγματογηνή and probably used for
stuffing and padding) were produced in Gujarat and exported to East Africa from Barygaza together with muslins
and girdles and a third kind of coarse "mallow-coloured"
(μολοχινή) cotton cloth, dyed, we must suppose, with a product of some Indian hibiscus, unless we are to assume that
in dealing with cottons the author uses Greek corruptions
of Indian names, and moreover cotton belongs to the
Order of Mallows. Similar kinds were sent to Arabia from
Barygaza, large quantities being conveyed to this place from
the inland centres Ozene and Tagara; all three kinds were
also sent to Egypt, some also to Socotra. The Indus seems
to have exported muslins of some kind and the districts of
Trichinopoly and Tanjore sent "Argaritic" muslins, and to
these were added muslins of Ceylon, muslins of Masulipatam
(Masalia) in large quantities, and the finest of all, called
Gangetic, which came from the Dacca district. Tamil
literature shews that cotton fabrics could be got in Kaviripaddinam and possibly at Madura (45). Thus it is clear
that woven Indian cottons and muslins were displacing
those which were produced elsewhere, and so we have in
the Digest-list cotton cloth (opus byssicum), raw cotton,
(carpasum) and dyed cotton muslins. References to cotton

as Indian are rare, but there are signs that the ordinary man knew Indian muslins when he saw them. These fine fabrics were called ventus textilis or nebula, and Pollux distinguishes the Egyptian cotton (which he calls "tree-wool") from what he calls byssos, a kind of flax found among the Indians, and he says that the Egyptians mixed cotton and linen in making cloth from the wool of the "nut," so that the woof was of cotton, the warp of linen, and this quality of cloth is still manufactured in Egypt. Perhaps the word "byssos" was at last being confined gradually to cotton. Arrian again says that Indian cottons are whiter and brighter than were those of any other region, and Lucian says that "Indian fabrics" (muslins?) are lighter and softer than the Greek. From about A.D. 100 onwards much raw cotton was submitted to the looms of Alexandria and Syria (46) and to the looms of private houses.

As in the case of silk, most but not all the imported cotton passed straight through Egypt, where emperors possessed imperial weaving and dyeing manufactories, some worked by the priests. Thus we have Philostratos' statement that Indian cotton (byssos) was imported to Egypt for many sacred purposes; the edict of Diocletian shews that stuffed mattresses and pillows were made from Indian raw cotton (doubtless from the σαγματογηνή of the *Periplus*) at Tralles, at Damascus, and at Antinoöpolis in Egypt; in Egyptian documents we have an unknown due referring apparently to raw cotton (κιαρβασᾶις, cp. carpasum of the Digest-list); we have also the weaving of cotton as reported by Pollux, and some many-coloured cotton fabrics have been found near Memphis and at Panopolis (Achmim), and some of the fabrics contain Indian elements in their designs (47). The weaving would be done in the linen manufactories. Palestine also received much Indian cloth.

The woods imported by the Romans from India may be

divided into two classes—(*a*) ornamental and timber-woods and (*b*) fragrant woods used as medicines. The most definite announcement of conditions of traffic in Indian woods occurs in the *Periplus*, which says that together with sandal-wood, teak-wood timber and logs of blackwood and ebony were brought regularly to Apologos and Ommana by vessels coming from Barygaza. Of these the most important was Ebony, obtained from various species of African and Indian *Diospyros,* and much in demand among the Romans since the time of Pompey, who exhibited the wood at his triumph over Mithradates; this would be the Indian ebony, which became so familiar after Alexander's conquests that Theophrastos and also Virgil (copying, I think, his Greek predecessor) ascribe the wood to India only; the Persian Gulf traffic in Indian ebony was one of long standing, for it is mentioned by Ezekiel, and a much-favoured and variegated kind was obtained by the Romans from India, perhaps from *D. quaesita* now growing chiefly in Ceylon. But they also obtained, especially after Nero's reign, a good black Ethiopian sort from the interior of Africa. It is strange that the author of the *Periplus* did not notice ebony at any Indian or African mart, and it is by no means certain that the wood is included in the Digest-list; so that we must conclude that African ebony was obtained from the interior of Africa by land and so does not appear as liable to the Red Sea due, according to the Digest-list, and that Indian ebony (together with the other valuable Indian woods which we shall describe) was nearly always obtained from the Persian Gulf whither the Indians brought it; and the exports in return from Apologos and Ommana were sent by Arabians, as the *Periplus* shews, not Romans. In other words, so far as we can tell, the Romans left the trade of Indian ebony in the hands of Arabians. The wood was used chiefly for furniture and in

statuary and for durability ranked with Cypress and
Cedar (48). In the Persian Gulf, shews Theophrastos, men
built ships of Teak-wood (*Tectona grandis*) of India, particularly the forests of Malabar, Canara, Travancore,
Gujarat, and the Malay Peninsula; it has the advantage of
being able to resist the action of water, and is thus the most
valuable of all building timber. It is found also in Burma,
Siam, Java, and so on; the town of Siraf on the Persian Gulf
was wholly built of it, and in 1811 teak was found in the walls
of a Persian palace near Baghdad pillaged in the seventh
century A.C.; moreover it was used in the time of Nabonidus
during the sixth century B.C., so that some must have
reached the Roman Empire even if it went no farther than
the eastern provinces (49), Blackwood, that is the East
Indian Rosewood (*Dalbergia latifolia* and varieties), was
valuable for similar reasons, and Theophrastos says that it
was used for making beds, couches, and other things of taste.
The *Periplus* shews that it was exported from Barygaza
to the Persian Gulf, but in succeeding centuries the place
of export was shifted, if we may so judge from the statements of Cosmas, to Kalyana. In the Roman Empire the
wood was sometimes sold as ebony. The name (*sesamin*)
under which the Greeks knew it and the mention of northern
parts of the west coast of India in connexion with its
exportation point to the two varieties called *Dalbergia
Ougeinensis* and *D. sissoo* (the true Blackwood) respectively,
the last named being called in India *Shisham* or *Sisam* and
found in the districts of Coromandel, the Indus, Gujarat,
and Bengal (50). Bankot, which is perhaps the Mandagora
of the *Periplus,* once possessed a great trade in both blackwood and teak. Broach was clearly the centre of the trade
in the first century, supplies from the inner parts of India
being supplemented by wood from the trees which still
grow by the Nerbudda.

The fourth wood mentioned by the *Periplus* as a peculiar part of the trade of Broach with the Persian Gulf is Sandalwood, which brings us into the class of fragrant woods. Sandal-wood (σάνταλον, τζανδάνα, Sanskrit *chandana, Santalum album*, Linn.), native to South India, especially the Mysore, Coimbatore, and Salem districts, entered apparently into the trade of the near East at a very early era, but the identification of the "almug" or "algum" trees of the Old Testament with the sandal-wood is uncertain, though the derivation from the Sanskrit *valgu*, Malabar *valgum*, is tempting. It was sold in the bazaars of Kaviripaddinam of the Chola Kingdom with Red Sanders wood (*Pterocarpus santalinus*) of South India and Ceylon. In the time of Cosmas it was an important article of commerce brought from southern districts of the east coast of India (not China, as Cosmas thought) up to marts of the west coast. The Indians used the wood in many ways, but as far as we can tell the Romans used it only as a purgative (51). Carved wood may have been sent by the far East, but so-called "Chinese" bows, arrows, and quivers of which we hear were apparently not Chinese or Tamil (Chera) but Parthian (52).

Of some importance was the aromatic wood variously called heart-, agal-, aghil-, eagle-, or aloes-wood or lign-aloes, Sanskrit *agaru*, known to the Greeks as ἀγάλλοχον and produced partly from *Aquilaria agallochum* of East India, Assam, and China, and more from *A. malaccensis*. The wood seems to have been well known to the Hebrews but no mention is made in writers of the imperial age previous to the discovery of the monsoons and even after that development we find that the author of the *Periplus* does not know of it at all. It was known however to Dioscurides and is called Arabian and Indian by him, which means of course that the Arabians maintained part of their ancient trade in the wood. The same author states that it was used to sprinkle over the body and for such complaints as pleurisy and dysentery. A Tamil poem states that the wood was brought to the bazaars of Kaviripaddinam of the Chola Kingdom, and Cosmas says that in his time (sixth century A.C.) this "aloes-wood" was being obtained by the Ceylonese from countries east of Cape Comorin and sent by them to marts on the west coast of India. Thus it played a part in Rome's Indian trade in order to provide a medicine (53). In 284 Roman subjects trading in Indian seas sent a large quantity to China (54).

The last of the aromatic woods with which we have to deal is one of which the identification is uncertain; this is the μάκειρ, imported chiefly to the East African coast and thence to Arabia; the author of the *Periplus* knew no more than that it was an Indian product sent to Africa, apparently in Indian ships, and Pliny, Dioscurides, and Galen throw no further light upon the subject except to shew that the Romans knew the material as an Indian aromatic bark, reddish in colour, useful for dysentery as a decoction mixed with honey. Lassen identifies it with a Malabar tree which he omits to specify, and it is now considered to be "Tellicherry bark," that is the root-bark of *Holarrhena antidysenterica*, found throughout India to Burma (55).

We need not doubt that in the course of a flourishing trade various fruits were imported from India, but it is difficult to trace any with certainty. The reference (56) which we have to unspecified "Indian" fruits to be seen at Clysma, an important point of departure to and arrival from the Indian Ocean, belongs to a period when the term Indian could mean very often nothing more than East Africa with South Arabia, but we may count as Indian importations the following fruits and fruit-products. The Palm-oil (*nargilios Periplus, argellion* Cosmas, Sanskrit *variker(l)a*) exported, according to the *Periplus*, in small quantity from East Africa is the oil of the Coco-nut (*Cocos nucifera*); the trees and the nuts seem to be referred to by Pliny, and Philostratos shews that coco-nuts were to be seen as curiosities in Greek temples; likewise the very large Indian nuts mentioned by Cedrenus are coco-nuts, and Cosmas of the sixth century A.C. knew the trees well as growing on the Maldive Islands. The coco-nut, native in the Indian archipelago, spread westwards by means of Hindu activity and probably by means of the nuts floating in the sea; in the time of the *Periplus* coco-nut trees grew on Sarapis island (Masira) and the sewed boats of Ommana were made partly, it is thought, of the husks (57).

Pliny speaks very distinctly of the Banana, the fruit of the Plantain tree (*Musa paradisiaca sapientium*) of India, and although it is possible that his description comes solely from Hellenistic sources, he speaks in a manner suggesting that he had seen bunches of the fruit, and he mentions the name *pala*, which is the Malayalam name to-day, and is used on the Malabar coast (58). It is possible too that Sepistan or Sebesten plums (from *Cordia Myxa* and *C. latifolia,* ranging from China to Egypt) were occasionally imported from India but of this we cannot be sure, but we can speak with more certainty of Melons (melones, melo-pepones) which were obtained from districts north of India and transplanted as far as Campania, so that Pliny could speak of the wonderful new Campanian "melopepones" and an Egyptian papyrus of the second or third century A.C. mentions the dispatch of good melon-seeds (59).

Of the more delicious table-fruits the following may be included: (*a*) the Peach, and probably the Nectarine, of China, which had spread westward through Persia before the Roman Empire began, and hence the Peach tree was called *Arbor Persica* and the Nectarine *Persea,* fine examples of nectarines being probably called "duracina" (60); (*b*) the

Apricot of North China and North-west India, already much cultivated in Armenia, whence we find the epithets "Sericum," "Armenium," and "Persicum" (61); (c) the Citron, native to North-west India, already cultivated in Media, whence come the names *Malus assyria, medica, persica* (sometimes with confusion with the name of the Peach); the fruit and leaves were used as a counter-poison and as a protection for clothes against the ravages of moth-caterpillars, and so the fruits with leaves attached may have reached Rome even from India especially in times of war with Parthia. Virgil knew of the fruit only and seems to take his description from Theophrastos, but in Petronius, Trimalchio grows his own citrons and the papyri refer to the cultivation of them in Egypt. All these fruits then may have been an incidental portion of Rome's Indian trade; but the orange and the lemon were not known (at least evidence is wanting) to the West until the Arabs brought them shortly before the ninth century (62).

Vegetables such as cucumber, culcas, skirret, coriander, ajowan (*Carum copticum*, brought by way of Egypt), onion, and leek, had an Indian or eastern origin, but were no longer articles of commerce with the far East, though the pumpkin (?) and the long gourd were still sometimes called Indian. The same must be said of a number of other plants which the Greeks and Romans knew were natives of India but did not use.

Skirret (*Sium Sisarum*, Linn.), apparently the "sisaron" of Dioscurides, the "siser" of Columella and Pliny, is a plant which seems to have travelled from East Asia by way of south Russia to Germany, whence Tiberius obtained much every year (63).

We can trace four kinds of cereals among the exports of India in ancient times. The most important of these was Rice (*oryza*, old Persian *virinzi*, Sanskrit *vrihi*, Tamil *arisi*),

Oryza sativa, which spread in Persia at an early date, rice-cake being mentioned apparently by Sophocles. The Greeks and Romans obtained it from Lower Syria, Susis and Bactriana, but the cultivation originated in India, Burma and South China and some rice was exported from Barygaza to East Africa and to Socotra even in Nero's time. Hence rice was connected by writers with Ethiopia. Greek merchants must have brought it home with them from the Indian Ocean on many an occasion. The Romans used it in various ways, for instance as broth or as a cake, and when kneaded with bean-meal as a preparation used by ladies for preserving the smoothness of the skin. Like all oriental wares, it fetched a high price (64).

Three kinds of millets are extensively cultivated in India now: the Great Millet (*Sorghum*), the Spiked Millet, and Ragi, none of which is a true millet, and the first of them (perhaps a Sweet Sorghum) perhaps provided the black Indian millet which Pliny says had been imported into the Empire less than ten years before his time of writing, while the βόσμορος of Greek writers was perhaps the Ragi or *Panicum Crus-galli.* Millets were clearly no more than incidental importations (65).

Wheat seems to have been passed to and fro in Indian seas for use among ships' crews; the Egyptian Greeks sent much to Muziris and Nelcynda in India for the use of sailors only, and it appears as an export from India to Moscha in Arabia, to Socotra and East Africa, with Egyptian wheat, but beyond this we can say nothing (66).

Some plant-products seem to have been brought as curiosities or as useful ornaments; the coco-nuts have already been mentioned as curiosities found in temples. Pliny says reeds, like tree-trunks, were often seen in temples, and were brought from India, and since the large size of them seems to refer not to height but to girth, we must understand not bamboo but some such palm as the Palmyra Palm (*Borassus flabellifer*), which provided perhaps the φλαγέλλιον καλάμου Ἰνδικοῦ mentioned as part of household furniture in a papyrus of the early part of the second century A.C. (67).

We may conclude this survey of plant-products by indicating one more problem and adding a supplementary list. Virgil Ovid and Martial speak of Roses flowering twice a year in the flower-gardens of Paestum in Lucania, and the only kind of rose which flowers twice a year is the China Rose (*Rosa Indica*) which is not recorded as having reached Europe before the sixteenth century A.C. Nevertheless the twice-flowering roses of Paestum may have been cultivated from a chance importation of the China Rose in a living state, perhaps by an embassy, perhaps by merchants engaged in the new silk traffic, or together with Cabbage roses which the Romans obtained from Persia, or Provins roses which they obtained from the Caucasus. The most likely solution is that the plants came with a consignment of silk which was first introduced about the Augustan period (68).

The Arabians established traffic in the following medicinal plant-products known also perhaps to the earlier Romans: (*a*) Camphor, not the gum-camphor, but the product of the camphor tree (*Dryobalanops camphora*) of Sumatra and Borneo, obtained as a rare and precious medicine from the fourth century until the Arabians made it better known together with the modern camphor from *Cinnamomum camphora* of Japan, Formosa and Central China; (*b*) the pulp of Purging Cassia (*Cassia fistula*) of India, Babylonia, and Arabia, Senna from species of *C*. native to Nubia, Arabia, and India, and "alkelkel" from *C. tora*; (*c*) "Guinea-grains" (*Amomum Grana Paradisi*) of Yemen and India; (*d*) Nutmeg (*Myristica officinalis* of India); (*e*) Coco-nut as a medicine; (*f*) Tamarinds of India (?); (*g*) the stone fruits (myrobalans) of *Terminalia chebula*, known to the Arabs as Black or Indian, citrine, and chebulic; of *T. Belerica*, known to them as Beleric; and apparently of *Emblica officinalis*, known to them as Chinese; (*h*) "Dende" of India, China, and so on, of disputed identity; (*i*) Molucca grains of *Croton Tiglium*; (*j*) a product of the Deodar or Indian Pine (*Pinus Deodara*); (*k*) the Betel-leaf of *Chavica betle* and the Betel-nut of *Areca catechu*, both of India; (*l*) Cubebs (*Piper Cubeba*) of Java; (*m*) Indian and Arabian Memecyls (*Memecylon tinctorium*); (*n*) juice of Orchids from India; (*o*) seeds of *Cocculus Indicus*; (*p*) "Abrong," "Abrugi," apparently a species of pea (*Pisa*) from China; (*q*) the Orange (*Citrus Aurantium*) and the Lemon (*C. medica Limon*) of China; (*r*) Galangal from the Chinese *Alpinia officinarum*; (*s*) "Zedoary root" from species of *Curcuma* native to India and China; (*t*) Turpeth-root, of *Convolvulus Turpethum*, from Ceylon, Malabar and Australia; (*u*) leaves of *Melia azedarach* (Bead-tree) native to North India; (*v*) seeds of species of *Xanthoxylon* of India, China and Japan; (*w*) nut of *Datura Methel*; (*x*) the Mangosteen of the Malay Peninsula; (*y*) Banana as a medicine; (*z*) kernels of *Cerbera manghas* of the East Indies (69); and a few others. To what extent any of these reached the earlier Romans even as an incidental part of the oriental trade it is impossible to tell.

From this survey of Indian plant-products it is clear that there was a tendency to use them for display and for that form of luxury which expresses itself in the use of perfumes. This is illustrated by many a remark made by the ordinary writers of the imperial period, and by the remarks of Pliny in his twelfth book and by the lists which he and Dioscurides give of mixed unguents and flavoured wines; but this last point brings us at once to a different point of view, namely, the use of many Indian plant-products in drugs and medicines; this is clear from all medical writers com-

mencing with Hippocrates in the fifth century B.C., and
I have illustrated these uses by frequent references in the
notes to various medical writers in the separate accounts of
each plant-product. Besides this, the work of Caelius Apicius,
which gives us so many culinary receipts typical of the
Roman Empire, shews that Indian products took a place at
the Roman meal-tables, but with the exception of pepper
and ginger, a small one, and confined almost without exception to the use of spikenard and cinnamon in expensive
sauces of peculiar delicacy; the pepper however is universal,
and it is clear that two uses alone—as a table-spice, and
as a medicine—made pepper the most important of all the
foreign plant-products used by the Romans. Malaria may
well have been partly the cause of this, and the demand
never waned even in the most troubled period of later
Roman history; when for example Serenus Sammonicus
culled his prescriptions from Pliny and Dioscurides perhaps
in the time of Caracalla, he included very few Indian spices,
but pepper constantly. But as we have said, other Indian
products were rarely used in foods; Apicius is a better
source for this than Athenaeos, who spends so much of his
energy in quoting much earlier Greek writers, in order to
display his wide reading, and his only reference to contemporary habit is to say that Roman subjects used unguents of such great worth as to eclipse the expense of
previous ages; nevertheless the Indian spices which he does
deal with are similar to those given by Apicius:—pepper,
nard, and cinnamon, though he shews that as foods the
last two were not commonly used (70).

I am of the opinion that the medical writers of the Roman
period, that is to say from Celsus onward, can be used
fairly as evidence for estimating progress made in Indian
trade with Rome. It is true that they represent a progres-
sion chiefly in the art of drug-making, and that they use

authorities of the Hellenistic period as well, but the theory appears to me to hold good. Cornelius Celsus was a Roman patrician who apparently studied medicine as a branch of general knowledge under Tiberius, and although his pre-scriptions are taken from Greek authors and Alexandrian method (one only (71) being Arabian), although further the maxims and rules of Greek surgery in books VII and VIII of his work are no advance on the early Brahmanical *Sastras*, and although his well-known account of lithotomy is taken from the way in which that operation was per-formed long before by the Indians and by the Alexandrians and probably the Cnidian school of medicine which bor-rowed from the Indians, nevertheless this practical Roman writer who apparently performed a physician's duty among his friends must have used medicines obtainable at Rome, and in his various drug-prescriptions for external and in-ternal complaints, in his decoctions, poultices, salves and antidotes, there are frequent references to Indian plant-products. Again, Scribonius Largus wrote his compilation in Claudius' reign, but in fact before the monsoons were being used fully by the Greeks. Both these writers, there-fore, represent the period of the early Empire previous to the developments of Hippalos' discovery, and in both the references to Indian plant-products as used in medicine occur in much the same proportion, as given on the following page in order of frequency.

But the correspondence is closer than this; for in both writers ginger occurs very rarely, and in neither writer do sugar, aghal-wood, and copal occur at all. On the other hand in medical writers living subsequent to the full dis-covery of the monsoons the three last named products occur, while pepper, spikenard and cinnamon continue to be the three Indian plant-products used most frequently in medi-cine, and it must be noticed that these same three aromatics

VERY FREQUENT	VERY FREQUENT
Celsus	*Largus*
Pepper (most common)	Pepper (most common)
Nard	Nard
Cinnamon and Casia	Cinnamon and Casia
Costus	Costus
Cardamomum	Grass-nard
Grass-nard	

INFREQUENT	INFREQUENT
Ebony	Cardamomum
Lycium	Lycium
Bdellium	

are the three Indian plant-products most frequently in demand for purposes other than medicinal both before and after Hippalos' discovery. Thus we are not dealing with coincidences. We find an increase in the use of the favourite aromatics in medicine and the adoption of new ones after full discovery of the monsoons and the development is reflected in contemporary medical writers, who shew likewise that the trade in eastern aromatics and spices was considerable (especially after the end of the Roman Republic) even before that development. And I think farther that although these two Roman writers and also those writing after the discovery do draw upon and as it were summarise Greek knowledge, yet the very much more extensive knowledge shewn by Dioscurides, Pliny and Galen is due to their unconscious reflection of knowledge which had become the common property of druggists and medical men as a result of the use of the monsoon winds by Roman subjects. Dioscurides illustrates the sudden advance made since the times of Celsus and Largus, and Galen at a later date vividly reflects the results of the most flourishing period of Rome's Indian trade, and he wrote his voluminous treatises when Rome had perhaps passed the highest point of her prosperity. All the Indian plant-products mentioned in other writers as used in medicines and described above are mentioned by him, sometimes with considerable detail, in all kinds of prescriptions, many of which are Arabian, and some of them come from Indian physicians; thus there was an ointment for the eyes called Indian "basilicon" and also a plaster called Indian, the prescription and preparation of which were provided by a surgeon with a Greek name Tharseos or Thrasos, who was either an Indian who had visited the Roman Empire or a Greek who had been to India and there learnt of the prescription (72). But Indian medicine as a whole did not spread westwards until the period of the Arabian conquests, as we have shewn.

A few tentative conclusions may be drawn from an investigation of the retail prices which Pliny sometimes gives in his descriptions of the products of nature, warning us that these prices varied continually, a fact noticed also by the writer of a papyrus which gives us a glimpse of the bazaar of Coptos. We may take it that generally the prices which Pliny gives apply to his own age—to a period subsequent to the discovery of the monsoons. Below is given a list of most of these references to prices (73), arranged in six groups, namely, of prices of products obtained (i) within the Roman Empire; (ii) from the Arabians, as merchandise native to them; (iii) from the Arabians and Somali as intermediaries between the Empire and the far East; (iv) from the Somali, as merchandise native to them; (v) from the Somali as intermediaries between the Empire and the far East; (vi) from India direct. I have confined myself to Pliny's prices because for the most part he gives the prices within the Empire at a given period, but others might be added, for instance, oleum 4 asses per lb. at Pompeii. The Axumites were of course only just rising.

(i) *From within the Empire*

Gallic nard	3 denarii for one pound	
Mastic, black	2 ,, ,, ,, ,,	
,, white	10 ,, ,, ,, ,,	
Myrobalanum	2 ,, ,, ,, ,,	
Cyperos	5 ,, ,, ,, ,,	
Rosewood (Aspalathus)	5 ,, ,, ,, ,,	
Balsamum, real	1000 ,, ,, ,, sext.	
,, false	300 ,, •,, ,, ,,	
Xylobalsamum	6 ,, ,, ,, pound	
Styrax, best	17 ,, ,, ,, ,,	
Sour grape-juice	6 ,, ,, ,, ,,	
Gum	3 ,, ,, ,, ,,	
Goat's Thorn	3 ,, ,, ten pounds	
All-Heal	2 ,, ,, one pound	
Calamus aromaticus (Sweet Flag)	1 denarius ,, ,, ,,	

Compare the following Mineral- and Animal-products:

Blue	8 and 1 denarii for one pound
Lomentum	5 asses for one pound
Armenian Blue	6 (once 30) denarii for one pound
Appian Green	1 sestert. for one pound
Cinnabar	50 ,, ,, ,, ,,
Melian White	1 ,, ,, ,, ,,
White Chalk (paraetonium)	50 denarii for six pounds
Chrysocolla	7, 5, and 3 denarii for one pound
Red Lead	6 denarii for one pound
Minium	70 sesterces for one pound
Yellow Ochre (sil)	2 ,, ,, ,, ,,
,, ,, ,,	2 denarii ,, ,, ,,
Sandarache	5 asses ,, ,, ,,
Sandyx	2½ ,, ,, ,, ,,
Red Ochre, African	8 ,, ,, ,, ,,
,, ,, best	2 ,, ,, ,, ,,
Auripigmentum	4 denarii ,, ,, ,,
Purple	1–30 denarii for one pound (74)

(ii) *From the Arabians, as native produce*

Frankincense by way of the Gebbanite Arabs
688 denarii per camel-load wholesale

Myrrh, stacte		3 to 50 denarii for one pound					
,,	sativa	11	,,	,,	,,	,,	
,,	Erythraean	16	,,	,,	,,	,,	
,,	odoraria	14	,,	,,	,,	,,	
Ladanum		40 asses	,,	,,	,,		

(iii) *From the Arabians as intermediaries*

Ginger		6 denarii for one pound			
Cardamomum ("Arabian")		3	,,	,, ,,	,,
Cinnamon flower-juice (by way of Gebbanites)	1000	,,	,, ,,		
Cinnamon flower-juice (by way of Gebbanites) even	1500	,,	,,	,,	,,
Syrian comacum (?)		40 asses	,,	,,	,,
Serichatum		6	,,	,, ,,	,,
Calamus iuncus (Ginger Grass)		5 denarii	,,	,,	,,

(iv) *From the Somali, as native produce*

Myrrh, Troglodytic			$16\frac{1}{2}$ denarii for one pound				
,,	,,	odoraria	12	,,	,,	,,	,,
Frankincense	Somali	best	6	,,	,,	,,	,,
,,	and	next	5	,,	,,	,,	,,
,,	Arabian	third	3	,,	,,	,,	,,
Hammoniaci lacrima?			40 asses	,,	,,	,,	

(v) *From the Somali as intermediaries*

Ginger	6	denarii for one pound			
Xylocinnamon	10	,,	,,	,,	,,
Casia, best	50	,,	,,	,,	,,
Casia (others, including doubtless adulterated sorts)	5	,,	,,	,,	,,
Casia, Daphnis	300	,,	,,	,,	,,
Cinnamon oil (mixed cinnamominon) made from imported raw spice	35–300	,,	,,	,,	,,

(vi) *From India direct*

Cinnamon-leaf		60 denarii for one pound
Cinnamon leaf-oil (made from imported raw spice)	1 to 300 or 400	,, ,, ,, ,,
Long Pepper	15	,, ,, ,, ,,
White Pepper	7	,, ,, ,, ,,
Black Pepper	4	,, ,, ,, ,,
Ginger Grass (Calamus iuncus)	5	,, ,, ,, ,,
,, ,, ,, aromaticus?	5	,, ,, ,, ,,
Spikenard-spike, St Mark ⎱ ,, ,, St John ⎰	more than 300 denarii	,, ,, litra
,, ,, Pliny	100	,, ,, ,, pound
Spikenard-leaf, large-ball	40	,, ,, ,, ,,
,, ,, medium-ball	60	,, ,, ,, ,,
,, ,, small-ball	75	,, ,, ,, ,,
(This perhaps applies to balls of cinnamon-leaf as well)		
Amomum	60	,, ,, ,, ,,
,, friatum	49	,, ,, ,, ,,
Costus	5½	,, ,, ,, ,,
Bdellium, pure Bactrian	3	,, ,, ,, ,,
Indigo, black	7	,, ,, ,, ,,
Indigo prepared after importation, blue	20	,, ,, ,, ,,

The first thing which strikes us after a comparison of the groups in this list is the much smaller price generally paid for plant-products obtained from plants growing within the Empire than the price paid for those which came from oriental races outside the Empire. The imperial products had no frontier dues, no foreign exactions, and no heavy carriage expenses such as contributed to raise the price of external commodities; they had to bear merely the costs of Mediterranean travel and customs-dues within the Empire, so that with the exception of the more valuable products such as styrax (which was used as an export to India and China as we shall see) the average prices ranged from two to eight denarii a pound.

We get a very different impression from the prices paid for plant-products which came from the East. The obtaining of supplies from foreign powers, the introduction of the intermediaries with their additional exactions, and the much larger distances over which the materials were brought from their foreign sources to the consumers of the Roman Empire greatly increased the prices. The prices paid for plant-products obtained from the Arabians and those paid for products from the Somali (see groups (ii) and (iv)) in each case as native produce of the people were roughly similar and both the Arabians and Somali probably traded with the Romans on equal terms; both peoples (except the Nabataean) were quite free from Roman customs-control, and would naturally agree to adopt a mutual arrangement with each other in dealing with those western Greeks. Thus myrrh (except the finest stacte) cost roughly the same whether obtained from the East Africans or the Arabians, and the same appears to have been the case with frankincense; it is only where the Gebbanite Arabs were concerned (and they seem to have possessed the most grasping elements in their commercial population) that the most absurd demands were presented to and apparently accepted by the Romans.

But it is when the Somali and the Arabians acted as intermediaries for the provision of wares which came from India and China that the prices became extremely high when the wares reached the Roman Empire, and here again it is probable that both the Somali and the Arabians charged each the same price at a given period for any given article of merchandise when offering it to the Romans, and here again the Gebbanite Arabs seem to have surpassed all others in commercial avarice and deception, and the Axumites too had a reputation for miserliness. Cinnamon must have passed through Somali hands above all, Arabian sometimes, and sometimes both, but the real causes of the peculiarly variable price of cinnamon at all times in the early part of the Roman Empire were the many varieties of the spice which flooded the market and the frequent adulteration.

When we come to products obtained from India direct, we find that the conditions are different. The Somali and Arabian intermediaries are cut out and the considerations affecting the price, besides imperial customs-dues, are a long sea-voyage, the conditions under which the wares were obtained in India, and the permanent esteem in which a thing was held to necessitate its being brought from India, together with the extensive adulteration and imitation which took place as a result. In the examples which Pliny gives, the prices are high, except bdellium which was an inferior kind of myrrh, and pepper, which I shall deal with below. If we exclude these exceptions, and look at the prices paid for amomum, nard-leaf and cinnamon-leaf, we find that the average prices ranged from forty to seventy-five denarii a pound in Pliny's time, though nard-spike oil and good cinnamon-leaf oil sometimes fetched very much more. Why did not direct trade in these products make the prices low? Long sea-journeys and possibly heavy export duties imposed by Indian kings contributed to this result, and it must be remembered that spikenard produced the most highly prized of all perfumes in ancient times, and cinnamon oil came close behind, but there were, I think, other considerations beside these, for although the raw material was obtained in India, the trade was not altogether direct. In the case of spikenard it came through disturbed Saka regions, and the Kushan monarchy must have controlled nearly all the Indian spikenard trade in Pliny's time, and much of the raw plant came from regions very far from the west coast of India, as Ptolemy shews; in the case of cinnamon-leaf, all the best kinds came from regions beyond India or at least remote vales of the Himalayas; and I have tried to shew that amomum, until shortly before Pliny wrote, seems to have come by the land-routes, and the prices which he quotes may refer to those current during the early part of the first century.

Lastly, all three aromatics must have been of great importance to the imperial manufactories of aromatics in Egypt, and the imperial authority would tend to keep up the price of articles much in demand among the wealthy classes of the Roman Empire.

One other important thing is revealed by this group of the list gleaned from Pliny, and that is that the discovery of the monsoons undoubtedly did cause a drop in the prices paid for Indian commodities that came to the West by sea. Three items, I think, reveal this. The maximum price of true spikenard raw was one hundred denarii a pound in Pliny's time, but great as this is, the one pound's weight (litra) of spikenard oil which Mary poured over the feet and head of Jesus was worth three times as much, that is, in the words of St John, three hundred denarii a litra, and though after manufacture the price was naturally increased, yet this instance surely illustrates the difference in prices brought about in Indian trade by the discovery of the monsoons, for in the early imperial period, although Greeks were already sailing to the Indus with the monsoon, this aromatic came by the land-routes quite as much as by sea, as we stated above, and there were Parthian and Arabian intermediaries to heighten the price of an already valuable product, very precious says Pliny, among the Indians themselves. But the full use of the monsoons to reach the Malabar coast changed everything not only by opening up all sea-routes to Roman subjects (though it did not eliminate the Yue(h)-chi or Kushan monarchy in the districts of North-west India) but vastly increasing the sailings to all districts of India, including the Indus, to which Roman subjects sailed apparently direct, as we saw, even during the time of Jesus.

Again, Pliny gives $5\frac{1}{2}$ denarii only as the price paid for one Roman pound of costus, but this is hardly reconcilable with his inclusion at the end of his work of the root of costus among the most costly merchandise and his statement that it was the most expensive of roots. It seems most likely that in giving the definite price he quotes from contemporary sources but at the end of his work remembered only the higher prices which he knew had been paid for costus in days gone by, before the discovery of the monsoons cheapened the product.

And thirdly, while the "long pepper," being the species less abundantly brought to the Roman Empire, cost fifteen denarii a pound in Pliny's time, the "black pepper" cost only four and the superior "white" preparation seven. We should expect these prices to be greater, and so they must have been at the beginning of the Roman Empire, and even in the time of Persius pepper is called "sacrum." But we have shewn that this was the spice brought more abundantly than any other, perhaps more than any other merchandise whatever, from India; it was the staple article of commerce between that region and Rome along the sea-route after the discovery of Hippalos, and thus its very abundance tended to cheapen it: it had to be procurable at a low price, for the ordinary man who bought it in paper packets demanded it as much as anyone else, we may surmise in an adulterated form, and it may be said almost to have ceased to be a luxury from the reign of Nero onwards. The great profits reaped by dealers in pepper were due not to the price of pepper, but to large demand for it all over the Roman Empire (particularly perhaps in the Romanised

West, where Roman pepper pots have been found) not only as a table-spice but also as a valued medicine, and so merchants, as we have seen, sent their especially large ships to Muziris and Nelcynda and paid for the pepper in gold and brought back huge quantities upon which the ordinary man could draw at a reasonable price. Now in the Digest-list of wares subject to duty on entering Egypt from the Red Sea long pepper and white pepper are mentioned, but black pepper is absent, and elsewhere to distinguish the commoner kind from the long, not "white" but "black" or "round" pepper is used. Is it possible that black pepper, the common man's spice, inferior in quality to the other varieties, was purposely exempted from the Red Sea customs-due so as to render the price low? The inclusion of white pepper shews that the spice often came to Egypt in an already prepared form. Of all three the imperial authority had a wide control in Egypt and Greek merchants would be ordered to charge a low price for black pepper which had not paid due. It might well be a way of providing a concession to the common people of Rome without acting contrary to the interests of the pepper-merchants, and if such an arrangement really came about, we may attribute it to Nero who planned to abolish dues in general.

At any rate the price of black and white pepper was not so great as we should expect, and I think we may attribute this ultimately to the results of Hippalos' discovery. The excessively high price of pepper during the Middle Ages was one of the reasons why the Portuguese were led to seek a sea-route to India, and when such a route was made available by the discovery of the passage round the Cape of Good Hope in 1498 a considerable fall in the price of pepper took place as a result. Discovery of the monsoons may have had a similar effect. In two places Pliny remarks upon dishonest methods employed in the ointment trade; in one passage he complains of the surreptitious adulterations of the Capuan ointment-street, and in the other he speaks of one Demetrios who in the principate of Nero was unanimously accused in the presence of the consuls by that same centre for engrossing the market and so heightening the price of unguents (75). Of these complaints one certainly and both probably apply to a time soon after the discovery of the direct passage to Malabar—the last stage in the use of the monsoons.

CHAPTER III

Mineral-Products

EQUALLY important in Rome's trade with the East were mineral-products, in particular the precious stones, for the most valued of these came from India, to which with its rivers the epithet "gem-bearing" was particularly applied(1). We obtain glimpses of these stones from various classical writers but our chief sources of information are Pliny's thirty-seventh book, and the collections of Greek and Roman gem-stones, rings, and jewelry. These, together with Theophrastos and passages in Strabo and ordinary writers, shew that the oriental stones, brought westwards plentifully after Alexander's conquests and introduced to the Romans particularly by the downfall of Perseus and of Mithradates, and by the trade of the Seleucids and the Ptolemies, were soon avidly sought after by the Romans, who constantly shewed a low taste by a love of coarse massiveness, by excessive decoration of the fingers, and by the use of gems to cover couches, garlands, armour, walls, and so on. The practice of collecting gems became common during the first century B.C. and Scaurus, Julius Caesar, Marcellus, Maecenas, Vespasian and Hadrian were collectors. All who could afford one obtained a gem-signet from the guilds of ring-makers, and the gem-cabinet (often itself decked with gems) was an essential part of every rich home; the poor used glass imitations, while the rich bought the largest and rarest genuine specimens and the imperial house encouraged the new art of cameo-engraving (2).

In all these luxurious demands, which became so great at the beginning of the Empire, the Romans looked for artists and material to the Greeks, and the Greeks looked to the Indians, who provided nearly all of the best stones, and knowing that the road to wealth was to seek for gems,

set up rows of jewellers' shops in their marts. Of the stones
given in three lists, in the book of Revelation, in Dionysios
Periegetes, and in the Digest-list—all have Indian sources (3).
I have here tried to trace the Roman trade in each one, as
shewn by the evidence of collections, of Theophrastos,
Solinus, Pliny, and ordinary writers, adopting with slight
modifications the modern classification recommended in
E. S. Dana's *System of Mineralogy*.

There can be no doubt that the Romans obtained the
true diamond, which they called "adamas." For Pliny speaks
of the "adamas" as the most precious of all possessions,
known for a long time only to very few kings; his Indian
"adamas" is a true diamond; he describes too the use of
diamond splinters by gem-engravers, and the point of the
diamond was, according to Manilius, more precious than
gold; the hardest stones, even sapphires, could be cut by
it, and there are extant examples of softer stones apparently
cut by Greeks with the diamond. But the final proof that
of Pliny's six "adamantes" one at least was the true diamond, is provided by the antique diamonds set in several
rings and one gold seal in the British Museum, and all the
evidence points to India as the sole source (4). In the first
century they were bought at Muziris and Nelcynda, but
if Ptolemy's "adamas" is not steel, diamonds were traced
during the second century to the Sabarae (near Sambhalpur?), to Cosa (near Betul?) and to the Sank branch of
the Brahmani river (5). To-day the Indian mines form five
groups (6) on the east side of the Deccan plateau in the
districts of Chennur, Kurnool, Kollar, Sambhalpur, and
Panna. The ancient Indians seem to have checked the exportation of large diamonds, but still the Romans obtained
large and famous specimens, perhaps used as amulets after
the Indian example (7).

Of the oxides of silicon grouped as quartzes and opals the

most frequently used were the chalcedonies called agate, carnelian, sard, onyx, and so on. The evidence of all the great collections—British Museum, Paris, Berlin, Vienna, Florence, Leningrad and others, and private collections, intact or dispersed, shews this. To-day India is an important source for these stones, but the workings of Germany come first; yet the ancient accounts which we have of German tribes, the absence of undue preponderance of Bohemian, German and Hungarian stones, such as chalcedonies, garnets, emeralds, opals, in Henkel's catalogue (8) of Roman rings found in the Rhine districts, and the almost entire absence of German stones from Pliny's account, convinces me that the now famous Bohemian German and Hungarian sources for these and other stones, like the Silesian silver mines, were unknown to the Romans, who obtained from India what are now equally European minerals. This will become clearer as we deal with the different kinds of stones. From the north the Romans obtained amber, slaves, and skins—not precious stones.

Of the chalcedony-quartzes, used from very early times (9), the most abundant were the Sard and Carnelian which really form one species and are not always distinguished in the catalogues of the great collections, which contain hundreds of them and bear out Pliny's remark that no gem was commoner "apud antiquos" than the sard (10); and the collections shew that the ubiquitous common sard or carnelian, together with the banded agate, began to go out of fashion only about the beginning of the imperial period—completely supplanted by the finer oriental kinds (11), particularly the Indian sard. There was a great influx of Persian and Indian sards after Alexander's campaigns (12), and of the various sources the Persian (which supplied the fine red-brown sard, Persian *sered* = yellowish-red) which had been known since Ctesias frequented the Persian court, Pliny believed were failing (13). But Ctesias had learnt of the Indian sources as well; and Pliny gives us three Indian varieties of sard, all still found in India, one of them, the red kind, being almost confined to that region, the most brilliant examples appearing in collections as hyacinthine sard (14); we have, too, antique rings and vase-fragments of fine sard-carnelian. India has always been the most plentiful source of the finest red sard which comes chiefly from the Deccan traps, especially with agates from Ratanpur near Broach in Rajpipla, where are the Sard or Sardonyx Mountains of the Greeks. Burma and Japan also produce carnelian in abundance. Hence, as the *Periplus* shews, the Greeks obtained their fine sards and carnelians with other agates at Barygaza (15), whither the Parthians in my opinion sent large supplies also, especially after Hippalos' time, so that the Romans thought that Persian supplies were running short (16). The much-discussed "myrrhina (or murrea) vasa," so greatly valued by the Hellenistic Greeks and by the Romans, were, to judge from the descriptions of ancient writers, vessels neither of fluor-spar, nor of porcelain, but of best oriental sard and carnelian obtained mostly from India (17). They were first brought to Rome after Pompey's victories and at once be-came a form of luxury, increasing even in Pliny's time, as we naturally expect since Hippalos had made his discovery, and glass imitations were frequent. See p. 393. Pliny laments that Romans should hold India in the hand in order to be drunken, and even under Augustus the material was a favourite one among the wealthy for sideboard-tops, vases, wine-scoops, and vessels for drinking and eating (18). Now Propertius, living before Hippalos, speaks of the treatment of these cups by heat in Parthia; Pliny, too, attributes them to the East, especially Parthia, the best to Carmania, but the *Periplus* says that they were brought from Ujjain to

Broach for exportation to Egypt [19]. Here therefore we have an example of transfer of trade from the overland to the sea-routes, the Arabians and Parthians striving to keep a secret in the traffic so that only the author of the *Periplus* definitely called the myrrhina "Indian." After Hippalos' time the references in ancient writers are frequent, and we have examples of the high prices paid for them, of large collections of them, and of the extraordinary whims of rich men like Nero and Petronius [20]. Martial enumerates myrrhina vessels, with silver plate, tables, house and estate, as possessions to sell if ready money be required [21]. Typical cups were ὀνύχινοι σκύφοι, holding about a pint, larger cups being rare, but Pompey obtained a board 4 ft. by 3 ft. made of two slabs. Our extant examples, as we shall see, are made of finer agates, but fragments of large vessels even of ordinary carnelian have been found on Roman soil. So also to-day large agates and carnelians are rare, but blocks weighing up to three pounds still come from the Rajpipla hills and are cut in Cambay, while the cups are sold [22] in Cambay and Broach. The Romans obtained theirs from the East ready-made, but sometimes perhaps they were manufactured on the way in Alexandria [23]. With the discovery of the monsoons, therefore, the trade in carnelian-agates vastly increased, especially when men like Nero set an example.

Among the quartzes more particularly classed as Agates, besides those particularly named onyx and so on, are some known as moss agate, banded agate, or simply agate, and of these we have numerous antique examples engraved, mounted in jewelry, and worked "in the round." Agates are common in many countries, and the Romans came to prefer onyxes by Pliny's time, rejecting the common agates [24]. But Pliny and Philostratos draw special attention to the Indian kinds, of large size, and there is extant a splendid large antique agate worked as a leopard's head. Even Pliny knows nothing of the now famous German sources round Oberstein, so that we may conclude safely that the Romans obtained their best and largest pieces from India where to-day agates are abundant still in the Deccan and the Rajmahal traps of Bengal and in Jubbulpore; the finest, coming from the agate-gravels near Ratanpur, are cut, polished, and sold largely in Cambay; the agate area, including the Deccan traps, covers over one thousand square miles, and there are many Indian sources outside this area. The chief mines are in Rewa Kantha and in north-east Kathiawar. The Mocha-stone of the Deccan traps, the veined agate from Ranpur, and the moss agate ("dendrachates" in Pliny?) from the Godavari, Kistna, and Bhima river-beds and from Morvi, all occur in extant collections. Burnt agates are also very common in collections, and are produced by the Indians to-day; the Romans got them doubtless at Barygaza (25).

The fresh impulses to Indian trade that came about under Augustus brought the fine layered agates onyx, sardonyx, and nicolo into sudden importance—the first two above all for cameos, the nicolo for ring-stone intaglios (26). Of the typical two-layered Onyx Pliny gives an Arabian and an Indian species, but in reality both were Indian, coming as the Greeks knew from mountains which supplied Barygaza in quantities and from regions far inland by way of Ozene —in other words from the various sources in the Deccan and the district of Jubbulpore, supplemented by the nearer sources of Rajpipla. No other sources were of importance. Besides being used in jewelry, the largest and finest from India were used for making cups, toilet articles, statuettes, and so on, and many of these still survive to-day, famous examples being a bust of Livia, a bust of Pertinax, the famous coronation of Augustus (a cameo), and splendid onyx vessels such as the Brunswick perfume-jar, the Vienna perfume-jar, the Waddesdon vase, and lastly the Berlin and St Maurice bowls (27). Onyx occurs as a gem-stone from Minoan times onwards, but the finer ones became known only during the Hellenistic period (28). The best onyxes now come from the districts of Betul and Chhindwara, though large ones are rare (29).

The Sardonyx (an agate of several layers, including sard) was also divided into Arabian and Indian kinds, and came from the same sources, was used by the same rich classes for the same objects, and became popular at the same period, as the onyx. A perforation was considered a proof of a true Indian kind, and the tastes of the Romans reacted upon the Indians themselves (30). Extant examples include small cups and jars, the splendid "Cup of the Ptolemies" (Nero's time?), the Farnese Tazza (recently broken), the Great Agate of France (the largest cameo known, celebrating the mission of Germanicus to the East in A.D. 17, an "Indian" sardonyx), the Apotheosis of Augustus, a double cameo in the British Museum, and many splendid cameo-portraits, especially of imperial personages, above all of the family of Claudius, who we know was very fond of sardonyxes (31). Good examples were valued at Rome almost as much as the opal, and imitations of glass or of artificially united layers of good stones were so great that detection was difficult; of these imitations large numbers have come down to us (32). Large cameos (perhaps with the supply of large pieces) cease before A.D. 100 but the material was sought after throughout the imperial period and in the Byzantine era as well. The Nicolo (an onyx with a dark layer) came into fashion during the first century A.C. and increased in popularity, as collections shew, during the period of decline, perhaps because of its supposed magical properties, and was much favoured by the Sassanids. The

Marlborough collection contained a perforated nicolo and another huge example, both of which doubtless came from India. The material was perhaps Pliny's "Aegyptilla," named from its trade-route (33).

The quartz known particularly as Chalcedony was called "iaspis" by the Greeks and perhaps "leucachates" and "cerachates." It was a very popular gem-stone and an important article of trade with Persia until Hellenistic times, and never went entirely out of fashion, though the finer green variety and the finer agates tended to displace it; besides, the stone is common only in South America, Germany, and India (34), and since the first two sources were unknown to the Romans, from India probably came the enormous chalcedony once in the Marlborough collection, and the large statuette and cups of "iaspis" of which Pliny speaks. Collections reveal the use of the stone in various ways, and that it sometimes appeared as part of a sardonyx (35). The sapphirine chalcedony, much favoured by the Persians and known to the Romans, is an uncommon stone from Siberia, Transylvania, and India, while a separate and rare mineral called Sapphirine (the Persian "iaspis aerizusa" of Pliny?), of which there are at least two antique examples extant, has been found only in Greenland and in the Vizagapatam district in India, so that India was the source of these (36).

Of other chalcedonies, the apple-green Chrysoprase (not Pliny's "chrysoprasus," but his emerald-green Indian "iaspis") found in the Urals, in India (whence come very fine examples), and since 1740 in Silesia, seems to occur in collections (37), while the green kinds known as Prase and Plasma (or "mother-of-emerald") are abundant, especially for the later period of the Roman era, and unworked lumps of plasma have been found on Roman sites. How much of it came from India we cannot tell, but at any rate it seems to be included by Pliny under the names iaspis, smaragdus, and prasius of which the last named was a common green stone found (if Pliny was right) only in India, and again a valueless apple-green stone "sandaresus" was named after its Indian source, and to-day much plasma comes from India, particularly north of the Bhima river, from the Kistna and Godavari river-beds, and from Kandahar, besides Egypt and Germany. When Pliny speaks of very large "emeralds," and of the Indian chrysoprase capable of being hollowed into cups, I take it that he refers to Indian plasmas (38).

The opaque "Bloodstone" and the translucent "Heliotrope" or "girasol," both of them in reality one species heliotrope, are red-marked green chalcedonies which, as collections shew, came into favour only from the second century A.C. onwards. In Pliny the opaque red-spotted prasius (blood-stone) appears among the less important stones, and he gives only India as a source; unimportant too was the translucent heliotrope reputed to come from Ethiopia, Africa, and Cyprus. Perhaps Pliny was relying upon information derived long before from the secretive Phoenicians, for these stones now come almost entirely from India with agates (39), being brought from the Deccan traps, especially the Kathiawar district, to Cambay for polishing, other regions being unimportant. Before passing on to the jaspers, into which the heliotrope merges, we must notice that Pliny's white-striped species of prasius coming from India is a striped chalcedony which occurs in collections (40).

It is difficult to trace definitely to India the various Jaspers used by the Romans, but Pliny's emerald-green iaspis from India perhaps includes the green jasper of the Urals and India but we cannot tell whether or not Indian iaspis means chalcedony. Green jaspers were much favoured in the near East because of their supposed value as amulets (41).

Red jasper was much esteemed in the Roman Empire, especially in its decline, and was known as "haematitis," attributed to Africa, Arabia, and above all Ethiopia by Pliny, who knew nothing of the British and German sources. Bright red stones are common in the rocks of the Nerbudda and Sone valleys, and ordinary red jasper often occurs among Deccan agates, polished at Cambay. The very fine vermilion and the rarer deep crimson kind of our antique collections are now found only in Mexico, but Pliny's haematitis (which seems to have been got originally from Arabian and African intermediaries) seems to be the deep red kind and his vermilion "corallis" (the coral of Northwest India in Dionysios Periegetes?) from India and Syene (which indicates African intermediaries) the vermilion kind. The best pieces of black jasper or touchstone, occurring in collections, now come from India, and black jasper is found often on antique nicolos, more rarely on onyxes and sardonyxes, and jaspers of other colours occur on onyxes and chalcedonies. Pliny speaks of a pale tawny variety of haematitis called "menui" by the Indians, and the ribbon, blue, and yellow jaspers (all of which have Indian sources) occur in extant collections (42).

The "asteria" of India and Carmania, or else the "zmilampis," which was supposed to be found in the Euphrates, included apparently the quartz Cat's-eye which comes to Cambay from near Madras, from Burma, perhaps from Malabar, but above all from Ceylon and the Deccan traps, especially Ratanpur (43), while another quartz called Aventurine, found chiefly in the Urals but also apparently in Bellary, Madras, and occurring in collections, was perhaps the very brilliant and costly Indian "sandastros" of Pliny, who by indicating South Arabia and the Garamantes as other sources, echoes the times when Carthaginians, Phoenicians, and Arabians brought the stone westwards (44).

The fine purple Amethyst was very popular in the Hellenistic and Roman periods, and fine extant examples and the amethyst cups of which we read shew that large pieces were often obtained (45). To-day good amethysts come from Germany, Hungary, Bohemia, the Urals, South America, and above all as pebbles from the gem-gravels of Ceylon, the rivers of India and Burma rarely producing them (46). The sources other than Indian were quite different in the time of Pliny, but even in his time "India" was the most renowned source, producing five kinds—purple, imitated by the purple-dyers, inferior sapphire-coloured (called socondion by the Indians), two kinds very pale, and another (garnet?) wine-red (47). The Romans obtained the Ceylonese pebbles in Tamil ports, probably through a secret of trade, for Pliny does not mention Ceylon here at all. At least one of our extant Roman amethysts is a polished pebble of the typical Ceylonese type, and one or two other splendid antique amethysts are perhaps similar in origin (48).

Some of the yellow quartz called "Citrine" comes from Ceylon and the Urals and was perhaps included in the "chrysolithoi" of the Greeks (49), while the pink Rose-quartz (Pliny's purple-tinged and rose-tinged "iaspides"?) comes from the Urals, India, and Ceylon besides Bavaria, Brazil, and so on. Both occur in collections (50).

Pure crystallised silica or rock Crystal, which was in use in very early times, was obtained in Alabanda, Orthosia, Cyprus, perhaps the Red Sea regions, and later on the Alps, but above all others was preferred Indian crystal, a statement of Pliny borne out by Strabo and Martial (51). The mineral has been worked in many places in India, particularly at Aurangpur near Delhi; Burma, Kalabagh, Kashmir, Sambhalpur, the Godavari basin, Morvi, Haiderabad, Tankara, the Rajmahal hills, and the Punjab still produce it, and Vellum is famous for cutting and polishing (52). The

Greeks and Romans used it (53) for ring-stones, models in the round, hand-balls, burning-lenses, and so on, but the wealthy Romans of the Empire used crystal above all as drinking cups, particularly for cool or iced drinks, and these vessels are frequently associated with the myrrhine as marks of wealth, luxury and extravagance. Pliny gives examples of these large cups and bowls, some of them from India, and of the high prices and foolish whims connected with the possession of them. The richer classes had keepers of crystal-cabinets and named their crystal cups. Most of the large examples came ready-made from India, but sometimes they were made on the way in Alexandria; the large masses noted by a Chinaman in Syrian architecture likewise surely came from India. In comparison an ordinary glass cup cost hardly anything (54).

Thus the trade in Indian crystal was an important one. When Pliny speaks of the unequalled excellence of Indian rock-crystal glass, he refers, it seems, not to Chinese porcelain but to a rock-glass made in Ceylon, if we may so judge from a passage in the Sinhalese *Mahavamsa*; even to-day what is apparently rock-crystal glass is made by the Chinese at Po-shan-hien in Shantung (55). The Greeks knew well that the Indians could stain rock-crystal into the colours of real precious stones, and Pliny refuses to give information about the treatises extant on the subject! The Indians still make these imitations (56).

The case of the Opal, highly prized in ancient times, is curious. To-day it comes from America, Australia, and above all Hungary; not from India, which Pliny expressly states was the sole source. Perhaps the opal, beloved by Indians, was obtained by them through Scythian tribes and then sent westwards. The same applies to the hydrophane opal of Saxony, known to the Romans; on the other hand, the cacholong opal comes chiefly from Central Asia and this stone too the Romans obtained, while Pliny's "sandastros" from India was perhaps matrix of opal, and non-opalescent opals are fairly common now in the Deccan traps. Thus perhaps all opals came from India and through India, the Sanskrit "upala" (precious stone) being perhaps borrowed by the East from North Europe and then passed on by India to the Greeks. Pliny shews how valuable the stone was, how frequently it was imitated, and how huge a price could be paid for fine large examples, apparently two million sesterces (57).

Of the stones produced by oxides of metals, the hard corundums of to-day (Tamil *kurrandam*) formed an important part of Rome's oriental trade, for the coloured kinds (notably ruby and sapphire) fit for gem-stones come chiefly from Ceylon, and also from Salem, Rewa, Burma, and Siam. For marble-sawing and polishing the Romans often used excellent "Ethiopian" and slightly inferior "Indian sand" (all of it coming really from India)—that is, either Emery-powder which is frequent in South India and abundant in the Rewa State, or the common Corundum from Malabar, the Carnatic, Bengal, Tibet, China, and so on, still used for stone-working. Sometimes this corundum forms gem-stones of which antique collections have a few examples (58).

The Sapphire (*hyacinthos*, Arabic *jacut*) was very well known to the Romans and the Byzantines and received names according to its colour. Ceylon has always been renowned for its sapphires of Ratnapura, Rakwane, Matara, and other places; Battambang in Siam (since 1870), Chantabun and Krat, the Zanskar range of Kashmir, and Upper Burma, also produce them; the only African source is Madagascar; the European sources are unimportant; the Bohemian sources were unknown to the Romans; Australia and America were outside their range (59); Pliny's European sapphires seem to be really amethyst and citrine quartzes. We are left then with this: sapphires and golden yellow chrysolithi were sent by Ethiopia, but the Indian and sometimes the Bactrian were preferred, the Arabian being despised; leucochrysi, melichrysi, and xanthi (pale, honey-coloured, and orange-coloured sapphires or corundums) were sent from India, which with Ethiopia sent also the "nilion" (another sapphire—Sanskrit *nilamani* and *nila-ratna*, *nila* = dark blue). I take Pliny's Bactrian stones to be Kashmirian sapphires, the Ethiopian to be Indian stones in the hands of Abyssinians, and the Indian chrysolithi to be yellowish sapphires such as are still sold in Ceylon to-day as "topazes." For the author of the *Periplus* found sapphires at Muziris and Nelcynda only, whither evidently all sapphires, including the now scarce Indian supplies from Salem, Malabar, the Cauvery, and the Upper Godavari, were sent, for Ptolemy is the first to give Ceylon as a source and much later Cosmas knew that they were abundant there and implies that they were a cause of the localisation of trade there in his day, and extant Byzantine sapphires include many fine stones.

Probably a considerable quantity of sapphires and other corundums was brought by the Indians to the Axumites and passed on by them and the Arabians, perhaps by land, for at one time Meroe was a depôt for precious stones and Ethiopia and North Africa are frequently mentioned as sources for gems and marbles. Otherwise we must deduce exhaustion or loss of once productive African mines (60). Ptolemy, Solinus, and Cosmas reveal the increase of knowledge of sapphires, but of course in later writers India means no more than East Africa (61). The hard sapphire first came into use as a gem-stone in the Graeco-Roman period, and extant examples shew us its use (generally unengraved, as was natural) in jewellery and rings and shew too the quantities obtained under the Byzantine Empire. Engraved sapphires one-half and even one inch wide, the so-called signet of Constantius II (a sapphire of 53 carats) and a perforated stone of Hadrian's time are all extant examples of ancient trade in splendid oriental sapphires (62).

The identification of Pliny's "asteria" from India (difficult to cut) and Carmania (preferred) and of his "astrion" from Patalene and Carmania (whence came the best) is uncertain. They seem to include sunstone, moonstone, and girasol or star sapphire, at any rate the last named which comes largely from Ceylon and India (63). A very rare corundum called the green ruby may be included in Pliny's "Scythian emerald," but this is quite uncertain (64).

Generally we cannot tell when the words "lychnis" and "anthrax" (Latin "carbunculus") mean garnet, and when they mean ruby, but the fine red Ruby was used by the Romans unengraved, as collections shew, in rings and jewellery, and one of the "anthraces" of Theophrastos, the "lychnitis" of Solinus, and the best "lychnis" of Pliny found in Indian regions and attributed by one writer to the Hydaspes, are probably the ruby, which now comes above all from Upper Burma, Siam and the gem-gravels of Ceylon, much more rarely from Mysore and Salem, the Cauvery and other rivers, and Badakshan and Jagdalak, near Kabul; hence perhaps the "Hydaspes" rubies (65). The inferior spinel ruby coming chiefly from Upper Burma, and then Ceylon, Siam, and Badakshan, and the balas or balais ruby from Badakshan are both represented among extant Roman gem-stones (66). The Romans may also have known the corundum Cat's-eye (not quartz cat's-eye) which occurs above all in Ceylon; much of it is really a form of our very hard Chrysoberyl of which only the kind called cymophane can possibly have reached the Romans, chiefly from Ceylon and also from Burma and India, especially Rajpipla; it is almost certainly Pliny's "chrysoprasus" of India, and a few antique examples of this chrysoberyl still survive. Whether the variety called Alexandrite, from the Urals and the gem-gravels of Ceylon, was known to the Romans we cannot tell (67).

The emerald and the beryl (closely related stones, as Pliny knew) were very highly prized by the Romans. As a general rule the Emerald was not an export from but an import (68) into India sent in the Byzantine era at least through the Axumites, but Indian emeralds are referred to, a Sanskrit name *marakata* (*smaragdos*) is borrowed for the stone, and Pliny's best "Scythian" emeralds must have come from a source in the Urals rediscovered in 1830, and his "Bactrian" were perhaps the same (unless both kinds were aquamarine-beryls of the Ural and Altai mountains). The Indians made crystal "beryls" and "emeralds" and perhaps sent them by land-routes with real stones, whence we get supposed Pontic beryls and Persian and Median emeralds in Pliny (69).

The Beryl or Aquamarine was also very highly favoured by the Romans; the sea-green aquamarines were valued more than the blue, and were more preferred than gold, but nine kinds are given by Isidore, seven by Pliny, who says they were rarely found outside India. All Pliny's oriental emeralds may have been aquamarines, revealed to the West by Alexander's conquests. Beryls are found not only in Brazil and Saxony, but also in the Ural and Altai mountains (whence come very large masses which remind us of the huge "emeralds" spoken of by ancient writers), in the Toda hills, at Padiyur in Coimbatore, and at Kangayam in the Punjab; they are rare in Burma and in the gem-gravels of Ceylon. Three important Indian mines are recorded: at Padiyur, at Punnata in the south-west of Mysore, and at Vaniyambadi in the district of Salem. The beryls of Coimbatore were at least partly controlled by the Cheras—they would be sent down the Ponnani to Tyndis and so to Muziris; those from Punnata would be sent to Naura (Cannanore) and so to Muziris; those of Salem would go to the Chola coast and then round. At any rate the Pandya Kingdom cannot be said to have been famous for its beryls. By the time of Ptolemy sources Punnata and Ceylon were known or heard of—a distinct advance upon the knowledge of Pliny and the author of the *Periplus* (70). Soon the Romans knew that the name βήρυλλος was derived from the Indian (Sanskrit *Vaidurya, Veluriya*). Of the large quantities of Roman coins found in the Coimbatore district, where splendid six-sided beryl-prisms are found, many were possibly given in exchange for beryls. The stones were often polished in their original shape and worn by ladies as "cylindri" in their ears, and two inscriptions of Spain shew how highly valued they were; the Romans even decorated bowls with them, and they seem to have been even more widely used among the ancient Indians, according to Pliny, and good forgeries were frequent (71). At Rome they became suddenly popular, as Propertius and other writers and Augustus himself shew, at the beginning of the Empire, and Beryllus occurs as a name. Splendid engraved examples are extant and also splendid polygonal columns which are doubtless relics of Rome's Indian trade (72).

Lapis Lazuli (σάπφειρος, κύανος), which comes from Persia, Tatary, Tibet, China, and above all Badakshan, hence being attributed to Scythia, Persia, and the Hindu Kush, was nevertheless ascribed to India and Ethiopia as well, because as the *Periplus* shews, this non-Indian material reached the Greeks at Barbaricon on the Indus and it appears in the Digest-list. Collections shew that though known very early, it was used by the Romans chiefly at a

late period (73). It passes through India on its way to Europe
even to-day.

Certain Garnets, popular among the Greeks and Romans,
especially in jewellery (74), were included under ἄνθραξ,
ἀμέθυστος and λύχνις; common garnets are found in many
regions, but Alexander's campaigns first made them
popular. There is no sign whatever that the Romans knew
anything of the sources in Bohemia, Silesia, Tyrol and
Hungary whence come deep red pyropes and other garnets,
so that the extant antique pyropes must have come from
India, where they are extensively worked, especially at
Jeypore (Jaipur). To India also we must attribute the
extant examples of purple-tinted pyropes called to-day
Almandines, clearly in my opinion to be identified with
Pliny's "Carthaginian carbunculi" and with his gem called
"Indica," and the violet-tinted pyropes called Syriam (not
Syrian) garnets, which I take to be Pliny's "amethystizontes carbunculi," the best of all, and his Indian stone
called "Ion" (75). The almandines, common in India, are cut
in Delhi, Jaipur, Kishangarh, Godavari, Orissa, Haiderabad,
and so on; they occur with other garnets in Vizagapatam,
Trichinopoly, Tinnevelly, and Burma, but they are found
above all in the gem-gravels of Ceylon. Jaipur produces
the best Syriams, and Cambay and Broach have always
been the chief emporia for convex-cut garnets called car-
buncles, so that the Romans also got them at Barygaza;
yet they are prepared also in South India, Ceylon, Calcutta,
and Pegu, so that we may identify the alabandenon
exported from Kaviripaddinam, according to Cosmas, with
these garnets, and similar stones were got perhaps at
Muziris and Nelcynda also with other transparent gems (76).
The magnificent antique examples of pyrope, almandine,
and Syriam garnets still surviving (77) are sure relics of the
trade in smaller Indian garnets. But Indian almandine and

common garnets are often found as large pieces and in India small dishes are carved out of them. The Romans must have traded in these, for Pliny speaks of cups cut out of "lychnis," and vessels capable of holding a pint and cut out of Indian "carbunculi," and there are extant large antique garnet cups and also flat garnet plates obtained from Etruscan and Byzantine remains. Some may have come from the large masses of garnet still found in East Africa—for Pliny mentions Ethiopian "carbunculi" (78).

The reddish-brown garnets called "Cinnamon-stones" (or hessonite), which as gem-stones come almost entirely from Ceylon as pebbles, are found in collections and are perhaps Pliny's "chryselectri" (79).

The Chrysolite or peridot, which seems to have been the "topazios" of the Greeks, was an export from Egypt and a Red Sea island (probably the island of St John or Zeboiget) to India, and the "topazios" is not attributed to India except by Dionysios; yet the chrysolite is found in Ceylon and Pegu and may have been one of Pliny's "chrysolithi," "chrysoberulli," or "chrysoprasi" (80).

Zircon or Zirconium Silicate is called also Hyacinth or Jacinth when it is red or orange, Jargoon if it is not. Almost all that is used as gem-stones comes as pebbles from the gem-gravels of Ceylon and New South Wales; Indian, Bohemian, and other sources being unimportant (81). There are extant many small Hellenistic and Roman jacinths, but there is also a fine model of a bull and other fine jacinths, and cameos which indicate Roman trade with Ceylon (82). Jacinths were perhaps known to Pliny as honey-coloured or tawny "chrysolithi," or more likely porous "Arabian chrysolithi" and amber-coloured "lyncuria"—stones which both Pliny and extant collections shew were going out of fashion during the first century A.C. (83). Both jacinth and jargoon seem to be included in Pliny's Indian "morio," *var. lect.* "mormorio," and large extant jargoons of ancient date have been discovered. I do not know what the "pantarbes" was, but if the mormorio was a scare-goblin amulet, the similarity in the meaning of the names suggests to me the same stone—jargoon (84).

The widely distributed Tourmalines are commonest in India, most of the gem-stones coming from Ceylon, but we have black and white from the Shan States, green from Ceylon, Bengal, Seringapatam, Burma, blue from Bengal, yellow and brown from Ceylon, and red (called rubellite, and perhaps included among the "carbunculi" and "lychnides") from the Urals, Upper Burma and so on (85). All may have reached the Romans through trade.

I do not think that the felspar called Moonstone is Pliny's "astrion" or his "ceraunia," for nearly all the moonstone of commerce comes from the gem-gravels of Ceylon, especially Dumbara, but it may have been his "Solis gemma" or his "selenitis"; at any rate the Romans used it as a gem-stone (86). It is doubtful too whether the felspar Sunstone of Siberia, Norway, and perhaps India and Ceylon, and the Amazon(e)-stone of America, Madagascar, and the Urals, can be identified in Pliny, unless we seek the amazon-stone (of which there are ancient cylinders but no genuine Roman examples) in Pliny's Persian "tanos" and Assyrian "eumitres." Both perhaps reached marts of North-west India (87).

Since the discovery of Jadeite and Nephrite in the earth in Europe and America there has been no need to suppose a prehistoric traffic in Chinese jade, yet in ancient times no reference is made to any green or opaque white stone from Silesia, Austria, North Germany and the Alps where jadeite and nephrite have been found, and the word "iaspis" (which must have included jade) seems to be cognate with the Turkestan *yashm, yeshm*, Arabic *yeshb*, so that we may suppose that the ancient world did obtain nephrite from the now famous sources in Turkestan, Siberia, China and Bengal, and jade from Turkestan, China and Upper Burma—particularly Khotan in East Turkestan. We have antique examples of both jade and nephrite extending from early Babylonian and Egyptian eras to Gnostic times. All the East, says Pliny, wore "iaspis" as an amulet (88), but these minerals do not seem to have been favoured by the Romans.

The account given by Pliny of "asbestos" *growing* in the desert places of India and discoveries made in Italian and Roman sepulchres shew that the wealthy Romans obtained the incombustible fibrous mineral called asbestos or Chrysotile, valued it as highly as best pearls, and had it woven into wicks, handkerchiefs and shrouds, chiefly perhaps in Syria, where Kan Ying noticed it in A.D. 97. It is now found in many places, especially Italy, and also Tyrol, Hungary, and Russia, but with the exception of the Greek supplies the Romans must have obtained all theirs from Cherchen, Badakshan, Afghanistan, Punjab, Garhwal, Bhopawar, Chota Nagpur, and Mysore—the chief oriental sources (89).

The phosphate Turquoise (green, blue) is found to-day chiefly in Persia (Khorasan) and Turkestan, and especially near Maaden, stones of Silesia and Saxony being much inferior; the Romans knew of the oriental sources only, for the "callaina" (with the turbid "callaica") or green turquoise came from peoples of the "Caucasos" or Hindu Kush, and (best) from Carmania, and was exported from Barbaricon on the Indus, appearing in the Digest-list. India is the centre of distribution even to-day. The stone became popular quite suddenly in the Augustan period, the emerald-green stones being valued most highly; apparently it is the green kind which gave its name, as papyri indicate,

to coloured fabrics, and we have excellent antique examples
in jewellery, engraved with cameos, and modelled in the
round. Collections too shew that the Romans used the blue
turquoise also—Pliny's "callais," enumerated among the
less important stones (90).

Sometimes the Romans obtained the fossil resin Amber
from India, as well as the German tribes, if we are to
believe that Archelaos, King of Cappadocia under Tiberius,
really received supplies from India with the pine bark still
sticking on! If not copal, this would be Burmese amber
from the Hukawng valley, or else Baltic amber sent to
India (as it is to China to-day) and then to the West (91).
Normally however amber was imported to India by the
Romans, as we shall see.

I cannot identify the stones atizoe, amphidanes, chelonia,
eumeces, zoranisceus, and others resembling obsidian, all
attributed by Pliny to India, and therefore pass them
over (92). Nor is it possible to prove any trade in such Indian
stones as are found in large bulk; nevertheless the magnificent Indian columns which adorned the dining-room of
Ptolemy Philopator's famous ship may have been made of
Indian Marble such as is quarried at Makrana in Rajputana,
in the Nerbudda valley, and at Raialo in Ulwar (93), while
the oriental Alabaster, a marble so popular in ancient times
for making perfume boxes or jars, came at least in part
from Carmania and India, according to statements made
by Pliny (94). It was called "onyx."

What we have said so far about mineral-products illustrates the abiding characteristic of Rome's traffic with
India—it was a traffic in luxuries (95). As we shall see,
the metals were more important as articles of importation
to, rather than exportation from, India, but there was too
a considerable importation of oriental metals to the Roman
Empire.

About the time of Augustus Chinese Tutenag(ue)or white copper seems to have reached the Roman Empire as a substitute for silver, for we hear of a "copper" flagon of "Indian" workmanship, exactly resembling silver (96). But there can have been no extensive trade here. Copper itself was exported from Barygaza to the Persian Gulf when the *Periplus* was written, and from Kalyana in the time of Cosmas five centuries later, and this was either Indian copper from Kullu, Garhwal, Nepal, Sikkim, and Bhutan in the Himalayas, and from Rajputana and southern districts; or it was re-exported European metal (97).

Fine swords made of Indian steel had been famous since the time of Ctesias, and the Roman trade in Indian Iron and Steel was an important one. Since Pliny says that the finest of all iron was sent by the Seres with their tissues and skins the natural conclusion is that this metal was from the province of Shan-Si in China or at least from Ferghana. But, as Schoff has pointed out, the *Periplus* does not indicate the exportation of silk and steel together at the same marts, and we must take Seres as being the Cheras of the Malabar coast (98); "Indian" is the epithet applied by the *Periplus* and by others, and by the Digest-list. Now the *Periplus* gives Indian iron with sword-blades at Adulis and other African ports, and the author knew it came from the interior of Ariace, yet did not see the metal at any Indian port; so that the Indians sent it in their own ships to the Axumites, who kept the secret of production, perhaps allowing the Romans to attribute the metal to remote China. To-day the Indians make steel in Madras, Mysore, Punjab, Kashmir, Bengal, Rajputana, Assam, Burma, and so on, but especially Haiderabad; it is no wonder therefore that the Greeks attributed it to Ariace and the Chera Kingdom. Their excellent Parthian metal was perhaps really Indian. Eventually they learnt the

secret of production, for Saumaise points out a special Greek
treatise on the tempering of Indian steel. Chwostow may
be right in supposing that the bulk of Roman importation
consisted not of large quantities of ore, but objects made of
iron and steel. The Romans worked it into fancy cutlery,
as Clemens shews, and perhaps into armour at Damascus
(whither Indian metal was sent) and at Irenopolis (99). The
excellence of the steel would heighten the value of the untouched iron, but neither would come from distant China.

Gold was not regularly an article of trade with India, but
Pliny distinctly states that gold from the Ganges (where
an Indian gold coin was current) reached the Empire, and
implies the same of the famous "ant-gold" of the miners of
Dardistan and Tibet, whose pick-axes seem to have been
a curiosity at Erythrae (100). The gold of the Ganges would
be alluvial gold of the rivers in the Chota Nagpur plateau;
the gold used by goldsmiths in Madura and sold by traders
in Kaviripaddinam and apparently Malabar marts also
would be gold of Mysore; the washings of Assam and
Burma still produce gold which was at one time exchanged
for Chinese silver, the Irawadi, Sitang, Salween, Mekong,
and Yang-tse-Kiang rivers being productive sources of
gold. Hence the mysterious "gold" and "silver (?)" countries
of the East in ancient writers, and the name Chryse given
to Malay, the Irawadi delta, and Burma. For the rest, gold
was imported into India as Roman coin in the south or as
Arabian bullion in the north-west—this last perhaps for
the Kushan coinage (101).

Before discussing the products which the Romans exported to India, we must recapitulate the trade-secrets
which, in spite of the loss of their greatest secret the monsoon, the Arabians and Somali managed to retain wholly
or partly in their possession. The secret of cinnamon was
the most remarkable, being a double one, for the Romans

found the bark and shoots at Somali and Arabian ports, not knowing that they came from India and China, and found the leaves at Indian centres without knowing that they belonged to cinnamons, the veil being drawn closer after Hippalos' discovery. The spice ginger was in the hands of the Nabataeans and Trogodytae and was not traced to any far eastern regions until the second century; cardamom of Malabar was attributed to Assyria, Syria, Armenia, Media, Pontus, Arabia, India (where the author of the *Periplus* however did not see it) and so on throughout the first century, and seems to have been a secret of the Palmyrenes and of the Parthians, and also of the Arabians and others until the second century, when it was included in the Red Sea duty-list; and Indian copal was a possession of Somali Trogodytes Nabataeans, and other Arabians. In certain products there was a partial secret; thus Indian iron and steel were known by the Romans to be Indian but were not found in India by them if the intermediaries (Arabians, Axumites, Palmyrenes, Parthians) could help it (102); again, lac, sugar, makir, ghi, and gingelly-oil, all Indian, were found by the author of the *Periplus* in East African ports, were known by him to come from India, and yet he never found them there, though the first three products are ascribed wholly or partly to India by other writers also; again, the Arabians succeeded even in Roman times in making the Romans believe that a certain type of onyx- and sardonyx-agate was "Arabian" and not Indian, and the best agate and carnelian (myrrhine) was kept secret by Arabians and Parthians until after Hippalos' discovery men like the writer of the *Periplus* knew well the true Indian source; again certain other precious stones, notably sapphires and other corundums, were attributed by the Romans to East Africa as well as to India, though here again the same writer knew that oriental sapphires were Indian only. Lastly the Chinese kept the true nature of silk-production secret for centuries, and so did the Indians and Parthians when they discovered it; before the second century there *is* slender evidence to shew that there was a leakage along the sea-route under Augustus, but until the second century true Chinese silk was regarded by the Romans as a plant-product. We must of course remember that some of Pliny's information came from Hellenistic writers of an age when trade with India was almost entirely conducted through intermediaries, and that the partial use of such inter-mediaries was geographically inevitable even under the Empire, so that Indian products might be ascribed to them without any intentional secrecy or deception on their part, but in my opinion the secrets which I have traced above are established facts.

We can state with certainty that in no instance did the Greeks themselves by any agreement at all gather in person the products of Arabia, Africa, or India; hence the ignorance of cinnamon and the very vague knowledge which they had for instance of the climbing pepper-plant and the cardamom. Pliny gives hardly any exact localities of Indian products, and even Ptolemy adds only a few, while according to Philostratos the gathering of pepper is done by apes (103). Evidently gathering of all products was in the hands of the Indians themselves, even in the case of beryls, in spite of the Roman coins from Coimbatore; no Roman coins have been found at the pearl-centre Colchoi or near the pearl-harbours of Ceylon. The Indians kept their own sources secret, while the Tamils kept secret the Ceylonese origin of a good deal of what they sold to Roman subjects.

THE OBJECTS OF EXPORTATION TO INDIA AND THE "DRAIN" OF SPECIE THITHER

CHAPTER IV

A. *Articles of Exportation*

IN dealing with the imperial products which the Romans exported to India in the course of their trade we are confined to sea-traffic only, because we have no means of telling what merchandise was sent to India by land. But we have a complete list of the merchandise which was exported by sea from the Empire to India, and we also have a complete list of the Indian merchandise which was sent by sea to the Roman Empire, and we have shewn that with a few exceptions these Indian imports were sent by sea only as forming the most natural means of carriage during the Roman Empire. Therefore we will be justified in taking each list as a complete one representing the products forming the articles of trade between India and the Roman Empire respectively. Our information comes chiefly from the *Periplus*, from remarks scattered here and there in Pliny, from oriental sources, and from remarks in other Roman writers such as the passage where Philostratos speaks of an Egyptian ship such as took Egyptian wares to India and exchanged them for Indian merchandise (1).

That there was a regular commerce in slaves as imports of India from the West we may judge from the following evidence. A company of Yavana women attendants is a regular "feature of the Raja's court in Indian dramas"; for example, "Dushyanta Raja has such a company in the '*Sakuntala*' of Kalidasa," and the practice can be traced back as far as Chandragupta. Eudoxos, that remarkable man who sought what is now called the Cape Route to

India, intended to take to India a supply of young singing slaves for Indian princes, and the *Periplus* says that handsome girls were presented to the king at Barygaza for use in his harem, while the μουσικά, which the *Periplus* says were presented to the same king, were apparently not simply musical instruments but young slaves with good voices, bringing musical instruments as well perhaps; for a legend about St Thomas makes an Indian king engage a Jewish slave-girl to entertain by her flute-playing his guests on their disembarking, while the dumb Mlecchas who acted as guards to Tamil kings were perhaps slaves when they were not mercenaries naturally inclined to be loyal to their employer rather than to take sides in any dispute. Thus in India the slaves who were imported from the West were always destined to be presents, or at least specially selected merchandise, for Indian potentates, and the same may be said of the slave trade which existed even with China at this era; thus Chinese records state that jugglers were sent between 140 and 86 B.C. from "Syria" to China by the Parthians (a glimpse this of the land-traffic), and in A.D. 120 musicians and jugglers were sent from "Syria" to China along the sea-route. On the whole, therefore, the traffic in slaves exported to the far East from the Roman Empire (the eastern part of which is called "Syria" in Chinese records with special reference to Syria proper) may be regarded as having been an important one (2).

Of the rest of the animal kingdom we can trace nothing definite except in one instance; certain animals and shells were exported from the Roman Empire even as far as China, but the horses which were imported into Kaviri-paddinam from "distant lands beyond the seas" were surely sent from Parthia, for Cosmas makes the trade in horses between Persia and Ceylon an important one during the sixth century (3). Again, the purple which the Arabians exported from Apologos and Ommana in the Persian Gulf to Barygaza was doubtless Tyrian, but it counts only as an Arabian export to India. But one animal-product stands out as the most remarkable of the wares exported to the far East—and this is the fine red coral of the Mediterranean (*Corallium rubrum*). The *Periplus* says that coral was exported to Barbaricon, Barygaza, Muziris, and Nelcynda in India, and also to the Arabian port Cane, probably for re-shipment to India, and the quantities sent were so large that by Pliny's time the supplies were being exhausted even in places where they had been plentiful. The chief sources of supply were Sicily, Sardinia, Corsica, the Balearics, and the coasts of Italy, Spain and North Africa. In Gaul, shews Pliny, the tribes were ceasing to adorn profusely their swords shields and helmets with coral because the demand for it among the Indians was causing it to become rare even in its chief sources. Now Pliny says that the Indian pearl was as highly prized by a Roman lady as a bead of coral was by an Indian man, and coral was held by the Brahmans to be a sacred amulet besides an attractive adornment; it is thus possible that the Greek merchants exchanged their coral at the Indian marts which we mentioned for pearls brought up the coasts from the Gulf of Manaar for that purpose. Indian literature tells us that traders in coral and pearls frequented Kaviripaddinam of the Chola Kingdom, and this town contained resident Greek merchants; similarly, a poet who visited Uraiyur, the ancient Chola capital, speaks of coral and pearls together, with rare gems also, and as is shewn by the passage in the "Toy cart," jewellers' shops in India regularly sold coral. Dionysios Perigetes says that towards the west of India (he is talking of people round Patalene, that is, the Indus delta) "red coral" was found everywhere, and unless he refers to a red stone, he indicates the abundance of export from the West in days gone by. Centuries later coral was in much demand in the times of Marco Polo (who notices the great demand for it in Tibet), of Vasco da Gama, and of Tavernier, and it was undoubtedly of immense value to the Romans in their trade with India and also with China (4), and Chinese records indicate that the inferior black coral of the Red Sea and Persian Gulf was sent as well to the far East (5). To-day India is the chief market for it. By the Romans it was not admired.

The exportation of plant-products was considerable, but they came for the most part from the eastern regions of the Empire only. That clothing of flax was widely exported to the East from Egypt is clear from the outburst of Pliny on this subject, and the *Periplus* shews that much thin and a little spurious (νόθος) clothing, as well as figured linens (πολύμιτα), was sent from Egypt to Barbaricon; that all sorts were sent to Barygaza, the finest being set apart for the king, and that a little thin clothing and figured linens were sent also to Muziris and Nelcynda. The brightly coloured girdles imported into Barygaza were intended probably for the Bhils, a Dravidian tribe, who still work the carnelian mines. We need not doubt that some of this clothing had come from the inland district of Arsinoë, which produced stuffs mentioned on a papyrus and which were exported to African marts, and a papyrus records the absence in India of a man of Arsinoë; some of the inferior stuff may have been brought even from Spain and northern Gaul. The looms of Syria too must have contributed a share in these exportations; thus the clothing exported by the Arabians from Apologos and Ommana in the Persian Gulf to Barygaza and Arabia to suit the tastes of the receivers would include naturally Syrian fabrics, while Claudian, as some interpret, says that coloured garments made in Palestine were worked up by the "Indians"—perhaps real Indians—and Chinese records shew that the embroidered fabrics of the eastern part of the Roman Empire were preferred by the Chinese to the Babylonian fabrics, because they were "polymita" (6).

In the third century there were considerable opportunities for trading in Egyptian papyrus—at least Firmus, who caused much trouble to Aurelian, seems to have carried on a great and profitable trade with India (?) in papyrus and glue, and it is strange that we have no earlier examples of the use of papyrus as an export to the far East (7). At any rate there must have been a great demand for it in India beginning perhaps only in the third century A.C.

The Romans made considerable use of their wines (which could be carried as part of a ship's ballast) in their trade with the far East; Laodicean and Italian wines were sent to various places in Africa and Arabia; unspecified wines in small quantity to Barbaricon; Italian, Laodicean and Arabian (date?) wine to Barygaza, where the Italian was preferred, and about the same quantity and apparently of the same kinds to Muziris and Nelcynda. So far the *Periplus* is our authority (8), but the famous Roman wines perhaps reached even more distant regions, for the Indian poet Nakkirar exhorts a Pandya prince to drink in peace the cool and fragrant wine brought by the Yavana in their good ships (or bottles). Of these wines which were evidently so much esteemed by the Indians, the Italian kinds must have been largely produced from the plains of Campania, whence were obtained the Falernian, the Statanian, and the Calenian, while the Laodicean speaks for itself; for Laodicea abounded in wine of which most was imported into Alexandria and so passed on to more eastern lands (9).

Another important product was styrax or storax (apparently the liquid kind obtained from the sap of *Liquidambar orientalis*) sent to Barbaricon and Barygaza for use in medicines, and exported from Egypt, and, if we may so judge from Chinese records, Syria also (10). In A.D. 97 Kan Ying reported to the Chinese that the Syrians, after extracting as storax the finest qualities from odoriferous plants, sold the residue to foreign peoples, and that the storax sent to China passed through many hands and lost fragrance. This may account for the cheap ointment sent to Barygaza besides the very finest quality given to the king there (11). Another interesting fact is revealed by Chinese literature, and that is the transplantation to Canton before A.D. 300 of the finger-nail flower or Henna, not from India or Parthia, where the plant grows besides the Levant, but from "Syria" (12); and things like this make us wonder how much exportation of Roman goods to the far East increased during the period of prosperity in the second century, and during the monetary decline of the third century.

The trade in the remaining plant-products which we can trace stands on a different footing from the others, as will be seen. Thus it has been conjectured that the Sweet Clover (*Trifolium melilotus*), obtained chiefly in Campania, Crete, Chalcidice, and at Cape Sunion, and sent from Egypt to Barygaza, was destined to be manufactured into chaplets by Indians for re-exportation back to the Roman Empire, though the plant had medicinal uses as well (13), while the following were not imperial exports at all— dates, which were imported from the Persian Gulf to Barygaza (14) and probably did not enter into Rome's export trade, and frankincense, which must have been used for exchange both by Arabians and by Roman subjects. For it has been supposed that frankincense, which was imported into Barbaricon alone of Indian marts known to the author of the *Periplus*, was given there in exchange for silk yarn or thread brought thither from China; both Arabians and Roman subjects would naturally bring the incense—(the Romans procuring it on their way to India)—which would ultimately reach the Chinese by whom it was highly prized; and in return the silk yarn sent from China to the mouth of the Indus would ultimately reach Arabia and Syria for making the part-silk fabrics for which those regions were so famous (15). We can guess too that the Somali sent frankincense in exchange for Chinese cinnamons which they passed on to the Romans. A Tamil poem speaks perhaps of frankincense in Kaviripaddinam of the Chola Kingdom, and even to-day frankincense is sent to Bombay for exportation to Europe and to China (16).

The mineral-products which were exported by the Roman Empire were few but striking. In the first place the Indians required during the period of the Roman Empire supplies of base metals chiefly for the native currency, which was of lead mostly, alloyed with copper or tin, and the Roman Empire supplied that demand chiefly from the western provinces. As for silver and gold, silver was uncommonly, gold hardly ever used by the ancient Indians for coinage, but both metals were legal tender. Now Cosmas says that copper was found at Kalyana in his day, and at a much earlier date Ptolemy speaks of numerous copper mines in further India, but Pliny says that India had neither brass nor lead, but exchanged precious stones and pearls for those metals, and the *Periplus* says that lead, copper, and tin were imported into Barygaza and into Muziris and Nelcynda, and so we may conclude that India was not producing those metals in the first century A.C., but depended on the West for her supplies (17).

The exportation of lead seems to have exceeded that of the other two metals. Together with copper, it was imported into the chief western marts of India mainly for the native coinages, but it was also alloyed with a little tin (imported from the Roman Empire to the same Indian marts) and made into thin sheets for providing foils in the manufacture of mirrors (18). It was in providing this lead and tin that the most western provinces of the Roman Empire were particularly important from the point of view of its trade with India. The finest lead came from Spain, the mine at Baebelo having yielded at one time as much as 300 pounds daily; the central source was Carthago Nova, and other supplies were obtained from the Ebro valley, Baetica, Gaul and other regions, including Capraria of the Balearic islands, but both for ordinary uses and for exportation to India the lead of Britain (from the Mendips, from near Wroxeter, Tamworth, Matlock, and so on) was taking the place of supplies from other sources; it was easier, Pliny implies, to dig up lead in Britain than it was in Spain, and it is probable that the demand for lead within the Roman Empire and without in the far East was exhausting the mines of Spain (whence lead with tin, iron, and silver had been brought eastwards before the destruction of Tyre), for the hoards of lead stamps found at Carthago Nova dwindle in the second century A.C. (19).

The copper too was required for coinage by the Indians, and ancient Indian inscriptions frequently occur on that metal. The copper which the *Periplus* says was exported from Barygaza to Ommana and Apologos in the Persian Gulf was perhaps surplus European metal exported to Malabar and Barygaza and thence re-shipped by Indians to the Persian Gulf, probably when Rome and Parthia were at war. Pliny, too, has iron, copper, arsenic, and red lead as products of Carmania shipped to the Persian Gulf and the Red Sea ports for marketing. The main source of European copper was the island of Cyprus with its mines at Amathos, Soli, and Curion, of which the Roman government had complete control. The mines of the Lelantine plain had long been exhausted and more recently the mine in Gaul owned by Livia had failed likewise; but the Vaudrevange of to-day, and also Lyon, the Bergomates, Comum, Sulmo, and North Wales all supplied the metal, and sources other than these and those of Cyprus were insignificant [20].

The importance of tin as a western import into India is shewn by the fact that at a fairly late date the Sanskrit tongue borrowed its word (*kastira*) for tin from the Greek κασσίτερος; the Indians used it with lead to make mirror foils, and in other ways. European tin, with copper, coral, and storax was often re-shipped from Cane to India, but most of it was brought directly in Greek shipping [21]. The Romans of the early Empire obtained nearly all their tin from the mines of Lusitania and Gallaecia in Spain, especially after Pliny's time, the Cornish and Irish sources being hardly touched, and the metal was brought by sea through the Straits of Gibraltar rather than by land. Now the metals, coral, and perhaps clothing from these western and north-western regions were exported in very large quantities to India, which sent, in return for British lead for instance, pearls and gems as Pliny says, besides spices and so on in order to supply the rich and "Romanised" populations of Gaul and Spain especially. Hence at Malaca in Spain Syrians exchanged oriental wares for Spanish metals, and an oriental pearl-merchant traded at Emerita. In Gaul, too, dwelt Orientals, and Massiliotes frequented Egypt where Narbonese pottery has been found. Perhaps then in the early Empire western merchants went all the way to India through Egypt and back after Hippalos' discovery. We hear of voyages from Massilia, from Narbo, and from Spain to Alexandria; Seneca notes the shortness of a voyage between Spain and India, and Lucian suggests travel from the Pillars of Heracles to India. Moreover about A.D. 600 direct voyages between Britain and Alexandria for tin caused no surprise (22).

Syria and Egypt sent asbestos-cloth to China, but we cannot tell whether the fabrics were sent also to India, which was itself a source of the raw mineral, as we have seen. Such an article of commerce would tempt rich buyers anywhere (23), and probably India got some from Rome.

Three other minerals have a place here, but their use by the Romans as exports to India was peculiar, like their importation thither of frankincense. Thus the sulphide of antimony (στίμμι), used for ointments and eye-tinctures and found chiefly in East Arabia and in Carmania, was sent to Barygaza and to Muziris and Nelcynda; to the same marts was brought the red sulphide of arsenic called realgar obtained in Persia and Carmania for use as a medicine; while to Muziris and Nelcynda alone was brought orpiment to provide a yellow paint (24). The Romans must have obtained these chiefly on the way to India; all three substances are still important as articles of commerce sent thither. The last occurs on old Indian and Ceylon paintings.

It is interesting to note here that the ancient Indians must have used widely the products of Roman industries in lamps and vases, for in Tamil poems occur references to Yavana vases and lamps, and bronze vessels of a European and first-century type have been found in megalithie tombs of the Nilghiri hills (Chera Kingdom) (25). Costly silver vessels too were presented to the Sakas of Barbaricon and Barygaza, who were as grasping as the Arabian potentates (26). The gold which the Arabians exported as bullion from Apologos and Ommana to Barygaza was perhaps destined for the Kushan monarchs, as we shall indicate (27).

Amber is not mentioned by the *Periplus* as an imperial import to the East, but Pliny says that amber was exchanged in India for pearls and other precious things, and it even reached China from the Roman Empire; but the Indians must have obtained most of their amber from the Baltic across south Russia through the "Scythian" tribes (28). The *Periplus* does not mention articles of jewelry either, but western gems have occurred in India and were imitated there, and they reached China by the sea-route. We should expect too that reference would be made to the emeralds of Egypt, which were certainly exported to India by the Axumites in the sixth century A.C., but in fact the only gem-stone recorded by the *Periplus* as an export to India is the chrysolite sent from Ethiopia and the Red Sea to Barbaricon, Barygaza, and Muziris and Nelcynda. Probably the emeralds would have to compete with Indian beryls and Bactrian emeralds and so appeared only late in Indian commerce (29). The idea of taking precious stones of any kind to India would appear unnatural to most merchants who knew India as the most famous source for them.

The last of the imperial exports to the East with which we have to deal is glass, and this material was of considerable importance in Rome's trade with India. Alexandria, Tyre and Sidon were famous for their works in glass, which spread all over the Empire and very far beyond (30). Thus crude glass was exported from Alexandria to Barygaza, Nelcynda and Muziris, doubtless for making mirrors besides vessels, and vessels of glass were imported into Barbaricon; and moreover much Greek glass reached even China as is shewn by Chinese annals which record glass of several different colours, received as a present (it is said) from the West by the Emperor Tsaou-tsaou in the beginning of the third century A.C. Glass vases imitating metal vases have been found both in Kuban and in the far East, and these appear to have been made in Alexandria. A fine Alexandrian glass vase was found in the Chinese province of Honan. Khotan in East Turkestan was famous during the early centuries of the Christian era for its glass wares and for its copper tankards, the materials having come presumably from the West. By way of Khotan or from Khotan must have come the Yue(h)-chi glass-maker who arrived in China soon after the Emperor Tsaou-tsaou had received his "gift" of western glass, and who taught the art of glass-making to the natives. Tsaou-tsaou belonged to the Wei dynasty and reigned in North China, where at Poshan-hien in Shantung glass-making from native rock still goes on. Even in 140 B.C. the Emperor Wu-ti of the Han dynasty had a manufactory probably of opaque glass. In India, a few small glass objects found in topes, for example at Manikyala in the Punjab, and dating from the Christian era, were probably made from crude glass imported from the West, while fragments found at Bahmanabad in the Indus region are "hardly distinguishable from the Roman glass of the imperial period" (31).

B. *The Adverse Balance*

Our list is now complete, and we cannot help being struck by its smallness in comparison with the list of imports received by the Empire from India, and that the noteworthy difference between the respective quantities is no mere accidental illusion produced from any lack of material in our extant sources is revealed with certainty by other considerations. Thus within the Empire we find that ships plying between Puteoli and Alexandria (the route taken by the greater part of Rome's trade with the far East) always returned to the Egyptian capital less heavily laden than when they left for Italy, and the inner parts of Alexandria were fuller of bustle and life than the regions fronting the Mediterranean; still more striking is the fact of a guild of "saburrarii" or stevedores, who carried ballast into ships which, having arrived with a cargo at the Tiber, needed a make-up load for a return journey eastwards (32). Again, outside the eastern boundaries of the Empire the specially large ships being sent to the coast of Malabar, and the need felt at Mosyllon for ships still larger than those being used when the *Periplus* was written—in other words all larger vessels used or needed by the Romans in the Indian Ocean were not so much for taking imperial products to India as for bringing large quantities of Indian products into the Roman Empire; and, to speak generally, the very nature of the articles of merchandise which formed this trade reveals that the *separate* articles of exportation from the Empire to India, often suited to the tastes of the receivers, consisted largely of materials much weightier and bulkier than those which were brought from India, if we except the larger animals which as we have seen came by land and formed in reality a part of Rome's trade with the Parthians: in other words, the general quality of Rome's exports was weight and bulk rather than large variety and there was a tendency to sell inferior goods to people of slight culture. The conclusion to be drawn is that not only did Italy consume more than she produced, not only was Rome a city and Latium a district poor in manufactures, so that neither is mentioned in the lists of exports in the *Periplus*, but the Empire taken as one unit was often unable to offer to foreign regions in general and to oriental nations in particular sufficient products of its own to balance the articles imported from them in large quantities, and the result of this was the draining away from the Empire of precious metals in the form of coined money without any adequate return. Our task is now to consider this pheno- menon from an economic point of view and to form so far as possible an estimate of its effect upon the Roman Empire.

The movement of specie eastwards took place in two forms; merchants carrying on large transactions with foreign countries found gold coin a necessity for a condition of wealth and for external commerce, while silver was essential for small change, and so, much Roman money was taken by Roman subjects to India in order to buy up in bulk what they were unable to get by exchanging imperial products in bulk. But besides this natural condition of wholesale trade there was a deliberate exportation of Roman money to India to create a Roman currency there, and it is our business to find the real significance of this very dangerous use of state coinage. Such references as occur in extant classical writers apply to exportation of coin for the first reason. The Emperor Tiberius had already expressed disapproval of the manner in which Roman wealth was being drawn away to foreign lands, but full discovery of the monsoons must have increased the tendency for we find complaints made by writers of the times of Nero and Vespasian. Thus Pliny says that at the lowest computation India, Seres (= Cheras ?), (see p. 393), and Arabia drained from the Empire a hundred million sesterces (about £1,087,500) every year—"so dearly do we pay for our luxury and our women" [33]; again, in a more important passage he tells us that India took away from Rome not less than fifty-five million sesterces (about £600,000) yearly, giving in return merchandise which was sold for one hundred times its original cost, that is to say through expenses incurred on the journey. This is confirmed by Chinese sources, for in the Chin-shu annals we are told that the Parthians and Indians traded with the Roman Empire by sea, reaping one-hundredfold profit, and although a corresponding passage in the Later Han annals reads tenfold and implies that "Syria" made the profit, Pliny's statement seems to confirm the higher estimate (34). The Chinese wrote according as they viewed the Roman or Indian side of the trade and noted everywhere the high profits made by the carriers and the capitalists of the trade. The outburst of Dion Chrysostom is a remarkable one (35). He says that the Celts, Indians, Iberians, Arabians, and Babylonians levy tribute from the Roman subjects not in land or cattle but through Roman foolishness. If it is true that some men through senseless and luxurious desire send money willingly over long stretches of land and sea to people who cannot easily set foot upon our territory, surely (says Dion) it is altogether a wicked and a shameless thing. The foreigners providing miserable little stones, yes, and the bones of wild beasts, take money, rendering worthless things in return for good. Pliny is the only one to give us figures, and it is to be noted that of the whole amount one-half and more was pouring into India—a proof perhaps of the extent to which India had supplanted Arabia and Africa since the discovery made by Hippalos; the two passages which we gave above have caused much controversy. There are those who believe that Pliny was referring only to such traffic between India and the West as was conducted along the northern route by way of the Caspian and the Black Sea (36); others again take it that he omits the cost of the pearl trade (37), but I think he refers to the sea-trade by way of Alexandria, and that Hirth, Chwostow and others are right in believing that Pliny meant to point out that over and above the articles actually exported from the Roman Empire in return for oriental goods, and the cost of carriage and so on of both exports and imports, the oriental commerce brought with it a further heavy cost because of the necessity of sending away the precious metals in order to pay for merchandise not obtained by barter, and that the ultimate balance of trade was in favour of the far East and Arabia, however much individuals might profit. Chwostow points out that the cost of Asiatic importation to the Roman Empire in the time of Pliny nearly equals the cost of such importation into Europe during the period 1788–1810, and gives the tentative conclusion of Beloch that the cost of Indian imports per head of population in the Roman Empire during the reign of Vespasian was only 30 per cent. lower than the cost per head of the population of Europe in 1835; and although, as Salvioli well illustrates, the total energy of commerce and industry in the ancient world was feeble when compared with the conditions of to-day, I think Rome's Indian trade does stand apart, and that Chwostow is right when he concludes that the volume of exports from India during the epoch of the Roman Empire can compare not unfavourably with the conditions of more modern times (38). One has only to consider the extravagant expenditure incurred (as we have seen) in the purchase of oriental luxuries and the wealth accumulated at this period by such men as Seneca (300,000,000 sesterces) and the imperial freedmen Narcissus (400,000,000 sesterces) and Pallas (300,000,000 sesterces) in order to be convinced that the amounts which were quoted above from Pliny cannot have represented the value of the whole of the trade with oriental countries and in particular India (39). I am inclined to think that in this passage Pliny excludes from his India the Tamils, including them instead under the name Seres with special reference to the Cheras, whose ports received the bulk of Roman money. The *Periplus* shews that in the time of Nero merchants brought money to two important regions of India, and of these regions the author is careful to give a list of the exports and imports as well. At Barbaricon no coin was noted as an import, but to Barygaza were brought silver denarii and gold aurei, which were exchanged profitably with the local currency, and to Muziris and Nelcynda a very large amount of Roman money was sent, of which the *Periplus* does not specify the metal, but undoubtedly both gold and silver were included, the gold being brought to pay for large loads, particularly of pepper and malabathrum, for a Tamil poem speaks of Yavana ships bringing gold and taking away pepper (40). The *Periplus* shews that the taking of money to the Chera Kingdom was much more important than the taking thither of imperial wares; it shews too that bringing of coin into Barbaricon was on a less important scale than it was to other places, and we shall see the reason for this shortly.

Exportation of Roman money to India was really inevitable, for the dearth of a commercial coinage was felt so much by Sakas that coins of Apollodotos and Menander were still current in Nero's time (41); the Indian coinage was made chiefly from base metals of little exchange-value in international commerce, yet the Tamils, tending to stay in India, and allowing the Romans to come to them bringing their light and valuable western money with them, accepted that money without imitating it. In the story of Apollonios by Philostratos the question arises of exchanging good Roman and Parthian money for "Indian stuff of orichalc and black brass with which all who come to India have to buy things" (42), but the *Periplus* shews that at Barygaza (for instance) the exchange was made to the advantage of the Romans (43). In my judgment these two statements reveal two different conditions of exchange. Roman money imported into Barygaza was exchanged partly with issues of Saka satraps centred in Kathiawar and Malwa and striking chiefly silver coins, and partly with issues of Andhra kings, who coined chiefly in lead but at least partly in silver, besides copper. The advantage in the coin-exchange was therefore in exchange of precious metal on both sides. On the other hand Roman money imported into the lands of the Tamils could only be exchanged (if at all) for coin of base metal, for the Tamils did not coin the precious metals gold and silver. Now the Greeks would not want to carry away base Tamil coin in large bulk received as small change, and so in dealing with the coinage imported into marts of Malabar the *Periplus* does not mention anything about the coin-exchange. Instead the Greeks deliberately established a Roman currency of Roman coins in Tamil districts. This might explain the abundance of Roman coins found in South India only. Roman subjects were bound to bring their money if they could not persuade the Indians to coin in precious metals, and they had to use the Indian coinage of baser metal in any case for very small change, so that Roman coinage of base metal rarely reached India until a late period.

Of the several thousand Roman coins which have been found in India the greater part had been brought to the three Tamil Kingdoms during the first century of the Roman Empire, and while the discovery of coins is regulated by chance alone, the available evidence seems to admit certain conclusions which may be regarded as fairly certain. We will take first the finds made in the Deccan; an enormous number of silver coins and a large number of gold coins have been found in regions corresponding to the three old Tamil States and issued under. the stamps of Augustus, Tiberius, Gaius, and Claudius, but the coins with stamps of Tiberius' reign exceed in number by far those of any other reign. With Nero a change takes place—his gold coins have occurred frequently but only two silver coins have been found, and of reigns subsequent to Nero no silver coins have been found at all in South India. Parallel with this there are two other developments to note—gold coins of Vespasian and of many succeeding emperors occur in India, but never in large numbers; we find groups of less than six instead of hoards consisting of even more than one hundred and fifty coins. The other development is a sudden cessation of the discoveries in the more southern parts of the Tamil States and a shifting to more northern districts, both on the west and on the east sides of the Indian peninsula, in some cases beyond the limits of the Tamil States altogether, and although all theories built on this evidence are liable to be overthrown by new discoveries of coins, nevertheless I think that in certain directions the evidence is too strong to be resisted.

A gold currency was necessary for a condition of wealth and for foreign commerce and the imperial government of Rome knew this well and took the initiative in conducting commerce by means of gold; during the first century even the Parthians were sufficiently uncommercial to leave the Roman emperors a free field for monetary circulation in the East, and they allowed the Roman government to have the sole right of coining gold for universal use, for the Arsacids of Parthia coined no gold at all and left the silver and copper coinage of Parthia to the satraps and to the towns; only later did the Sassanid rulers of a new Persia adopt a system of gold coin of their own. Now in the course of their sea-trade with India, Roman subjects naturally brought gold with them to India in order to pay for large cargoes of Indian wares; we know even from literary sources that they did this, but the question arises—did the Romans deliberately export their gold and silver in large quantities with the definite object of exchanging it in India for native coinage and of creating a Roman currency in India? The *Periplus* shews that importation of both metals took place into Barygaza for exchanging, but the same object was absent in the case of the more southern Tamil States. Numismatic evidence is valuable here.

Let us consider the following single hoards of gold coins and then single hoards of silver coins, and see if they offer any sure evidence on which to base any sort of conclusions. The different finds are compiled from the list which Sewell gives according to the reigns of the different emperors, and from Thurston's *Catalogue*, but the conclusions drawn are independent of their commentaries (44).

Gold

(a) Found at Pudukottai, Chola Kingdom (probably), 1898.

Of the reign of	Augustus	51	coins
,,	,,	Tiberius	193	,,
,,	,,	Gaius	5	,,
,,	,,	Claudius	126	,,
,,	,,	Nero	123	,,
,,	,,	Vespasian	3	,,

Total number in one hoard 501 coins.

Many were much worn and nearly all ultimately put out of circulation by a chisel-cut across the head, Nero, Claudius, and above all Tiberius, being well represented.

(b) Found at Kalliyamputtur, Madura district (Pandya Kingdom, but near the boundary of Coimbatore), 1856.

Of the reign of	Augustus	2	coins
,,	,,	Tiberius	11	,,
,,	,,	Gaius	1	coin
,,	,,	Claudius	11	coins
,,	,,	Nero	17	,,
,,	,,	Domitian	5	,,
,,	,,	Nerva	2	,,

Total surviving in one hoard of 63:—49 coins.

Some coins up to Commodus have been lost from this hoard.

(c) Found in 1850 at Kottayam, the old Nelcynda, belonging of right to the Chera Kingdom, whither a Tamil poem shews that the Romans sent gold in order to pay for pepper (chiefly Cottonaric, from the Sanskrit *Kuddanadu*), an enormous hoard of five "cooly-loads" of which the following known examples are:—

Of the reign of	Augustus		several coins	
,,	,,	Tiberius	at least 30 coins	
,,	,,	Gaius	,, 2 ,,	
,,	,,	Claudius	about 20 ,,	
,,	,,	Nero	,, 16 ,,	
,,	,,	Antoninus Pius	1 coin	

Those of Tiberius' reign perhaps predominated in the total. The coins were very fresh, new, and pure (45).

(d) Found at Karuvur, Coimbatore, Pandya Kingdom, 1806.

Of the reign of	Augustus	1 coin	
,,	,,	Tiberius	2 coins
,,	,,	Claudius	2 ,,
		Total	5 coins.

(e) Found near Nellore, north Chola Kingdom, 1786.

Of the reign of	Trajan	a number of coins	
,,	,,	Hadrian	6 coins
,,	,,	Antoninus Pius	1 coin

Total in one hoard at Nellore about 12 coins.

Some of Trajan's were quite fresh and new and of pure gold (46).

(*f*) Found at Vinukonda, Kistna district (Andhra kingdom), 1889.

Of the reign of		Tiberius	2 coins
,,	,,	Vespasian	1 coin
,,	,,	Domitian	1 ,,
,,	,,	Hadrian	5 coins
,,	,,	Antoninus Pius	5 ,,
,,	,,	Marcus Aurelius	2 ,,
,,	,,	Commodus	1 coin
,,	,,	Caracalla	1 ,,

Total of the Kistna find 18 coins.

(*g*) Found at Darphal, near Sholapur, 1840.

A few of Antoninus Pius, Lucius Verus, Commodus,
Septimius Severus, and Geta.

(*h*) Found at Pudankavu, Travancore (Pandya), 1903.

Struck under		Theodosius II	1 coin at least
,,	,,	Marcian	1 ,, ,,
,,	,,	Leo I	1 ,, ,,
,,	,,	Zeno	1 ,, ,,
,,	,,	Anastasius I	1 ,, ,,
,,	,,	Justinus I	1 ,, ,,

Total at least 6 coins.

Coins after the time of Septimius Severus are rare, and
when emperors are represented it is chiefly by single
examples.

So much for the gold coin; but the money substance under
the Roman Empire was silver, a necessary medium for small
change, and the most important medium of commercial
relations in oriental countries, so that we find the number
of silver coins of the Empire found in India to be very large,

and it is the word "denarius" which, together with faint
traces of Roman law and procedure, appears ultimately
in Indian records(47), transferred however to a gold coin
when only Roman gold had value.

The following finds of Roman silver in India are worth
consideration; in some instances the numbers were so large
that they were never counted before they were lost again.

Silver

(*a*) Found at Pollachi, Coimbatore, Chera Kingdom, 1800.
Large numbers of the reigns of Augustus and Tiberius: a
further find of large numbers belonging to the same reigns
and presumably made of silver occurred in 1810; these seem
to count as one hoard, of coins of like weight and value.

(*b*) Found at Karuvur, Coimbatore, about 1856. A great
hoard of from fifteen to twenty pints (making several
thousand silver coins) struck under Augustus and succeeding emperors. They were apparently melted down soon after
discovery.

(*c*) Found at Karuvur, Coimbatore, 1878.

Of the reign of Augustus 27 coins (Gaius and Lucius); of
the reign of Tiberius 90 coins. Total in one hoard 117, but
there were originally 500 altogether. Of the surviving remainder most were of one type struck in Tiberius' reign.
Most of them were very fresh (48).

(*d*) Found at Vellalur, Coimbatore, 1842.

Of the reign of Augustus		136 coins	
,,	,,	Tiberius	380 ,,
,,	,,	Gaius	1 coin
,,	,,	Claudius	5 coins

Total 522 coins,

nearly all belonging to the reigns of Augustus and Tiberius,
and many being of one type.

(e) Found at Vellalur, Coimbatore, 1891.

Of the reign of Augustus			189 coins
,,	,,	Tiberius	331 ,,
,,	,,	Gaius	8 ,,
,,	,,	Claudius	14 ,,
,,	,,	Nero	2 ,,

Total 544 coins,

of which an extraordinarily large number were struck in Tiberius' reign and many in Augustus' reign. Many of them were very fresh.

(f) Found at Yeshovantpur, near Bangalore, Chera Kingdom, 1891: many coins of Augustus, Tiberius, Gaius, and Claudius, the total being 163 in this case.

From the lists given above we may conclude with safety that down to the time of Nero deliberate exportation of both metals took place not only for wholesale purchases but in order to create in India a gold and silver currency of a Roman type among the Tamils in general, and any one of the separate hoards may include the relics of definite importations, the coins being lost before being long in circulation. The strangest thing is the extraordinarily large proportion of coins, both of gold and silver, belonging to the reign of Tiberius—finds (a), (c) of gold and finds (a), (c), (d), (e) of silver illustrate this fully—and it may be that the exportation commenced on a large scale in his reign or in the reign of Augustus, for the plated coins of one type (Augustus' reign) found in India seem to have been struck for special use in that country (49); moreover, though I hesitate to take single hoards as evidence in themselves that the coins composing them were brought in bulk in single shipments, the finds (a) and (c) and probably finds (d) and (e) of silver do include single loads of coins belonging only to the reigns of Augustus and Tiberius, and the one completely certain thing we know is that Tiberius had complaints to make about the drainage of specie eastwards from the Roman Empire.

But there is another possibility— we know for certain that after the discovery of the monsoons exportation of gold and silver coin took place into the most important marts of the western coast of India, and when we consider the effects likely to be produced upon this tendency by the use of the monsoons combined with the proved and notorious extravagance of Nero, it is possible that we are not wrong in suggesting that Nero himself, who debased the silver currency, caused merchants to collect and take with them to India good coins belonging to previous emperors and so to create as far as possible a really good Roman currency in Tamil-land. Be this as it may, coins of Tiberius went to India in abundance; the only ones found in the Kistna district well up the east coast and dating previous to Vespasian are two gold coins of Tiberius (find (f) of gold). Chwostow and others suggest that the Indians so much admired the coinage of the earlier Roman emperors that subsequent emperors may have struck coins with the stamp of those emperors and had them sent out to India (50). If this be true, it helps to account for the next phenomenon presented by the finds—namely, the entire absence of silver coins after Nero's reign except in the north of India and Ceylon, about which we deal elsewhere. This development is so clearly indicated that we must perforce conclude that after Nero's reign the exportation of silver to India from the Roman Empire was wisely discouraged except in so far as it was necessary for a prosperous oriental commerce—for as I shall shew, there was no real decline in trade after Nero's death. The emperor we naturally think of is Vespasian; he may well have checked the outflow of silver as part of his national economy, but the finds shew that the bringing out of gold naturally continued as a necessity. Perhaps after the decline of Roman trade, the Indians melted down quantities of the depreciated coins as they have melted down in recent times the imported gold bars and newly found hoards of Roman coins, and so helped to cause the dearth of silver coins in finds dating after Nero's reign. Good coins of early reigns they found it worth while to keep in circulation.

But even in the case of the gold coins there is a change in the localities which have produced the finds; with few exceptions, no coins dating after Nero have been found in the Tamil regions until a much later stage of the Roman Empire is reached. See find (*h*) of gold and compare the numbers of copper coins of Arcadius and Honorius and other emperors discovered in Madura and Ceylon, and also the great numbers of oboli found on the Coromandel coast (51). But instead gold coins of various emperors have been found in districts farther towards the north of the Indian peninsula. Sewell, who notes that these districts are cotton-growing regions just as they were apparently in the time of the *Periplus*, denies the possibility of Romans having given up the practice of residing in Tamil States through wars between the Pandya and the Chola Kingdoms (though some of the finds seem to indicate that hoards of coins were hidden away hastily), and concludes (52) that the appearance of gold coins in more northern districts contrasted with the meagre finds made in the Tamil Kingdoms (three finds only having occurred in the district of Madura and none at all in the district of Coimbatore) points to a partial cessation in demand for luxuries paid for by coin and a new impulse of trade towards the acquisition of raw necessaries such as cotton goods paid for by barter, and that the whole development indicates a decline of trade helped by the disastrous fire of A.D. 64, by the extinction of the

Claudian line of emperors, by the frugal example of Vespasian, by the cruelty of Domitian, and by the moderation shewn by succeeding emperors in their expenditures (53). I have shewn that any examination made of the literature of the later part of the first century and of the second century reveals that there was no decrease in Rome's trade with India but rather a still further increase, at least in the wide sphere covered by Roman traders in Indian seas and on overland routes. Sewell actually says that the trade in spices, perfumes, and stones almost ceased with Nero's death—a statement which, as we have seen, is in reality quite contrary to the truth. Chwostow also differs from Sewell's conclusion, and, having pointed out the fact that not only the higher classes but the population of the whole Empire were consumers of Indian products, dissents from a view which attributes a change affecting a large section of the known world to changes which took place in the way of living of a court aristocracy. He thinks that down to the time of Nero, when Rome's sea-trade was developing, the attention of merchants was drawn to the more costly wares, and that if there was to be a profitable trade in the cheaper goods such as cotton fabrics, it was necessary for the population to get used to such goods first and demand for them to grow, and that relations with India should become regular, safer, and thus cheaper—developments which could only come in course of time, and which, as we have seen, did so. Chwostow attributes the abundance of coins of Augustus and Tiberius and their successors, as far as the epoch of Vespasian, to a natural trust placed by the uncultured Indian in the good Roman coinage of that age, and that emperors from Nero onwards struck coins similar to those of earlier emperors which were accepted by the Indians who at the same time got rid of such as were felt to be unsatisfactory (54).

But these explanations take no real account of the double development which the finds of coins dating after Nero's time indicate, so far as I can judge. Coins shew firstly a development of commerce up the east side of the Indian peninsula after the time of Nero, and after the *Periplus* was written; thus near Nellore at the northern extremity of the old Chola Kingdom a number of gold coins of the reigns of Trajan and Hadrian have been found, and farther north beyond the limits of the Tamils a find of gold coins was made at Fort Vinukonda in the Kistna district, that is the district of Maesolia, well up the east coast of India; it consisted of 18 coins struck by emperors from Vespasian to Caracalla (and especially Hadrian and Pius) together with two struck in the time of Tiberius (see finds (*e*) and (*f*) of gold). Far from indicating a decline of Rome's trade with India, these finds shew an advance made in frequency and scope of voyages made round Cape Comorin and up the east coast of India by Roman merchants the results of which are revealed by the geography of Ptolemy; about the time of Hadrian, too, we may suspect that men like Alexander were making their voyages to the Ganges and to regions beyond India—men upon whom Ptolemy relied so much in his work. Moreover the Romans found their way to the inland districts of the Tamil and of other kingdoms during the second century—another fact revealed by Ptolemy's geographical details, as we have seen, and perhaps reflected in the find of a gold coin of Trajan at Athiral in the district of Cuddapah, north Chola Kingdom, and in the find made in Fort Vinukonda.

Secondly, gold coins in northern districts of the Indian peninsula reached from the west coast have a somewhat different significance. It appears to me that one reason why Roman silver coins are absent N.W. of the Cheras is that Sakas coined silver, and Andhras also helped their own issues of lead and copper by issues of silver, importation of which was thus found by the Romans to be at last unnecessary; what they did bring and exchanged was perhaps melted down and then reissued by Andhras and Sakas who coined no gold. Now at Darphal near Sholapur was found a quantity of gold coins of which the surviving number represent emperors from Antoninus Pius to Geta; at Nagdhara in the district of Surat a coin of Lucius Verus turned up, and in the region of Khandeish one of Septimius Severus. Chwostow suggests naturally that these coins penetrated into India through Barygaza, and I agree with the exception of the find made at Darphal; the coins discovered here found entry, I think, at the modern Chaul, the ancient Simylla, which while not of much importance when the *Periplus* was written, appears as a flourishing mart in the geography of Ptolemy frequented by resident Roman traders, and we may go so far as to conjecture that just as the agate trade perhaps caused the rise of Barygaza, so the cotton trade caused the rise of Simylla from Vespasian's reign onwards. Gold therefore was often brought to districts of Saka and Andhra kings from Claudius onwards (55).

But what is the significance of this apparent increase of trade up the west coast of India? Had it commenced already when the *Periplus* was written? It is noticeable that the only place where the author specifies by metal the coinage imported is Barygaza, and yet the coins that have turned up in this district (in a wide sense) reach a very small number, and unless we can explain this dearth by melting down on the part of the Sakas and of the Andhras of the district, or by a possible recall of the silver currency in India (except in the Tamil districts where trade was so great), by the Roman government for reissue in a more debased form—as happened at the end of the reign of Aurelius—we have here a circumstance which warns us that all evidence based on the discoveries of coins rests upon unstable foundations. But I think that a definite conclusion can be reached in general terms. In this case also no decline of trade took place. The author of the *Periplus* shews that in his time trade with Barygaza was almost equal in importance to the trade with each Tamil State, and the absence of coins of the earlier emperors in the more northern region (see p. 393) I attribute to melting down and reissuing of Roman silver by Andhras and Sakas, notably Nahapana, as his coins suggest. This and cessation of coins in the Tamil States seem to reflect a tendency which we may trace or deduce from other material. In the latter half of the first century and the second century there was an undiminished demand for spices, perfumes, precious stones, and so on among the Romans, and perhaps an increase in the demand for cotton, but there seems to have been a tendency to shift some of the trade from the Tamil Kingdoms to north-western districts of India, causing the rise of such towns as Simylla, as Ptolemy shews, while at the same time *exchange* of Indian and Roman wares in Tamil-land continued unabated and voyages of Romans beyond the Tamils to the East increased largely; but the Tamils themselves started to send their wares so far as possible up the western coast of India in order to find a more crowded market of Greeks, Syrians, Arabians, Persians, Sakas, Andhras, Kushans. Ceylon, too, adopted the same methods and was seldom visited by "Roman" subjects. The Chera Kingdom was more fertile, more peaceful, more easily reached by western merchants than were other Tamils, and places like Barbaricon, Barygaza, were more easily reached by Persians, Arabians, Syrians, Palmyrenes, Kushans, and so on, than were any of the Tamil Kingdoms. The *Periplus* shews clearly that the pearls of the more southern Tamil States and tortoiseshell from various sources were brought to the Malabar marts in order to find a market, that the iron and steel of India (chiefly the central district, not the Sind town, of Haiderabad) was exported solely from North-west India, that the products of Ceylon (and especially the sapphires of Ceylon, Burma, and Siam) were brought to the marts of Malabar which were in constant connexion with the marts on the eastern coast of India. And gradually more trade shifted definitely to the north-western districts of India which were so conveniently reached from all directions. For Barygaza communicated with the interior of Central and of North India to the Himalayas and the Ganges; the Indus was connected with Central Asia and with the great overland routes through Parthia and was the natural centre of commerce for the Kushan monarchs with their gold currency; by sea too the north-west of India could be reached by the simplest use of the monsoons; the journey to the Persian Gulf and the Syrian and even many Arabian towns was not a very long one; all those who still preferred a coasting voyage to India naturally reached the north-west first. The tendency of Indian trade to shift northwards was probably assisted by Trajan's visit to the Persian Gulf and his regulation of the trade in those regions followed by Hadrian's policy of peace and by the rise of Palmyra in constant communication with the Persian Gulf. The rise of Palmyra seems to have given a fresh impetus to inland traffic through Parthia, and the Romans themselves sought to improve the northern route from India by taking action in the regions of the Caucasus and of the Euxine, while the unification of the dominions of the Yue(h)-chi under Kadphises II and Kanishka helped to draw trade northwards. All these tendencies would react on Indian trade and draw it to the north-west of the country. One general result seems to me to consist in the detailed account given by Ptolemy of North-west and North India, perhaps the regions of the Ganges, and certainly the regions of the Indus, even to distances far inland, while the good knowledge which he reveals of the inland districts of the Tamil Kingdoms and his altogether peculiar knowledge of Ceylon shew how active was the traffic still conducted by Roman subjects with South India, but now chiefly by barter.

The general conclusions are therefore that from the time of Augustus to the death of Nero there was an exportation of gold and silver coin of the Roman Empire, and generally of good standard, to the marts of the west coast of India and round Cape Comorin as far as Pudukottai in order to pay for many Indian wares in exchange for which imperial exports were not forthcoming; that to the Tamil States in particular specie was brought in quantities in order also to produce a Roman currency in those regions, employed by Indians and by visiting and resident Roman subjects; that the same system was increased in Nero's reign so as to include Barygaza and so on; that the Tamils used the coins but Andhras and Sakas melted down the Roman silver and reissued it as Indian coins; that at first the Romans sent out under Augustus and Tiberius very fine pure gold and silver coins but at the same time tried the effect of bad coins, for instance the plated examples of Gaius and Lucius (56), upon uncultured minds, and that after a little, perhaps under Caligula and Claudius (whose coins as found in India are not numerous) and especially as the use of the monsoons developed, the Romans, moved by the admiration of the Indians (for example of the Raja of Ceylon in Pliny) for the better coins of constant weight, sent out silver and gold of the very best standard and with the stamps of Augustus' and Tiberius' reigns, or struck a new issue of coins of similar weight and stamp (in order to please the Indians who had learnt to admire them (57)), ceasing to include bad coins. The same system was continued under Nero (of whose coins not very many have been found in India) though the silver denarius was being depreciated. We may conclude farther that either the merchants on their own initiative, or else the economical Vespasian, who had to meet a huge state deficit, discouraged and checked the exportation of gold and silver except so much as was necessary to maintain an efficient and sufficient commerce, and directed that merchants should, in large dealings, continue to pay the Indians in gold (see p. 393), which was still pure and plentiful, and in imperial products by barter, and not as a rule in silver, of which supplies were running short, which was debased and so distrusted by the Indians; and that the exports from the Empire to India increased greatly in quantity, and that new ones were added or increased so that Firmus in the third century traffics in Egyptian papyrus and glue (58) and the Axumites in the sixth century take Egyptian emeralds to India (59)—such articles not being given as exports thither even by the *Periplus*. Evidently the Greek merchants of Egypt, where the emperor almost monopolised the economic system, faithfully carried out the new policy during the second century, and pushed up the east coast of India, as Ptolemy shews and states, and traded frequently though not regularly as far as the district of Kistna but beyond that to a much less extent, paying gold and imperial exports wherever possible, the importations of coin of previous reigns remaining in circulation in the Tamil Kingdoms (which made the change easier to bring about) but being recalled perhaps at the end of Aurelius' reign (60) from Sakas and Andhras or melted down by them. Thus the return to natural economy which developed when Rome declined had its beginning quite early in the Indian trade— even when the *Periplus* was written Egyptians were exporting to the Chola Kingdom native wares on a larger scale than elsewhere, but not money (61).

The evidence of coins appears to me to shew that from Vespasian onwards the important change was not, as Sewell holds, so much a shifting of trade to cotton-growing districts and a cessation of traffic in luxuries, as an expansion and a more equal spreading of trade both with the western and eastern coasts of India by barter, the undue exportation of gold and silver to Barygaza during Nero's reign being promptly checked, and payment by gold only (together with imperial products) being adopted in return for the products obtained, while Sakas reissued the earlier silver. That is why the coins (which are of gold, not silver) in the more northern districts are so very few compared with the very large numbers of earlier reigns found in the southern states, where the earlier importations remained in circulation, and where the finds almost stop through substitution of a large system of barter. The development of barter and the cessation of unwise exportation of silver, and even gold, to the East from Vespasian's time onwards seem to me to be established facts. Complaints about the eastward drain of the Empire's wealth cease after Vespasian's time, and in the second century Pausanias implies the development of barter when he says the Indians give their own wares in exchange for those of the Greeks without understanding the use of money, though they have gold and bronze (presumably Roman imported and native Indian money respectively) in abundance (62), and Philostratos also speaks particularly of special Egyptian ships for Indian barter-trade (63). In the period of decline Rome ceased to trade direct with India, with few exceptions, and we find that the wealth of Firmus was due apparently to his Indian, or at least African, trade in Egyptian products. It was the "Indians" who brought him riches, not the Romans, who in times gone by would have done so by demanding Indian products at high prices. The Roman coins of the latter part of the third century and of the Byzantine era found in India were probably brought by the middlemen—Abyssinians, Arabians, and Persians(64), and the alleged admiration of Byzantine coinage by Ceylon in the sixth century (65) must be taken not as a fact, but as a mournful reflection upon what really happened in days gone by.

In the first two centuries the principle of the Romans was to send out to India not the local coinage of Egypt, but official coinage of Rome—the aureus and the denarius. In Egypt, where the denarius was not current but passed through to the East, Roman gold, too, being uncommon, local needs were met by a special Alexandrian currency, of which we have to deal with silver only. This was founded on the debased silver tetradrachms of the later Ptolemies, and, established by Tiberius still in a debased form but equated with the Roman denarius, continued until A.D. 296(66). As a rule these tetradrachms, debased from the start, were not taken to India, though they drifted thither in some numbers, but I believe the Indian trade affected the Alexandrian currency in Egypt. Thus the first real burst of activity in the issue of the new silver tetradrachms occurred in the second year of Claudius, and this, I take it, was due to the voyage of Plocamus' freedman, and perhaps progress in using the monsoon winds, and this activity culminated in the twelfth year of Nero's reign, at a time when he consumed a huge quantity of oriental spices. In that year so many tetradrachms were issued that they formed about one-tenth of the silver currency for more than a century(67), and the currency was stabilised. With few exceptions the output was regular until A.D. 170, and the bronze currency, related to the silver, reached its highest importance in the time of Trajan. After Marcus Aurelius the tetradrachm depreciated more and was abolished by Diocletian. With the depreciation, too, of the Roman denarius, coins of local mints of the Empire were brought to India, and also Ceylon, more than before.

These conclusions are suggestions only, which I make with the knowledge that I may have over-estimated the force of the evidence. Turning to the commercial relations of Rome with the most northern regions of India, as revealed by numismatic evidence, we find that here, curiously enough, the initiative was taken by the eastern power, though in imitation of western example. The regions which include the valley of Kabul with the districts north-west of Peshawar, the Indus, and Punjab were for a long time ruled by Greek princes, either independent or subject to the over-lordship of Parthia, and we have seen how this system was broken up by the invasion of the Yue-chi after the Roman Empire began. After A.D. 25 the Kushans, one of the five Yue-chi tribes, gained supremacy over the rest, according to Chinese records, and created a united power, which, before A.D. 50, spread from Bactria, and under Kujula Kadphises mastered the land south of the Hindu Kush, that is, part of Afghanistan and Kabul with Kandahar, thus controlling the gates of India. The last Greek prince succumbed and over this united empire Kadphises I (Kujula Kadphises) began to rule, perhaps in A.D. 50(68). The bronze or copper coins of this Kadphises were struck at first in his own name and that of the Greek prince (Hermaeos); then in his own name only. The next development is a curious one, the bust of the Greek prince being replaced by an effigy which has caused considerable discussion. V. A. Smith is quite certain that there is a likeness to the head of Augustus and no other, and he denies that the alleged resemblance to a Roman is either fanciful or accidental; others see in the stamp a resemblance to Gaius and Lucius, grandsons of Augustus. Professor Rapson was once sure that the resemblance is to Augustus, but he tells me that he is now not so certain. Now it must be admitted that most of the coins of the first Kadphises, which were struck chiefly in the Kabul valley, are utterly un-Roman in look, and those which appear to resemble the Roman are very rare and belong to one mint only in a place perhaps exposed to Roman influence; but a personal inspection of coin No. 28 in case No. 59 (Ancient and Mediaeval India) in the British Museum, a coin of "Kozola Kadaphes," convinces me that it is stamped with a likeness of Augustus in the usual profile. It is noteworthy too that an embassy from North India had reached Augustus not very long before Kadphises began to rule, and that the controversy about the coins centres round supposed imitations of coins of which large numbers have turned up in South India (Augustus, Gaius and Lucius, Tiberius). The alleged resemblances are carried even farther than this, for some authorities think that many of the coins found at Jogaltembhi in the Nasik district and issued by Nahapana, who was apparently a Saka viceroy of Kushans and naturally coined according to the stamp of his superior, have on their obverse imitations of the heads on Roman coins struck between 30 B.C. and A.D. 150, and in support of this we have the importation of Roman money into Barygaza, a port controlled by "Nambanos." It has even been suggested tentatively that the modifications in the heads on Kushan coins and those in busts of the earlier emperors are similar. Again, upon the coins of Kharamosta (c. A.D. 15–30) and later upon some of this western Kshatrapa Nahapana appears a single trace of the Roman alphabet intermingled with the Greek. At any rate the Yue-chi by their unifying conquests helped to open up commerce by land between the Roman Empire and India, for this commerce had been accidental hitherto, the Parthians not having been able to control the traffic so far east. Kujula's successor, Kadphises II, who ruled from before 64 until 78, initiated and carried out Indian conquests, which reached as far as Benares and Ghazipur on the river Ganges before 78, and although driving south of the Indo-Parthian Sakas is revealed in the reference by the *Periplus* to warlike kings of the Indus delta and the warlike Bactrians inland (69), the creation of a stable power in the Indus valley and Afghanistan encouraged a regular trade from the Ganges to the Euphrates by land, and from the Ganges to the Persian Gulf by way of the mouths of the Indus. Greek or Syrian merchants, we may suppose, who had penetrated to the Kabul valley, had suggested to Kadphises I the idea of imitating in some way the Roman coinage; but this had only taken place in bronze or copper of little commercial significance. It was Kadphises II who grasped, either on his own initiative or by Roman persuasion, what was really required. There was already a large importation of Roman gold and silver coin into the marts of India, and Kadphises II, seeing the advantage of a gold currency, struck a plentiful issue of what we may call oriental aurei, for they agree in weight with the Roman aurei, and are but little inferior in purity; and, moreover, the one known silver coin struck by Kadphises II corresponds with one weight of the Roman denarius (70). These provide striking evidence of the new developments in Indo-European commerce. However doubtful may be the head of a Roman emperor on some of these Kushan coins, the correspondence in weight between Kushan and Roman coins of the same metal and purity leaves no doubt, as equality in weight is a very fair test of a lively commerce, and in this respect at least the two coinages were alike, all other likenesses or differences being unimportant. Influenced therefore by Rome, Kadphises struck a gold coinage, perhaps in special connexion with the silk traffic directed to the Indus, but whence did he obtain his gold? Not from the Roman Empire; India, and especially the Ganges, and even the Indus may have yielded it, but it is probable that he got most of it from the near East through the rulers of Mesene and Characene by way of the Persian Gulf, through which there is no doubt the Kushans naturally conducted most of their sea-trade with the West(71). In the time of the *Periplus* the Arabians were exporting from Apologos and Ommana to Barygaza gold as bullion, and it is natural to suppose that Kadphises soon had it sent by them to the mouths of the Indus as well(72). Thus the fame and purity of the Roman coinage had more effect among the northern potentates than had been the case with the Raja of Ceylon in the time of Claudius, and Indian gold coinage of Roman weight continued, it seems, in the Kabul valley and Punjab until about the year 425. Kanishka, the successor of Kadphises II in 78, shews little Roman influence in his currency outside the all-important correspondence in weight, but he adopted the title "Caesar" and apparently the Roman system of hours. The next Kushan ruler, by name Huvishka, struck coins stamped with the inscription RIOM, and perhaps with Rome personified as a goddess Roma; he introduced the Alexandrian Serapis (as Sarapo) on some of his coins, a change due to the constant traffic with India conducted by Alexandrian merchants during the second century A.C., and reflected in the detailed knowledge shewn by Ptolemy, especially of regions which were under Kushan control(73).

What was the Roman attitude towards their trade with the regions conquered by the Kushans during the first century? The Ptolemies had coasted from the Red Sea to India, and this system continued at the beginning of the Roman Empire, so that the regions of the Indus were the first to be visited; it is not surprising, therefore, that in most northern districts of India Roman coins have been

found of earlier date than any in South India. In the
district of Kohat have been found about 70 Roman coins,
most of them being late Republican, and all of silver,
except five of copper. In 1830 seven silver coins of consular
families (chiefly 43 B.C.) were found in the Manikyala tope (74),
and in 1898 or 1899 a large find was made in the Hazara
district of the Punjab, and of this hoard twenty-three
silver coins survive, including one each of Caesar, Antony,
and Brutus, twelve of Augustus, two of Tiberius, and one
of Hadrian. Again, in the Ahin Posh tope at Jellalabad,
in the Kabul valley, where Roman influence in architecture
has been traced, were discovered one gold coin each of
Domitian, Trajan, and Sabina, together with seventeen of
Kadphises II, Kanishka, and Huvishka. A few copper coins
of emperors were also found somewhere in North India.
These are the only records for the early emperors, unless
we include the single silver coins of Augustus, Germanicus,
Tiberius, and Vespasian, lying in the Calcutta Museum in
1832. But trade continued with the north of India through
the centuries, the chief records being single copper coins of
Gordian, Gallienus, Salonina, Postumus, Victorinus, Claudius Gothicus, Tacitus, Probus, Maximian, Constantine,
and Theodosius I, found somewhere in North India; gold
coins of Theodosius II, Marcian, and Leo I, found at Hidda
near Jellalabad; and a large number of gold coins of Gordian,
Constantine, and others found at Bamanghati in South-east
Bengal, on the main road due west from Tamluk on the
Hughli. Other finds are doubtful and of little value (75).

Thus the discoveries do not compare for a moment with
those made in South India, and I am convinced that the
Romans never imported their coinage into North-west India
on any large scale, and the *Periplus* does not include money
among the imports to Barbaricon on the Indus. Nevertheless, a good deal seems to have been brought (if we may

so judge from the finds) until Kadphises II struck his gold (and perhaps silver) currency in imitation of the Roman, and the close relations favoured by Trajan perhaps fostered large trading by gold coin for some time. The presence of imperial copper coins possibly points to residence of Roman subjects, a fact proved, I think, from Ptolemy's geography. We may take it, then, that trade by means of money, besides barter, was opened up at the end of the Republic, and increased after an embassy sent to Augustus until the Kushans saw that the Roman currency might well be imitated; the Romans then ceased to import specie so much as they did before, since it was no longer required. The partial cessation of exportations of silver into the Tamil Kingdoms after Nero's reign was adopted as a wise piece of caution, the quantity already sent remaining in circulation and filling the gap caused by the omission of the Tamils to imitate the Roman currency. Vespasian, perhaps, checked the importation of specie into the north of India also; the system had not been adopted on such a scale as in the case of the Tamils, but here Kadphises II stepped in and created a half-Roman currency of his own, which must have attracted Greeks and Syrians in large numbers, and relations with the West were established on a sound economic basis. A coin of the Graeco-Bactrian king Menander was discovered, together with one of Vespasian, at Tenby in Pembrokeshire, where there was, it seems, a Roman trading station. The Indian coin must have been a curiosity in the possession of a "Roman" trader. Now the author of the *Periplus* found coins of Apollodotos and Menander still current in his day at Barygaza, whence this stray coin may have been brought by a Roman subject. The temptation is obvious to conclude that we have here a relic of a Greek who in the course of his life had been both to India and to Britain in the pursuit of trade. After all, the coin would not be current legally in the Roman Empire, and was perhaps lost by its original possessor. But other North Indian coins and imitations of them have been found in Scandinavia (76), and the one found in Pembrokeshire may be, like these, a relic of the oriental trade of the Oxus-Caspian route.

Rome's trade with North-west India was therefore peculiar; there Orientals melted down and reissued the Roman coinage, besides striking from their own imported bullion, so that the Roman merchants tended to receive some of their money-wealth back again (77). A general discussion on the economic aspects of Rome's relations with India from the point of view of exchange by means of money will be given later, for the first thing to be considered is how far the trade which we have described helped Roman industries; how far it was conducted by private activity; and how far it was assisted by the use of capital. After that is done we shall be able to estimate whether this oriental commerce as a whole was detrimental to the Roman Empire from an economic point of view.

To a certain extent we can trace with success the progress of Indian wares from the time they reached the Roman Empire to their reception by the consumer. The staple article of trade with India varied along different trade-routes: it was always some article of luxury, the price of which, when it reached its destination, heightened by the cost of transport and of customs and other dues, and by the profit expected by the merchant, was yet no bar to a persistent demand. Thus on the sea-route to the Malabar coast by way of the Red Sea the staple article was pepper and other eastern spices; on the overland route to China it was silks.

Alexandria possessed, for storing eastern goods, most carefully protected warehouses (78), but storage in these was only

for short periods, for the bulk of oriental cargoes of the Red
Sea was directed ultimately towards Italy, with its two main
ports, Ostia and Puteoli. In spite of the dangers of the Tiber
and the scarcity of return cargoes obtainable at Rome, a
good deal of merchandise was sent to Ostia, especially
after the improvements made by Claudius and by Trajan,
and was stored in the large public warehouses (*horrea*) at
Ostia, or those in the "emporium" of the Tiber, and in many
places in Rome itself (79). The most important of these warehouses were the ἀποθῆκαι τῶν τε Αἰγυπτίων καὶ τῶν Ἀραβίων
φορτίων situated near the Temple of Peace, and including
after A.D. 92 special spice warehouses (*horrea piperataria*)
adjacent to the Sacra Via (80). The position of these shews
perhaps that they received most of their stores not from
Ostia, but from Puteoli, where in a safe harbour merchants,
with reasonable hopes of return cargoes, landed their wares
for manufacture in Campanian towns, or for land transport
to Rome, where the business centre was the Forum. From
the warehouses goods were transferred to the shops for
retail trade, particular trades tending to be concentrated
in their own quarters. Thus the chief centre for the sale of
precious articles in hard materials produced largely by the
"fabri" was the Saepta in the Campus Martius with its fine
shops; here were sold ivory, tortoiseshell couches, crystal
and agate vessels, pearls, and precious stones—all Indian
wares (81), while close by was the Porticus Argonautarum
(or Agrippae) where crystal and agate vessels and diamonds were sold (82). Pearls were also sold in the Forum,
where there were officinae margaritariorum, and on the Sacra
Via, the centre of the gem-cutting and jewellery trade.
There were a porticus margaritaria, guilds of margaritarii,
dealers in pearls (who existed everywhere), and pearl
drillers (diatretarii) (83). The dealers in precious stones were
generally also the artizans who cut and set them; in Rome

they worked in shops on the Via Sacra (84), but the bulk of the stones were worked into jewellery in Syria and Alexandria, which also produced articles of ivory and ebony, and reaped thereby perhaps as much wealth as it did from its transit-trade, and we may say that Indian trade helped inter-provincial commerce, which was the chief source of the wealth of provincial towns. Much Indian produce was worked up by the workers in ivory, wood and tortoise-shell, and in spite of the general scantiness of household furniture in ancient times, there was perhaps even factory work in Campania, near Puteoli (85). Perhaps, too, Delos, Miletos, Chios, Corinth, and Carthage were still famed for their fine tortoiseshell veneered ivory bedsteads (86). Indian iron, not worked up in India or Damascus, was probably dealt with at Puteoli, Cales, and Minturnae (87). Vessels of agate were made in India, Parthia, and Alexandria; crystal vessels in India and Alexandria, and perhaps Syria. At Rome the agate and crystal vessels were sold in the Saepta, the Porticus Argonautarum, and the Via Sacra (88). Indian animals found accommodation in cages on the wharves near the Campus Martius (89), while the pet parrots would be sold by the bird-dealers in the quarter of the Vicus Tuscus.

As we have seen, the plant traffic, particularly in Indian products, was of great importance, and the manufacture was carried on most extensively in regions towards which flowed Indian trade. Thus the unguents of Arabia and Parthia were well known, and in the Roman Empire three regions were famous: (a) Egypt, a most suitable region for unguents, says Pliny, where the Roman emperors possessed state manufactories and shops (a legacy from the mono-polies of the Ptolemies) (90), often let and sublet; that is why the aromatics and spices are so carefully given in the Digest-list, and it was easy for voluptuaries like Gaius, Nero, Commodus, and Elagabalus to indulge their tastes in aromatics. The importations were carried out by private individuals, and when consignments were not destined for state manufactories in Egypt, they paid transit-dues, as a papyrus shews(91). (b) Syria, always famous for unguents, and various districts of Asia Minor, were well placed for the reception of raw material; Lycia was well known for its preparation of raisin-barberry and Laodicea, Tarsos and Commagene were famous for nard oil, and some towns in Greece itself were not unimportant. (c) But the chief consumers were the rich women of Rome(92), so that with Puteoli as the port, Capua, Cumae, and Naples formed a western centre of manufacture in Italy, while the construction by Domitian in 95 of a shorter road between Puteoli and Rome by way of Cumae instead of Capua, and the building of spice warehouses at Rome in 92, point to the spread of unguent-manufacture to Rome itself, where Galen says nard essences were prepared. Men like Cosmus and Niceros flourished from Nero's reign onwards, but especially under Domitian, and the whole tendency appears as a result of the monsoons, bringing a slight decline in the previous importance of Ephesos, Syria, and Pergamos(93). From the horrea piperataria the stuff reached the drug and ointment sellers, the herbalists, and the medici, and in Rome, as in the provinces, the unguents were sold in a special street (Vicus Unguentarius—Galen's Street) with various aromatics and spices, and in the Via Sacra(94). The Vicus Tuscus was another centre of sale, ultimately named Vicus Turarius(95). The lists in Dioscurides and Pliny, the numerous references to unguent-makers, shops, ointment boxes, guilds of aromatarii, turarii, unguentarii, and to private caretakers of the ointment cupboard, shew the great importance of this traffic. Many ointment sellers, whether at Capua or not, were called Seplasiarii, from the "Seplasia" —the unguent centre in Capua(96).

Indian cotton and Chinese silk, when raw and unspun, were worked up (by vestifici(-ae), or vestitores) and perhaps dyed chiefly in Alexandria, Galilee, and Syria, or in private homes. The dealers were vestiarii, and both in Rome and in the provinces clothing was sold in a special forum, or in shops connected with private horrea. Much fine stuff was worked up by the tenuiarii (97). Sometimes perhaps pure silk fabrics from China were undone in the centres of silk industry and the thread rewoven with cotton or wool (98). Sometimes, too, linen fabrics were coated or covered with silk. Syrians, Jews, and Greeks of both sexes were active in the silk trade in Syria, Italy and Rome, and, as we have seen, this traffic brought much Indian produce along with it. The centre of sale of silk in Rome was the Vicus Tuscus, and the imperial families and the richer classes generally possessed special silk wardrobes (99).

The high price demanded for Indian and Chinese luxuries brought wealth inevitably to those who employed their resources of capital in their own oriental trading or in helping others; and the Indian trade helped to produce hereditary merchants like Maes. The emperors, too, and the Roman state received large profits from the trade; thus the frontier and other dues paid in the spheres formed by the eastern frontiers of the Empire, by the fiscal unit of Bithynia, Paphlagonia, and Pontus, by the fiscal unit of Asia ($2\frac{1}{2}$ °/。 for both these), and by Italy, must have been lucrative, but less so than the levies made in Egypt, which included transit-dues, carriage-dues (100), and levies in kind on production and sale, besides the all-important Red Sea dues. In a passage in Statius (101) describing the duties of the emperor's "a rationibus," we find that with the products of Spain and other regions are mentioned the products of Egypt, and also oriental pearls and Indian ivory. Statius gives us no more than a poetic outline, so that we can con-

clude that the "a rationibus" had to look after much revenue
derived from Indian merchandise coming into the Roman
Empire, and Nero's scheme of abolition in A.D. 58 would
have had an immeasurable effect on the economy of the
Empire(102). The most important part of the revenue derived by the Empire from import and export dues was
naturally the Red Sea due(103) (*vectigal Maris Rubri*), levied
upon all Arabian, African, Indian, and other wares when
they entered Egyptian territory. The collection of it was
let to farmers during the first century A.C. as the account
of Annius Plocamus and his freedman shews(104) and its
importance is illustrated by the Digest-list of oriental
merchandise liable to the due; the list as we have it was
drawn up in the time of Marcus Aurelius and formed
a basis for subsequent ages and was not obsolete even
under the Byzantine Empire, but I believe it goes back
farther than the Antonines, and the "first edition," so to
speak, was, I think, issued by Nero; it was during his reign
that the effects of Hippalos' discovery developed trade
with the Indian Ocean on a great scale, so that disputes
between merchants and collectors (indicated and provided for in the Digest passage) became very frequent;
it was Nero, too, who first published tariff-lists with reference
to such disputes(105). We do not know the amount of the
due in the case of Egypt, but we can form some idea of
the localities where it was levied. There are some(106) who
think that Roman influence spread so far as to include
the island of Socotra within the sphere of Roman customs-
levies and to maintain a garrison on the Syagros promontory—in other words, that the Romans levied dues outside
the Strait of Bab-el-Mandeb. Rostowzew thinks that the
due was levied at the Strait itself; there are others who
hold that the Romans controlled all the dues of the Red
Sea (that is to say, of both coasts)(107). The first view is

an untenable extreme; Rostowzew's opinion lacks confirmation—surely if he were right the author of the *Periplus* and even Pliny would make some mention of a great customs-station at the Strait. As for the third, Muza, on the Arabian coast of the Red Sea, is manifestly an Arabian port where Arabian dues were levied; and Ocelis, at the mouth, is a watering-station, not a customs-station, subject to an Arabian chief.

I think that the Romans confined their financial activities to the Egyptian side of the Red Sea and levied the Red Sea due at Myos Hormos and Berenice, which the *Periplus* calls official ports (that is ports where trade was officially allowed and customs were levied), through the agency of an official (not a tax-farmer) resident in S. Thebais, as had been the case under Ptolemaic rule[108]. He would control the exactions of the farmers made at the ports. I am not sure about Adulis, another legal mart; it appears to have belonged to the Axumites in Nero's time, and yet an inscription of Augustan time shews that the receiver of Red Sea dues was then resident at Ombos or Elephantine which perhaps means that goods of a certain type (other than inner African goods) coming from the Indian Ocean and the East African ports, including perhaps even Adulis, overland to the Nile and the southern frontiers of Egypt, were regarded as "Red Sea" products and paid due at Syene[109]; the freedman of Annius Plocamus, who was sailing round Arabia, was perhaps investigating the uncertain status of African ports of the Somali, or doing official business with Arabians in connexion with differential dues levied at Egyptian ports. Likewise there must have been a Red Sea customs-station at Arsinoë, which does not appear in the *Periplus*, the author of which never visited it; perhaps, too, it was not important until fresh developments took place under Trajan. It is possible, too, that the

Romans levied differential customs-dues at Egyptian ports against non-Roman vessels, but I do not think that they controlled entirely the activities of the Arabians on the eastern side of the Red Sea. There is evidence to shew that for protective purposes (not for purposes of revenue) a due of 25 °/₀ or thereabouts was levied in Egypt, and this fact, together with the presence of a "centurion," has been held to prove that the 25 °/₀ due levied at Leuce Come was a Roman one. I think that it was a protective due levied by the orders of the Romans for the Nabataean treasury to induce ships to go to the cheaper Egyptian ports—with the result that, as the *Periplus* shews, only small Arabian vessels used Leuce Come (110).

Turning to India, we find that the kings controlled the shipping, maintained special service at estuaries, fixed official marts where export and import dues were levied, issued the coinage and possessed storehouses of their own. In the earlier Maurya empire were levied frontier dues (20 °/₀ of value), road-taxes, and "octroi" tolls at city-gates, and merchants had to shew passports and render full information about themselves and their goods, commerce being controlled by special boards (111). Early Buddhist literature reveals the hereditary nature of commerce, industry, and leadership of caravans, while all kinds of guide work, land and sea trading, and ivory-working, weaving, jewel-making, pottery, and garland-making were counted honourable, unlike hunting, trapping, and snake-charming. Much of the produce destined for Rome was dealt with by craft-villages of wood-wrights, ironsmiths, potters, and trappers who supplied game, skins, ivory, and so on. In the towns too there was localisation of industries, for instance of ivory-working, dyeing, weaving, and so on, and the wares were sold in bazaars. But the extensive Roman trade of the Tamils required market-places, and Tamil poems give us glimpses of the pepper trade of Muziris, the commercial quarters of Madura, and the river-trade, market, warehouses, traders and trading streets and arrangements of Kaviripaddinam (112). The details shew a brisk commerce in luxuries but no extensive production by large industries, and the chief traders are the Yavana—the Roman Greeks.

Turning back once more to the point of view of the western merchants in the Indian Ocean, we find that the Roman government undertook to protect trade-routes within the borders of the Empire and to conduct when occasion offered diplomatic relations with the oriental peoples, but no more. Under the early Ptolemies large commercial enterprises had been conducted officially by the state, but under the later Lagid rulers the traffic became a matter of private enterprise, and this system was perpetuated by the imperial government of Rome (113). The traders whom Pliny, Ptolemy, the author of the *Periplus* (himself a trader working with his own capital?) and others describe as trading in the Indian Ocean are private individuals; so also was the Egyptian of Arsinoë registered in 72–3 as absent in India; the Syrian merchants who went to China in 166; the Arabian Scythianos who traded between Alexandria and India; Firmus whose activities were similar until he was put down by Aurelian ; and the Roman merchant Lun of whom Chinese records tell (114). Sometimes perhaps the state (that is the fiscus) had something to do with lending money and sending out merchants in connexion with state manufactories in Egypt, but on this point and in many aspects of the entirely independent trading we are at present uninformed. It is true that persons who traded with India on any large scale would have to possess (as Chwostow remarks, giving the instances of Scythianos and Firmus) (115) ample means for buying an out-going cargo, equipping and even building large ships, providing armed guards, and so on, and in many cases doubtless the man behind the Greek merchants was a stay-at-home Roman capitalist, often a member of the urban classes of imperial cities. Perhaps the Calpurnii of Puteoli who traded with Alexandria, Asia, and Syria were examples of those who helped oriental traders (116), but there is nothing to shew that Scythianos and Firmus did not obtain their wealth gradually as a result of unaided but steady trading upon small beginnings. The author of the *Periplus* seems to have been a man independent of state control and capitalistic help, such as it was in his day. The richer, of course, could employ agents, but others went from port to port in person.

The Indian trade, in spite of sums paid for obtaining and carrying the goods, brought a good profit, for Pliny says that Indian wares cost a hundred times more in Roman markets than they did in Indian markets, and Chinese records give the profit as tenfold or a hundredfold (117). Many people have thought this traffic was economically harmful to the Roman Empire in the long run. The Roman products failed to balance the Indian imports, and the exportation of money, discouraged even from Italy (118) in the first century B.C., was freely allowed to altogether foreign lands under Augustus and his successors. We must consider the use of wealth by the Romans and estimate whether the exportation of the money substance, silver, and of gold was detrimental to the Empire. It is a fact that as early as 62 the ruinous system of depreciation had begun; an alloy of from 5°/₀ to 20°/₀ added before the death of Nero increased to 30°/₀ under Trajan, 50°/₀ and more under Severus, until finally after 218 the denarius ceased to be a silver coin and there was a return to the system of payment in kind. The aureus too was depreciated (119), but gold, which plays a different part in economics from silver, did not become so scarce, though the aureus decreased in weight from $\frac{1}{40}$ lb. to $\frac{1}{72}$ lb. between Augustus and Constantine. Throughout monetary history there has been a struggle between the tendencies which produce deterioration and those which maintain a good currency, and when currency is purely metallic, debasement always threatens. A country needs for the good working of its industries enough money to keep its prices in due level with those of the countries with which it trades, otherwise a preponderance of its imports over its exports will necessitate a transfer of money to make a balance. To-day international trade tends to produce the necessary level by distributing money, with one striking exception—for to-day, just as in the first century, and in the Middle Ages, large quantities of precious money-metals move in a direction contrary to that of civilisation, and the chief manifestation of it is the "drain" to the East, a process we have seen in its birth, for the Roman silver exported from the Empire to the north and into Africa was little compared with the quantity sent to China(?), Arabia, and above all India, with no similar return. In the Middle Ages, too, the oriental luxuries were paid for by European silver, especially after the discovery of the Cape route, and during last century the amount increased farther (between 1851 and 1862, £110,000,000 value of metals went to India) followed by the addition of a drainage to India of gold bars and, until 1914, sovereigns. In 1905–6, out of £82,500,000 value of imports £14,000,000 consisted of the precious metals. For the silver currency there silver is purchased and converted into rupees (120).

The "drain" to the East has continued therefore for nearly 2000 years. In the Roman world Italy, not unproductive (though Rome and Latium are not mentioned by the *Periplus*), kept her balance through good investments of capital and provincial tribute and by the activities of

Campania, Etruria, and, in the north, Aquileia, but the Empire as a unit (for even the local currencies were really imperial) could only make her balance with foreign countries by exporting her precious metals, a process theoretically unsound, but did it cause harm?

Before the Roman Empire began, war rather than commerce distributed wealth gained by slave-labour, and through war Republican Rome became rich by the plunder of the East with its hoarded wealth and possession of the mines of Spain and other regions. Roman capitalists speculators and money-lenders came to regard money as the only riches and valuable only in exchange; hence the new wealth was spent not upon productive enterprises, but (and this was the weak point in the Roman economic scheme) in unproductive ways (121). Lucky trade-secrets and accidents alone caused large industries, except where a hard-working, free population (as in Syria and Egypt) built up some sort of factory-production (122). Indeed, industry can flourish only when wealth, spread through large masses of people as it is to-day, causes wide consumption of products, and in the ancient world where wealth was attracted rather to one pole, the demand was rather for luxuries for a few only, and this process did not help Roman industries (see p. 394), which were unable to compete with foreign luxuries brought from outside. Within the Empire industry was normally production by slaves or by despised artizans with their simple instruments in their small work-shops, with or without the aid of a richer man's capital (123). The household of slaves was generally a cheap device, patent-laws did not exist, and transport was slow. So the wealthy Roman either invested his capital in agriculture, land, and houses, or more often he lent it to some merchant in order to carry on commerce, which consisted consequently in a traffic in luxuries largely for the wealthy, with exceptions such as pepper which brought wealth because all demanded it. Exactly of this type was Rome's commerce with India—a traffic in luxuries conducted by travelling merchants using another's capital and then more and more their own, so that the "negotiator" was the "mercator"; the lucky ones looked forward to a comfortable old age in the knowledge that their families were well provided for —they looked back on their years of commerce—they did not die as owners of great industries built up for themselves. In other respects Roman commerce, conducted (in an age when the standard of life was not high) by the low-born to produce articles of ordinary luxury for the use of rich urban classes, did not produce a large commercial class (124), but I feel confident that the commerce with India as conducted after Hippalos' discovery was an exception from this rule. Anything may be called a luxury, and pepper at least became an article of general consumption, and large numbers of the imperial population, especially the female population, must have obtained the Indian aromatics without difficulty, at least in adulterated forms. Moreover, as Rostowzew well points out, wealth became more widely spread than before through the growth of urban classes in the cities of the Empire from Augustus onwards and especially during the second century (125) and industry was less despised.

In the Indian trade the Greeks were enterprising, the ships large, and the monsoons were as a mariner's compass for them, and although the quantity of precious metal sent in modern times is from twenty to thirty times as great as the figure given by Pliny, we must remember the difference in population tastes and purchasing-power of money. Imperial industries, especially industries of unguent-making and weaving and dyeing, were helped by the trade, especially when the oriental products were sent raw and could be worked up chiefly in the eastern provinces, which also prepared goods, such as glass and clothing, for exportation to the East. But we have shewn how insufficient the total amount of exportation was; it consisted so much of metal simply dug up; of wines carried as ballast; of articles of small trades, no effort being made (except in Egypt and Syria) to build up industries which would prosper upon export trade to India; typical of the mentality of the time was the enormous exportation of coral to India until the supplies ran short; typical, too, was the complete lack of capitalistic methods (126) in the case of the jewelry and gem trades, which remained small industries working to individual order. On the whole, then, a traffic which brought profit to individuals did not create large industries out of small trades, and the same held good among the Indians, who did not use much money of precious metals except where the Romans imported it or the Kushans held sway. Unproductive luxury in gold and silver plate, in villas, marbles, and so on stands upon a different footing as it did not draw wealth out of the Empire, but it is none the less typical of the day.

The very peace which Augustus brought to the Roman world put an end to acquisition of new wealth by war, and Italy ceased to be the centre of capitalisation. Unfortunately, the wealth of the Empire gained by tribute was dissipated in unproductive ways, though we must not forget that the pictures drawn by moralists give us only the abnormal side of imperial luxury, and when we consider the large state deficit faced by Vespasian we are inclined to ask whether the Empire was bankrupt when it began (127). We cannot tell, but it is a fact that in the third century the Empire declined and the economic system collapsed. Economic questions had not received much attention from the government. The process shewed itself in the exhaustion of the supplies of silver (obtained chiefly from Spain, the

Silesian mines not being known (128) until very much later),
and the causes of the economic collapse may be arranged
according to their importance thus:—

(i) Perhaps the root of all the trouble was the fact that
the great wealth of Rome had been the "spoils of war"
taken in a wide sense of the phrase (129), and this source
of revenue (if we except the mines and the money brought
in by peaceful and prosperous provinces) ceased when the
Empire brought peace without a sufficient substitute being
discovered (130).

(ii) The bulk of Roman money was used in unproductive
ways of all kinds, even in the matters of industry and commerce. The rich urban classes looked to their own interests
while the poor could not rise to a higher level.

(iii) The maintenance of a good supply of silver coinage
was impossible for the following reasons:—

(a) Under the Empire, mining was one of the departments
still let to farmers who worked them in a wasteful manner,
and their chief means of production were handicapped by
a reduction in the supply of slaves, and the decline in the
stores of money manifested itself from Augustus onwards.

(b) The total amount of silver (and, of course, gold) suffered from the wear and tear of general circulation, and
was much more liable to loss than when it was stored up
in temples and in the treasuries of oriental potentates.
There was not a sufficient amount of either metal in circulation during the Roman Empire.

(c) The drainage of precious metal (particularly silver)
to northern tribes (131), to East Africa, China? and Arabia,
but above all to India, was unwise, particularly in the
freedom with which it was allowed until Vespasian (perhaps,
or the merchants themselves) succeeded at least in confining
it within certain bounds.

(*d*) Moreover, in the middle of the third century, at the very time when these tendencies were producing most clearly visible effects, the barbarians dealt a worse blow by "drawing off the mining population and damaging" the mines themselves which thus fell into disuse. The development became worse from 406–7 onwards. Jacob has conjectured that from a possible highest accumulation in money of £358,000,000 at the death of Augustus in A.D. 14 the supply had dwindled to £33,000,000 (about one-eleventh of what it had been) by about A.D. 800 (132). From that period a new era in the history of gold and silver commenced, for the Moors re-opened the mines in Spain, and the mines of Austria, Saxony, and the Harz mountains soon came into use and were the chief sources of supply for the Middle Ages, and it may be said that only after 800 A.D. was the supply sufficient to make up for loss caused by abrasion and exportation. The supply remained roughly fixed until the American sources were discovered.

Of the developments detrimental to the silver currency of the Roman Empire the exportation of it to India was at first the most serious because the trade between India and the Roman Empire was the greatest traffic of antiquity, and while approaching in a way that of more modern times, was at the same time conducted without the economic background which was required for a state of economic safety. But of these same developments it appears to me to have been in the long run not the most detrimental because it was the only one which was checked in any way. There was no economic reserve—that was the fault: we must not accuse the Romans of blindly meeting their economic collapse as though it were caused only or primarily because of their Indian trade. Chwostow rightly points out that history has shewn examples of preponderance of import over export without disastrous consequences, though he appears to think that the serious part of Rome's Indian trade was the flow of gold to the East; this certainly was continuous, as finds of coins shew, but we have shewn above that the drain of silver, though apparently checked in time, was the more serious (133). The ultimate conclusion of Chwostow is that no harm is noticeable as a direct result of this passive trade of Rome and that if the flow of coin to the East was undesirable, on the other hand trade with the East stimulated barter and tended to develop industries (134). The drain perhaps did no more than hasten a little a financial collapse which would have come in any case.

CONCLUSION

IN our survey of the Indian commerce of the Roman
Empire during two centuries we have in reality watched
the splendour of a great power as reflected in one branch
of its commerce; we have seen that Empire feeling its way
towards a direct commerce with the far East; we have seen
the complete attainment of that aim during the first two
centuries after Christ; we have indicated the close relations
reached between Roman subjects and Indian races, and
have watched the activities of Syrians and Egyptian Greeks
backed by private capital; we have indicated the collapse
of this direct trade as a sign of the economic and political
disintegration of the Western Empire, and the reversion
of control into the hands of Persian, Arabian, and Abys-
sinian middlemen. Did this traffic have any influence upon
the institutions or habits of the Roman Empire and India?
On the whole the answer must be no, but the fact that
Roman subjects constantly visited India but Indians seldom
visited the Roman Empire (except Alexandria and Asia
Minor) is reflected in such evidence which we can collect.
Thus, almost the only traces of Indian influence upon the
West are the adoption of Jataka stories, the presence of
Indian elements in Manichean, Gnostic, and especially
Neo-Platonic tenets and possibly the presence of grotesque
"grylli" as Roman talismans and amulets[1]. Indian ele-
ments are found in Roman work of silver and ivory, and in
Egyptian fabrics[2]. Traces of Roman influence upon India
are more substantial, but even many of these are doubtful.
Thus the Krishna legend seems to owe something to the
West[3]; the visit of Pantaenos, alleged by Eusebius and
Jerome, possibly influenced Tamil philosophy [4], and the

debt of India to Alexandrian merchants for Greek astronomy was a real one, as is shewn by the titles and contents of five early Indian writings on astronomy; the influence seems to have reached China (5), and the Jewish calendar of the week-days was brought to India from Syria. In the matter of literature, there are distinct traces of Greek influence in the ancient Indian drama and theatre, but the resemblances occur mostly in one play (6). In art we have the "Gandhara School" of sculpture in North India, and influences upon Indian building elsewhere, the surest evidence being the presence of the "composite" Roman capital, at a place where Roman coins have turned up (6). Again, Indian filigree workers retain to this day the same patterns as the ancient Greeks devised, and Indian jewellers imitated Greek styles. Lastly, the Roman connexions influenced the Indian system of commerce. In the North the coinage was affected, since the Kushans and the Guptas struck coins of equal weight to the Roman, and in the fifth century A.D. the word "dinar" (denarius) was being used in Indian records; the gold coin of the Ganges region was struck perhaps under Roman influence. In the South, Roman law and procedure influenced the Tamils of Malabar, and the Greek troy scales of weight perhaps reached India and China (7).

We have seen how Rome strove to remedy what ancient commerce lacked—adequate means of transport, freedom of labour, security along trade-routes; her roads were splendid and her ships built according to the demands of oriental trade; her population possessed the elements of free labour, and the Red Sea, the Euxine Sea, the Mediterranean Sea, and the wilds of Asia Minor felt her strength, though inadequately, for the pirates of the Black Sea and of Indian seas were never thoroughly put down. Excepting where rivers and sea were used, we find that the transport of very large quantities of wares in bulk (8) was impossible by mere beasts of burden—hence the high price of oriental wares especially before Hippalos' discovery. But Rome possessed remarkable commercial honour in the eyes of the Orientals: the Indians and Ceylonese admired her early imperial coinage and the Chinese her honesty; under her imperial rule commerce became less an armed force than it had been before, and the first two centuries of it, like the nineteenth century of our era, were an age of great discoveries, and without the aid of the compass, of steam, of electricity, the Roman subjects made full use of their means with the encouragement, if not with the assistance, of the emperors, and trade flourished from Spain to China. With the highest point of Rome's imperial splendour came the highest point in her imperial commerce, and when this passed, Rome allowed Palmyra, one of her half-independent intermediaries, to rise to greatness through its oriental traffic at the very time when the troubles of Egypt demanded some remedy, only to destroy the upstart city and the prosperity of the land-trade. Mediterranean and Egyptian commerce was ruined in the general decline, and the Indian trade fell back into the control of Abyssinians, Arabians, and Persians. The rise of Constantinople caused a partial revival of indirect trade with the East, but the sackings of Rome herself (which had ceased to be the main focus of commerce before the foundation of Constantinople) and the fall of the Western Empire marked the end of the commerce between the Roman Empire and India. The strife of Constantinople with the Persians and with the Arabians, the ultimate supremacy of these in commerce, and the rise of new nationalities in the West led to the commerce of the Middle Ages. The nineteenth century and the twentieth have witnessed brilliant developments in mechanical arts and inventions, more extended commercial settlements, discovery of the use of steam, the opening of China to the world's commerce, improved methods of production, highly organised division of labour, and the use of telegraphy which to-day is possible with and without the use of wires. Yet, in spite of the absence of these and other advantages, Rome, as we have seen, carried on successfully a tolerably peaceful traffic with the far East for more than two centuries, and this, like the reduction of much of the known world to peace and order, was no mean achievement for an ancient people.

ABBREVIATIONS

Abh. d. K. Akad. d. W. Abhandlungen der Königlichen Akademie der Wissenschaften, Berlin.

Acad. des Inscr. (et B.-L.), C.-R. Académie des Inscriptions et Belles-Lettres, Comptes Rendus.

Acad. des Inscr. (et B.-L.), Mém. Académie etc. Mémoires.

Adams, *Paul. Aegin.* F. Adams, *The Seven Books of Paulus Aegineta.*

d'Alviella. Le Comte G. d'Alviella, *Ce que l'Inde doit à la Grèce* (1897).

Amer. Philol., Amer. Journ. Philol. American Journal of Philology.

Amh. Pap. The Amherst Papyri. Grenfell and Hunt.

Ann. Rep. Amer. Hist. Assoc. Annual Report of the American Historical Association.

Arch., Archaeol. Surv. Ind. Archaeological Survey of India.

Arch.
Archiv. } *Archiv für Papyrusforschung.*
Arch. f. Pap.

Bauer. M. Bauer, *Precious Stones*, translated with additions by L. J. Spencer.

Berlin. Klassikert. Berliner Klassikertexte. Herausgegeben v. d. General-verwaltung d. Kön. Museen z. Berlin.

B.G.U. Ägyptische Urkunden aus den Kön. Museen z. Berlin. Griechische Urkunden.

Bibl. Nat. Bronzes. E. Babelon et J. Blanchet, *Catalogue des bronzes antiques de la Bibliothèque Nationale.*

Blümner. } *Technologie und Terminologie der Gewerbe und Künste bei*
Bl. } *Griechen und Römern.* H. Blümner.

B.M. Bronzes. Catalogue of the Bronzes, Greek, Roman, and Etruscan, in the British Museum. H. B. Walters.

B.M. } *Catalogue of the Engraved Gems, Greek, Roman, and Etrus-*
B.M. Gems. } *can...in the British Museum.* H. B. Walters, 1926.

B.M. Jew. Catalogue of the Jewelry, Greek, Roman, and Etruscan in the ...British Museum. F. H. Marshall.

B.M. Rings. Catalogue of the Finger-Rings, Greek, Roman, and Etruscan in the...British Museum. F. H. Marshall.

Bomb. Gaz. Gazetteer of the Bombay Presidency.

Bouché-Leclercq. A. Bouché-Leclercq, *Histoire des Lagides.*

Brünn. u. Domas. *Pr. Ar.* R. E. Brünnow und A. v. Domaszewski, *Die Provincia Arabia.*

Bunbury. E. H. Bunbury, *History of Ancient Geography.*

Bury, *St. R. E.* J. B. Bury, *The Student's Roman Empire.*

Cagn. } *Inscriptiones Graecae ad res Romanas pertinentes.*
Cagn.-Laf. *I.G.R.* } R. Cagnat, etc. Paris.

Camb. Hist. Ind. The Cambridge History of India. Ed. E. J. Rapson.

de Candolle. A. de Candolle, *Origin of Cultivated Plants.*

Chab. *Catalogue général et raisonné des camées et pierres gravées de la Bibliothèque impériale.* M. Chabouillet.

Charlesworth. M. P. Charlesworth, *Trade-Routes and Commerce of the Roman Empire.* 2nd ed.

Chrest. See *Grundz.*

Chwostow. M. Khvostoff, *Istoriia vostochnoi torgovli Greko-rimskago Egipta* (in Russian). History of the Oriental Commerce in Graeco-Roman Egypt (*Studies in the History of Exchange,* I).

C.I.G. Corpus Inscriptionum Graecarum.

C.I.L. Corpus Inscriptionum Latinarum.

Class. Philol. Classical Philology.

Class. Quart. The Classical Quarterly.

Coedès, *Textes.* G. Coedès, *Textes d'auteurs grecs et latins relatifs à l'Extrême-Orient.*

Cooke, *N.S.I.* G. A. Cooke, *A Text-book of North-Semitic Inscriptions.*

Corn. Pap. Greek Papyri in the Library of Cornell University (W. L. Westermann and J. Kraemer).

Dahlmann. J. Dahlmann, *Die Thomas-Legende.*

Daremb.-Sagl. Ch. Daremberg et E. Saglio, *Dictionnaire des Antiquités grecques et romaines.*

Dessau. H. Dessau, *Inscriptiones Latinae Selectae.*

Dessau, *Röm. K.* H. Dessau, *Geschichte der Römischen Kaiserzeit.*

Ditt. }
Ditt. *S.* } *Orientis Graeci Inscriptiones Selectae, Supplementum Sylloges Inscriptionum Graecarum.* W. Dittenberger.
Ditt. *Suppl.* }

Eckhel, *Doctr. Num. Vet.* J. H. von Eckhel, *Doctrina Numorum Veterum.*

E. E., Ephem. Epig. Ephemeris Epigraphica. Corporis I. L. Suppl.

Eichler-Kris. F. Eichler v. E. Kris, *Die Kameen im Kunsthist. Mus. Wien.*

Encycl. Brit. Encyclopaedia Britannica. 11th ed.

Fay. Pap. Fayum Towns and their Papyri (Grenfell, Hunt, Hogarth).

Ferrand. G. Ferrand, *Relations de voyages et Textes géographiques arabes.*

Fitz. *The Engraved Gems of Classical Times, with a Catalogue of the Engraved Gems in the Fitzwilliam Museum, Cambridge.* J. H. Middleton.

Flor. *Papiri Fiorentini,* I ff. (Vitelli and Comparetti).

Forrer. R. Forrer, *Römische u. Byzantinische Seiden-Textilien aus dem Gräberfelde von Achmim-Panopolis.*

Frank. T. Frank, *An Economic History of Rome.* 2nd ed.

Friedländer. L. Friedländer, *Darstellungen, etc.* 9th ed. G. Wissowa.

Furtw. 〉 A. Furtwängler, *Die Antiken Gemmen.*
Furtwängler. 〉

Gall. Fir. *Reale Galleria di Firenze, Serie V, Cammei ed Intagli.*

Gardthausen (*Aug. u. s. Z.*). V. Gardthausen, *Augustus und seine Zeit.*

Gerini. G. E. Gerini in *Journal of the Royal Asiatic Society,* 1897, pp. 551–577 with Tables (abbr. T., Tab.).

Giess. Pap. *Griechische Papyri im Museum...zu Giessen,* Leipzig (E. Kornemann u. P. M. Meyer). (=*P. Giss.*)

Glaser, *Sk.* E. Glaser, *Skizze d. Geschichte u. Geographie Arabiens.*

Götz. W. Götz, *Die Verkehrswege im Dienste des Welthandels.*

Grundz., Gr. u. Chr. 〉 *Grundzüge und Chrestomathie der Papyruskunde.*
Grundz. u. Chrest. 〉 L. Mitteis u. U. Wilcken.

Hawara Pap. See J. G. Milne in *Archiv f. Papyrusforschung,* y. 378 ff.

Heeren, *As. Nat.* A. H. L. Heeren, *Ideen über die Politik, den Verkehr, und den Handel der vornehmsten Völker der alten Welt.* English trans. 1846. Vol. II, *Asiatic Nations.*

Hehn. V. Hehn, *Kulturpflanzen u. Hausthiere.* 7th ed. 1902.

Herm. *Corpus Papyrorum Hermopolitanorum* (Wessely).

Herrmann, *Verkehrswege.* A. Herrmann, *Die Verkehrswege zwischen China, Indien, und Rom.*

Hibeh Pap. *The Hibeh Papyri* (Grenfell and Hunt).

Hirschfeld, *K. V.* H. O. Hirschfeld, *Die Kaiserlichen Verwaltungsbeamten.*

Hirth. F. Hirth, *China and the Roman Orient.*

Hl. 〉 F. Henkel, *Die Römischen Fingerringe der Rheinlande.*
Henkel. 〉

Holdich. Sir T. Holdich, *The Gates of India.*

Imhoof-Blumer. 〉 F. Imhoof-Blumer u. O. Keller, *Tier- und Pflanzenbilder*
Imh. Blum. 〉 *auf Münzen u. Gemmen des klassischen Altertums.*

Imper. Gaz. (Ind.). *Imperial Gazetteer of India.*

Ind. Antiqu. *Indian Antiquary.*

Jacoby. F. Jacoby, *Fragmente der Griechischen Historiker.*

Jahr. d. (K.) D. Arch. Instit. *Jahrbuch des Kaiserlich Deutschen Archäologischen Instituts.*

Jahr. d. (K.) D. Arch. Instit., Anz. Jahrbuch des Kaiserlich Deutschen Archäologischen Instituts, Anzeiger.

Jahrb. f. Nationalök. u. Stat. Jahrbücher für Nationalökonomie und Statistik.

J.A.O.S. Journal of the American Oriental Society.

J.A.S.B. Journal of the Asiatic Society of Bengal.

J. E(g). Arch. Journal of Egyptian Archaeology.

J., Journ. Hellen. Stud. Journal of Hellenic Studies.

Jordan, *Topogr.* H. Jordan, *Topographie der Stadt Rom in Alterthum.*

Journ. Asiat. Journal Asiatique.

J.R.A.S. Journal of the Royal Asiatic Society.

J.R.A.S. Bomb. Br. Journal of the Royal Asiatic Society, Bombay Branch.

J.R.A.S. Ceyl. Br. Journal of the Royal Asiatic Society, Ceylon Branch.

J.R. Stud. ⎱
J. Rom. St. ⎰ *Journal of Roman Studies.*

Kenyon, *Gk. Pap.* See *Lond. P.*

King. ⎱ C. W. King, *Natural History of Precious Stones and Gems.*
King, *P.S.* ⎰ (Ed. 1865.)

King, *E.G.* C. W. King, *The Handbook of Engraved Gems.*

K.M.B. Königliche Museen zu Berlin. Beschreibung der geschnittenen Steine im Antiquarium. A. Furtwängler.

Kornemann, *Jan. Festschrift zu C. F. Lehmann-Haupts sechzigstem Geburtstage (Janus. Heft I).*

Krause. ⎱
Krause, *Pyrgot.* ⎰ J. H. Krause, *Pyrgoteles.*

Lacouperie. T. de Lacouperie, *The Western Origin of Chinese Civilisation.*

Lassen. C. Lassen, *Indische Altertumskunde.* Vols. I and II of ed. 1867–74; Vols. III and IV of ed. 1847–62.

Layard. A. H. Layard, *Nineveh and Babylon.*

Lewes. The Lewes House Collection of Ancient Gems. J. D. Beazley.

Lewis. The Lewis Collection of Gems and Rings. J. H. Middleton.

Lips. Griechische Urkunden...zu Leipzig (Mitteis).

Lond. P. Greek Papyri in the British Museum (F. G. Kenyon and H. I. Bell).

Louvre. Musée National du Louvre. Catalogue Sommaire des Bijoux antiques. A. de Ridder.

Marlb. (Cat.). Sale-Catalogue of the Marlborough Gems. M. H. N. Story-Maskelyne.

Maskel. | *Sale-Catalogue of the Marlborough Gems.* M. H. N. Story-
Mask. | Maskelyne.

Masp. *Papyrus grecs d'époque Byzantine,* i ff. Maspero (*Catal. général des antiqu. égypt. du Mus. du Caire*).

McCr. *Anc. Ind.* J. W. McCrindle, *Ancient India as described in Classical Literature.*

McCr. *Ctes.* J. W. McCrindle, *Ancient India as described by Ktesias.*

McCr. *Ptol.* J. W. McCrindle, *Ancient India as described by Ptolemy.*

Middleton. See *Fitz.*

Miller, *Itin.* C. Miller, *Itineraria Romana.*

Milne. J. G. Milne, *A History of Egypt under Roman Rule,* 1924.

Minns. E. H. Minns, *Scythians and Greeks.*

Mommsen, *Prov.* T. Mommsen, *The Provinces of the Roman Empire,* trans. W. P. Dickson.

Momms.-(trans.) Blacas. *Histoire de la Monnaie Romaine.* T. Mommsen, trans. Blacas.

Mommsen-Marqu. *Manuel des Antiquités Romaines.* T. Mommsen et J. Marquardt.

Monahan. F. J. Monahan, *The Early History of Bengal.*

Mosaïques. *Inventaire des Mosaïques de la Gaule et de l'Afrique* (Lafaye, Gauckler, et de Pachtere; ed. R. Cagnat).

Müller, Müller, *Geog. Gr. Min.* C. Müller, *Geographi Graeci Minores.*

Nissen, *Verein.* Nissen in *Verein von Altertumsfreunden im Rheinlande, Jahrbücher.*

Num. Chron. | *Numismatic Chronicle.*
Numism. Chron. |

N.Y. *Metropolitan Museum of Art* (New York) *Catalogue of the Engraved Gems of the Classical Style.* G. M. A. Richter.

O.P. *The Oxyrhynchus Papyri.* Grenfell and Hunt.

Palazzo d. Conserv. *Catalogue of the Palazzo dei Conservatori, Text.* Ed. H. Stuart Jones.

Pauly. *Paulys Real-Encyclopädie der Classischen Altertumswissenschaft* (Wissowa u. Kroll).

P. Brem. See Wilcken, *Chrest.* i (ii). 28.

Penny Cycl. *Penny Cyclopaedia.*

Persson. A. W. Persson, *Staat u. Manufaktur im römischen Reiche.*

P. Hamb. *Griech. Papyrusurk. d. Hamburger...Bibl.* P. Meyer.

P. Heidelberg. F. Bilabel, *Griechische Papyri.*

Phil. | *Philologus. Zeitschrift für das Klassische Altertum.*
Philolog. |

Philolog. Woch. *Philologische Wochenschrift* (supersedes *Wochenschrift für Klassische Philologie*).

Pillai. Kanakasabhai Pillai, *The Tamils eighteen hundred years ago.*

Preisigke, *Wörterb.* *Wörterbuch der griechischen Papyrusurkunden.* F. Preisigke (ed. E. Kiessling).

Priaulx. O. de B. Priaulx, *The Indian travels of Apollonius of Tyana and the Indian Embassies to Rome.*

P.Z. C. Edgar, *Selected Papyri from the Archives of Zeno. Annales du Service des Antiquités de l'Égypte.*

Ransom. C. L. Ransom, *Studies in Ancient Furniture.*

Rawlinson. ⎱ H. G. Rawlinson, *Intercourse between India and the*
Rawlinson, *Interc.* ⎰ *Western World,* 1926.

Reinaud. J. T. Reinaud, *Relations politiques et commerciales de l'Empire Romain avec l'Asie Orientale* (also in *Journal Asiatique,* 1863).

Rev. Arch. Revue Archéologique.

Rev. Numism. Revue Numismatique.

Rev. Pap. Revenue Laws of Ptolemy Philadelphus (Grenfell).

Richter. See *N.Y.*

Rostowzew, *Ir. and Gr.* M. Rostovtzeff, *Iranians and Greeks in South Russia.*

Rostowzew, *Soc. and Econ.* M. Rostovtzeff, *The Social and Economic History of the Roman Empire.*

Rylands. T. G. Rylands, *The Geography of Ptolemy Elucidated.*

Rylands P. Catalogue of the Greek Papyri in the John Rylands Library, Manchester (Johnson, Martin, Hunt).

Salvioli. G. Salvioli, *Le Capitalisme dans le monde antique.*

SB. Sammelbuch griechischer Urkunden aus Ägypten (F. Preisigke). As cited by Preisigke, *Wörterbuch.* (See above under Preisigke.)

Schiller. H. Schiller, *Geschichte der Römischen Kaiserzeit.*

Schmidt. A. Schmidt, *Drogen und Drogenhandel im Altertum.*

Schoff, (ad) *Peripl.* W. H. Schoff, *The Periplus of the Erythraean Sea.*

Sk. Catalogue of the Collection of Antique Gems formed by the ninth Earl of Southesk. Ed. Lady H. Carnegie. (*Not* Glaser, *Sk.* q.v.)

Smith. V. A. Smith, *The Early History of India,* 1924.

Smith, *Hist. of Fine Art.* ⎱ V. A. Smith, *History of Fine Art in India*
Smith, *Fine Art.* ⎰ *and Ceylon.*

Soc. Papiri greci e latini (Pubblicazioni della Società Italiana, I ff.).

Stud. Studien zur Paläographie u. Papyruskunde (Wessely).

Tab. Peut. Miller. C. Miller, *Itineraria Romana.*

Tebt. Pap. The Tebtunis Papyri (Grenfell, Hunt, Smyly).

Tesserar. Syll. Tesserarum urbis Romae et suburbi plumbearum Sylloge. Ed. M. Rostovtzeff.

Thompson, *Gloss.* D'Arcy W. Thompson, *A Glossary of Greek Birds.*
Trans. and Proc. Amer. Philol. Transactions and Proceedings of the American Philological Association.

Verh. d. Gesells. f. Erdk. Gesellschaft für Erdkunde, Verhandlungen (1873 onwards).
Veröffentlichungen, etc. *Veröffentlichungen des Forschungsinstituts für Vergleichende Religionsgeschichte.*
Vienna. Die Sammlungen des K. K. Münz- u. Antiken-Cabinetes (Wien). E. v. Sacken u. F. Kenner. (When nothing is added after *Vienna,* except K. and a number, Section IX (*Antike Geschnittene Steine*) is meant.)
Vincent. W. Vincent, *The Periplus of the Erythraean Sea.*

Wartena. J. Wartena, *Inleiding op een Uitgave der Tabula Peutingeriana.*
Watt. Sir G. Watt, *Commercial Products of India,* abridged from:—
Watt, *Dict.* Sir G. Watt, *Dictionary of the Economic Products of India.*
Wessely. *Griechische Zauberpapyrus v. Paris u. London.* C. Wessely.
Wilcken, *Ostr.* U. Wilcken, *Griechische Ostraka.*
Wochenschrift etc. See *Philolog. Woch.*

Yates, *Textr. Antiqu.* J. Yates, *Textrinum Antiquorum.*
Yule. Sir H. Yule, *Cathay and the Way Thither.*

Zeits., Zeitschrift d. G. f. Erd. Zeitschrift der Gesellschaft für Erdkunde zu Berlin (1866 onwards).

NOTES

PART I

INTRODUCTION

(1) For the progress of Roman commerce see e.g. Momms. *H.R.* Bk. II. Ch. 8; III. 12–13; IV. 11; V. 11. Frank, 16 ff., 69 ff., 108 ff., 298 ff. For India see Smith, *Early Hist. of India.*

(2) Strabo V. 3. 5; V. 4. 6. Dionys. Hal. III. 44 (more favourable). Cp. *Anth. Pal.* VII. 379. Plut. *Caes.* 58. Suet. *Aug.* 30.

(3) Strabo XVII. 1. 7. Suet. *Aug.* 98. Sen. *Ep.* 77. 1. *Anth. Pal.* VII. 379. Cic. *ad Att.* I. 4; XIV. 7 etc. *Acts* xxviii. 13. Cic. *Pro Planco,* 26. Pliny XXXVII. 70. *C.I.G.* 5853. Momms. *I.R.N.* 2488. *C.I.L.* X. 1797. Cp. Philostrat. *Apoll.* VII. 10, 12, 15. Ch. Dubois, *Pouzzoles Antique.* Rostowzew, *Soc. and Econ.* 150–1. *Klio,* Beih. XIV. 1923, 163 ff. Add Ptol. III. 1. 5, 6. Philo, *Leg.* 29.

(4) Tac. *Ann.* II. 55 (Athens—Rhodes—Syria), cp. 53–4. *Acts* xxi. 1–3 (Ephesos—Rhodes—Cyprus on left—Tyre). Joseph. *A.J.* XVI. 62 (Samos—Caesarea). Philo, *in Flacc.* 5 (25–8). Strabo VII. 7. 4 (Via Egnatia). Cic. *ad Att.* III. 7. 3.

(5) Sir W. Ramsay, *Dict. of the Bible,* suppl. vol. s.v. *Trade and Commerce.* Suet. *Aug.* 98. Pliny XIX. 3, 4. Cels. *de Med.* III. 22. 8. Sulp. Sev. *Dial.* 3. 14. G. Kaibel, *I.G.* XIV. 917, cp. 916. Waltzing, 3. 2308. Cp. Jer. *Epp.* 97. 1. *B.G.U.* 27 etc. *Hist. Aug. 'Aurelian.'* 47. Joseph. *A.J.* XVIII. 155–160 (Palestine—Alexandria—Puteoli). Lucian, *Navig.* 1, 7–9 (Alexandria—Sidon—S. coast of Asia Minor—Aegaean —Crete on right—Malea—Italy). Cp. *Anth. Pal.* XI. 306. *Acts* xxvii. 2–5, 6–7, 14 ff.; xxviii. 11–13. Philo, *in Flacc.* 5. 25–8 (Italy— Alexandria—Syria advised in place of any other route to Syria). Cp. also L. C. West in *J. Rom. St.* 1917, 48–9.

(6) Caes. *B.C.* III. 107. Tac. *H.* II. 98. Pliny II. 127. *Joseph. vita,* 3. *Acts* xiii. 4 ff.; xxvii. 2 ff., 37 (Alex. MS. 276; Vat. MS. 76). Cassian. *Instit.* 4. 31. *Miracles of St George* (Budge), 263. Cp. *C.I.L.* III. 1. 3. Strabo X. 4. 5.

(7) Philo, *Leg.* 29 (190). Cp. Jos. *A.J.* XVI. 15. Hor. *Od.* III. 24. 35; *Ep.* I. 16. 71. Tac. *Ann.* III. 1.

(8) Juv. xiv. 278 ff. Philo, *Leg.* 21 (146-7). Pers. v. 141-2. Cp. Hor. *Ep.* i. 6. 32; *A.P.* 117; *Od.* iii. 24. 35; *S.* i. 4. 29; *Ep.* i. 6. 17; *Od.* i. 115. Sen. *ad Paul.* 2. Ov. *Tr.* i. 2. 75.

CHAPTER I

(1) Strabo xvii. 1. 44 fin.-45. Pliny vi. 102. Solin. 54. 8. Lucian, *Philopseud.* 33. *P. Giess.* 47. 29. Xen. *Ephes.* 4. 1. Aristeid. *Or.* xlviii. p. 485 (361). Dind. etc. *Pauly,* s.v. *Koptos.* G. W. Murray in *J. Eg. Archaeol.* 1925, pp. 138 ff. Petrie, *Koptos,* etc. *Hist. Aug. 'Prob.'* 17. 3.

(2) Strabo *loc. cit.* Pliny vi. 102-3. *Anton. Itin.* 172-3 (ed. Parth. and Pind.). *Tab. Peut.* (Miller, *Itin.*), 862-3. *C.I.L.* iii. S. i. 6627. *Geog. Ravenn.* ii. 7. Petrie, *Koptos,* ch. 5. Jer. *Epp.* 125. 3.

(3) Strabo *loc. cit.* Pliny vi. 168 (Myos H.), 103 and 168 (Ber.). See also Strabo xvi. 4. 5. Pompon. Mela iii. 8. 7. Steph. Byz. s.v. Βερενῖκαι. Ptol. iv. 5. 14. P. Collart, *Les Papyrus Bouriant,* 15, 103, apparently. On Myos Hormos and Berenice see Müller, *Geog. Gr. Min.* i. 167 ff., 257; Chwostow, 190 (he translates Myos Hormos into 'Mouse Harbour'), 191, 369, 380 (Berenice). Murray, *op. cit.* 141-3 (cp. 133-4, 146-7). *Pauly,* s.v. *Berenike.* The enumeration of the 'hydreumata' on the Coptos—Berenice route shews the paramount importance of that track, cp. *Lond. P.* 328.

(4) Ptol. iv. 5. 14, 73; 7, 7. Strabo xvi. 4. 5 ff. Steph. Byz. s.v. Ὄμβοι. *Anton. Itin.* 165. Juv. xv. 35; *Q.P.* iv. 384 etc. Chwostow, 189-194, 357, 380. Rawlinson, *Hist. of Ancient Eg.* ii. 133-4, 378. Petrie, *Koptos,* p. 32 (correcting Leuce Come).

(5) Chwostow, 189-195, 380. Schwarz, *Inschr. d. Wüst.* 3, 16, 48-9. Ditt. *S.* ii. 660 (between Coptos and Kosseir); *C.I.L.* iii. 1. 27-9. Ditt. *S.* i. 70-4 (Redesiya). Götz, 46. 442. Murray, *op. cit.* 142, 145-6.

(6) Chwostow, 180-8, 357. Petrie, *Researches in Sinai,* 48 (a modern Red Sea storm).

(7) There was also a road from the Nile to Suez. Chwostow, 188. Götz, 445-6. Rawlinson, *op. cit.* ii. 297-8, 472-4. *Bull. de l'Inst. Franç. d'Arch. Or.* xxiii. 27-84. St Hilaire, *Eg. and Suez Canal,* 4. Wilkinson, *Anc. Eg.* ed. Birch, i. 47-9. Birch, *Records of the Past,* ix. 80-1. Herod. ii. 158. Pliny vi. 167. Diodor. i. 33. 8-12; iii. 39. 1. Jacoby ii. p. 212. Ptol. iv. 5. 14. Suet. *Aug.* 18. Dio Cass. lxxviii.

32. 'Vict.' *Ep.* 1, 5. Strabo XVII. 1. 25–6; XVI. 46. Euseb. *H.E.* IV. 2. John of Nikiou, 72. Journey 96 miles in all. West end kept open by dredging.

(8) Strabo XVI. 4. 24; XVII. 1. 13 (does India mean Somali here? Ethiopian ἄκραι were Cape Guardafui), 44 fin.–45, cp. XVII. 1. 5; XVI. 4. 14. Diodor. I. 50. 7; XVII. 52. 5. The Cinnamon country was the coast of the Somali and Guardafui. Some think that the fleets belonged to Arabia Eudaemon. Milne, 294. Cp. also Schur, *Klio*, XX. 1926, 221, and Kornemann, *Jan.* I. 70–1.

(9) *Peripl.* 57, 20, 21. Pliny VI. 101. Strabo XVI. 4. 5. Philostr. *Apollon.* III. 35. Dangers, guides, and records of perils escaped: Chwostow, 180–8, 323 ff., 371 ff. Ditt. *S.* I. 69–74; 69, saved from the Red Sea; *C.I.G.* 4838, saved from Arabia; 4838 c, saved from Trogodytica (both found at Apollinopolis). *C.I.G.* 4712 b records murder by robbers in the ὅρμος of Puchis. See also Petrie, *Kopt.*, Tariff-list line 10 κυβερνητὴς ἐρυθραϊκός, cp. *C.I.G.* 4712 b κυβερνητής, and Petrie, *op. cit.* pp. 34–5, No. VIII. See also Chwostow, 571–2.

(10) *Peripl.* 25–6, 28, 32. *Ezek.* xxvii. 3 and 23 (Eden, Canneh). Muza rose to importance after the fall of Arabia Eudaemon, for which see below, pp. 15–16, 53.

(11) *Peripl.* 38–9, 41, 43–6, 54–60. Steph. Byz. s.v. Βαρύγαζα. *Pauly*, s.v. *India*, 1212, 1272, 1280–1, but Muziris and Nelcynda are no longer identified with Mangalore and Nileswara respectively, at least by those who know the ancient geography of Malabar.

(12) Strabo XV. 1. 3–4; 2. 12–13; II. 5. 14. Monahan, 10–11.

(13) Chwostow, 347–9, 360, and Kornemann, *Jan.* I. 57–8, think that men sailed direct to Sigerus in India in Augustus' time; for this, see below, pp. 45 ff.

(14) Attributions of the farce on *O.P.* III. 413 to the Ptolemaic period, e.g. by Charlesworth, p. 59, are untenable.

(15) Plut. *Ant.* 27.

(16) Gardthausen, *Aug. u. s. Z.* I. 2. 792–3. Herrmann, *Verkehrswege*, 4. *Encycl. Brit.* s.v. *Arabia*. Müller, *Geog. Gr. Min.* I. pp. 186–191 from Agatharchides. Strabo XVI. 4. 2, 19. *Peripl.* 26.

(17) E.g. Hor. *Odes*, III. 24. 2; *Ep.* I. 6. 6. Tibull. III. 8 (IV. 2), 16–20. Prop. III. (IV) 13. 1–8. Cp. Virg. *G.* I. 57; II. 116–117. Roman coins even in Central Arabia, Chwostow, 382.

(18) Glaser, *Sk.* II. 4 ff., 93 ff. Qataban and Gaba'an were now

Sabaean. See Joseph. *B.J.* IV. 115 = 659–663 ; IV. 7. 1. II *Kings* xiv. 7, and perhaps *Isaiah* xvi. 1. *Judges* i. 36. Jer. *Qu. in Gen.* XIV. Strabo XVI. 4. 18, 21–4. Diodor. III. 42. Müller I. 176–8. Cp. Diodor. I. 60. 5. Dio Cass. LXVII. 14. Ammian. Marcell. XIV. 8. 13. Pliny VI. 144–5 (Petra—Forath, then by river to Charax). Strabo XVI. 2. 30. Hirth, 158–160, 173, 183. De Lacouperie, 243. Chwostow, 199 (Aelana), 205–6 (Rhinocolura), 208–211, 252 ff. Cp. also *Antonin. Itin.* 147–154 (= p. 68, Parth. and Pind.). Ptol. IV. 5. 12 ; v. 19. 7 ; 20. 4 ; VI. 7. 16 ; v. 17. 1. The track Red Sea—Syria became later Trajan's road. Journey Aelana to Minaeans of Jauf took 70 days. Route Alexandria—Palestine via Pelusium difficult, Chwostow, 203–7. Nabataean port Egra (Ghar) was not important, Gardthausen I. 2. 793–4, 796. See also *Pauly*, s.v. *Gabaeoi, Gebbanitae, Catabanes, Gerrha.*

(19) Glaser, *Sk.* Ch. XVIII. H. Dillmann, *Abh. d. K. Akad. d. W.* 1878, pp. 177 ff.; id. 1880, 3 ff. Glaser, *Die Abessin. in Arab. u. Afr.* (1895). *Punt u. die Südarab. Reiche* (1899). *Peripl.* 3–14. Pliny VI. 104. Birch, *Records of the Past,* x. 14 etc. Vincent I. 111 ff. Cp. *C.I.G.* 5127. Ptol. IV. 7. 25. The Greeks called the Somali coast 'Barbari(c)a.'

(20) Pliny VI. 174–5. Schoff, *Peripl.* p. 64. J. Fergusson, *Hist. of Architect.* I. 149–150 (3rd ed. 1893).

(21) E.g. Plut. *Ant.* 81 where India = East Africa as Dio Cass. LI. 15, I think, shews. Cp. Virg. *G.* IV. 286–294 = Ethiopia. Reinaud, pp. 180–3, vainly tries another explanation. Should we, with Wagner and others, bracket 291–3 as a late insertion ? Cp. Κινναμωμοφόρου ['Ἰνδικῆς] of Strabo II. 1. 17. The source of Cinnamon was always regarded as Arabia and Africa falsely, and that supposed source was later called Indian falsely, e.g. Sidon. Apoll. *C.* IX. 325.

(22) *Peripl.* 2. Diodor. I. 30. Pliny v. 53. Strabo XVII. 1. 5. Seneca, *N.Q.* VI. 8. Cp. Pliny XII. 19. Chwostow, 63.

(23) *Peripl.* 30. Pliny VI. 172–3. Cosmas III. 169 B. Chwostow, 195–8. Götz, 447 ff. When the *Periplus* was written, Somali marts were still under independent chiefs.

(24) Suet. *Aug.* 18. Dio Cass. LI. 18. Vict. *Ep.* I. 5 ; *C.I.L.* III. Suppl. I. 6627 (found at Coptos); III. Suppl. II. 12046. *Rev. Arch.* Sér. IV. 6, p. 190. Cp. Ael. *d. A.* VII. 18.

(25) *C.I.G.* 5075 belongs to Augustus' time.

(26) Chwostow, 187, 372–3. See Ditt. *Suppl.* I. 202 ; *C.I.G.* 5075. Wilck. *Ostr.* I. 584. *Arch. f. Pap.* III. 196–7 ; IV. 309–310. Rostowzew

in *Phil. Suppl.-B.* IX. 596. Armed guards on merchant ships were probably hired privately. See also Petrie, *Kopt.* 26.

(**27**) Ditt. *op. cit.* I. 132 (130 B.C.); *C.I.G.* 4896, l. 16. Ditt. I. 190; *C.I.G.* 4933. Ditt. I. 186 (62 B.C.); *C.I.G.* 4751, 4897 *b*; *C.I.L.* III. 13, 580; *Arch.* IV. 305. *Grundz.* I. (i) 264. M. L. Strack, *Die Dyn. der Ptol.* 257, No. 109; *C.I.L.* IX. 3083; III. 32, 55, but not 40; X. 1129. Dessau, 2700. Ditt. *S.* II. 674. 9; Hogarth in Flinders Petrie, *Koptos,* 26–32. Ditt. *S.* II. 700.

(**28**) Milne, 162 and note. Ditt. *Suppl.* II. 674 (tariff of Coptos).

(**29**) Glaser, *Sk.* II. 43 ff. H. Krüger, *Der Feldzug des Ael. Gall.* Gardthausen, *Aug. u. s. Z.* I. 2. 789–796 and II. 3. 449 ff., 452, 454–5. Strabo XVI. 4. 22; II. 15. 12. Pliny VI. 160–1. Hor. *Od.* I. 291; 35. 8; II. 12. 24; III. 24. 1; *Ep.* I. 7. 35. Prop. II. 8. 19. *Mon. Ancyr.* (Lat.) V. 18–23. Dio Cass. LIII. 29. Dessau, *Röm. K.* I. 381. Schiller I. 198–201. Rostowzew, *Soc. and Econ.* 53, 91. *Arch.* IV. 306 ff. *J.R.A.S.* N.S. VI. 1872, 121 ff. Glaser, *Sk.* 56–9. Chwostow, 26 ff., 352–4. *J.A.S.B.* I. 50, 1881, 96. The Nabataeans, of course, wished to keep the Sabaean trade unimpaired. Cf. also Mommsen, *Prov.* II. 290 ff.

(**30**) Pliny XII. 56; II. 168; VI. 141, 160; XXXII. 10 etc. Isid. ap. Athenae. III. 14. 93 = 46. Momms. *Prov.* II. 39, 293. Chwostow, 354–5.

(**31**) E.g. Prop. II. (III) 10. 13–16 (Parthia, India, Arabia); III. 1. 16; IV. 3. 10; III. 4. 1–6. Hor. *Od.* I. 12. 55–6 (Indians and Chinese?). Cp. III. 29. 27–8; IV. 15. 23; IV. 14. 41–6. *Anth. Pal.* IX. 59 and 297.

(**32**) Charlesworth, 61. Schur, *Klio,* Beih. XV. 1923, 46; XX. 1926, 221. Kornemann, *Jan.* I. 61 ff. Momms. *Prov.* II. 294. Rostowzew in *Arch.* IV. 308–9. Kennedy, *J.R.A.S.* 1916, 832–4. Schwanbeck, *Rhein. Mus. Phil.* VII. 1850, 352 ff., 328. Schoff, Fabric., and Müller, ad *Peripl.* 26. Schwanbeck reads Charibael, Fabric. and Müller Elisar = Eleazos = Iliazzu, King of Cane and Hadramaut. If he destroyed Ar. Eud., he wished to benefit his port Cane—see Chwostow, 216–217. Cp. Bunbury II. 478. See *Peripl.* 26. Philostorg. *H.E.* III. 4. Glaser, *Die Abessinier,* 34, 37, 38.

(**33**) Strabo XVI. 4. 18. Götz, 435. Cp. Diodor. III. 43.

(**34**) Charlesworth, pp. 9 and 254; Strabo XVI. 4. 21 settles the matter, I think.

(**35**) *Peripl.* 19. Different opinions:—that it was a Nabataean due—

Schoff, *J.A.O.S.* 35, p. 38. Fabric., Müller, and Schoff, ad *Peripl.* 19. Wilck. *Arch.* III. 198–9 (changed from his opinion in *Ostr.* I. 398–9). Bouché-Leclercq III. 322; that it was Ptolemaic and Roman— Lumbroso, *Rech.* 312. Wilck. *Ostr., loc. cit.* Momms. *Prov.* II. 151. Rostowzew, *Arch.* IV. 306–7. Cp. *Wochenschr. f. Klass. Phil.* 1900, p. 116. *Gesch. d. Staatsp.* in *Philol. Suppl.-B.* IX. 397. *Soc. and Econ.* p. 513, n. 18 (correcting Myos Hormos to Leuce Come). Vincent II. 315. Cagnat, *Imp. Ind.* 78. Kornemann, *Jan.* I. 62. Hirschfeld, *Unters.* 20; *K. V.* 80–1. Kennedy, *J.R.A.S.* 1916, p. 832. Cp. Chwostow, pp. 375–6, 200–1. Dessau, *Röm. K.* 381 n.; add Pliny XII. 63–5, Roman dues paid first at Gaza on wares coming through Nabataean territory.

(**36**) Strabo XVI. 4. 21. Pliny VI. 32.

(**37**) Strabo XVII. 1. 53. Cp. Cagnat, *I.G.R.* I. 1293; *C.I.L.* III. S. II. 14147[5]. Gardthausen I. 1. 454; I. 2. 787–8.

(**38**) Strabo XVI. 4. 22; *Mon. Ancyr.* (Lat.) v. 18–23.

(**39**) Strabo XVII. 1. 54. Pliny VI. 181. Dio Cass. LIV. 5. *Grundz.* 29; *Arch. f. Pap.* v. 321. Chwostow, 29. Gardthausen I. 2. 796–8.

(**40**) Cagnat, *I.G.R.* I. 1359. Hierasycaminos a mart for gold, linen, ivory or elephants, roots, myrrh, and spices, sold apparently by silent trade—Philostrat. *Apoll.* VI. 2. Cp. silent trade of Axumites—Cosmas II. 100 B–C.

(**41**) Momms. *Prov.* II. 299.

(**42**) Strabo II. 3. 4–5. Cp. Pliny II. 169 (Red Sea to Gades!).

(**43**) Suet. *Aug.* 98. Charlesworth, 9, with notes, adding *C.I.L.* X. 1613. Philae, of course, was not on any main route to the East. *Tab. Peut.* Miller, 790. Kornemann, *Jan.* I. 61–3, 71, 66–7. Schur, *Klio*, Beih. XV. 1923, 45 ff.; XX. 1926, 221.

(**44**) Convergence of trade in Phoenicia (Tyre)—*Ezek.* xxvii, esp. 6, 7, 10, 12, 13, 15–17, 19, 21–4. Commercial Syria—L. C. West in *Trans. and Proc. Amer. Philol.* LV. 1924, 159–189.

(**45**) C. Skeel, *Travel in First Cent.* pp. 118–120, map p. 111.

(**46**) Tac. *Ann.* XII. 12. Pliny V. 86. Bunbury II. 107. Philostr. *Apoll.* I. 20. B. W. Henderson, *Five R. Emperors*, 64 ff.

(**47**) Arrian, *Anab.* III. 7; *Geog. Rev.* Sept. 1919, 153–179. Dio Cass. LXVIII. 19; XL. 17; XLIX. 19. Tac. *Ann.* XII. 12–13.

(**48**) Maes, according to Ptolemy, makes the route to China begin at the Bay of Issos, Cilicia.

(**49**) I *Kings* iv. 24? Strabo XVI. 1. 21. Curt. X. 1. Xen. *Anab.* I.

4. 11. Arr. *A*. II. 13; III. 7 etc. Ptol. v. 19. 3. It ceased to be important after Pliny's time. J. Peters, *Nation*, May 23, 1889. *Nippur*, 196 ff. *Sitz.-Ber. d. Berl. Akad.* July 25, 1889, B. Moritz.

(50) Isid. Char. *Mans. Parth.* 1. Strabo XVI. 1. 27–8. Plut. *Luc.* 21. 5. Kennedy, *J.R.A.S.* 1912, 1013–14.

(51) Dio Cass. LXVIII. 30.

(52) E.g. Philostrat. *Apoll.* II. 2. 4. Generally Caucasos = Pamirs + Himalayas + Hindu Kush, but Paropanisos = Hindu Kush, Imaos (or Emodos) = Himalayas, and Imaos ultimately = the Pamirs and Tian Shan.

(53) These points are from *Encycl. Brit.* s.v. *Asia*, s.v. *Hindu Kush*. *Camb. Hist. Ind.* I. pp. 27–9, 31, 542. Lassen I. 24–9, 37–41. Sir T. Holdich, *The Gates of India*, esp. pp. 48–9, 51, 69, 87. The Khyber is again becoming important.

(54) Pliny VI. 122. Joseph. *A.J.* XVIII. 9. 8. Strabo XVI. 1. 5, 16. Polyb. v. 45.

(55) Isid. 3–8; *J.R.A.S.* XII. 1850, 97–124. Strabo XI. 9. 1; 13. 5–8. Ptol. VI. 2. 7. Polyb. v. 44. Arr. *Anab.* III. 19–20. Pliny VI. 42–3. Μηδικὴ πύλη, αἱ τοῦ Ζάγρου πύλαι = Rowandiz Pass? *Tab. Peut.* Miller, 781, 792.

(56) Pliny VI. 44–5. Isid. 8–14, 19. Ptol. I. 12. Kandahar was the frontier-town of Parthia.

(57) Strabo XI. 11. 1; XV. 1. 34, 37. Hor. *Od.* I. 12. 56; III. 29. 27; IV. 15. 23. After Crassus' defeat the Roman prisoners had been taken to Merv—Pliny VI. 47.

(58) Ptol. I. 12. 3–11; I. 11. 4, 6; VI. 10. 4; 11. 9; 13. 23. Ammian. Marcell. XXIII. 6. 60, 67–8. A. Herrmann, *Die alten Seidenstrassen zw. China u. Syrien, Qu. u. Forsch. z. a. Gesch. u. Geog.* Heft 21, 1910; *Verkehrsw. zw. Ch., Ind., u. R. um* 100 A.D. (with map) pp. 4–6. Chwostow, 281. Friedländer I. 369 and notes. Nissen, *Verein*, H. 95, 1894, 1 ff. Yule I, 189 ff. Götz, 500–511. *Verh. d. Gesell. f. Erdk.* IV. 1877, 104–7. Richtofen, *China*, I. 454 ff. Coedès, *Textes*, XX–XXIII. Stein, *Sand-buried Ruins of Khotan*, ch. v and map. McCrindle, *Ptol.* p. 12; *J. R. Geog. Soc.* XLIII. 579. Authorities in Herrmann, *Verkehrswege*, p. 3 and *Pauly*, s.v. *India*, 1927. *Journ. Asiat.* Sér. IV. vol. 8, 1846, 228–252. The Tashkurgan near Balkh was apparently called Aornos. See also *Pauly*, s.v. *Sera*; but Singanfu was really Daxata—Gerini, T. v; Ptol. VI. 16. 8.

(**59**) Cosmas II. 97 B (via Nisibis).

(**60**) *Pauly*, s.v. *Sakai*, 1707, s.v. *India*, 1297–8. *Camb. Hist. Ind.*
I, map between pp. 26–7. *Harmsworth Atlas*, Nos. 115–16. Ortospana
was also called Cabura. Ptol. I. 12. 7 ff., esp. 9; 17. 5; VI. 18. 5.
Tab. Peut. Miller, 787, 799–802. Pliny VI. 61–3. McCr. *Ptol.* 312.
The Greeks called Mathura 'Modura of the Gods.'

(**61**) Strabo XI. 8. 9; XV. 2. 8. Pliny VI. 61–3. Isid. *op. cit.* 14–19.
Lassen I. 30–6, 434. Ptol. VI. 19–20. McCr. *Ptol.* 315.

(**62**) On the 'three roads' from Bactria. *Camb. Hist. Ind.* I. 28–9.

(**63**) See *Peripl.* 37, adding Rhambacia in the lacuna. Arr. *Anab.*
VI. 21. 5–22; *Ind.* 21. 24–5. Diodor. XVI. 104. Strabo XV. 2. 2.
Holdich, 320, 372. Schoff, ad *Peripl.* pp. 161–3.

(**64**) *Tab. Peut.* Miller, 785–8 (with map). Müller, *Geog. Gr. Min.*
I, XCIV, XCV. Ptol. VI. 5. 4 and 19. 4. Supposed Makran route on
Tab. Peut.: Miller, 786–8 (with road to Palibothra). Cp. Ptol. VI.
21. 1–6.

(**65**) Kennedy, *J.R.A.S.* 1893, pp. 241–284. Rawlinson, *Intercourse*,
1–31.

(**66**) Ammian. Marcell. XXIII. 6. 69–71. Kennedy, *J.R.A.S.* 1912,
990 ff. Schoff, *J.A.O.S.* 35, 32 ff. Kushan coins in a Characene hoard:
B.M. Cat. of Gk. coins, Arabia, Mesopotamia, Persia (G. F. Hill),
CXCVI, cp. CXIV ff.

(**67**) See Strabo XI. 5. 8; XI. 7. 3; II. 1. 15; XI. 11. 6—exaggerated
report. Lassen I. 619 (ed. 1849); II. 536–7, 624–5 (ed. 1874). Routes in
N. India by way of Ozene and Minnagara led through Peucelaotis
and Kabulistan to Bactria and so to the Oxus, *Peripl.* 47 ff.

(**68**) Pliny VI. 52, from Varro.

(**69**) *Amer. Journ. Philol.* XXVII. 137–8. Rostowzew, *Ir. and Gr.*
203, thinks Iranian influence reached China through Sarmatian
tribes. There is numismatic evidence of Scandinavian trade with
N. and N.W. India—d'Alviella, 56. Cp. trade-route, India—Nov-
gorod—Baltic, 8th–11th cent. A.D. and Samanid coins (*c.* 900–1000)
in Sweden.

(**70**) See W. W. Tarn in *Journ. Hellen. Stud.* XXI, esp. pp. 23–4,
18–19, 21, 28, but cp. Magie in *Ann. Rep. of Amer. Hist. Assoc.* 1919,
297–304. Minns, 443. Von Humboldt, *Asie Centrale*, II. 162–297.
Encycl. Brit. s.v. *Oxus*, s.v. *Turkestan*, s.v. *Asia.* *Geog. Journ.* XII.
306–310; XLII. 396. *Camb. Hist. Ind.* I. 69–70. Holdich, *op. cit.* p. 89.

Iaxartes and Ochos navigable—Strabo XI. 11. 5. See also Götz, 403–4. For S. Russian trade see Rostowzew, *Ir. and Gr.* and *Soc. and Econ.* 146, 531–2. Minns, 445 ff. (the towns).

(71) Hor. *Od.* II. 22. 7. Stat. *S.* I. 6. 55, 77; IV. 4. 63–4 (he means Caucasian); cp. III. 2. 92 etc. Strabo XI. 2. 14–19. Pompon. Mela III. 5. 38. Dionys. Perieg. 719–720. Tac. *Ann.* XII. 20.

(72) Pliny II. 170. Pompon. Mela III. 5. 45 (reading Boii). Lassen III. 58. In Tac. *Ann.* III. 42, Indus is a European name—see *Pauly*, s.v. *Julius*, X. 652, and s.v. *ala*, I. 1243–4. *Rev. Arch.* 1881, 198–9. Perhaps the "Indians" of the Suevi were merely Europeans.

(73) *J.R.A.S.* 1904, pp. 309–312. They may have come through Parthia.

(74) Tarn, *op. cit.* 28.

(75) *Encycl. Brit.* s.v. *Caspian Sea.*

(76) Strabo XII. 3. 14. Diodor. XIV. 30, 31. Manetho, *Fr. Hist. Gr.* II. 614. Müller, No. 78.

(77) For Caspian tribes see esp. Strabo XI. 7. 3; 1. 6–7; 2. 3; 2. 12; 2. 19; 3. 1–6; 4. 1–8; XI. 61. 2; VII. 3. 17. Pompon. Mela I. 19. 108 ff.; II. 1. 119. Pliny VI. 15 ff.; IV. 84. Ptol. V. 8, 9, 10. Herod. IV. 20, 104. Minns, 445 ff.

(78) Strabo XVI. 3. 3. Müller, *Geog. Gr. Min.* I. 176–7, 189 (Agatharch.).

(79) Cooke, *N.S.I.* 114–115. Pliny VI. 140, 145. *Peripl.* 34.

(80) Kennedy, *J.R.A.S.* 1917, pp. 231, 237; 1912, 981–1009. Chwostow, 285–6. *Peripl.* 35. Pliny VI. 140.

(81) *Peripl.* 35–6. Cp. *Ezek.* xxvii. 15, 19. Ptol. VI. 7. 36. Pliny IV. 138; IX. 106.

(82) Birch, *Records of the Past*, IX. 80. Hirth, 39–40, 43, 158. Cp. Alexander's scheme of circumnavigating Arabia.

(83) Use of camels and guides on the routes and in India—Philostrat. *Apoll.* I. 40; II. 6, 17, 40.

(84) The whole route from Hamadan: Pliny VI. 43–5, 61–3, measured for Alexander to the Hyphasis, for Seleucos to the mouth of the Ganges. Cp. Ptol. I. 12. 9; VII. 1. 53; 2. 22. McCr. *Ptol.* 227–8. *Tab. Peut.* Miller, 791–802. Rawlinson, *Intercourse*, 42, 64–5. Cp. *Arch. Surv. Ind.* (Reports, Old Series), VIII. 50. *Camb. Hist. Ind.* I. 543.

(85) *Peripl.* 48. *Camb. Hist. Ind.* 517, 543. *Tab. Peut.* Miller, 789, 786. Roads in India kept in repair, *Ramayana*, III. 226 ff. etc.

(86) *J.R.A.S.* 1901, pp. 537–552, esp. 547–8, 538, 540. *Peripl.* 51–2. Cp. *Arch. Surv. Ind.* (Reports, Old Series), VII. 140.

(87) *Vin. Texts*, III. 401, 382. *Jat.* I. 98, 107.

(88) *Camb. Hist. Ind.* vol. I. 561. Herrmann, *op. cit.* 4.

(89) For the state of trade along the land-routes see Chwostow, 278 ff. Schoff, *J.A.O.S.* 35, pp. 31–41.

(90) Pliny XXXVII. 14–18; XII. 20; VIII. 71; VI. 52. Athenae. VI. 275=109. Plut. *Pomp.* 34, 36, 37, 41. Joseph. *A.J.* XIV. 29 ff.; *B.J.* I. 4. Strabo XI. 7. 3. Dio Cass. XLIX. 24. Strabo XIV. 3. 3. Petron. 123, lines 238–9, 241–2. 'Erythraean Sea' included the Red Sea, Persian Gulf, Arabian Sea, and Indian Ocean, see Schoff, *J.A.O.S.* 33. 349–362.

(91) Plut. *Caes.* 58. Dio Cass. XLIII. 50. Suet. *Iul.* 41. Pliny IV. 10.

(92) Strabo XVI. 2. 20. Joseph. *A.J.* XVI. 282. Cagn.-Laf. *I.G.R.* III. 1223.

(93) Strabo XVI. 1. 28. St Chrys. *ad Stag.* II. 6. Stat. *S.* III. 2. 136–8.

(94) Pliny VI. 141 (query—read Isidorum). Vitruv. VIII. 26. Cp. Ditt. *Suppl.* I. 205 (A.D. 33).

(95) Suet. *Aug.* 101.

(96) *Tab. Peut.* Miller, 647–655. Charlesworth, 104–7. Lassen III. 2. Momms. *Prov.* 19–20. Magie in *Ann. Rep. of Amer. Hist. Assoc.* 1919, 297–304, esp. 302. Strabo XII. 3. 35 etc. Tac. *Ann.* II. 3, 56.

(97) Pliny VI. 3, 37, 39; *Monum. Ancyr.* Lat. V. 53, Gk. XVI. 21; *Monum. Antioch.* (in *Klio*, Beih. XIX. 1927), 31—embassies from Scythians and Sarmatians beyond the Tanais, and Albani and Iberi. Cp. Hor. *Odes*, III. 29. 28; IV. 15. 24. Virg. *Aen.* VI. 799 etc. Tac. *Ann.* XIII. 34. G. Rawlinson, *Sixth Oriental Monarchy*, ch. IX ff.

CHAPTER II

(1) See Lucan X. 33; VII. 429. Cic. *Verr.* II. L. 5. 166. Plut. *Ant.* 37, Indians stirred! cp. perhaps Virg. *Aen.* VIII. 705, 688.

(2) Pliny VI. 58. Strabo II. 1. 9; XV. 35. 36. Arr. *Ind.* 10. Müll. *Fr. Hist. Gr.* IV. 421. V. Smith, *Asoka*, p. 43, rock-edicts II and XIII. *Archaeol. Surv. Ind.* II. 124–5.

(3) *Monum. Ancyr.* (*C.I.G.* 4040. v), Lat. V. 50–1, Gk. XVI. 16, ed. Hardy, pp. 43–4. *Monum. Antioch., loc. cit.* in Ch. I. n. 97.

(**4**) Strabo xv. 1. 4 and 73, cp. 60. Dio Cass. LIV. 9, cp. Zonar. *A*. x. 34. D p. 415 *Corp. Hist. Scr. Byz.* Plut. *Alex.* 69. Rawlinson, *Intercourse*, p. 108. *Ind. Antiqu.* XIV. p. 305 on Ael. XVI. 2.

(**5**) See Flor. *Ep.* II. 34. Hor. *Carm. Saec.* 55–6; *Odes*, I. 12. 56; IV. 14. 41–3; IV. 15. 23; III. 29. 27–8. Prop. II. 10 (III. 1), 15. Virg. *Aen.* VI. 795; VIII. 705; *G.* II. 170. Jer. *Chron.* Ol. 188. Syncell. 248 (589 ed. Bonn, Πανδίων). Suet. *Aug.* 21. Oros. *Hist.* VI. 21. 19; auct. *Vir. Ill.* 79. 1. *Epit.* 1. 9. Vict. *de Caes.* 1. 7. Prop. gives (IV. 3. 7) Bactrians and perhaps (8) Seres. Cp. *Hist. Aug.* '*Aurel.*' 41. The Bactrians (Yueh-chi?) came about silk, or about the Sakas.

(**6**) *Priap.* XLVI. 5 (Müller).

(**7**) Suet. *Aug.* 43.

(**8**) Chwostow, 355–6, wrongly, I think, makes Poros a Pandyan king, but rightly points out that the Pandyan embassy was not the only one.

(**9**) Letronne, *Acad. d. Inscr. et B.-L.*, *Mém.* vᵉ S. x. 226, has needless doubts. See Lassen III. 59; I. 158 (ed. 1849). Friedländer IV. 8–9. Priaulx, 65–87 (and in *J.R.A.S.* 1860). Mommsen, *R.G.D.A.* (1883), pp. 132 ff. Bunbury II. 167. Hirth, 304 ff. Cp. Friedländer IV. 9. See also Charlesworth, 62. Vincent II. 463. Gardthausen I. 2. 832. Nissen, *Verein*, H. 95, 1894, p. 13. If Seres were Cheras, then Horace as cited above, Ch. I. n. 31, and perhaps Prop. IV. 3. 8; Luc. I. 19 (cp. *Hist. Aug.* '*Aurelian*,' 41, Flor. II. 34, Juv. VI. 403, Claudian 8. 258; and so on) do not give mere boasting. Augustus does not speak of Seres at all. Ptol. VII. 1. 45–6 (Pandoouoi of N.W. India) does not invalidate the theory of a Pandyan embassy from S. India.

(**10**) Augustus had Caesarion recalled not from India as Plutarch says (*Ant.* 81), but from Ethiopia (Dio Cass. LI. 15, cp. Suet. *Aug.* 17) though Plutarch's words are indeed 'to India through Ethiopia,' i.e. through Meroe to the Axumites or the Somali.

(**11**) *Ind. Antiqu.* II. 145.

(**12**) Sewell, *J.R.A.S.* 1904, esp. pp. 620–636, cf. also pp. 280–4 of this book.

(**13**) *J.R.A.S.* 1904, p. 403 (Hultzsch). Sewell, *op. cit.* 594, 620–1. Smith, 270–1, n. 1. *J.A.S.B.* I. 32–3. A few Republican coins went to Ceylon and all perhaps came under the Empire.

(**14**) Sewell, *op. cit.* 623–5.

(**15**) *Numism. Chron.* 1898, 319 and No. 4 in list. C. v. Ernst, *Numism. Zeitschr.* (*Wien*), XII. 1880, 46 f. Momms.-Blac. III. 337–8. Eckhel, *Doctr. Num. Vet.* VI. 171. A single type of Tiberius is also common, *Num. Chron., loc. cit.*

(**16**) Sewell, *op. cit.* 596, 621. *Numism. Chron.* 1899, 263–5.

(**17**) The gingelly-oil plant, rice, and the citron, peach, and apricot trees had already spread westwards as cultivated plants, as we shall see. References in Augustan writers to the Indian products here mentioned will be found in the notes of Part II.

(**18**) Cic. *Verr.* II. 5. 56; 4. 41; 4. 27.

(**19**) Lucan X. 155 ff. Plut. *Ant.* 58, 84. Suet. *Aug.* 71. *Hist. Aug.* '*Trig. Tyr.*' 32, 6. Tac. *Ann.* III. 55.

(**20**) Dio Cass. LVII. 15. Tac. *Ann.* III. 53; II. 33.

(**21**) Sewell, *op. cit.* 621, 626–7, 596. *Num. Chron.* 1898, p. 319. No. 16 in list especially. *J.R.A.S. Bomb. Br.* I. 294. *J.A.S.B.* XX. 372.

(**22**) Chwostow, 400. E. Thurston, *Madras Gov. Mus.* Cat. 2, pp. 7, 8, 10, 21.

(**23**) Dio Cass. LVII. 17. 7. Joseph. *A.J.* XVIII. 5. Tac. *Ann.* II. 42, 56–7. Suet. *Tib.* 37. Strabo XVI. 2. 3. Pliny XXXVII. 37, 46. Cooke, *N.S.I.* 147, pp. 329–330. Suet. *Tib.* 41, cp. *Calig.* 14. Joseph. *A.J.* XVIII. 4. 4. Tac. *Ann.* VI. 33 ff., Iberians take Artaxata; Parthians fail against them. Cp. IV. 5.

(**24**) Pliny XXXVII. 17; cp. XIII. 22. Seneca, *ad Helv.* 10. Suet. *Calig.* 37, 52, 55. Joseph. *A.J.* XIX. 1. Pliny XIX. 117–118. Dio Cass. LIX. 26. 10. Zonar. *Ep.* XI. 5.

(**25**) Ostia also got a brigade. Suet. *Claud.* 18, 19, 20, 25.

(**26**) Philostrat. *Apollon.* I. 20. Tac. *Ann.* XII. 12, 15–17. Pliny V. 86.

(**27**) Tac. *Ann.* XI. 8 ff. Cp. XII. 44 ff. Iberians involved.

(**28**) Diodor. II. 55–60. Cp. Lucian, *Ver. Hist.* Introd. 3. Lassen III. 253–269. E. Rohde, *der Griech. Roman.* pp. 241 ff. -

(**29**) Pliny VI. 84–91. Priaulx, *op. cit.* 91–122. Was he sailing round Africa in pursuit of customs-defaulters?

(**30**) Ferguson, *J.R.A.S.* 1904, pp. 539–541. Kennedy, *J.R.A.S.* 1904, 359–362. Priaulx, 98–9. Vincent II. 48. Chwostow, 365–6. Friedländer IV. 9. In Pliny VI. 84, I would correct XV to XL, thus making the voyage one of 40 days.

(**31**) *Peripl.* 57. Pliny VI. 100, 101–6.

(**32**) *Peripl.* 57, 26. Pliny VI. 100.

(**33**) *Peripl.* 57. Return voyages were probably very soon found out. The *Itin. Alex.* 110 seems to put the Hippalus Sea near the Persian Gulf—this points to Hippalos as the discoverer of the direct voyage to the Indus rather than all the stages.

(**34**) *Peripl.* 31. Some still returned by way of Moscha late in the season, perhaps by coasting in the old way, id. 32.

(**35**) Pliny VI. 101.

(**36**) Pliny VI. 100, 172. Ptol. IV. 7. 12. *Itin. Alex.* 110. Vincent II. 56. Schoff, ad *Peripl.* p. 227.

(**37**) *J.R.A.S.* 1898, 248–287. Cp. Kornemann, *Jan.* I. 57.

(**38**) Chwostow, 346–9, 360, 386–7, 433. Cp. Kornemann, *Jan.* I. 57–8. Schur in *Klio*, XX. 1926, 220. See also *Pauly*, VIII. 2, s.v. *Hippalos*, 1660–1. Lassen III. 3–4. Dahlmann, 24 ff.

(**39**) Chwostow, 363. Some (e.g. Richter, *Hand. u. Verk.* 121) put Hippalos in Nero's reign. We cannot be sure. Rostowzew, *Soc. and Econ.* 93 (reading Hippalus).

(**40**) See the whole journey from Alexandria in Pliny VI. 100–6 (cp. *Anton. Itin.* 172–3, pp. 76–7, ed. Parth. and Pind.).

(**41**) *Penny Cyclopaedia*, s.v. *Monsoon*, a good account which I have used. Chwostow, 212.

(**42**) Ptol. I. 9. 1.

(**43**) Pliny II. 169–170. (The Indians were perhaps victims of storms on the Caspian Sea, see above, Ch. I. note 72.) Through ignorance the freedman of Annius Plocamus had been caught while going the other way and blown to Ceylon, probably in October.

(**44**) Chwostow, 183–5, 213. Fabric. ad *Peripl.* pp. 114–115.

(**45**) *C.I.G.* 4957 (news of Galba). *B.G.U.* 646 (Pertinax). Wilcken, *Ostr.* 800 (Nero). Cp. *O.P.* VII. 1021. Did report of Nero's death come by the Via Egnatia—Troas—Syria—Palestine—Egypt, by imperial post?

(**46**) Ptol. I. 9 and 17. *Peripl.* 39, 49, 56 (July), 15.

(**47**) Figures from Pliny VI. 101–6; cp. VI. 175, 163 (reading quadraginta dierum).

(**48**) Except possibly a Chinese record of a voyage from India to the Roman Empire lasting more than one month—Hirth, 168–9. Cp. Pliny's 40 days Ocelis—Muziris.

(**49**) Pliny VI. 106.

(**50**) Lucian, *Navig.* 7 ff.; cp. *Anth. Pal.* XI. 306 (Alex.—Syria—Italy); IX. 90 (Syria—Greece); cp. IX. 384, 9; X. 1–7, and 14, 16, 25.

(**51**) Schoff, *Peripl.* 8–16, but see also *J.R.A.S.* 1916, 836 (Kennedy); 1917, 827–830 (Schoff); 1918, 111 ff. (Kennedy). The latest tendency is to put the author in Domitian's reign—Schur, *Klio*, Beih. XV. 1923, pp. 43–4; XX. 1926, 222. Kornemann, *Jan.* I. 58 ff., 55 and n. 4. Rostowzew, *Soc. and Econ.* 91–3. See also Chwostow, 426–9, with authorities there referred to. The very survival of such a work shews the new importance of the Indian trade; cp. Dahlmann, 30 ff. Modern names given are those accepted by Schoff.

(**52**) The fabrics of Arsinoë mentioned by the *Periplus* came from the inland nome, not the Gulf of Suez—see a Hawara Papyrus, *Arch. f. Pap.* V. p. 389.

(**53**) Steph. Byz. s.v. *Ἄξουμις* and s.v. *Ἄδουλις*. *Peripl.* 4–14. Pliny VI. 173. Ptol. IV. 7. Roman authority surely ended at Bab-el-Mandeb if indeed it extended so far.

(**54**) *Peripl.* 15–17. Pliny VI. 158.

(**55**) *Peripl.* 16, 21–5, 31. Change of capital from Marib to Saphar was perhaps due to Gallus' expedition. Glaser, *Die Abessin.* 37–8.

(**56**) *Id.* 30–1. Cosmas III. 169 B. Virgil, *G.* I. 213 (Panchaia?). Dues of Socotra farmed to the Romans? Kornemann, *Jan.* I. 11.

(**57**) That is, by Persis=Parthia, *Peripl.* 33, 36. Hirth, 38, 68, 145. Schoff, *J.A.O.S.* 35, pp. 35–9. Muza not used, Pliny VI. 104. Note that Parthia controlled the Arabian coast from Kuria Muria Islands onwards—*Peripl.* 33. Glaser, *op. cit.* 34.

(**58**) *Peripl.* 32, 34–6. Pliny VI. 149. Ptol. VI. 7. 36 (his distortion of the gulf is less than Mela's, III. 8. 73). Glaser, *Sk.* 189–194, Chwostow, 218–9, 287, and others place Ommana on the wrong side of the gulf. Naturally Mela is more correct with regard to the Red Sea. Pompon. Mela III. 8. 74. Wartena, 10.

(**59**) Pliny VI. 104.

(**60**) Ocelis was distinctly Arabian, controlled by Muza(?), not by Rome. *Peripl.* 25. Pliny, *loc. cit.* But note that the *Periplus* says it was the 'first landing for those sailing into the gulf'—in this chapter the only gulf mentioned is the Avalitic=Gulf of Aden.

(**61**) *Peripl.* 38–9, 47. The Minnagara in the district of the Indus is not Patala, for Ptol. gives both Patala and a 'Binagara' in the regions of the Indus—Ptol. VII. 1. 17; 1. 59, 61. J. Marshall, *Guide to Taxila*, 13 (Maues). Rapson, *Indian Coins*, 8. Dahlmann, 41.

(62) *Pauly*, s.v. *India*, 1280. Lassen I. 108.

(63) *Peripl.* 41 ff. and in 47 read μαχιμώτατον ἔθνος Βακτριανῶν ὑπὸ βασιλέα Κοῦσαν ἰδιότοπον—Kennedy in *J.R.A.S.* 1916, p. 831; cp. 1913, p. 128. Steph. Byz. s.v. Βαρύγαζα, *Imper. Gaz.* IX. 297. *Bomb. Gaz.* I. Pt. I. 26 ff. ἀπὸ τῶν ἄλλων ἐμπορίων refers apparently to regions of E. India or east coast marts, say of the Kistna district. Nahapana (Kushan viceroy?) was overthrown by the Andhra Gautamiputra Sri Satakarni, who re-stamped the Saka coins.

(64) *Peripl.* 52–3. *Bomb. Gaz.* I. Pt. I. pp. 44–5 (note 2 of p. 44). *J.A.S.B.* 1904, 272–3 (Wilson). *J.R.A.S.* 1917, 829 (Schoff); 1918, 109–110 (Kennedy). *Ind. Antiqu.* XLII. 279; cp. Schoff, ad *Peripl.* 197–200. Tagara and Paethana—cf. also *Archaeol. Surv. Western Ind.* III. 54–5. Kalyana flourished later and St Thomas was connected with it—Cosmas 445 D–448 A. Dahlmann, 58–9, 153 ff., 161, 164–5. *Archaeol. Surv. Western Ind.* IV. p. 93, No. 5; p. 95, No. 16.

(65) *Peripl.* 53–4. W. Logan, *Malabar*, I. 77. Lassen III. 6. Damirice (Dravida-desam) from *Tab. Peut.* Segm. XII (Miller, 627); Limyrice in *Peripl.*; Dimirice in Ptol. I. 76; VII. 1. 8, 85. See also Pliny VI. 104. Strong Andrae with 30 cities—id. VI. 67. *Tab. Peut.* Miller, 627, has Andre Indi. Andrapolis: *Apocryph. N.T.* trans. M. R. James, p. 366. The Syriac text has Sandaruk (or Sanadruk) instead (cp. Sandanes of *Peripl.*) = Calliena? Cf. Dahlmann, 51 ff., 64 ff. Smith, *Asoka*, p. 161. Have we a record of service against Indian pirates in *C.I.G.* 6195, line 8, or is it an allusion to Dionysos? 'Pirates' are marked on *Tab. Peut.* Miller, 628, cp. Ch. III. n. 85.

(66) *Peripl.* 54–6, reading in 54 Arabia for Ariace. Miller, *Itin.* 790; *Imper. Gaz.* XVI. 6–7; XX. 21. Pillai, 19, 16. De Lacouperie, 253. Pliny VI. 88, 104–5. Lucian, *Q. Hist. S. Scrib.* 31. *Ind. Antiqu.* I. 194, 229–230; III. 333–4; XXXI. 338 ff., esp. 342–3. W. Logan, *Malabar*, I. 76, 80, 254. *J.R.A.S.* 1913, 130–1. Schoff, *J.A.O.S.* 33, p. 211. Smith, 464 ff. Chwostow, 227. Schur, *Klio*, XX. 1926, 220–1 (Mangalore and Nileswara, identifications now rejected). St Thomas: *J.R.A.S.* 1924, Far Eastern section, pp. 215 ff.—a legend which makes St Thomas land near Cranganore and go overland to the Chola Kingdom and still farther. Cp. vol. I. pp. 171 ff. Bunbury II. 468.

Pillai, 19, who denies the existence of the backwaters until after Ptolemy, identifies Bacare with Vaikkarai. Cp. Smith, 477.

(**67**) *Peripl.* 58–9. Pliny VI. 105. Pillai, 12 and 37–8. Cp. Mookerji, *Indian Shipping*, 128–9. V. A. Smith, 462–3.

(**68**) *Peripl.* 59–60. Ptol. VII. 1. 13. Smith, 462–3. Pillai, 24–5. Strabo II. 3. 4–5. *Apocryph. Acts of Apost.* trans. Wright, pp. 146–7. *Apocryph. N.T.* trans. James, 365. *Ind. Antiqu.* XXXII. 151. Dahlmann, esp. 34 ff., 103 ff., 151. *Veröffentlichungen des Forschungsinst.* No. 5, 60–1; cp. 140–1. Euseb. *H.E.* III. 1. 1 ; V. 10. *C.I.G.* 2545.

(**69**) *Peripl.* 60. Pillai, 23–4. Smith, 463. Ptol. VII. 1. 88. It is put inland by Ptol. Schoff puts Camara (Caber in Cosmas XI. 448 B) near Karikal.

(**70**) *Peripl.* 61. Pompon. Mela III. 7. 70. Marcianus, *Geog. Gr. Min.* I. p. 535. Pliny VI. 24. Steph. Byz. s.v. Ταπροβάνη. Lassen I. 232 ff., 286–7 ; and see also J. E. Tennent, *Ceylon*, I. 549 ff.

(**71**) *Peripl.* 62, Maesolia in Ptolemy.

(**72**) North of the Tamil regions both coasts of India were controlled by Andhra Kings.

(**73**) *Peripl.* 63.

(**74**) Schoff, *Peripl.* p. 255. Monahan, 15.

(**75**) *Peripl.* 62–5. Pompon. Mela I. 2. 11 ; III. 6. 60. Ptol. VII. 2. 2, 15, 16. McCrindle, *Ptol.* 191–2, 218, 246. Lassen III. 38, 235–7 ; I. 523–537. Pseudo-Callisth. III. 8. Roughly the Besatae dwelt in Sikkim, the Cirrhadae in Morung west of Sikkim—Schoff, ad *Peripl.* pp. 253, 278–9.

(**76**) Mookerji, *Indian Shipping*, 19–53. *J.R.A.S.* 1898, pp. 241–272. Lassen II. 583.

(**77**) *Peripl.* 16, 21, 27, 31, 32, 54.

(**78**) *Peripl.* 6, 14, 36. Agatharch. in Müller I. 191.

(**79**) *Peripl.* 36. 6, 14 ; 44. 39. Lassen II. 584. *Archaeol. Surv. Ind.* 1913–14, 129–130—river-boat. Cp. 1905–6, 145 ff. Schoff, ad *Peripl.* 245.

(**80**) Pliny VI. 105. Pillai, 16. *Peripl.* 55.

(**81**) Pliny VI. 82. *Peripl.* 61.

(**82**) *Peripl.* 60. *J.A.S.B.* 1847, 1–78. Heeren, *Ideen über die Polit.* etc. I. iii. 361. Pillai, 29. *Camb. Hist. Ind.* I. 212–214. Schoff, 243, 246.

(**83**) Sir W. Elliott, *Coins of S. India*, Pl. I. Fig. 38. *Peripl.* 63–4.

(**84**) *Jahr. d. K. D. Arch. Instit.* VII. 50–1. Philostrat. *Apollon*, III. 50.

(85) See the curious story in Philostrat. *Apollon.* III. 35; from Ptolemaic era when Arabians may have persuaded the Indians to treat Greeks in this way? But mention of Erythras seems to take us back to a much earlier age. Chwostow believes the prohibition was an Indian one (Chwostow, 405–6).

(86) *Peripl.* 56. Pillai, 16. *Peripl.* 10; and see Chwostow, 405–6. Hirth, 169.

(87) *Acts* xxvii. 6 and 37; xxviii. 11. *Josephi vita*, 3. Lucian, *Navig.* 5–6, 13, 18. Suet. *Claud.* 18–19.

(88) Frank, 300 ff.

(89) Philo, *de Leg.* 21. Pers. v. 141–2. Juv. XIV. 278 ff.

(90) *O.P.* II. 300 (CCC).

(91) Catull. XI. 2. Prop. II. 9. 29–30; IV. (v) 3. 7–10. Hor. *Ep.* I. 1. 4; *Odes*, II. 22. 7 etc. Romans: *Mahabharata* II. 51. 17.

(92) Kenyon, *Gk. Pap.* II. p. 48, no. 260, lines 41–2. Pliny VI. 101–6. Greeks: *Mahabharata* II. 14. 4; III. 254. 18; XII. 207. 43.

(93) Priaulx, *Apollon.* p. 161. Vidal de Lablache, *Acad. d. Inscr. et B.-L., C.-R.* 1896, p. 462.

(94) Pompon. Mela I. 61; III. 7. 22 ff. ; I. 2. 12, 14. Pliny VI. 149. Strabo XVI 4. 14. Notu Ceras=Guardafui.

(95) Pompon. Mela III. 68–9, 61, 70, 71. Of the Indus, Strabo gives two, Mela several, the *Periplus* and Ptolemy seven mouths.

(96) Pliny VI. 142–162.

(97) Pliny VI. 57.

(98) Pompon. Mela III. 7. 70. *Peripl.* 56, 63.

(99) Joseph. *A.J.* VIII. 1. 64. Pliny has 'Chryse promunturium': VI. 55. Pliny's Perimula, more than 60 Roman miles from Patala, should be located in India. Pliny VI. 72 ; IX. 106. Ael. XV. 8. McCrindle, *Ptol.* 201 (at Simylla). The idea of Chryse would be caused by reports of Sumatra, of Argyre perhaps by reports of Java— Bunbury II. 475.

(100) *Isaiah* xlix. 12. Yule, I. 3 ff., 14 ff., 20.

(101) Strabo II. 3. 4–5. Pliny II. 169–170. Seneca, *Q.N.* Prol. 11. Cp. *ad Paulin.* 2. Lucian, *Hermotim.* 4. Voyages between Egypt and Massilia—Sulp. Sev. *Dial.* I. 1; Narbo—id. I. 3; Spain—Pallad. *Hist.* I. 14; Britain—Leontius, *V.S.J.E.* 13. The merchants of Spain and Gaul would call at Puteoli and there take in Italian goods.

(102) Philostrat. *Apollon.* III. 35.

(**103**) Chwostow, 406. Götz, 486–7.

(**104**) *Milindapañha*, 359; trans. II. 269 (*S.B.E.* XXXVI), quoted by *Camb. Hist. Ind.* I. 212. *Ramayana*, III. 237.

(**105**) Dio Chrys. *Or.* LXXIX. 287, Dind.=5, ed. Arnim.

(**106**) Id. *Or.* XXXV. 271, Dind.=22–3, ed. Arnim.

(**107**) Mommsen, *Prov.* II. 299 ff. Cp. Strabo XVII. 1. 15. Ethiopians (which includes Abyssinians) did not use the Red Sea much, until of course the Axumites were established ; these let Indians into Adulis though the Romans proceeded to exclude them from Muza.

(**108**) Dio Chrys. *Or.* XXXII. 413, 20, Dind.=40, ed. Arnim.

(**109**) Id. *Or.* XXXV. 271=22, Arnim.

(**110**) Id. XXXII. 36, Arnim.

(**111**) Hultzsch, *J.R.A.S.* 1904, p. 402. *Hermes*, XXXIX. 307 ff. Lepsius, *Denkm.* VI. 166, p. 81; *Ind. Antiqu.* III. 229, n. We may suppose that the Redesiya route would be free from traffic and used by men not bringing large loads. Bronze bust of an Indian?—Greek work—*Jahrb. d. D. Arch. Inst.* XXXII, *Anz.* 69–71.

(**112**) Dio Chrys. *Or.* LIII. 6, Arnim. Sen. *ad Helv.* 6. Ael. XII. 18.

(**113**) *J.R.A.S.* 1917, 227.

(**114**) Mart. *Spect.* 3. *Epig.* I. 104. 10. Juv. VI. 585–6. Representations of Indians, except in connexion with Dionysos or Alexander occur generally in the eastern part of the Empire.

(**115**) Traders in the East, e.g. Black Sea, Arr. *Peripl.* 9. 5; Red Sea, Diodor. III. 18; Charax, Pliny VI. 140, were of course Roman subjects, not generally true Romans.

(**116**) J. Marshall, *Guide to Taxila*, 14–16. Priaulx gives full details. See Philostrat. *Apollon.* I. 19 ff., esp. 20, 40 ; II. 2, 4, and his return, III. 53 ff. Much of the account is mere story-telling.

(**117**) Milne, *Eg. under R. Rule* (ed. 1924), pp. 14, 15, 25, 56.

(**118**) Pliny VI. 104. Philo, *de Somn.* II. 7–9 (48–63), *de Vit. Contempl.* 6, 49 ff.

(**119**) See Pliny XII. 82–4; XXXVII. 17; VI. 101.

(**120**) Suet. *Nero*, 31. Cp. *Galba*, 18; *Nero*, 11. Plut. *Galba*, 19. Sen. *Ep.* XIV. 2 (90), 15. Pliny XIII. 32 ; XV. 105. Cp. XXIV. 5. Petron. *S.* 38, cp. 60, 65, 70, 77, 78, 71, 76, 119 line 12. *Peripl.* 10, 56. Sen. *de Benef.* VII. 9. Cp. *Ep.* 86. Pliny XIV. 52. Dio Cass. LXI. 10 ; LXII. 2. Pliny XV. 105. Petron. *S.* 67, 55. Juv. VI. 466. Cp. I *Tim.* ii. 9. Clem. Alex. *Paed.* III. 4. 271 P; II. 12. Tertull. *de* *cult. fem.* I. 1. 6–8. Extant collections shew the use of glass paste for gems.

CHAPTER III

(1) Schur, *Klio*, Beih. xv. 1923, and *Klio*, xx. 1926, 215 ff., and critics there mentioned. Milne (ed. 1924), p. 22. Rostowzew, *Soc. and Econ.* 513 (correcting Myos Hormos to Leuce Come).

(2) Pliny vi. 181; xii. 19. Tac. *Hist.* i. 31. Cp. Joseph. *B.J.* iii. 65. Suet. *Nero*, 19, 47. Compare also Dio Cass. lxiii. 8. 1. Plut. *Galba*, 2. Sen. *Q.N.* vi. 8. *C.I.G.* iii. 4699 and possibly *Anth. Pal.* ix. 352. Tac. *Ann.* xiv. 27. Vespasian added colonists and territory to Puteoli. On Meroe see Chwostow, 63, 71–2.

(3) Tac. *Ann.* xiv. 25. *Bombay Gaz.* i. Pt. i. 490, n. 2. *Peripl.* 39, 46.

(4) Tac. *Hist.* i. 6. Suet. *Nero*, 19. Tac. *Ann.* vi. 33. See also Dio Cass. lxiii. 8. 1. Pliny corrects to Caucasian, vi. 30, 40, and mentions (40) map of Armenia and Caspian regions sent to Rome by Corbulo's staff in A.D. 58. Schur, *op. cit.* 62–9. Hudson, *Class. Rev.* Nov.—Dec., 1924, p. 161. Tyras was not added permanently.

(5) Suet. *Vesp.* 8. Cagn.-Laf. iii. 133; *C.I.L.* iii. 312. Dio Cass. lxviii. 19. See also *C.I.L.* iii. 306, 14184. 48.

(6) Tac. *Ann.* xi. 8 ff.

(7) Pliny vi. 122. Ammian. Marcell. xxiii. 6. 23.

(8) Pliny v. 88. App. *B.C.* v. 9. Cooke, *N.S.I.* 113–115, 147, pp. 329–330. *J.A.O.S.* 1904, 320. Momms. *Prov.* ii. 93.

(9) Id. 138, cp. Momms.-Blac. iii. 322.

(10) Hirth, 41 ff., cp. 3, 165–6.

(11) Id. 62, cp. 70 etc.

(12) Id. 219, 187, 239.

(13) Momms. *Prov.* ii. 94.

(14) Schoff, ad *Peripl.* p. 268. See also Yule, i. 57 ff. The Persepolis—Carmana route now became quite unimportant—Schoff, *J.A.O.S.* 35, p. 38.

(15) Pompon. Mela iii. 8. 60; cp. *Peripl.* 65.

(16) Priaulx, *Apollon.* 1–61. Philostrat. *Apollon.* i. 19 ff., 20, 40; ii. 2, 4 ff.; iii. 53 ff.

(17) Joseph. *B.J.* vii. 54. Cp. Tac. *Ann.* iii. 55.

(**18**) The references in Mart. and Stat. will be found in notes to Part II.

(**19**) Quintil. XI. 1. 3; XII. 10. 47.

(**20**) Jer. *Chron.* Ol. 217, A.D. 92. Dio Cass. LXVII. 14. Stat. *S.* IV. 3. Under Titus, Canobic arm of Nile cleared out—Cagn.-Laf. *I.G.R.* I. 1098, cp. 1099. Ditt. *S.* II. 672. Under Domitian, canal Schedia—Alexandria cleared out, id. 673, and bridge built near Coptos, Petrie, *Kopt.* p. 26. *C.I.L.* III. S. II. 13,580. Chwostow, 369.

(**21**) Mart. I. 87. 2; III. 82. 6; XI. 15. 6; III. 55. 1–3; XI. 8. 9, 15. 6, 18. 9; XII. 55. 7, 65. 4. Juv. VIII. 86. Petron. *Fragm.* 18.

(**22**) Mart. IV. 13. 3; XI. 27. 9–11; XIV. 110; X. 38. 8; VI. 55. 3. Cp. Sid. Apoll. *C.* IX. 323.

(**23**) Suet. *Domit.* 18.

(**24**) *C.I.L.* III. 312, 318, 14184. 48.

(**25**) Stat. *S.* III. 2. 136–8; I. 6. 55, 77; VI. 4. 63–4; V. 3. 185–8; III. 12. 92. Suet. *Domit.* 2.

(**26**) Stat. *S.* III. 2. 21–4. Mart. XII. 74. 1.

(**27**) Dio Cass. LXVIII. 17 ff. Different views of Trajan: Schiller, *Gesch. d. R. Kaiserz.* I. 2, 546, 554–563. De la Berge, *Essai*, 180–2, 288 ff. Bury, *St. R. E.* 455–6 (favourable). Rostowzew, *Soc. and Econ.* 307–311. B. W. Henderson, *Five R. Emperors*, 308 ff., 339 ff.

(**28**) Liebenam, *d. R. Leg.* p. 175. *Prosopogr. Imp. R.* II. p. 164. Damascus:—*Pauly*, s.v. *Damaskos.*

(**29**) Eckhel VI. 420. Dio Cass. LXVIII. 14; LXXV. 1. 2. Eutrop. VIII. 18. *Notit. Dign.* III. 1. 203. *Chron. Pasch.* I. p. 472. Ptol. V. 16. 1. Renewed? prosperity of Petra after destruction of Palmyra—see Ammian. Marcell. XIV. 8. 13. Province of Arabia: Brünn. u. Domas, *Pr. Ar.* III. 250 ff.

(**30**) Commercial importance of Petra, etc.: Pliny VI. 144. Strabo XVI. 4. 24. *Peripl.* 19. Hirth, 159–163. Ptol. V. 17. 5.

(**31**) Brünn. u. Domas, *op. cit.* II. 177–244 (Trajan's road). *C.I.L.* III. 14149. 30, 6715, 6722, the road being maintained for centuries. Ptol. V. 175 (Auara near Petra is not Leuce Come? Cp. Steph. Byz. s.v. Αὔαρα. *Geog. Ravenn.* II. 6). If the inscription of Adulis is late, we have merely a translation back into Leuce Come—Cosmas II. 104 C ff., 105 C. *C.I.G.* 5172 B. *J. E. Arch.* 1915, p. 112.

(**32**) Eckhel III. 500 ff. Ditt. *S.* 626. *Chron. Pasch.* 472 (Bonn). John Mal. *Chron.* IX. 223 (Bonn, correcting Augustus to Trajan).

Damasc. ap. *Phot. Cod.* 272 (347). Ptol. v. 17. 7. Entitled Metropolis by Philip; prospered—Ammian. Marcell. xiv. 8. 13 etc. Rostowzew, *Soc. and Econ.* 251–3. *Pauly*, s.v. *Bostra.*

(**33**) Dio Cass. lxviii. 17, 18. Eutrop. viii. 3. Fronto, *Pr. Hist.* 9. vol. ii. p. 204, Haines. Pliny min. *Ep. ad Traj.* x. 74.

(**34**) Dio Cass. lxviii. 19–20. Procop. *de Aedif.* iii. 4. Eutrop. viii. 3. Cohen, *Med. Traj.* 206–7, 372. Arr. *Peripl.* 11. *C.I.L.* x. 8291, Armenia put under legate of Cappadocia?

(**35**) Cohen, *Med. Traj.* 29, 318. Eckhel vi. 438.

(**36**) Dio Cass. lxviii. 28. Cohen, 184. Vict. *Caes.* 13. 3. Eutrop. viii. 3. Arr. *Fr. Hist. Gr.* vol. iii. 590. Chwostow, 366–7.

(**37**) Fronto, *op. cit.* 16 = vol. ii. p. 214, Haines. On Mesene see Reinaud in *Journ. Asiat.* vᵉ Sér. T. xviii. 161 ff. etc.

(**38**) Trajan's activities reflected in the Wei-lio: Hirth, 71 (341), 146, 151.

(**39**) Stat. *S.* iv. 1. 40–2; cp. iv. 3. 155. Cp. also the general tone of iii. 3; iii. 4. 57–63. Sil. Ital. *Bell. Pun.* iii. 612–615. Mart. xii. 8. 8–10. Plut. *Pomp.* 70.

(**40**) Dio Cass. lxviii. 28–9. Zonar. *Ann.* xi. 22. Eutrop. viii. 3. P. Gardner, *Gk. and Scyth. Kings*, Pl. xxviii. 20, RIOM and goddess Roma. B. W. Henderson, *Five R. Emperors*, 330–1.

(**41**) Dio Cass. lxviii. 15. Smith, 275.

(**42**) *Ind. Antiqu.* vols. lii. 53; xlii. 136–7; xl. 179. Smith, *Fine Art*, 133–4,155,379,358,cp. 355–6. Agisala = Agesilaos,Kanishka's overseer.

(**43**) Ptol. iv. 5. Sext. Ruf. 20. Eutrop. viii. 3. John of Nikiou, 72. Dio Cass. lxviii. 32. Euseb. *H.E.* iv. 2; *P. Giess.* 24, 27, 41; *P. Brem.* 40; *P. Heidelb.* 36. Cp. *O.P.* 705. *C.I.G.* 4713 C? *C.I.L.* iii. 1. 24? *O.P.* xii. 1426; another given there; *P. Hamb.* 39. Epiphan. *ad Haer.* 46 = 66. Antonin. Martyr. 41. Lucian, *Pseudomant.* 44 (voyage Clysma—India). *J.R.A.S.* 1916, 833–4. Clysma is Qulzum. Ormerod. 258. Chwostow, 367, 371–2. Strabo xvi. 4. 23. Pliny vi. 167 ff., 176. Ptol. vii. 1. 84. A road ran generally close to the canal.

(**44**) Charlesworth, 177–8. Chwostow, 208–9, 211, notes how the canal-route to Clysma helped to link Egypt with Petra and its trade. Route via Pelusium—id. 206–7. Joseph. *B.J.* iv. 10. 5; iv. 11. 5.

(**45**) Juv. xii. 75–81, and Schol. *ad loc.* Pliny min. *Panegyr.* 29–31. *Hist. Aug.* '*Aurelian.*' 45. 2; '*Tac.*' 10. 5 etc. Cagnat, *I.G.R.* i. 421 = *C.I.G.* 5853.

(46) *J.A.S.B.* vol. I. p. 397. *J.R.A.S.* 1904, 620, 630.

(47) Bury, *St. R. E.* 493. B. W. Henderson, *Life and Principate of Hadrian,* 140. Schiller I. 2. 606.

(48) *Peripl.* 34–6. Pliny VI. 139–140. Cooke, *N.S.I.* 113–115.

(49) *Hist. Aug. 'Hadr.'* 21.

(50) Eckhel III. 504. *C.I.G.* 4667 etc.

(51) II *Chron.* viii. 4. Cooke, *N.S.I.* 147, pp. 329–330. Pliny V. 88. App. *B.C.* v. 9.

(52) Cooke, *N.S.I.* 113–115. Pliny VI. 145. Momms.-Marqu. IX. p. 362 with authorities. Chwostow, 283 ff. Rostowzew, *Soc. and Econ.* 147, 160, 531–2.

(53) Visit of Hadrian, Cooke, *N.S.I.* 122. Tariff-list—id. 147 = *C.I.G.* 6015, discussed by Hirschfeld, *K. V.* 81, n. 1. 90, n. 1. Dessau, *Hermes,* XIX. 486 ff. Rostowzew in *Philolog. Suppl.-B.* IX. 405–6. Cp. Priaulx, 164–5.

(54) Bury, *op. cit.* 507. Waddington, 2585 = *C.I.G.* 4482. Steph. Byz. s.v. Πάλμυρα (φρούριον Συρίας). The Palmyrenes who spread over the Empire were mostly soldiers, not merchants.

(55) *Peripl.* 36.

(56) Dio Cass. LXIX. 15.

(57) Arrian, *Peripl.* 9, 3; 95; 10, 3; 11, 2–3. Cagn.-Laf. *I.G.R.* III. 133. Joseph. *B.J.* II. 16. Pliny VI. 15. *Anth. Pal.* IX. 210. Ptol. v. 10. 2.

(58) Cagnat, *I.G.R.* I. 1207. Chwostow, 373–4.

(59) Cagn.-Laf. *I.G.R.* 1142. *Rev. Arch.* N.S. XXI. 1870, pp. 313–318. Ditt. *S.* II. 701. Dürr, *Arch-Ep. Semin. Wien,* 1880, No. 143. Momms. *Prov.* p. 297, n. 2. Chwostow, 192. *J. Eg. Arch.* 1925, 149–150.

(60) Aristeid. XLVIII. 485 (361), Dind. Juv. XV. 28. Berenice route still important :—*P. Lond.* 328 (A.D. 163); *P. Hamb.* 7. 3. Ael. VII. 18.

(61) *C.I.G.* 5127 B, 29–30. Cosmas II. 105 C. *J. E. Arch.* 1915, 112.

(62) *Hist. Aug. 'Saturnin.'* 8. Cp. Juv. *S.* xv.

(63) See Dio Cass. LXIX. 16. *Hist. Aug. 'Hadr.'* 19. 5. King, 149, 325, 220, 309. Juv. VI. 153–7, 380–2, 80, 585; VII. 144, 130, 133; XIII. 139; XI. 123–6; X. 150, 26–7; V. 38–43; IV. 108–9; XV. 28; XIV. 137, 308.

(64) 'Vict.' *Ep.* 15. 4. Cp. App. *Praef.* 7. Momms. *Prov.* II. 155. Reinaud, 235.

(65) *Hist. Aug. 'Aurel.'* 17. Sewell, *op. cit.* 602–3. King, *E.G.* 42,

58, 56. Schoff, ad *Peripl.* 219. Cp. Momms.-Blac. III. 24–5, 61. For supplies of gold and silver see E. Babelon, *Traité des Monn. Gr. et Rom.* I. 782–806. Cp. Rostowzew, *Soc. and Econ.* 417 ff., 421.

(**66**) Dio Cass. LXXI. 22, 28. *Hist. Aug. 'Comm.'* 17. Milne, 56–7 and note on p. 296 (Milne). Chwostow, 412.

(**67**) *Dig.* XXXIX. 4. 16. 7. Justinian, *Corp. Jur. Civ.*, Krueger, vol. I. p. 606.

(**68**) Aristeid. XIV. 326 (200), Dind. Cp. Philostrat. *Apollon.* III. 35. 1. Paus. III. 12. Xen. *Eph.* IV. 1. Cp. Aristeid. XLVIII. 485. Rohde, *Gr. R.* 392. Part of Mesopotamia became a dependency. Artaxata (destroyed) was replaced by Caenepolis.

(**69**) Lucian, *Hermotim.* 28. *Alex.* 43–4. *Toxar.* 34. *Q. Hist. S. Scrib.* 31. *Rhet. Praecept.* 5. *Philopseud.* 33. *Hermotim.* 4. Cp. *Lond. P.* 328 (A.D. 163).

. (**70**) Lucian, *Catapl.* = *Tyr.* 21 (cp. *Anth. Pal.* XI. 428). *Alex.* 44. *Hermotim.* 71. '*de Syr. D.*' 16 (cp. Paus. V. 12. 1). *Toxar.* 57. Indians and others in Hierapolis—'*de Syr. D.*' 32.

(**71**) Appian, *B.C.* V. 9. Plut. *Pomp.* 70.

(**72**) Full references will be given in Part II. See Lucian, *Amores,* 39 etc. '*de Syr. D.*' 16 and 32. Paus. II. 28; VI. 21; VIII. 18. 5. Arr. *Ind.* 8,9 ; 15,9 ; 16,1 ; cp. Pollux VII. 76. Lucian, *Musc. Encom.* 1 and perhaps *Dial. Meretr.* V. 4 etc. Vopisc. '*Sat.*' 8. Clem. Alex. *Paed.* II. 11. Dio Cass. LXXII. 17 ff. Herodian I. 15. 5. *Hist. Aug. 'Comm.'* 13, '*Pert.*' 8. '*Elagab.*' 28, 20, 21, 31 (cp. 21, 24), 26, 23, 27, 24, 33, 32 ; Ael. XVI. 2 ; XIII. 18. Dio Cass. LXXIX. 9 ; cp. *Hist. Aug. 'Sev.'* 41, 1 ; cp. 4, 40 ; 22, 39 ; '*Ver.*' 5, 3, 10. Clem. Alex., Tertull. and Cyprian as cited in Part II. Pisa Indica of Apic. V. 3. 3 (195) may be from an Indian recipe, but it looks as though in this passage 'indica' means 'black as indigo.'

(**73**) I find hardly any—Ptol. III. 4. 6.

(**74**) Id. I. 11. 8.

(**75**) Id. I. 14. 1–4 ; I. 17. 3–5 ; I. 9. Ptol. and Marinos, Nissen, *Verein,* H. 95, 1894, 14.

(**76**) Athenae. III. 13. 95 = 45. Cp. Ael. XVII. 1.

(**77**) In Ptol. I. 17, 3–4 we have Marinos corrected in favour of other merchants' reports. Cp. I. 19.

(**78**) Ptol. I. 11. 7, 8 ; 17. 3–5.

(**79**) Id. VII. 1. 2–3, 55–61. Upheavals had evidently affected Barbaricon the former legal mart. Monoglosson = Mangrol ?

(80) Id. 26-8, 42-61. *Tab. Peut.* Miller, 628. The readings are those of Renou (*Texte Établi*), as generally wherever Ptol. is the authority, and the identifications are generally those accepted by McCrindle which are as probable as the results of later attempts.

(81) Ptol. id. 31 ff., 44-7.

(82) Id. I. 17. 5—true; monsoons are irregular in B. of Bengal.

(83) Arr. *Ind.* 4. Ptol. VII. 1. 29-30. Monahan, 11.

(84) Ptol. VII. 1. 6 ; 62-3 ; I. 17. 3-4. *Peripl.* 52-3. Would T. be Rudradaman (grandson of Chastana) victor over the Andhra Puliman ?

(85) Ptol. VII. 1. 82-3. Paethana is Paithan on the Godavari. Sri-Puliman of dynasty of Andhrabhritya—*Pauly*, s.v. *India*, 1280. V. A. Smith, 222. Defeated by Rudradaman I (Saka).

(86) *Archaeol. Surv. of Western India*, IV. 38, 115, 4 (20); 5 (21), Nasik. But Ramanaka may be deceptive, and the Yavana (Dahlmann, 58-9; *Archaeol. Surv. Western India*, IV. 93, 95) of Kalyana might be visitors from North-west India, Gandhara, and so on. See also Ptol. id. 64-5, cp. 41. Vilivayakura=Gautamiputra.

(87) Ptol. id. 66-72, 74-80. d'Alviella, 80, 103. Hirth, 68. Smith, *Fine Art*, 178-9. *J.A.S.B.* 58. 1. 173. Dahlmann, 149.

(88) Ptol. id. 7 and 84. *Peripl.* 53-4. Pliny VI. 104. Marco Polo, III. 25. *Pauly*, s.v. *India*, 1280. Even in *Pauly* places like Byzantion (Vizadrog) are regarded as Greek colonies of Roman date—Lassen III. 6. 57. See also *Ind. Antiqu.* LII. 6-7. *Bomb. Gaz.* I. 541 ; X. 192, n. 3, cp. p. 57 of this book.

(89) *Peripl.* 54. Pliny VI. 105 ; possibly *Tab. Peut.* S. XII, Miller, 790 (Cotiara, Cottara). Ptol. VII. 1. 8-9 and 85 ; 9-10 and 87-8. W. Logan, *Malabar*, I. 252. For the trade in pearls, pepper, and cotton, see below. *Imper. Gaz.* XX. 21. 395 ; XVI. 6 (Punn.), XVI. 62 (Kar.) X. 358 (Coimb.). V. A. Smith, 461, 477. *Pauly*, *l.c.* Pillai, 20. Colchic Gulf = Gulf of Manaar. Ptolemy's Carura is *not* that Karur which is in Coimbatore.

(90) Schoff, *J.A.O.S.* 33, 210 ff. (209-213).

(91) Chola and Andhra regions : Ptol. id. 11-15, 68, 90-3. *Peripl.* 59, 62. *Imper. Gaz.* XVII. 215. McCrindle's notes *ad Ptol.* Pitura—thus Renou, but for Pityndra cp. Pitinna in *Tab. Peut.* Miller, 789. *Geog. Ravenn.* II. 1. Maesolia = roughly the district between the Kistna and the Godavari. Some take the Tyna to be the Kistna, the Maesolos the Godavari (in order to obviate the omission of an important river), Melange to be Bandar Malanka near one of the

mouths of the Godavari, and Malanga to be Ellore—McCrindle, *Ptol.*
p. 67. *Arch. Surv. Ind.* xv. 20. 1. 64. V. A. Smith, *Hist. of Fine Art*,
178–9 (an Aurangabad cave). d'Alviella, 11–12. Cp. Gerini, Tab. vi.
Pauly, s.v. *India*, 1316. Mitra, *Ant. of Or.* ii. 58–9 etc.

(**92**) Ptol. vii. 1. 85–91.

(**93**) Id. 16–17, 41, 81. *Arch. Surv. Western Ind.* xvii. 125. *Pauly*,
s.v. *India*, 1272, cp. id. s.v. *Adamas.*

(**94**) Ptol. id. 18, 13, 5, 7, 81, 73, 29–30, 51–4. Virg. *G.* iii. 27.
Val. Flacc. iv. 66. Curt. ix. 2 etc. Pliny vi. 65; cp. Ptol. vii. 2. 22.
McCr. *Ptol.* 227–8, 131–3. Monahan, 15.

(**95**) Dionys. Perieg. 710–712.

(**96**) Ptol. vii. 4. 1 ff.; cp. Steph. Byz. s.v. Ταπροβάνη. Pompon.
Mela iii. 7. 70. Ideas of Sumatra confused by Ptol.? Ferguson,
J.R.A.S. 1904, 54. Map, Codrington (H.W.), *A Short Hist. of Ceylon*,
4. *Tab. Peut.* Miller, *Itin.* 851–2. Wartena, 10.

(**97**) Strabo ii. 1. 14.

(**98**) Bunbury ii. 481. Dionys. Perieg. 709–714.

(**99**) Id. 596–604.

(**100**) Priaulx, 197. Pillai, 64–78. V. A. Smith, 475, 481, cp. 485. Cp.
Archaeol. Surv. Ind. 1905–6, 145 ff., record of ancient traffic between
Ceylon and Broach.

(**101**) See Codrington, *Ceylon Coins and Currency*, 31 ff., 36–8,
45–8. J. Still in *J.R.A.S. Ceylon Br.* xix. 1907, 161–190, cp. *J.R.A.S.*
1904, 609–615 (Madura). Chwostow, 232–4, 236. Dahlmann, 55.
Doubtful coins of Claudius, and one of Tiberius, *Ceylon Antiqu.* ii
(1916–17), p. 1, n. 45. *J.R.A.S. Ceylon Br.* xx. No. 60, 1908, 83–4.
J.R.A.S. 1905, 156–7, id. *Ceyl. Br.* i. 3, 1848, 73, 157; xi. 41, 454;
vii. 24, 50, 60. On the barbarous imitation sent to me see Codrington, *op. cit.* 33, 45–8. Still, *op. cit.* 168. Admiration of Roman
coins by Ceylonese: Pliny vi. 85, cp. Cosmas xi. 448 D. Silent trade
of Ceylonese with Tamils: Pliny vi. 88.

(**102**) *J.A.S.B.* xx. 379.

(**103**) Ptol. vii. 4. 11–12. Cosmas xi. 445 C. Ps.-Callisth. iii. 7
(there called Maniolae, not those of Ptol. vii. 2. 31). Pallad. *Hist.
Laus.* iii. 7, cp. Philostorg. *H.E.* iii. 5. Theophilos of 'Dibou' (but
perhaps Socotra or a Red Sea island). Ammian. Marcell. xxii. 7. 10
(Divi). Priaulx, 188. Heeren, *As. Nat.* 429 (Ptol.'s islands correctly
called Maldives), cp. Lassen i. 244–6.

(**104**) *Peripl.* 56, 63. Ptol. VII. 2. 15–17, 23 (gold mines of Pahang?).

(**105**) Joseph. *A.J.* VIII. 164, 176. Pompon. Mela III. 7. 70. Dionys. Perieg. knows no farther than Malay and to him India is the extreme east of the world, though he does mention the Seres—Dionys. Per. 1107–8, 752. For India beyond the Ganges, and China, according to Ptol., see G. E. Gerini, *J.R.A.S.* 1897, 551–577 (with map, and eleven Tables after p. 564) and id. *Researches on Ptolemy's Geog. of E. Asia, Asiat. Soc. Monogr.* I. 1909 and Herrmann in *Zeits. d. G. f. Erdk.* 1913, 771–787, map p. 773.

(**106**) McCr. *Ptol.* 9–11. Lassen III. 70. Rylands, 52, 54. Götz, 487, 497–8. Herrmann in *op. cit.* 772, 774, 780, favours Ha-tinh; Gerini favours Kampu near Hang-Chow. *Researches* as in last note, 302–4. Chwostow, 237–8 (favours Hanoi), 416. *Rev. Numism.* N.S. IX. 1864, 481. Nissen, *Verein*, H. 95, 1894, p. 5. In Chinese records Tong-king is the end of voyages from the West. Herrmann, *Verkehrswege*, 6–7. Cp. Yule, I. 4.

(**107**) Ptol. I. 13. 5–9; VII. 1. 12, 16; VII. 2, 3; 1, 15; 3, 6; I. 14. 1. *Pauly*, s.v. *India*, 1274. Hirth, 82.

(**108**) Ptol. I. 14. 1. Lassen III. 6. 70. For a later voyage of this type see McCr. *Ptol.* 69. Gerini identifies Palura = Conora, ἀφετήριον = Vizagapatam, Temala (near Cape Temala) = Old Bassein, Zabae = Baria. In Ptol. Sada is 70 miles north-west of Temala and so may not be Thade. Alexander: Herrmann, *Zeits. d. G. f. Erdk.* 1913, 779 ff. See also refs. of last note and Ptol. VII. 2. 6.

(**109**) Ptol. VII. 2, cp. I. 13. 7.

(**110**) Chinese annals reveal the use of some such rivers as the Irawadi or the Salween, or a road from Pegu to Yunnan, for western goods bound for China—Hirth, 179. Gerini: Baracura = old Arakan.

(**111**) Ptol. VII. 2. 24. Gerini makes Besynga Thatung or else Rangoon.

(**112**) Id. 5 and 8–12. Gerini: Tacola = near mouth of Pak Shan; Sabana = Syriam.

(**113**) Id. 6–7. (*Pauly, Ind.* 1274.) Gerini says Λῃσταί does not mean brigands here but people of Siam.

(**114**) Id. VII. 2. 13–16. *Peripl.* 62, 65. Pliny VI. 25, see above.

(**115**) Ptol. VII. 2. 17–19, 21. Gerini makes Argyre = Arakan, not 'Silver Country,' and 'Gold Country' = maritime Burma and Pegu.

(**116**) Id. 22–5. Gerini: Randamarta = Tung Liang, Tosale = Sylhet, Tugma = Manipur. Monahan, 205–7.

(**117**) Id. 29. Bunbury II. 608, 643–4. Ptol. id. 26–8, 30–1. Surely not the island of Diodor. II. 57–60. Rylands, 52, 54, thinks Ptol. meant Banca. See also Gerini, T. VII, T. XI.

(**118**) Ptol. VII. 3. 1–6.

(**119**) Paus. VI. 26. 4 (8–9). But see Schoff, ad *Peripl.* 33, p. 146. *J.A.O.S.* 35, 40.

(**120**) Hirth, 378, 174–8. Momms. *Prov.* II. 98–9. Priaulx, 129–130. Chwostow, 398. Letronne in *Mém. de l'Acad. d. Inscr.* vᵉ S. x. 227. Vidal de Lablache id. *C.R.* 1897, 525–7, cp. Götz, 496–8. Messengers from Emesa at Coptos (Petrie, *Kopt.* 23) were perhaps going east.

(**121**) Paus. VI. 26. 6. Reinaud, *Relations*, etc. 185–6. Pollux VII. 76.

(**122**) See Hirth, 39 ff., 42, 48, 167 ff.; and 272–5, 147, 306 ff.

(**123**) Hirth, 47. Priaulx, 249, cp. 178–9.

(**124**) *Ind. Antiqu.* II. 145. *J.R.A.S.* 1907, 969; 1898, 955–6; 1917, 482 ff. *Ind. Antiqu.* XXXIX. 237. XXXIII. 10–16. IV. 181–3. XXXII. 1–15, 145–160, esp. 149. Joseph. *A.J.* I. 6. 4 = 147. Jews settled near Kabul? Christians: *J.R.A.S.* 1917, 233 ff. Winstedt, *The Christian Topogr.* (Cosmas), 344–5. Christians in India perhaps quite early—Tertull. *Adv. Iud.* I. 7 (doubtful).

(**125**) *O.P.* III. 413, pp. 41–57. *J.R.A.S.* 1904, 399–401. L. D. Barnett in *J. E. Arch.* 1926, pp. 13–15, denies that the language is Canarese and does not know what it is. Clem. Alex. *Strom.* I. 15. 71 first mentions Buddha (*not* from Megasthenes?).

(**126**) *Camb. Hist. Ind.* I. 648. *Arch. Surv. Ind.* x. 428 (Tanjavur). Also a Jonaka occurs as a donor, id. 428. Dahlmann, 69 ff., 92–3, 107, 108, 119, 120, 125, 150, 151. *J. of the Royal Institute of Brit. Architects*, 3rd S. I. 1893, 93–115, 147–153. Smith, *Fine Art*, 155, 178–9, 352 ff. Classical gems of the West found in India (it seems): Furtw. XXXI. 40. *B.M. Rings*, 529, *K.M.B.* 1011. (Rawal Pindi, Punjab.) *B.M. Gems*, 192, 244, 254?, 3588. (Akra in Punjab.) For other western works of art found in India see J. Marshall, *A Guide to Taxila*, 77 (bronze Harpocrates), 77–9, 53. *J. Hellen. St.* 1926, 262–3. G. R. Kaye, *Index to the Ann. Reports of the Dir. Gen. of Archaeol. in India*, 1902–1916, s.v. *Hellenistic Influence in India*.

(**127**) Bunbury II. 609–610.

(**128**) Ptol. VI. 7. 1–47. Mesopotamian regions in detail: id. 1–13; 14; 21–47; VI. 3. 2; V. 18–20; IV. 7; esp. 10, 12, 25. Philostorg. *H. E.* III. 4, calls Aden a Roman mart, that is, where Roman subjects still traded.

(**129**) Ptol. I. 17. 6. Pliny VIII. 7.

(**130**) Ptol. I. 11. 4–8; 12. 5–11; VI. 16. 1–8, cp. Ammian. Marcell. XXIII. 6. 60, 67–8. Chwostow, 282. Dionys. Per. 713–714. Kwang Vouti had removed the capital to Loh-yang in Honan from Singanfu before A.D. 76. Gerini, T. V. Cp. *Pauly*, s.v. *Sera*.

(**131**) V. d. St Martin, *Ét.* pp. 258 ff. esp. 261. (*Acad. des Inscr. et B.-L.* 1860.) Ptol. I. 12. 9; IV. 13. 3; 14, 1. 3; etc. cp. Rohde, *Gr. R.* 217 ff. McCr. *Ptol.* 305, *Encycl. Brit.* s.v. *Ptolemy.*

(**132**) Sir M. A. Stein, *Ruins of Desert Cathay*, vol. I. pp. 410–411, 457–8, 471–2, 467, 480, 486–7, 492–3, 381. Smith, *Fine Art*, 358. Dahlmann, 106. The Romans had learnt of several routes between China and the West—see Gerini, T. XI. Roman influence of Gandhara may have been due partly to artists from the West.

(**133**) *J.A.S.B.* 58. I. Suppl. 1889, p. 3. *Acad.* 1886, No. 730, p. 316. *Rev. Numism.* N.S. IX. 1864, 481, Nissen, *Verein*, H. 95, 1894, p. 5.

(**134**) Ptol. V. 10–11; VI. 9–12. Beyond the Iaxartes to the north all is chaos in Ptolemy and the Iaxartes itself is vague.

(**135**) Ptol. VII. 5. 4 (Caspian); III. 5. 14; V. 9. 1–2 (Tanais, etc.); V. 9. 12, 17, 19, 21; VI. 14. 1, 4 (Rha).

THE DECLINE

For an outline of this development cf. Chwostow, 411–420, Priaulx, 163 ff., Reinaud, 236 ff.

(**136**) Cooke, *N.S.I.* 113–114, 116, 121–7. Kennedy, *J.R.A.S.* 1912, 990 ff., cp. Reinaud, 168. Priaulx, 132–3, thinks, wrongly in my opinion, that Indian trade was at its highest under Severus, Caracalla, and the pseudo-Antonines. Decline of coin-finds, especially after Septimius Severus: Sewell, *op. cit.* 601–3.

(**137**) Dio Cass. LXXVII. 22. Herodian IV. 158. *Hist. Aug.* '*Carac.*' 6. Kennedy, *J.R.A.S.* 1898, p. 954. Sewell, *op. cit.* 603.

(**138**) Dio Cass. LXXII. 17 ff. Herodian I. 15. 5. *Hist. Aug.* '*Comm.*' 13; '*Pert.*' 8; '*Aurel.*' 3. Priaulx, 172–3. *J.R.A.S.* XX. 267.

(**139**) *Hist. Aug. 'Elagab.'* 30–1, 23–4, 26–9, 31–3. Dio Cass. LXXIX. 9. Rawlinson, 142. Stob. *Ecl. Phys.* I. 3. 56. Priaulx, 52. Porphyr. *de Abst.* IV. 17, p. 355.

(**140**) *Hist. Aug. 'Alex. Sev.'* 41, cp. 4, 40, 22, 39.

(**141**) Cooke, *N.S.I.* 125. At this time perhaps the Syrians helped to produce the Gandhara School in sculpture in N.W. India. Rawlinson, 163–8. Smith, 255–6 etc. Cp. *J.R.A.S. Bomb. Br.* XXIII. p. 235. West Asiatic influence at Amaravati: Smith, *Fine Art*, 133.

(**142**) Chwostow, 288–9.

(**143**) Sewell, *op. cit.* 605.

(**144**) Stein as cited above, n. 132.

(**145**) Cooke, *N.S.I.* I. 127–8, 121, 126, 130, pp. 290–1 *Hist. Aug. 'Aurelian.'* 8. Zos. I. 61. Ammian. Marcell. XXII. 16. Euseb. *H.E.* VII. 21.

(**146**) Ammian. Marcell. XIV. 3. 3, 11. Procop. *de Bell. Pers.* II. 12. In the *'Meadows of Gold'* (Mas'udi) is a passage which speaks of ships from India and China lying at Hira, not far south-west of Babylon, in the 5th cent. A.C. Priaulx, 162.

(**147**) *Hist. Aug. 'Aurel.'* 33, 41, 29, 45 ; *'Prob.'* 17. Zosim. I. 71.

(**148**) King, *E.G.* 42, 58, 76 ; *P.S.* 306–7, 273–4, 197–200 etc. Middleton, 58, 141.

(**149**) Sewell, *op. cit.* 605, 608–9. Dues were levied at Iotabe.

(**150**) Euseb. *Vita Const.* IV. 7 ; IV. 50.

(**151**) Ammian. Marcell. XXII. 7. 10. Lassen III. 63. 'Vict.' *Ep.* 16. Ceylon: Cosmas XI. 445 B–449 D.

(**152**) Epiph. *ad Haer.* LXVI. 1. Cosmas II. 101 A. Philostorg. *H.* III. 6. Axumites: Cosmas II. 100 B, 101 A–C, 105 C, 97 C ; III. 169 C ; VI. 321 A, 324 A. Adulis: II. 97 D, 101 A, C, 105 C ; XI. 448 A–B, 449 A. Clysma: Philostorg. III. 6. Epiphan. *Haer.* II. 618.

(**153**) Sewell, *op. cit.* 608–9. Codrington, 33.—(See note 101.)

PART II

CHAPTER I

Cf. Lassen III. 44 ff. *Pauly*, s.v. *India*, 1303.

(**1**) Athenae. v. 8, 32, 201 (*a*). *Peripl.* 31. *Dig.* XXXIX. 4. 16. 7. Tibull. II. 3. 49–58. Cp. Ter. *Eun.* I. 2. 85–6. Hor. *Od.* I. 29. 7–10

(Chinese); *Sat.* II. 8. 14. Juv. VI. 585. (Bücheler's reading is 'et Indae.') Zonar. *Ep.* X. IV. 25. 18. Nicephor. *Corp. Script. Byz.* p. 52 C. Flinders Petrie, (Hogarth) *Kopt.*, Tariff, lines 16–17. Lassen III. 44. Chwostow, 115, Arr. *Ind.* 14, 5 etc.

(2) *Peripl.* 50.

(3) *Dig.*, *loc. cit.* Any heavier animals are absent. Unspecified Indian animals in Syria—Euseb. *Mart. Pal.* 6, 2.

(4) Diodor. Sic. II. 53. 2. The transport of elephants in the Red Sea by the Ptols. had been dangerous.

(5) *Camb. Hist. Ind.* I. 207–8. *Jat.* VI. 71, cp. III. 49. *Therig.* (Comm.) 220.

(6) Symm. *Epp.* v. 62 = 60; in his day it was $2\,°/_°$.

(7) Rawlinson, pp. 4–5. *Hist. Aug. 'Aurel.'* 5; cp. Ammian. Marcell. XVIII. 7. 4 ; XXIII. 6. 50.

(8) The langurs given are respectively *Semnopithecus entellus*, *S. priamus*, *S. hypoleucus*, *S. Johni*; add perhaps the purple-faced langur (*S. cephalopterus*) of Ceylon. *Ind. Antiqu.* vol. XIV. p. 279. Arr. *Ind.* 15, 9, cp. Strabo XV. 1. 37. Ael. *d. A.* XVII. 25, 39. XVI. 10. *Pauly*, s.v. *Affe*. McCrindle, *Ctes.* p. 8. Diodor. XVII. 90. Pliny VIII. 72, 76. Frazer, ad Paus. vol. III. p. 259 (calls the fowl a turkey, which is an American bird). Rostowzew, *Soc. and Econ.* Plate XVII. Fig. 1, p. 126 (larger in *Jahrb. d. Kais. Deutsch. Archäol. Inst.* XV (1900), p. 203), and frontispiece to Part II of this book; guinea-fowl (African) called Indian—Soph. ap. Pliny XXXVII. 40.

(9) Pliny VIII. 53. Catull. XLV. 6–7. Ael. XVII. 26. Strabo XVI. 1. 24 ; 4, 15 and 18; XVII. 2, 2 ; 3, 4 ff. Venationes : Mongez in *Mém. de l'Instit.* X. 360–460, esp. on lions, p. 390—thinks the maneless lions of India were leopards.

(10) Pliny VIII. 62, 65–6 (tigers of Ptol. IV. 9. 4 are incorrect). *B.M. Jew.* Introd. XXXIV and 1805. *B.M. Gems*, 2332 (2333 of old *B.M. Cat.* is now rejected). Representations in *C.I.G.* 6131 *b* do not appear to me to be tigers. So also *Tesserar. Syll.* 595 (Tab. IV. 65) is quite unrecognisable and the dish of Lampsacos (see frontispiece to Part II) does not clearly shew a tiger. Cp. A. Mau, *Pomp.* 295, Minns, 274–5. But the tiger appears often in Orpheus-scenes and in other ways : see *Vienna (Antike Bronzen)*, 1224, 1226, 1337, 1514, 1520, 1526, 1531. *Palazzo d. Conserv.* Text, pp. 260–1. Sc. VI. 3 ; cp. p. 264, VI. 8; p. 291, III. 21. *Mosaïques (de l'Afrique)*, II. 381

and 496 (with parrot), 74, 125, 136 etc.; id. (*de la Gaule*), I. 196, 207; id. (*de l'Afr.*), III. 221, 440 etc. *B.M. Bronzes*, 1767–8, 2471, 2502. Matz and v. Duhn, *Antike Bildwerke in Rom*, 3926. *Bibl. Nat., Bronzes*, 1122–4, 1130. *Jahr. d. D. Arch. Inst.* xv, *Anz.* 222. 37.

(11) Philemon ap. Athenae. XIII. 6. 57 = 590 (*a*). Varro *L.L.* v. 20. Virg. *Aen.* IV. 367. Suet. *Aug.* 43 (in scaena). Pliny VIII. 65–6. Petron. *S.* 119, lines 17–18. Pomp. Mela III. 5. 43. Sen. *Phaedra*, 352. *Herc. Oet.* 146. Mart. VIII. 26. 1–4, cp. I. 104. 2. *Spect.* 18, 1–2. Sil. Ital. v. 148. Juv. xv. 163. *Hist. Aug.* '*Gord.*' 33. Sewell, *J.R.A.S.* 1904, 605, cp. Paus. IX. 21. 4. Ael. *d. A.* VIII. I. xv. 14. Opp. *Cyneg.* III. 340 ff. Philostrat. *Apoll.* II. 14. Tigers of Antoninus Pius: *Hist. Aug.* '*Pi.*' 10; of Sept. Sev.: Dio Cass. LXXXVI. 7; of Elagabalus: *Hist. Aug.* '*Elagab.*' 28. Dio Cass. LXXIX. 9 (51 killed !); of Aurelian: *Hist. Aug.* '*Aurel.*' 33. Bunbury II. 201. Monahan, 114.

(12) Ptol. VII. 4. 1; VII. 2. 21.

(13) Herod. I. 192. McCr. *Ctes.* p. 9. Athenae. v. 8. 32 = 201 (*b*). Pollux v. 41. *Arch. f. Pap.* VI. 453–4. *P.Z.* 48, *Annales*, XIX. 101–4. Rostowzew, *A large Estate in Egypt*, 112. Layard, *Nin.* 527, 537, id. abr. 302–3. Dio Chrys. III. 130, Arnim. Lassen I. 350–1.

(14) Xen. *Cyn.* IX. 1. Pliny VII. 21. Ael. IV. 19; VIII. 1; xv. 14 etc.

(15) Layard, abr. 346. Athenae. *loc. cit.* 201 (*c*). *Bibl. Nat. Bronzes*, 1166; cp. Hirth, 38 and x–XI. Pollux v. 37. Cp. Plut. *de Is. et Os.* 362 B–C.

(16) Ael. XIII. 25 ? XVI. 11 (poephagos). Cosmas XI. 441 D, ταυρέ-λαφος = buffalo, 444 A, ἀγριόβους = yak. Cosmas describes either the chowri or the tail-standard. Aristotle, *H.A.* II. 1. 499 (*a*), 4–5. Paul. Diac. *H.* IV. 11. Hehn, 470–1, 610–611. 4th cent. mosaic of tiger and buffalo—*Palazzo d. Conserv.* Text, pp. 260–1.

(17) Paus. XI. 21. 2. Marcellin. *Chron.* ad 496. Cassian. Bass. *Geopon.* XVI. 22. 9. Cosmas XI. 441 D.

(18) Cagnat, *I.G.R.* I. 945, 65, p. 317. Cosmas XI. 449 C. Herod. VII. 86, 106. M. O. Dalton, *Treasure of the Oxus*, xx etc. Ael. XVI. 9, wild ass of western India ? Bactrian camel in Syria, Jer. *Vit. Hil.* 23, cp. Pliny VIII. 67. *Tesserar. Syll.* 703. *B.M. Gems*, 546–7. Did Cosmas see and eat in Ethiopia an Indian hog (*Sus babyrussa*) ? see Cosmas, 444 C (Winstedt, 351) (cp. Pliny VIII. 212).

(19) One-horned Agatharch, Müller I. 158. Diodor. III. 35. Ael. XVII. 44. Suet. *Aug.* 43. Dio Cass. LI. 22. Strabo XVI. 415. Pliny VIII. 71. Solin. 30 = 43. Oppian, *Cyneg.* II. 551–3. *Tesserar. Syll.* 446 (and

parrot), 625 (Tab. v. 1), 652 (Fig. 50), are clearly one-horned; so perhaps are 373 (Tab. IV. 8), 445–6 (Tab. IV. 9), 649 (Tab. V. 9) etc. *K.M.B.* 8490 = Imhoof-Blumer, Pl. XIX. No. 46. *C.I.G.* 6131, b, fig. (a mere caricature). Hirth, 38 and X–XII. Cp. Cosmas XI. 444 B, 445 B. Of the Indian species, *R. unicornis* is the best known: the Javan R. is smaller, while the Sumatran has two horns.

(**20**) Plut. *Pyrrh.* 20. Polyb. I. 40; III. 46; XI. 1; V. 84. Phylarch. ap. Athenae. XIII. 8. 85 = 606 f. Ter. *Eun.* III. 2. 23. Sen. *Dial.* x *ad Paul.* 13. Cosmas XI. 449 B–D. *Anth. Lat.* 375, 1–2. Strabo XV. 1. 14 and 42–3. Lucret. II. 540. Ptol. VII. 2. 21; VII. 4. 1. Juv. XII. 102; X. 150. Hor. *Ep.* II. 1. 196. Ael. *d. A.* III. 46; XVI. 18. Diodor. II. 16. 4; 35. 4; II. 42. Philostrat. *Apoll.* II. 6. 12–14. The Indian elephants are *E. maximus* with its local varieties. *Ind. Antiqu.* vol. XI. p. 543. Tarn in *Class. Quart.* 1926, 98–100, cp. specimens in the Museum at S. Kensington. Watt, *Dict.* s.v. *Elephas. Pauly*, s.v. *Elefant.* White variety in Africa? see Ptol. IV. 9. 4.

(**21**) E.g. *K.M.B.* 3282, 3284, Chab. 1985–9, *Vienna*, K IV. 1029.

(**22**) E.g. Imhoof-Blumer XXI. 1 (clearly Alexandrine); cp. Hl. 59, the parrot on the dish from Lampsacos (frontispiece to Part II), and perhaps *N.Y.* 258. So also *B.M. Bronzes*, 2493 and 1886; the latter is not a cockatoo nor is it a macaw (South American) as suggested. Cp. *Bibl. Nat. Bronzes*, 1258 (Fig.).

(**23**) See *K.M.B.* 7916.

(**24**) Chab. 1990. *K.M.B.* 7914, 7917. In Imh.-Blum. the parrots of Pl. XXI. 3 (= Chab. 1990) and XXI. 4 are stated to be *P. Alexandri* of Ceylon—the name should be really *P. eupatria.*

(**25**) Ctes. *Ind.* 3. See *Catal. of Birds in the Brit. Mus.* vol. XX. pp. 435–456 for these various parrots, and the examples in the Parrot House, Zoological Gardens, Regent's Park. The African type of *P. torquatus* is *P. docilis.*

(**26**) Ptol. VII. 2. 23. *B.M. Bronzes*, 1885 is stated to be a cockatoo, but I have not seen it.

(**27**) *K.M.B.* 5836–7, 7915–7, 8708. Chab. 1985–7, 1989. More examples of parrots: Hl. Pl. LXXVII. 268 = T. 199; id. 269 = 1531. *Palazzo d. Conserv.* Text, Galler. Sup. I. 18 (p. 277). *Mosaïques* I, *de la G.* 181, 220, 233, 369; III, *de l'Afr.* 291, 333 (ring-necked), 334, 440; II. 381 (with tiger etc.), 496 (with domesticated and pet birds). *Tesserar. Syll.* 445 (Tab. IV. 9 with rhinoceros), 446, 439 (Tab. IV.

12, with elephant, it seems). *Jahr. d. D. Arch. Instit.* XXVI. 8; XXXVII, *Anz.* 113. *Vienna (Antike Bronzen),* 1283.

(**28**) E.g. *B.M. Rings,* 182, *K.M.B.* 3282–3, 8563, 8707. See Aristotle, *H.A.* VIII. 14. 6. Diodor. Sic. II. 53. Athenae. v. 8. 32. 201 (*b*). Ov. *Am.* II. 6. *Anth. Pal.* IX. 562 (wicker cage). Pers. *Prol.* 8. Mart. x. 3. 7; XIV. 73, 77. Varro, *R.R.* III. 9. 17. Ael. XVI. 2; XIII. 8; XVI. 5; VI. 19. Pliny x. 117. Solin. 23. Apulei. *Flor.* 12. Oppian, *Cyneg.* II. 408–9. Stat. *S.* II. 4. Paus. II. 28. Philostr. *Soph.* I. 7. 2. *Anth. Lat.* Riese, II. 691. Clem. Alex. *Paed.* III. 4. 270–1 P ('Indian birds'), and Schol. *ad loc.* Prisc. *Perieg.* 1033–4. Arr. *Ind.* 15, 9. *Hist. Aug.* '*Elagab.*' 20–1. *B.M.* 2478–80, 2482. *K.M.B.* 7913–20, 8056, 8062 and others as cited above. Pliny min. *Ep.* IV. 2. Dion. *de Av.* I. 19. Marc. Empir. 8. Scribon. 27. Philostorg. *H.E.* 3. 11. *Ind. Antiqu.* XIV. 304. Thompson, *Gloss.* 198–9. Newton, *Dict. of Birds,* s.v. *Parrot. Penny Cycl.* s.v. *Psittacidae.* Inscription: *C.I.G.* 3846 Z[43] (Phrygia).

(**29**) See Diodor. II. 53. Frazer, ad Paus. vol. III. p. 259. Reinach, *Antiqu. d. Bosph. Cimm.* p. 58; cp. alleged derivation from Psittace near the Tigris and suggested derivation of Ctesias' βίττακος from the Persian tedek. Heeren, *As. Nat.* II. tr. 1846, 361.

(**30**) Sen. *Dial.* XII *ad Helv.* 10 etc. monal(?) in Ael. XVI. 2.— great Indian cock, cp. Ctes. *Ind.* 3. Yule, *Marco Polo,* I. 280.

(**31**) Thompson, *Gloss.* 182–4.

(**32**) Hehn, 363 (phoenix). Pliny x. 5 (x. 132 does not allude to silver or any but the common pheasants); XI. 121. Sid. Apoll. *C.* IX. 325. Philostrat. *Apollon.* III. 49. Herod. II. 73. Tac. *Ann.* VI. 28. Dio Cass. LVIII. 27. Dion. *de Av.* I. 32. Lucian, *Navig.* 44; *De morte peregr.* 27. *Pauly,* s.v. *Fasan,* 2002.

(**33**) Pliny x. 146, 156. Columella VIII. 2. 13. Hehn, 321. Indian jungle-fowl brought to ancient Egypt:—*J. E. Arch.* 1923, 1 ff. Median cocks:—Varro, *R.R.* III. 9. 6. See *J.A.O.S.* 33, 361 ff. Darwin, *The Variation of Animals and Plants under Domestication,* I. 236–289, ch. VII. 2nd ed.

(**34**) Lucian, *Navig.* 23, cp. Ael. XVI. 2. Hehn, 349 ff.

(**35**) Suet. *Aug.* 43. Strabo XV. 1. 45. Dio Cass. LXIX. 16. Ael. IV. 36; XII. 32; XVII. 2. *Pauly,* s.v. *Schlange,* 532, 548.

(**36**) Chinese literature shews that the skins and furs were important articles of the trade of the Chinese—Hirth, 226.

(37) *Peripl.* 39, 6.   Pliny XII. 31; XXXIV. 145; XXXVII. 204.
Dig. XXXIX. 4. 16. 7.   Arr. *Ind.* 15, 4–7.   Strabo XV. 1. 44; XI. 2. 3.
Cod. Just. X. 47. 7.   *Cod. Theod.* XIV. 10.   Herodian IV. 10.   Paul.
Silent. III. 6. 79.   Furs in India—*Ramayana*, I. 605 ff. (perhaps).
Mahabharata, II. 50; I. p. 373.   Lassen I. 373–4.   Watt, *Dict.* 458–
461 (a list).   *Camb. Hist. Ind.* 208.   Schoff, ad *Peripl.* 257.

(38) *Peripl.* 14, 41.   Pliny VIII. 176; XXVIII. 159.   Diosc. II. 72 etc.
Ctes. *Ind.* 22.   Heeren, *Asiat. Nat.* II. tr. 1846, p. 301 and n. 8.   In
Cosmas we have the statement that the tame ταυρέλαφοι of India
were used for carrying pepper and other wares, and produced milk
and butter—Cosmas XI. 441 D.

(39) Ael. *d. A.* III. 34 (arni-buffalo's horn? or rhinoceros-horn?).
Dig. XXXIX. 4. 16. 7.   Cosmas XI. 441 B, 444 B (McCrindle, p. 360).
Heeren, *As. Nat.* 364–9 (unicorn).   Ctes. *Ind.* 25.

(40) The Greeks perhaps could obtain ordinary woollen clothes in
Indian marts—for instance in Kaviripaddinam—Pillai, 25.

(41) *Hist. Aug. 'Aurel.'* 29.   G. Rawlinson, *7th Orient. Mon.* 106,
141. *Dig., loc. cit.* Ptol. VII. 1. 47–50.   Vincent, Appendix to vol. II.
p. 56.   *Grundz.* I. (i) pp. 249, 251.   Dirksen, *Abh. der K. Akad. d.
Wissensch. zu Berlin*, 1843, pp. 105–6.   Strabo XV. 3. 21.   Watt,
Dict. s.v. *Sheep and Goats*, p. 559.   Chwostow, 116.   Heeren, *op. cit.*
II. 273.   *Ramayana*, I. 201.   But Karakoram is Turkish.

(42) Cosmas XI. 444 B, 445 D–448 A.   Aetius, 16, 122.   Serapion,
de Simpl. 185 etc.   Lassen III. 45.   Watt, *Dict.* s.v. *Deer*, pp. 58 ff.
Ferrand I. pp. 292–5.   κοστό(ά)ριν in Cosmas might be costus.

(43) *Peripl.* 6, 17 (African).   Pliny VI. 173.   Mart. XIV. 52, in
lemm.   Juv. VII. 130.   Watt, *Dict.* s.v. *Rhinoceros.*   Philostr. *Apoll.*
III. 2.

(44) Chwostow, 398, and see below.

(45) Paus. V. 12. 3.   Lucian, *de Sacrif.* 11, cp. id. *Zeus Trag.* 8.
Virg. *G.* I. 57.   *Aen.* XII. 67–8.   Hor. *Od.* I. 31. 6.   Ov. *Met.* VIII. 288.
Catull. LXIV. 48 and so on.   Perrot et Chipiez II. 730, *Pauly*, s.v.
Elfenbein.   Much African ivory obtained by Ptolemy II before 250
decreased the price considerably—see Tarn in *Class. Quart.* 1926, 100.

(46) Homer, *Odyss.* XXIII. 200.   Pliny XXXVI. 22.   Dionys. Halic.
A.R. III. 62.   'Virg.' *Catal.* VIII. 23.   Ov. *P.* IV. 5. 18 etc.   Hor. *Od.*
II. 18. 1.   *Sat.* II. 6. 103.   Athenae. XV. 50=695 C.   Dio Chrys. *Or.
de Ven.* 7.   Galen V. 837.   Kühn. etc.   Varro, *L.L.* IX. 47.   Lucian,

Dial. Meretr. IX. 2. *de Sacr.* 11. Mart. I. 72. 4; V. 37. 5; II. 43. 9; X. 98. 6; apophoreta in XIV. 5, 12, 14, 77, 83 etc. Philo, *de Somn.* II. 8. 57.

(**47**) Ov. *Am.* II. 5. 40, cp. men of Dedan (on Persian Gulf) and ivory—*Ezek.* xxvii. 15, cp. xvii. 6.

(**48**) *Peripl.* 49, 56, 62 (African:—3–4, 6–7, 10, 16, 17). Suet. *Calig.* 55. *Nero,* 31. Dio Cass. LXI. 10. 3. Pliny VIII. 7. Lucian, *de Sacr.* 11. 'Indian' ivory:—Dio Chrys. LXXIX. 4 and 6, Arnim. *Anth. Lat.* 374. 1. Petron. *S.* 135. Ruf. Fest. Av. 1315. Prisc. *Perieg.* 1017 etc. Chwostow, 116. Ivory couches:—Clem. Alex. *Paed.* II. 3. 188. Hor. *Sat.* II. 6. 103. Macrob. *S.* III. 13. 11. Suet. *Iul.* 84.

(**49**) Stat. *S.* I. 3. 48–9; III. 3. 94–5; IV. 2. 38–9; III. 1. 38 and so on. Mart. as cited above.

(**50**) Cosmas XI. 449 C–D. Ceylon ivory not good. Sent to Indian marts in Hellenistic and Roman times:—Strabo II. 1. 14. *Peripl.* 61. African ivory sent to India:—Cosmas XI. 449 D.

(**51**) Watt, s.v. *Ivory.* Id. *Dict.* s.v. *Elephas,* esp. 226–7. A scarcity of Libyan elephants in the 4th cent.:—Themist. *Or.* x. 140 (*a*), partly because of demand for shows? The Indian elephant still flourishes.

(**52**) Sym. Seth. *de Alim.* 13 ('amber'). F. Adams, *Paul. Aegin.* III. pp. 130, 426. Schoff, *J.A.O.S.* 42, pp. 180–1.

(**53**) Pliny XXVIII. 119. Diosc. II. 66; III. 128. *Peripl.* 30. Avicenna II. 2. 596. Ebn Baithar II. 32. Paul. Aegin. VII. 3, s.v. σκίγκου. Ainslie, *Med. Ind.* II. 278.

(**54**) By 'Indian,' tortoiseshell from any coast of the Indian Ocean and Arabian Sea was meant.

(**55**) Before full discovery of monsoons:—Varro, *L.L.* IX. 47, ex testudine. Cic. *N.D.* II. 47, 144. Strabo II. 1. 14. Virg. *G.* II. 463. Ov. *Met.* II. 737. Prop. IV. (v) 6. 32. Tib. IV. 2. 22. Philo, *de Vit. Contempl.* 6. 49; *de Somn.* II. 8. 57 etc. After monsoons:— *Peripl.* 56, 61, 63. Lucan X. 120. Mart. XII. 66. 5; IX. 59. 9; IX. 60. 9. Juv. XIV. 308; VI. 80. *Dig.* XXXII. 1. 100. 4. Apulei. *Met.* X. 34 (Indian). Lucian, *Asin.* 53. Galen V. 837. Clem. Alex. *Paed.* II. 3. 35; III. 11. 71. Seneca, *de Benef.* VII. 9. 2. Ael. *N.H.A.* XVI. 17. *Anth. Pal.* VI. 118. 4. See also Pliny VI. 91, 109; IX. 12; XXXII. 32–41 etc. C. L. Ransom, 58.

(**56**) Modern fisheries of Tuticorin and Ceylon:—*Madras Gov. Mus. Bull.* vol. I. pp. 1–54. See Pliny IX. 123 from Stilo; XXXII. 62; XXXVII. 14–17, 62; IX. 106–123; XII. 84. *Peripl.* 36, 56, 59, 61, 63. Pillai, 16, 25. Cic. *Verr.* II. 4. 1; II. 5. 56 etc. Lucan X. 155 ff. *Hist. Aug. 'Trig. Tyr.'* 32. Suet. *Aug.* 41. Plut. *Ant.* 83. Hor. *Od.* v. 8. 13–16; *Sat.* I. 2. 80. Ov. *A.A.* III. 129; *Am.* II. 11. 13; *M.* IX. 260. Prop. I. 8. 39; III. (IV) 13. 6 etc. Tib. II. 2. 15–16; IV. 2. 19–20. 'Virg.' *Cul.* 67–8 (gloss?). Strabo XV. 1. 67. Suet. *Aug.* 30. Athenae. III. 14. 93=46, cp. 45. Suet. *Iul.* 50. Hor. *Sat.* II. 3. 239–241. Petron. *S.* 67, 63, 64. Juv. VI. 549. Suet. *Nero*, 11, 12. *C.I.L.* VI. 7884, 9544–9, 641, 1925 etc.; II. 2060, 3386. Pliny min. *Ep.* v. 16. Lucian, *Imag.* 9; *Cod. Theod.* XIII. 4. 2. Jordan, *Topogr.* II. 553. Quintil. *Declam.* XI. 1. 3 and *Declam.* No. 359; *O.P.* X. 1273 (A.D. 260); cp. *Les Pap. Gr., Mus. d. Louvre, Not. et Extr.* XVIII. 2; 10; 9–10. *Palazzo d. Conserv.* Text, Galler. Sup. I. 20 (*a*). T. H. Dyer, *Pomp.* 571. *B.M. Jew.* 2709, 2732; Introd. lviii. Chab. 2550, 2597. *Vienna*, Toreutische Arbeiten, Pultkasten, 160, 163, 165, 167, 196, 198–200 etc. See also Mart. I. 109. 4; v. 37. 4; IX. 2. 9; XI. 49. (50) 4; X. 38. 5. I *Tim.* ii. 9. *Matth.* xiii. 45–6, cp. vii. 6. *Rev.* xxi. 21. Tertull. *de cult. fem.* I. 6, 7, 13. Cyprian, *d. D. et H.* 14. Tertull. *ad Martyr.* 4. Clem. Alex. *Paed.* III. 4. 271 P; II. 12. Val. Max. IX. 1. 2. *Anth. Pal.* v. 270. 3; VIII. 21. 1. *Dig.* XXXIV. 2. 19. 15, 18 etc. Daremb.-Sagl. s.v. *Margarita.* Where was the pearl-producing Perimula of Pliny VI. 72; IX. 106? Monahan, 49.

(**57**) Suet. *Nero*, 31. *Louvre*, 645. Philo, *de Somn.* II. 8. 57. *Encycl. Brit.* s.v. *Pearl. Dig.* XXXIX. 4. 16. 7?

(**58**) Pliny VI. 80. Seneca, *Dial.* XII *ad Helv.* 10. Tertull. *de cult. fem.* I. 6–8 trans. Thelwall. Philostrat. *Apollon.* III. 53. Athenae. III. 13, 45=93 *b*. There are oyster-fisheries at Bentotte, and a chank-fishery at Manaar—Tennent, *Ceylon*, II. 129, 556.

(**59**) *Peripl.* 59, and Müller, Fabricius, and Schoff, *ad loc.* J. Yates, *Textr. Antiqu.* vol. I. pp. 177–189.

(**60**) Diosc. II. 8. *O.P.* VIII. 1142, lines 3–5. *Soc.* 297, 14 (v). Cp. Oribas. v. 77. Galen XIII. 320. Paul. Aegin. VII. 3, s.v. ὄνυχες. Avicenna II. 2. 78. Rhazes, *Cont. l. ult.* I. 127. Serapion, *de Simpl.* 443. Probably used with bdellium; cp. *Genesis* ii. 12?

(**61**) Cosmas XI. 448 B. Pillai, 22, 25. Smith, 469. *Madras Gov. Mus. Bull.* vol. I. pp. 55–62 (chank). J. E. Tennent, *Ceylon*, II. 556.

Heeren, *op. cit.* 419. Marallo = Maŕawar? Ptol. VII. 2. 2. Island Saline = Salang?

(**62**) Hirth, 80, 225. Pliny VI. 54; XI. 76. Lucan X. 141–3. *Pauly*, s.v. *Serica*, 1725–7. Chwostow, 151. Yule I. 199. *Hist. Aug. 'Aurel.'* 45. Cordier in *Mélanges Graux*, 720. Virg. *Aen.* VIII. 688, cp. 705 (Bactrians and Indians in Antony's army—possibly, if really given by the king of the Medes). Caesar and silk:—Dio Cass. XLIII. 24. Tac. *Ann.* II. 33.

(**63**) *Amos* iii. 12. *Ezek.* xvi. 10? and 13, cp. *Isaiah* xlix. 12 (Chinese). Lucan X. 142. Petron. *S.* 119, lines 11 and 25. Ov. *Am.* I. 14, 5–6. Virg. *G.* II. 121. Prop. II. 3. 15, cp. I. 14. 22; IV. 8. 23. Hor. *Epo.* VIII. 15–16. Strabo XV. 1. 20.

(**64**) Minns, 336. Frazer ad Paus., vol. IV. p. 112. Chwostow, 154. R. Forrer, *Röm. u. Byz. Seiden-Textil. a. d. Gräberfeld. von Achmim-Panopolis*, 10 ff. esp. 10—silk very rare; 10–12—whole silks extremely rare. Silk occurs chiefly as ornaments or trimmings to garments, cp. *Jahrb. d. K. D. Arch. Instit.* XXVII, *Anz.* 273.

(**65**) Schoff, *J.A.O.S.* 35, p. 34, 39. Kennedy, *J.R.A.S.* 1912, 981 ff. esp. 987. Yule I. 64 ff.

(**66**) *Peripl.* 39, 49, 56, 64. Pillai, 25, *Dig.* XXXIX. 4. 16. 7. Cosmas XI. 445 D, 448 B, cp. II. 96 C–97 B? *Ramayana*, I. 605 ff., 621 ff., cp. III. 204, 282 etc.

(**67**) Clem. Alex. *Paed.* II. 11. Vidal de Lablache in *Acad. des Inscr. C.-R.* 1897, 520–7, writes on early trade by sea.

(**68**) This trade with India through Assam was very early if it is reflected in the mouthless Astomi on the east side of India, clothed with down from trees. Pliny VII. 25, from Megasthenes. Cp. expedition of numerous Indians who lived near the Bactrians into the gold-desert—Ael. IV. 27, apparently from Ctesias.

(**69**) Schoff, ad *Peripl.* 257, 272. Cp. Gerini, map facing p. 564.

(**70**) Pompon. Mela III. 7. Sen. *Ep.* XIV. 2. (90) 15. *C.I.L.* VI. 1343, 9891, 9768, 9892; XIV. 3711–12, 2793, 2812 (Latium). *C.I.G.* 5834 (reading σηρικοποιός), Waddington, 1854. Sen. *Phaedr.* 389. *Thyest.* 378–9. *Fr.* XIII. 52. Pliny XXXVII. 204; XXI. 11; XIV. 22; VI. 54; XII. 2; XXXIV. 145. Stat. *S.* v. 1. 215. Sil. Ital. VI. 4; XVII. 595–6. Galen X. 942 etc. Dessau, 7599–7603. *C.I.L.* XIV. 2215.

(**71**) Ptol. I. 11. 7; 12, 3–10; 13, 1–14, 9, esp. 14, 1. Hirth, 173–8, cp. 183. Momms. *Prov.* II. 98–9. Priaulx, 129–130. Paus. VI. 26.

4 (6–8). Pollux VII. 76. Chwostow, 146–155, 443. *Pauly*, s.v. *Seres, Serica*, Daremb.-Sagl. s.v. *Sericum*. E. Pariset, *Histoire de la Soie*, I. Pardessus, *Acad. d. Inscr. et B.-L. Mém.* XV. 1842, 1–27. T. Yoshida, *Entwickelung des Seidenhandels*, 17–52. Lassen I. 369–375; III. 25–30. Dalton, *Byz. Art*, 583 ff.

(72) Stein, *Ruins of Desert Cathay*, I. pp. 410–411, 457–8, 471–2, 467, 480, 486–7, 492–3, 381. Gibbon, *Decline and Fall*, XLII. Zonar. *Ep.* XIV. 9. 16–20 = XIV. 9 P II 69.

(73) Ctes. ap. Phot. Bibl. 72, p. 152, McCrindle, *Ct.* 22–3, reading 'lac' for (the American!) cochineal and 52–3. Ael. *d. N. A.* IV. 46 (from Ctes.), cp. Pliny XXXVII. 36–7, 39, 40—appears to refer to lac, cp. XII. 98. *Peripl.* 6. *Lond. P.* II. No. 191 (pp. 264–5), line 10, but see Preisigke, *Wörterb.* s.v. λακκόω. Watt, *Dict.* s.v. *Coccus lacca*, esp. 411. Schoff, 73. In giving invertebrates, I reverse the usual order.

CHAPTER II

(1) See *Ezek.* xxvii passim, esp. 19, 22. *Exod.* xxx. 23–4. *Gen.* xxxvii. 25 etc. Strabo XV. 1. 22. Cp. Vitruv. VIII. 3. 8 and Celsus and Scribonius as cited below. Theophr. IV. 4. 14; IX. 7. 2; 15. 2. Philo, *de Somn.* II. 8, fin.

(2) Hor. *Ep.* II. 1. 270. *Sat.* II. 473–4. Ov. *A.A.* II. 417.

(3) *Peripl.* 56, 49. Pliny VI. 104. Theophr. IX. 20. 1. Pillai, 16. Athenae. II. 25. 73 = 66 *d–f.* Pliny XXXVI. 70; cf. XVI. 201. Cedren. 172 A–B, the figures are exaggerated but the pepper is typical. Torr, *Ancient Ships*, p. 27. Cosmas XI. 445 D, pepper of Male = Malabar. Pepper called Syrian at beginning of the Empire—Vitruv. VIII. 3. 13—Syrian and Arabian.

(4) Caelius Apicius (or perhaps it should be Caelius, '*Apicius*'), *de Re Coquinaria*, passim. Plut. *Q. Conv.* VIII. 9. iii. 26. Used by shepherds to stimulate mating. Ael. IX. 48.

(5) E.g. Cels. *de Med.* V. 23. 1 (white); V. 18. 7 (round and long); V. 23. 3 etc. Scribon. Larg. 94, 113, 121 etc. (black); 9, 10, 26, 32–4 etc. (white); 120–1, 176–7 (long) etc. Aretae. V. 2. 11. Galen XII. 97 et passim. *O.P.* 1299, 10. *Stud.* XX. 27. 3. *Rylands P.* 29 (*a*), lines 2, 4, 23, cp. 29 (*b*) (pepper thrice). *Tebt. P.* II. 273. *Lips.* 102, 11 (IV). *Berlin. Klassikert.* vol. III. p. 32, No. 7763 (i) 6.

(6) Sir T. Clifford Allbutt, *Gr. Med. in Rome*, pp. 26, 337, 379. Lassen I. 278.

(7) Pliny **XII.** 26–8. Solin. 55. White pepper in Dig. list (*Dig.* **XXXIX.** 4. 16. 7) shews that it was sometimes ground in India, cp. Wessely, 1309–10. Petron. *S.* 38, 44, 49. Juv. **XIV.** 137. Pers. **v.** 55, 134–6; **VI.** 37–40, cp. **III.** 75; **VI.** 21. Mart. **IV.** 46. 7; **III.** 2. 5; **VII.** 27. 7; **VIII.** 59. 4; **X.** 57. 2; **XI.** 18. 9; **XII.** 52. 1; **XIII.** 5. 2; 13. 2. Stat. *S.* **IV.** 9. 12. Plut. *loc. cit.* Diosc. **II.** 159. Colum. **XII.** 47 and 57. *Anth. Pal.* **IX.** 502. Hippocr. *Morb. Mulc.* **II.** 676, 740, Kühn. Cosmas **XI.** 444 D, 445 D, 441 D.

(8) Cosmas, 441 D. Jordan, *Topogr.* I. 3. 7. Jer. *Chron.* Ol. 217, **A.D.** 92. Hor. *Ep.* **II.** 1. 270. Paul. *Sent.* **III.** 6. 86. Daremb.-Sagl. **s.v.** *Piper.* Silver pepper-dish—*Corn. Pap.* 33, l. 15; *O.P.* 921, l. 26. Pollux **X.** 169. Pantry pepper-jar—*C.I.L.* **IV.** 5763. Chwostow, 120–2. Pepper adulterated with heavier substances to deceive buyers—Isid. *Or.* **XVII.** 8. 8. Cf. Lanciani, *New Tales of old R.* 84–6.

(9) Diosc. **II.** 160. Pliny **XII.** 28. Ptol. **VII.** 4. 1. *Dig., loc. cit.* Apic. **I.** 13. 18; **II.** 2; **III.** 3. 4; **IV.** 1. 5; **VII.** 9; **VIII.** 6. Cels. **v.** 23. 3. Id. *Agric.* Fr. xxx (Marx, p. 10). Scribon. 165. Galen **XIV.** 258; **VI.** 271; **XIV.** 761; **XIX.** 730, 725, 740 and esp. **XI.** 880 ff., Kühn. Cp. Aretae. **VII.** 4. 12 etc. *C.I.L.* **III.** S. **I.** p. 1953, 68–9. *Stud.* **XX.** 27. 4. Chwostow, 88–9. I feel sure that the plant had not yet been transplanted to Africa, but see Chwostow, p. 122. Pall. *R.R.* **XI.** 20. 2.

(10) Theophr. **IX.** 7. 2, 3. *de Od.* 32. 25. Virg. *E.* **IV.** 25. Ov. *P.* I. 9. 51–2. *Her.* **XXI.** 166. *Trist.* **III.** 3. 69. Cp. Tibull. **I.** 3, 7; I. 5. 36; **III.** 2. 24 (Assyrian products, cp. 'Malta' ivory to-day because trans-shipped there). Pliny **XII.** 48–50; **XV.** 135; **XXXVII.** 204. Diosc. **I.** 6, 15. Celsus, Scribon. and Galen in many places. Stat. *S.* **I.** 2. 111; **II.** 4. 34; **III.** 3. 132 and 212; **II.** 6. 86–7 etc. Pers. **III.** 104. Juv. **IV.** 108–9; **VIII.** 159. Sil. **XI.** 404; **XV.** 117. Luc. **X.** 168. 'Virg.' *Cir.* 512. Sall. *Hist. Fr.* **IV.** 60=72. Wessely, 1311 and index. Watt, *Dict.* **s.v.** *Elettaria. Pauly,* **s.v.** *Amomon.*

(11) Hence perhaps Statius, who represents the well-to-do class, mentions cinnamon rather than casia. Galen **XIV.** 64 ff.

(12) *Psl.* xlv. 8. *Ezek.* xxvii. 19. *Exod.* xxx. 23–4. Virg. *G.* **II.** 466. Ov. *F.* **III.** 731; *M.* **X.** 308; **XV.** 399. Prop. **III.** 27=**II.** 29. 177. Cp. Herod. **III.** 110; **II.** 86. Müller, *Geog. Gr. Min.* **I.** p. 186. *O.P.* **I.** 36, Col. I edited by Wilcken in *Gr. u. Chr.* **I.** ii, *Chrest.* p. 322. *Arch. f. Pap.* **III.** 186. Strabo **XVI.** 4. 19 (Sabaeans, but see note 13), cp. **XVI.** 4. 25. Theophr. **IX.** 4. 2 etc. In Virg. *E.* **II.** 49; *G.* **II.** 213;

IV. 30, 182; Ov. *F.* IV. 440; Pliny XXI. 53; XII. 98; XVI. 136 casia is not cinnamon at all, but *Daphne Cneorum*; cp. Columella III. 8. 4 (X. 301). *Arch. Surv. Ind.* X. 77.

(13) Strabo XVI. 4. 19; 4. 25; XV. 1. 22; cp. XVI. 4. 14; II. 1. 17. Cp. possibly Herod. III. 111, cinnamon in country where Dionysos was brought up. For the spice in general see Chwostow, 119–120, 381–2, 383. Malabathr.:—id. 183–4. Vincent, II. 130, 701–716. Coedès, *Textes*, XVIII. Lindsay, *Hist. of Merch. Shipping and Anc. Comm.* I. 156–7. Kennedy in *J.R.A.S.* 1918, 595, thinks the plant really grew in East Africa. Lassen I. 327–332; III. 35–6. See also Cooley in *J. of R. Geogr. Soc.* XIX (1849), 166–191, esp. 177 ff. *Pauly*, s.v. *Casia.* Schoff, 82–4, 87, 89, 216–218, 256, 281.

(14) *Peripl.* 8, 10, 13, 62, 63, 65, 56. Pliny XII. 82–98, 129; XIII. 8–18, esp. 15; XXIII. 93; VI. 174. Galen, *de Compos. Medic. sec. loc.* passim; XIV. 257; XII. 66, 153, 756; XIX. 735. Diosc. I. 12–14; V. 39, 54.

(15) *Peripl.* 62–5. Pompon. Mela I. 2. 11; III. 6. 60. Ptol. VII. 2. 2; 15–16. Strabo XV. 1. 57. Pliny VII. 25 (Sciritae). Pseudo-Callisth. III. 8. *Tab. Peut.* Miller, 626–7. Lassen III. 37–9, 235–7. Schoff, ad *Peripl.* pp. 84, 89, 216–218, 253–6, 278–9, 281. McCrindle, *Ptol.* pp. 218, 191–2.

(16) *Peripl.* 56. Renou reads Σαησάδαι in Ptol. Of course the names μαλάβαθρον and Malabar have no connexion.

(17) Pliny XII. 129. Apic. I. 15, 16; IX. 1. 7. Hor. *Od.* II. 7. 7–8. Wessely, 2680, *B.G.U.* III. 953. 2 and perhaps *B.G.U.* I. 93. 11, *Corn. Pap.* 35. 4. Scribon. 120. Isid. *Or.* XVIII. 9. Diosc. I. 12. Cels. V. 23. 1; V. 23. 3 (malab. folium). It has been taken as the sheath of the nutmeg—Schoff, *J.A.O.S.* 45, p. 80. Does folium pentasphaerum of *Dig.* XXXIX. 4. 16. 7 mean malabathrum?

(18) Pliny XII. 44. *Peripl.* 65.

(19) *Peripl.* 13, 10, 12, 9, 8. Mosyllon gave its name to varieties of cinnamon. Diosc. I. 13, 14.

(20) Apulei. *Flor.* 6, cp. *Met.* II. 8. Galen and cinnamon in the possession of emperors of the 2nd cent. A.C.—Galen XIV. 64 ff.

(21) The Arabians probably got much of the spice at Muziris (*Peripl.* 54, reading Arabia for Ariace) or even Ceylon. Perhaps they made a trading voyage like the modern Arabians:—Red Sea (August)—Muscat—Malabar—Africa (December) as far as Mada-

gascar and even Sofala; back to Red Sea not before May. H. Salt, *Voyage to Abyssinia*, 103. Sabaeans visited Chinese court with a rhinoceros early in 1st cent. A.D.—Herrmann (who thinks Ta-ts'in was Arabia), *Verkehrswege*, 8. Chinese and E. Africa—Herrmann in *Zeits. d. Ges. f. Erdk.* 1913, pp. 553–561.

(22) Tales about cinnamon and casia—Pliny XII. 87–8, 93. Herod. III. 110–111, cp. 107. Strabo XVI. 4. 14, 'from the far interior.' Pliny VI. 174 shews that cinnamon was *landed* at Mosyllon and in XII. 82 that Greeks now knew that cinnamon and casia were at least not Arabian. Besides the references given above, see *C.I.G.* 2852, lines 59–60. Petron. 78. 30 (as a name, cp. *Thes. Lingu. Lat. Onomast.* II. s.v. *Cinnamus*; *E.E.* VIII. 221). Dio Chrys. *Or.* XXXIII. 28, Arnim (φρύγανα). Pompon. Mela III. 8. 79 (of Arab. Eud.). Columella III. 8. Wessely, 1309 and index. *O.P.* VIII. 1088. *Flor.* I. 100. 32. *Tebt. P.* 190, 250. *Soc.* 628, 8. 9. *B.G.U.* 953, 4. Scribon. 70, 93, 106, 110 etc.; frequent in all medical writers. *C.I.L.* III. *S.* I. 1953, 32. Stat. *S.* v. 3. 42–3; IV. 5. 32; II. 6. 88, cp. Mart. IV. 13. 3; III. 63. 3–4; X. 97. 2; IV. 55. 1; III. 55. 1–3; VI. 54. 26. Pers. VI. 35–6. Virg. *G.* II. 466. Euseb. IV. 887–8 etc. Schoff, *J.A.O.S.* 40, 260–270. Vincent, II. 511–514. J. d'Alwis in *J.R.A.S. Ceylon Br.* III. No. 12, 1860–1, pp. 372–380. McCr. *Ptol.* 219–220. Chwostow, 91 ff., 104, 107, 441 (with authorities). *J. R. Stud.* 1917, p. 55. Perhaps κάρπιον of Ctes. 28 comes ultimately from Sinhalese Koredhu, whence Kirfah, κάρπιον. Heeren, *As. Nat.* 369.

(23) Scribon. 110, 113, 126, 173 etc. Pliny XII. 45–6 (Syriacum). Cels. v. 23. 1; VI. 7. 2 C; 3 B. Cp. nard of Commagene.

(24) The sea-route gave the epithet Alexandrinus which appears in Cels. v. 24. 1. Price of cal. arom.—5 den. (apparently) a pound. The Romans confused grass-nards with malabathrum, since they considered this a marsh-plant.

(25) *Nard*:—*St Mark* xiv. 3–5. *St John* xii. 3–6. *Song of Sol.* i. 12. *O.P.* 1088, 1384. Hor. *Od.* II. 11. 16. *Epode* XIII. 8–9; v. 59. *Od.* IV. 12. 17. Diosc. I. 7, cp. 17, 18. Tibull. II. 2. 7; III. 4. 27; III. 6. 64. *C.I.L.* x. 1284 (name). Prop. v. 7. 32. *Anth. Pal.* v. 1, 43, cp. VI. 250, 6; 254, 4; 231, 5. Pliny XIII. 15; XII. 42–7; XXXVII. 204. Grat. *Cyneg.* 314. *Peripl.* 46, 56, 63. Cosmas XI. 445 D. Prisc. *Perieg.* 984. Cels. v. 23. 2; VI. 6. 6, 9 A, cp. III. 21. 7–8 etc. Strabo XVI. 4, 25. Galen XIV. 73; XIX. 737 etc.; XII. 84–5. Wessely,

index, ναρδίνου, νάρδος. *Soc.* 628, 7. *P.Z.* 69. 5 (*Annales*, XXII. 221).
S.B. 5307, 1. The Celtic was a European plant. Galen X. 492;
VI. 439–440, 426; XII. 429, 604; X. 791 etc. *Dig.*, *loc. cit.* Apic. I.
15, 16; IX. 1, 7; VII. 6 (282); VIII. 2 (347), cp. IX. 8; I 16. Ptol
VII. 2. 23. I suspect that the 'nardinum' which is mentioned in
medical inscriptions of the West was made from 'Celtic nard'—see
Signacula Medicorum Oculariorum (A. Espérandieu), Nos. 2, 8, 31,
86, 140, 194–5, 208, and esp. 226. *Grass-nards:*—Schoff, ad *Peripl.*
p. 169. *Penny Cycl.* s.v. *Sweet Calamus* and s.v. *Sugar.* *Peripl.* 39.
Exod. XXX. 33. *Song of Sol.* vi. 14. *Is.* xliii. 24. *Jerem.* vi. 20.
Ezek. xxvii. 19. Pliny. XII. 104–6. Diosc. I. 17, 18 etc. Veget. *Ar.*
Vet. 4. 13. 4. Calamus aromaticus it seems included Sweet Flag,
partly Indian. Ginger-grass of India is also meant by Stat. *S.* II.
1. 160; V. 1. 212; IV. 5. 30–1. Cp. Cels. IV. 21. 2; III. 21. 7 etc.
Theophr. *H.P.* IX. 7. 1 and 3 etc., but not IV. 11. 13. See also Schoff,
J.A.O.S. 43, pp. 216 ff. Watt, s.v. *Acorus Calamus.*

(**26**) Pliny XII. 41; XXXVII. 204. *Peripl.* 39, 46. *Dig.*, *loc. cit.*
Cosmas XI. 445 D? Diosc. I. 16. Ov. *M.* X. 308. Hor. *Od.* III. 1. 44.
Prop. IV. (v) 6. 5. Lucan IX. 917. Colum. XII. 20, 5 etc. Pliny XII.
16, 50 etc. Galen V. 22; VII. 46 etc. *O.P.* XI. 1384 (5th cent. A.D.).
B.G.U. 953. 3. Wessely, 2680. Scribon. 70, 121, 125–6, 129, 144, 173,
176–7, 269 etc. Cels. III. 21. 7; IV. 21. 2; V. 3 etc. Aretae. v. 8. 5;
VIII. 13. 8. Strabo XVI. 4. 26, κοστάρια of the Nabataeans? cf. also
Theophr. *H.P.* IX. 7. 6; *de Od.* 28, 34.

(**27**) *Jat.* III. 405. *Camb. Hist. Ind.* I. p. 207. Pillai, 25. Pliny
XXI. 1–11. *Peripl.* 49. Schoff, id. p. 191. Pliny XII. 94. Garland-
shops in ancient India:—*Ramayana*, III. 128 ff. Inscript. in *Arch.*
Surv. Ind. X. p. 18.

(**28**) Pliny XII. 135; XIII. 18. Pallad. *de Gent. Ind. et. Br.* p. 4.
Theophr. *H.P.* IX. 7. 2.

(**29**) Pliny XII. 30. *Dig.*, *loc. cit.* Duchesne, *Lib. Pont.* I. p. 178.
Cosmas XI. 445 D, 448 B. *Soc.* 297, 19. Paul. Aegin. VII. 3, s.v.

(**30**) Diosc. I. 68. *Peripl.* 30, 39. Pillai, 25. *Encycl. Brit.* s.v.
Frankincense (quoted). Müller, *Geog. Gr. Min.*, Proleg. CVIII. Philo-
strat. *Apollon.* III. 4. *Dig.*, *loc. cit.*, cp. *Ramayana*, I. 636 ff. Lassen
I. 335; III. 39–40.

(**31**) Theophr. IV. 4. 12; IX. 1. 2. *Peripl.* 39, 48, 49. Pliny XII. 35–6,
71. Diosc. I. 67. Galen XI. 849 etc. Isid. *Orig.* XVII. 8. *O.P.* VIII.

1142 (3rd cent.). Cels. v. 4, 5, 15; 18, 7 etc. *C.I.L.* iii. S. i. 1953, 54–5.

(**32**) Pliny xii. 98. Diosc. i. 24. Cp. Paul. Aegin. vii. 3, s.v. κάγχαμον. Galen xii. 8. *Peripl.* 8. Schoff, ad *Peripl.* p. 80. Watt, *Dict.* s.v. *Vateria.* Electrum of Pliny xxxvii. 36, 39?

(**33**) *Peripl.* 27–8. Pliny xxvii. 14. Diosc. iii. 22. Galen xi. 821; xii. 216. Scribon. 21. Schoff, *J.A.O.S.* 42, pp. 174–5. Watt, 59.

(**34**) *Peripl.* 30. Diosc. v. 94 (he calls it Libyan and nothing else). Bent, *Southern Arabia*, 379, 381, 387.

(**35**) Pliny xxix. 35; xiii. 7, 9, 10; viii. 34; xxxiii. 115–116; xxxv. 30, 50. Chwostow, 111, 125.

(**36**) Pliny xix. 38–40, 45; xiii. 67; xxiv. 128; xii. 72; xxiv. 12 etc. *Exod.* xxx. 24. Paul. Aegin. vii. 3, s.v. ὀπός. Diosc. iii. 89. *Dig.* xxxix. 4. 16. 7. Watt, 534–5, 901–2. Cp. Diosc. iii. 85 (sarcocolla); iii. 83. χαλβάνη 'of Syria,' because of land or Persian Gulf trade. Cp. Pliny xii. 126. He confuses, I think, Indian mastic-plant with bdellium-plant. B. Laufer, *Sino-Iranica*, 353 ff.

(**37**) *Peripl.* 27–33.

(**38**) Strabo xvi. 1. 22. Vitruv. vii. 9, 6; 10, 4 (Ind. ink); 14, 2. *Peripl.* 39. Pliny xxxiii. 163, cp. xxxv. 30, 49, 42–3, 46, 50; xxxiii. 161. Diosc. v. 92. Lassen iii. 596. Götz, 119–120.

(**39**) *Peripl.* 39, 49. Pliny xii. 30–1; xxiv. 124–7. Aretae. viii. 13. 9. Diosc. i. 100. Galen xii. 63; xix. 724 (Indian best). Cp. Paul. Aegin. vii. 3, s.v. Λύκιον. Scribon. 19, 142 (Indian); 142 (Pataric). *Dig., loc. cit.* Watt, 130. *J.R.A.S.* 1843, pp. 74–7. Cels. vi. 6, 5, 8, 24, 30; v. 1. He does not call it Indian. Difficulty of getting real pure Indian—Galen xii. 216.

(**40**) *Peripl.* 14, 41, 32. *Hibeh Pap.* 43 (B.C. 261). *Rev. Pap.*, Cols. 41–4, 61–72 etc. Cels. iv. 15. 3; v. 15. Pliny xv. 28. Philostrat. *Apoll.* iii. 5. Columella xi. 2. 50, 56 (Cilicia, Pamphylia).

(**41**) *Dig., loc. cit. Encycl. Brit.* s.v. *Poppy, Poppy-oil, Opium.* Watt, s.v. *Papaver*, 845 ff. L. West in *J. R. Stud.* 1917, p. 55.

(**42**) Diosc. iii. 2. Ammian. Marcell. xxii. 8. 28. Radix Pontica of Cels. v. 23. 3. Paul. Aegin. vii. 3, s.v. 'Ρῆον. These refer probably to vegetable rhubarb only. Averrhoes, *Collig.* v. 42. Mesua, *de Simpl.* v etc. Ferrand, 265–274. Vincent, ii. 389. *Encycl. Brit.* s.v. *Rhubarb, Penny Cyclopaedia*, s.v. *Rheum* (2 articles). Would folium barbaricum be cinnamon-leaf or nard got in Somali marts?

(**43**) Isid. xvii. 7. 58, quoting Varro. Strabo xv. 1. 20, from Nearchos.

(44) Seneca, *Ep.* 84. 4. Diosc. II. 82, 104; I. 41, 185. Pliny XII. 32. Solin. 52, 48. *Peripl.* 14. Stat. *S.* I. 615. Lucan III. 237. *Anth. Pal.* X. 221. Ptol. VII. 4. 1 (μέλι of Ceylon). Alex. Aphrod. II. 74. Oribas. XI. 205. Isidore, *loc. cit.* Paul. Aeg. VII. 3, s.v. Μέλι (speaks of σάχαρ from Arab. Eudaemon). Galen XII. 71; XIX. 727. Perhaps *Dig.* XXXIX. 4. 16. 7. Did Chinese white sugar-candy come westwards so long ago? Watt, s.v. *Saccharum*, 930–1. *Pauly*, s.v. Σάκχαρον. Lassen I. 317–322. W. Falconer, *Sketch of Hist. of Sugar.*

(45) Pillai, 13, 25. At first Rome imported cloth only.

(46) *Esther* i. 6. *Ezek.* xxvii. 23–4? Virg. *Aen.* VIII. 33–4. Theophrast. *H.P.* IV. 4. 8; IV. 7. 7–8. Philo, *de Somn.* II. 7. 53. Herod. IV. 193. Cic. *in Verr.* V. 12. 30. Lucret. V. 108 etc. Strabo XV. 1. 20–1. *Peripl.* 6, 14, 41, 49, 51, 31, 59, 63, 61. Cosmas XI. 445 D. Pliny XIX. 14–15; XII. 38–40; XIII. 90. *Dig.* XXXII. 70. 4. 9; XXXIX. 4. 16. 7. Petron. 65. Pollux VII. 75–6. *Hist. Aug. 'Saturn.'* 8. Arr. *Ind.* 16, 1. Lucian, *Musc. Encom.* I. Cp. *Dialog. Meretr.* V. 4. Lucan III. 237–9. *Anth. Pal.* IX. 415. 5–6. Philostrat. *Apollon.* II. 9. Isid. *Orig.* XIX. 22, 15; 27, 4. *Lond. P.* III. No. 928 (p. 190), l. 1. Müller, *Geog. Gr. Min.* I. 262–3. Yates, *Textr. Antiqu.* I. 334–354, 470 ff. McCrindle, *Anc. Ind.* 26. H. Brandes, *Baumvolle im Alterthum*, esp. 111 ff. Indian dress, value 8 minas, worn in Judaea, *Veröffentlichungen des Forschungsinst.* No. 5, p. 157. Chwostow, 130–146 —an interesting account; see especially authorities on p. 130. Daremberg-Saglio, s.v. *Byssus*, s.v. *Carbasus.* Lassen I. 295–8; III. 23 ff. *Pauly*, s.v. *Byssos*, s.v. *Carbasus.* Heeren, *As. Nat.* II. 272 ff.

(47) Philostrat. *Apollon.* II. 20. Chwostow, 143–4. Wilcken, *Ostr.* I. p. 380. Pollux, *l.c.* Claudian, *in Eutrop.* I. 357.

(48) Chwostow, 7–8, 126. Arist. *Meteor.* IV. 7. 16; *de Pl.* II. 96. Theophrast. *H.P.* IV. 4. 6 etc.; V. 4. 7. Herod. V. 97. Virg. *G.* II. 116–117. Pliny XII. 17–20. *Peripl.* 36, cp. *Ezek.* xxvii. 15. Paus. I. 42. 5; II. 22. 5; VIII. 53. 11. Athenae. V. 8 = 201. *Anth. Pal.* XII. 163. 3. Watt, *Dict.* s.v. *Diospyros*, 136 ff. Cels. III. 21. 7; V. 7, 12, 13.

(49) *Encycl. Brit.* s.v. *Teak.* Not in Torr, *Ancient Ships*, 31–4. See also Fabric. ad *Peripl.*, *l.c.* p. 75. Lassen III. 31. Chwostow, 126. Theophrast. V. 4. 7. Pliny XVI. 221. *Peripl.*, *l.c.*

(50) *Peripl.* 36, 53. Cosmas XI. 445 D. Fabric. needlessly alters the text of the *Peripl.* to συκαμινίνων. See also Theophr. V. 3. 2.

(51) *Peripl.* 36. Cosmas XI. 445 D. II *Chron.* ix. 10; ii. 8; I *Kings* x. 11. Celsius, *Hierobot.* I. 173. Galen XIV. 759. *Paddinappalai*, 185–191, Pillai, 27. Avicenna II. 2. 649 attributes it to Sini (China? wrongly, if so). Lassen I. 336; III. 40. *Arthasastra*, II. 1 (16 kinds). *Ramayana*, III. 125 etc. *Gitagovinda*, pp. 58, 65 etc.

(52) Charit. *Chaer. et Call.* IV. 4. Hor. *Od.* I. 29. 9 and Acron and Porphyr. *ad loc.* We have a Chinese carriage in Prop. IV. 8. 23, or perhaps he means a silk-hung carriage.

(53) It is perhaps aloes (ahaloth, ahil, *pl.* ahilim) in *Prov.* vii. 17. *Psl.* xlv. 8 (but not *Numb.* xxiv. 6); cp. I *Enoch* 28–31. *Canticles* iv. 13–14. *St John* xix. 39. But see Schoff, *J.A.O.S.* 42, 177–180. Cf. also Diosc. I. 22. Galen XIX. 723, 731, 733. Pillai, 27, Cosmas 445 D. The Malay word is agila or garoo. Chwostow, 106. Perhaps also in *Dig.* XXXIX. 4. 16. 7. Paul. Aegin. VII. 3, s.v. ἀγάλοχον, calls this an Indian wood. *Arthasastra*, II. 1.

(54) Hirth, 272–5.

(55) Pliny XII. 32. Diosc. I. 82 (from τῆς βαρβάρου, North-east Africa). Galen XII. 66 (of India). Cp. Paul. Aegin. VII. 3, s.v. Μάκερ. *Peripl.* 8. Lassen III. 31. Schoff, ad *Peripl.* pp. 80–1. Chwostow, 99, 441. Watt, 640, s.v. *Holarrhena*.

(56) Antonin. Martyr. 41.

(57) *Peripl.* 17, 36, 33. Pliny XIII. 62? Philostrat. *Apollon.* III. 5. Cosmas XI. 444 D–445 A, 445 C (on the Maldives). Cedren. 152 D. Pallad. *de Gent. Ind. et Br.* p. 4; cf. de Candolle, 435. Müller, *Geog. Gr. Min.* vol. I. Proleg. CIX. Lassen I. 314–317. Chwostow, 99.

(58) Pliny XII. 24. de Candolle, 306–7. Lassen I. 307–311. Cp. Theophr. IV. 4. 5. Arr. *Ind.* II. Curt. XI. 1. 10.

(59) Pliny XIX. 65–7; xx. 11. Pallad. *R.R.* IV. 9. 6 (melones). *O.P.* I. 117, ls. 11–12. Cp. *SB.* 4483, 13, 15; 4485, 5, 7. *Hist. Aug. 'Clod. Alb.'* 11. 3 (melones Ostienses). de Candolle, 262. Hehn, *Kulturpfl. u. Hausth.* 313–315.

(60) *Persica*: Pliny XV. 39–45, 109, 112–114; XII. 14; XV. 45; XVI. 138 etc. Columella XI. 2. 11. *SB.* 4483, 14; 15. 4485, 6; 7. *O.P.* 1631, 23; 1764. *Herm.* 29. 6. Pliny XIII. 63 (at Thebes, indicating the sea-route from India). *Hist. Aug. 'Clod. Alb.'* 11. 3, Persica Campana. *Persea*: Pliny XV. 45. *Soc.* 285. 10. *O.P.* 53. 7. Cp. *B.G.U.* 1028, 9. *O.P.* 1188, 21. Duracina, a var. of Persica: Pliny XV. 39, 109, 113; cp. Diosc. I. 115. de Candolle, 221–9. Hehn, *op. cit.* 424–8.

(61) Columella XI. 296; cp. X. 404. Galen XII. 77; VI. 594, 785. de Candolle, 215–218.

(62) Pliny XII. 15–16; XVI. 107; XV. 110. Diosc. I. 115. de Candolle, 178 ff. Hehn, 443–9. See also Plut. *Qu. Conv.* VIII. 9. iii. 26. Petron. *S.* 38, cp. 56. *O.P.* 1764; perhaps Joseph. *A.J.* XIII. 13. 5. *Cant.* ii. 3, 5. *Prov.* XXV. 11 etc. Theophr. I. 11. 4; 13. 4; IV. 4. 2–3.

(63) See de Candolle, 39, 73, 66, 101, 265, 346 etc. Athenae. II. 18. 58 *f*–59 *a* = 53. Diosc. II. 113. Columella XII. 56. Pliny XIX. 90 etc. Hehn, 309 ff.

(64) Hehn, 495 ff. Hor. *Sat.* II. 3. 155. Mart. III. 42. 1. Diosc. II. 98, 117. *Peripl.* 14, 41, 31. Pliny XVIII. 71; XV. 28. Galen VI. 525; XII. 71; XIX. 727. Apic. II. 2. Cels. II. 18. 10; 20, 1; 23, 1; 24, 1 (food); IV. 14. 7 (in medicine). *SB.* 5224, 36, 41. Cf. also Theophr. IV. 4. 10.

(65) Pliny XVIII. 55. Dionys. Perieget. 1126. Strabo XV. 1. 18 and 13. Philostrat. *Apollon.* III. 5. de Candolle, 381, 383. Chwostow, 117; cp. Theophr. IV. 4. 9.

(66) *Peripl.* 14, 32, 7, 8, 24, 28, 56, 17. Chwostow, 118. Cp. Theophrast. IV. 4. 9; VIII. 4. 2 (wheat and barley).

(67) Theophr. *H.P.* IV. 11, 13 (bamboo). Pliny XVI. 162. *P. Lond.* II. No. 191 (pp. 264–5), line 11. *Ind. Antiqu.* XIV. 335–6. Chwostow, 126.

(68) Virg. *G.* IV. 118. Ov. *M.* XV. 708. Mart. IV. 41. 10; VI. 80. 6.

(69) Add rhubarb. For camphor see Schoff, *J.A.O.S.* 42, p. 359. F. Adams, *Paul. Aegin.* III. 427–9. Serapion, *de Simpl.* 344. Avicenna II. 2. 130. Rhazes, *Contin. l. ult.* I. 147. *Ad Mans.* III. 22 etc. and for the other plant-products I give the following references as examples only:—Serapion, *de Simpl.* XII. 58, 275, 348 (from Arabian sources only), 388, 345, 288, 170, 260, 365, 153, 322, 172, 271 etc., 337, 257, 375, 79, 84. Ebn Baithar I. 272; II. 200; I. 30. Avicenna II. 2, 448; 2, 691; 2, 449; 2, 251; 2, 313; 2, 699; 2, 17; 2, 260; 2, 282. Rhazes, *Contin. l. ult.* I. 507, 506, 312. *Ad Mans.* III. 30. Nicol. Myreps. I. 24. Ainslie, *Mat. Ind.* I. 236 ff. I rely on F. Adams, *Paul. Aegin.* vol. III. Ferrand, I. 235–296. N.B. Casia and cassia (often both called cassia) are distinct; to the Roman list we might add (from Theophrastos):—Jack Fruit (IV. 4. 5; Pliny XII. 24?), Mango (Theophr. IV. 4. 5; Pliny XII. 24), Jujube (Theophr. IV. 4. 5) and others, but the evidence is slight.

(70) See references given above, also Pliny XII, passim; XIII. 4–

23; **xiv.** 107–8. Diosc. v. 57, 59, 54 etc. Cels., Scribon., Galen, Apic., as cited. Samm. Seren. *de Med.* 32. 323–4, 329, 332, 334, 343 etc. Athenae. **ii.** 73 = 66 *c–f*; **iii.** 100 = 126 f.; **xv.** 34 = 686 (cp. Lucian, *Lexiph.* 8); **xv.** 39 = 689; 40 = 690; 45 = 692.

(71) Cels. **v.** 18, 16.

(72) See esp. Galen, *de Compos. Medic. per gen.* and *sec. loc.* passim and in particular *per gen.* **xiii.** 741; *sec. loc.* **xii.** 782.

(73) Alphabetical list in Schmidt, 104–7, with which my readings of Pliny mostly coincide. Prices given of Parthian products by Pliny are too few to give a basis for any conclusion. See also Mau, *Pompeii*, 333, 497 (oleum, 4 asses per lb.), and price-list (chiefly from Papyri) by L. C. West in *Class. Phil.* 1916, pp. 306–314.

(74) See Pliny **xxxv.** 45; **ix.** 137–8 for purple, prices exceptionally high before the imperial period.

(75) Pliny **xxxiii.** 164; cp. **xxxiv.** 108.

CHAPTER III

(1) E.g. Pliny **xxxvii.** 200.

(2) Mart. **xi.** 59, 1–4; **v.** 61, 5; 11, 1–2. F. Henkel, vol. **i.** Glass in collections, passim, esp. *K.M.B.* index (nearly one-half). *B.M.* (about one-fourth). Guilds, *C.I.L.* **vi.** 9144. Cp. **xi.** 1235; **xii.** 4456; **vi.** 8734–6. Athenae. **v.** 199 *d, f*; 200 *b*; 202 *d, e.* Juv. **v.** 37–45; Virg. *Aen.* **i.** 654–5. Pliny **xxxvii.** 6. Suet. *Cal.* 50, 52. Luc. **x.** 111–112. Lucian, *Adv. Indoct.* 8 etc. Pliny on luxury in gems:—**xxxiii.** 22–3; **xxxvii.** 1, 50. Extant:—*B.M. Jew.* Introd. xvi–li. See also e.g. A. Odobescu, *Le Trés. de Pétrossa*, 91 ff. Pls. facing pp. 90, 92, 94. Lyd. *de Mag. R. R.* **ii.** 4. Pliny **xxxiii.** 22; **xxxvii.** 6, 11, 14–17, 81–2, 185, 200. Suet. *Iul.* 47, *Aug.* 30. Macrob. *S.* **ii.** 4. Petron. 119, l. 20; 120, l. 92. King, *E.G.* 319, 205. Lassen **i.** 229–243. Add Strabo **ii.** 3. 4. Claud. *in Eutr.* **xviii.** 225. *C.I.L.* **vi.** 1107. Philostrat. *Apollon.* **iii.** 27. Philo, *de Somn.* **ii.** 8. 57.

(3) *Jat.* 21, 139–141. *Camb. Hist. Ind.* **i.** 213. R. Mitra, *Antiqu. of Orissa*, **i.** p. 100. d'Alviella, 67. *Ind. Antiqu.* **xvi.** 7–8. *Rev.* xxi. 11 and 18–20. Cp. *Ezek.* xxvii. 13. *Exod.* xxviii. 16, 21; xxxix. 8–14. Joseph. *A.J.* **iii.** 7. 5. *Dig.* **xxxix.** 4. 16. 7. Cp. Ruf. Fest. Avien. *Descr. Or. Terr.* 1314–27. Prisc. *Perieg.* 1009–10, 1019–22.

Dionys. Perieg. 1104–24. Philostrat. *Apoll.* I. 10, cp. 11 and 33 (wealth); II. 40; III. 27. Diodor. II. 52 (var. stones). *Archaeol. Surv. Ind.* X. Introd. 16–17 (Indian inscriptions). *Ramayana*, I. 94 etc.

(4) Pliny XXXVII. 56–61, esp. 56. King, 31. Krause, *Pyrgot.* 30, cp. 32–3. *B.M. Rings*, 778–9, 885, 787–9, 790, Introd. lix. *B.M. Jew.* 2954. *Marlb.* 364–5, 367, 398, 426 etc. are not antique. King, 62, 417, 26. Blümner III. 229–233, 285, 295. *Pauly*, s.v. *Diamant.* Krause, 228 ff., 31. Richter, xlviii. *Marlb.* 25, 115. Furtw. III. p. 400. Pliny id. 60. Solin. 52, 56, 60, 33. Manil. *Astr.* IV. 926. Perhaps too *Fay. Pap.* 134. *Arthasastra*, II. 1.

(5) *Peripl.* 56. Ptol. VII. 1. 80, 64, 41. Lassen I. 286.

(6) Watt, s.v. *Gem-stones*, and Bauer, pp. 140–155, esp. 143–152. Lassen I. 284–5; III. 18–19.

(7) King, 21, 24. Juv. VI. 156 (Berenice's). *Hist. Aug.* '*Hadr.*' 3. 7 (Nerva's), see also Mart. V. 11. 1. *C.I.L.* II. 3386. Sen. *Dial.* II. 3. 5. Dionys. Per. 1119, 318. Prisc. *Perieg.* 1063. *Dig.* XXXIX. 4. 16. 7. Ruf. Fest. Av. 1321. Macrob. *Sat.* II. 4. Epiph. *de Gemm.* 231, 251.

(8) Henkel, vol. I. German agate-industry began in 14th cent. A.D. Silesian mines were first used in the 10th century. Pliny id. 60, discredits his authority. I have not generally mentioned American and Australian sources.

(9) See e.g. *Sk.*, Class O. Blümner III. 256 ff.

(10) Pliny id. 106.

(11) Richter, 34, 74, 83.

(12) Pliny id. Theophr. *de Lap.* 30, 31.

(13) Pliny id. 100. Ctes. ap. Phot. Cod. 72, p. 45. B. 14. Bekk. McCrindle, pp. 9, 10, 12.

(14) E.g. *Marlb.* 172, 313, 447. *B.M.* 1157, 1498.

(15) *Peripl.* 49. Blümner III. 257–9, 262–3. Watt, s.v. *Gem-stones*, and *Dict.* s.v. *Carnelian*, 173–4. Bauer, 509.

(16) But see Maskel. xii. Bl. III. 262–4. King, 296–300. *Encycl. Brit.* s.v. *Sard.*

(17) Watt, *Dict.* s.v. *Carnelian.* Mommsen-Marqu. XV. 430–2. King, 237–245. Bauer, 517–518, cp. Bl. III. 276–7. Chwostow, 129. *Pauly*, s.v. *Murrina.* Lassen III. 47–8. A. Kisa, *Das Glas*, 180, 531.

(18) Pliny id. 18. Prop. III. 10. 22; IV. 5. 26; III. 5. (IV. 4) 4.

Virg. *G.* II. 506. Ov. *Met.* XII. 572. Pliny XXXIII. 5; 2000 vessels of ὀνυχίτις in App. *M.* 115.

(19) Pliny XXXVII. 21. Prop. *loc. cit.*; cp. III. 5. 4. *Peripl.* 49.

(20) Pliny XXXIII. 5; XXXVI. 198; XXXII. 7 ff. Sen. *Ep.* XX. 6 (123), 7; 2 (119), 3. *Dig.* XXXIV. 2. 19. 19 etc. Suet. *Aug.* 71. Athenae. XI. 89. Pliny XXXVII. 13, 18–21.

(21) See Mart. IV. 85. 1; X. 80. 1, 70. 8; XIV. 113. 1; III. 82. 25.

(22) Athenae. *loc. cit.* Pliny id. 13. Chwostow, 129. Bauer, 509. Kohler, *Kl. Abh. z. Gemmenk.* I. 89. *J.R.A.S. Bomb. Br.* III. 318–327. Watt, *Dict.* s.v. *Carnelian*, p. 168. Chab. 285 etc. Cp. Philostrat. *Apollon.* III. 27—large vessels (of precious stones) made in India.

(23) *Hist. Aug.* ' *Ver.*' 5. Those in *Peripl.* 6 are glass imitations. Philostrat. *loc. cit.*

(24) Catalogues, passim. See e.g. *B.M.* 4030–3, 4035 etc., 277–8. Chab. 188–199 (cameos of Augustus). *Gall. Fir.* XXI. 1. Pliny XXXVII. 139. King, 15 ff.

(25) Pliny id. 139–142, cp. 153. Dionys. Per. 1075. *Orphic.* 230 ff. Theophr. *L.* 31. *B.M.* 3965 etc. Bauer, 517–518. Watt, s.v. *Gemstones*; *Dict.* s.v. *Carnelian*, pp. 171–4. Luc. X. 115. Pliny id. 139–140. *B.M.* 272, 913; *B.M.* has 25 burnt agates.

(26) E.g. *Onyx*, cameos :—*Marlb.* 57 out of 75; *Vienna* 118 out of 182. *Sardonyx*, cameos :—Chab. 186 out of 225; *Marlb.* at least 76 out of 88. *Nicolo*, intaglios :—*K.M.B.* 281 all; Hl. 74 out of 78; *B.M.* Gr.-Rom. nearly all; and so on.

(27) Pliny id. 90–1, 186. Ctes. *loc. cit. Peripl.* 48–9, 51. Theophr. *L.* 31. Ptol. VII. 1. 65. 6–7; I. 17. 3–4. The onyx of Pliny XXXVI. 59–61 (cp. Luc. X. 115 ff. and most 'onyx' perfume boxes) is alabaster. See also *B.M.* 3942, 3962, 4025. *Vienna*, K. 5. 32. Krause, 51, 221. *Vienna*, K. II. 19; Eichler-Kris, 7 (T. 4). Furt ... Pls. LIV, LV. Mommsen-Marqu. XV. 429. Psell. *de L.* 24. Rostowzew, *Ir. and Gr.* 135.

(28) *C.I.G.* 150, § 50; 151, § 29; 152? *Hibeh Pap.* I. 121, l. 23. Plut. *Ant.* 58. Collections, passim.

(29) Krause, 221, Bl. III. 264–7, 269–270. Watt, s.v. *Gem-stones.* King, 254–5, 307. Eichler-Kris, 4, 6, 18, 19, 26, 110 (T. 2, 3, 9, 10).

(30) Ptol. VII. 1. 20. 65. Pliny XXXVII. 85–9. Four in *K.M.B.* 1179–80, 1182–3 and two in Hl. Cp. Furtw. II. 348; I. Pl. LII. figs. 1–3, 6, answer to Pliny's account of the 'Indian' kind. Cp. Eichler-Kris, 3 (T. 1). King, 304. Krause, 55.

(31) *B.M.* 4017–24 etc. Chab. 282–3, 279, 209, cp. 188. Furtw. II. 257–8, 259–265; I. Pl. LVI; III. 314–320, 320 ff. (cp. Pliny id. 85). King, *P.S.* 309, *E.G.* 53 ff. *Marlb.* 482=*B.M.* 3619, cp. 3577, 3585 etc. esp. 3593, 3596. Bl. III. 267–9.

(32) Pliny id. 197. Mart. IX. 59. 19; X. 87. 14. *B.M.* 3720–3840, e.g. also Pers. I. 16. Lucian, *Dial. Meretr.* IX. 2. Ach. Tat. II. 1. Solin. 55. *Dig.* XXXIX. 4. 16. 7 etc.

(33) Richter, lvii–lviii; 88, 168. Mask. xvi–xvii. *Marlb.* 256, 309. Cp. Hl. Index. Pliny id. 148.

(34) Richter, lvi. 34, 38, 49, 60, 32, 83. Krause, 24. *Encycl. Brit.* s.v. *Chalcedony.* King, 16. Bauer, 506. Walters, *B.M. Introd.* XIV. Eichler-Kris, 6 (T. 3), 18 (T. 8).

(35) *Marlb.* 100. Pliny id. 118. *B.M.* 3948–9, 3951, 3953 etc., 3968, 3970. Chab. 975–1049 passim. *Louvre*, 588–590. *N.Y.* 343. 25 in Hl.

(36) *B.M.* 4054. Chab. 871, 907, 911 etc. (7 in all, being cylinders) and a good many cones, 122? Furtw. Pl. VI. 48 ff. King, 158–9. Bauer, 506. Sapphirine:—*Encycl. Brit.* s.v. *Chalcedony* and s.v. *Sapphire.* *B.M.* 1243, 1257. Pliny id. 115.

(37) Bauer, 498, Bl. III. 272. King, 163. *B.M.* 338, 2499. *Fitz.* 79. *Sk.* E. 21. Hl. 2119, 2149. *Louvre*, 1653. Pliny id. 115.

(38) Pliny id. 113–115, 102, 73–5. King, 288–290. Bauer, 510, 488. Watt, *Dict.* s.v. *Carnelian*, p. 172. Collections, passim. But see Walters, *B.M. Introd.* XIV. *Peripl.* 52—unfriendly Sandanes or Sandares at Calliena is mere coincidence of names?

(39) Pliny 113–114, 165. *Vienna*, K. I. 5, 19, 20; K. IV. 10, 18 etc. *Marlb.* 280, 641. Chab. has 23, *B.M.* has 14, e.g. 1659–60. Richter, lvi. 168. *N.Y.* Nos. 140, 361. Krause, 122, 287. Bl. III. 272. Mask. xiv. Bauer, 510. *Encycl. Brit.* s.v. *Bloodstone.* I am sure my identifications of Pliny's stones are correct in these two cases.

(40) Pliny id. 113–114.

(41) Richter, lvi. Mask. xii–xiv. Watt, s.v. *Gem-stones, Jasper.* Bauer, 501. Pliny, 115 ff. and 114. Galen XII. 207; XIX. 735. King, 209, 235. Collections, passim, esp. *B.M.* 349 ff. Maskel. xiii–xiv. Dionys. Per. 1120. Sid. Apoll. *C.* 11. 21.

(42) Pliny id. 169, 153, 177; cp. XXXVI. 196–7, 118. Watt, *loc. cit.* Bauer, 500–1. King, 172, 207, 212. Richter, lvii. Watt, *Dict.* s.v. *Carnelian*, 174. Cp. Plato, *Phaedo*, 110 D. Theophr. *L.* 23. *C.I.G.*

150, § 50. Macrob. *Sat.* ii. 4. 12. Isid. xix. 32. Virg. *Aen.* vi. 261.
Mart. v. 11. 1; ix. 59. 20 (iaspis). Cosmas xi. 452 B. *C.I.L.* ii.
2060 (Spain). Dionys. Per. 1103.

(**43**) Watt, s.v. *Gem-stones* and *Dict.* s.v. *Carnelian*, p. 175.
Bauer, 492. Pliny id. 131, 185. Solin. 20. Perhaps *Marlb.* 543.

(**44**) Pliny id. 139, 100–1. Bl. iii. 254. Bauer, 501. *Encycl. Brit.*
s.v. *Aventurine.* But see King, 16, 291–2.

(**45**) Richt. lviii. Bl. iii. 283. Many in collects. esp. *B.M.* 3542.
Anth. Pal. ix. 748, 752; v. 205; ix. 752. King, 52. Middleton,
Append. xvii. Cups:—Mart. ix. 49. 1 (garnet?).

(**46**) Bauer, 481–6, cp. 287. J. Marshall, *Guide to Taxila*, 118.

(**47**) Pliny id. 121–4, cp. Dionys. Per. 1122. Plut. *Q.C.* iii. 1. 3.
647 B. Theophr. *L.* 31, socondion, Sanskrit saguna. *Dig.* xxxiv.
2. 19. 15. 17. Mart. i. 97. 7; x. 49. 1. Rostowzew, *Ir. and Gr.*
135 etc. Minns, 233.

(**48**) *Marlb.* 5. Middleton, 76. King, 62.

(**49**) Pliny id. 127. Mask. xi. Bauer, 487. King, 167–8. *Marlb.*
493. *Fitz.* 29 (?). *Lewis*, A 7, B 5, 144, 172.

(**50**) Bauer, 488. Furtw. Pl. iii. 1 etc. Pliny id. 116. Hl. 1339?

(**51**) Pliny id. 23–4. Mart. xii. 74. 1. Strabo xv. 1. 67.

(**52**) Bauer, 476–8. Watt, s.v. *Gem-stones, Crystal. Dict.* s.v.
Carnelian, p. 170.

(**53**) *Vienna*, K. 1. 7. Hl. 1615, 1812, 428 etc. *Louvre*, 546–9, 561,
589, 678. *B.M.* 3646, 3957, 4016, 4027–8, 3984–3994 etc. King, 174.

(**54**) Theophr. *L.* 30. Pliny xxxiii. 5; xxxvii. 27–30, 79. Prop.
ii. (iv) 3. 52; ii. 24. 12=iii. 18. 12. Sen. *de Ira*, iii. 40. *Anth. Pal.*
ix. 776 (painted), 753; vi. 329, 1. Petron. *S.* 23, 64. *Hist. Aug.*
'*Ver.*' 5. Cp. '*Claud.*' 17. '*Ver.*' 10 etc. Achil. Tat. ii. 3. *C.I.L.*
iii. 536 ('a crystallinis'). Sen. *Ep.* xx. 6. (123) 6, 2. (119) 3, *N.Q.* iii.
25. 12. Plut. *Ant.* 58. Mommsen-Marquardt xv. 429. Hirth, 44 etc.
Strabo xvi. 2. 25. Frank, 225–6. Indian examples to-day reach
20 lbs. in weight, but the Romans got crystals up to 50 Roman
pounds.

(**55**) Pliny xxxvi. 192. R. Mitra, *Ant. of Orissa*, i. 101. King, 177.
Perhaps the Indians did not make glass so early, A. Kisa, *Das
Glas im Altert.* i. 105–6. But see J. Buchanan, *Journey through
Mysore*, i. 147 ff.; iii. 369 ff. A. Williamson, *Journeys in N. China*
etc. i. 131.

(**56**) Pliny XXXVII. 79, 197 (esp. beryls and emeralds). Watt, *Dict*. s.v. *Carnelian*, 170.

(**57**) Pliny id. 80–4. Isid. *Or*. XVI. 12. 3. Bl. III. 246, 273. Bauer, 388. Middleton, 146. Chab. 1485. *Sk*. C. 4 (antique?). *Vienna*, K. III. 222, 232; K. IV. 1273. King, 159, 271, 291–2. Krause, 44. The 'paederos' (Indian 'sangenon') was an opal.

(**58**) *Encycl. Brit*. s.v. *Corundum*. *B.M*. 1746? (Cat. of 1888, but now rejected). Chab. 1534. Pliny XXXVI. 51–2. King, *P.S*. 247. Bl. III. 77–8. Watt, *Dict*. s.v. *Corundum*. Perhaps too *O.P*. I. 36. *Gr. u. Chr*. I. ii. *Chrest*. pp. 321–2 (No. 273) but see Wilck. in *Arch. f. Pap*. III. 185 ff. esp. 188.

(**59**) Watt, s.v. *Gem-stones* and *Dict*. s.v. *Sapphire*. *Encycl. Brit*. id. Bauer, 283 ff. esp. 286. Pliny XXXVII. 125–8, reading Bactrianae, and in 128, xouthon or xanthon, 114. Diodor. II. 52. King, 193 ff. esp. 196. Walters, *B.M. Introd*. xii.

(**60**) *Peripl*. 56. Ptol. VII. 4. 1. Cosmas XI. 337. Diodor. I. 33. Cp. Iuba's derivation of Nilion from the Nile on the banks of which it was found! Yellow sapphires are common in Ceylon. In Tanjore inscriptions the Sapphire = 'nilam'—*Archaeol. Surv. Ind*. x, Introd. 17 etc.

(**61**) Solin. 30, 33. Prop. II. 16. 44 = III. 8. 44 (peridots?). *Anth. Pal*. IX. 75. 1; V. 270. 5. ¡Lucian, *Adv. Ind*. 9. *Dig*., *l.c*. and XXXIV. 2. 19. 25. 17. Prisc. *Per*. 1010. *Lond. P*. III. p. 191, No. 928, l. 15. King, 165–7, 200. Cp. *Soc*. 183, 5 (**v**).

(**62**) Sapphires: *B.M. Jew*. has 16 examples (e.g. 2396–8) all Roman, 1st to 3rd cent. A.C. (id. Introd. lxi); see also Chab. 2606. *Louvre*, 367, 431–2 etc. Five plain in rings, Hl. (e.g. 177, 183 etc.); only two *K.M.B*., fourteen *Vienna*, six *Marlb*., one *B.M. Marlb*. 98, 240 (pale), 485 (Caracalla). *Sk*. G. 7 (yellow). Bl. III. 233, 283. Krause, 197. Furtw. III. 364. *Marlb*. 485. *Gall. Fir*. I. XXI. 2, XXX. 1; II. XLVIII. 1 etc. King, 148, 198–200, 400, 403.

(**63**) Pliny id. 131–2, 134–5; cp. astriotes 133, astrobolos 133 (but see Dionys. Per. 328). King, 91–2, 201. Bl. III. 234. Bauer, 284.

(**64**) King, 315–316. Pliny id. 65.

(**65**) 'Lucian,' *de Syr. D*. 32. Plut. *de Fluv*. Hyd. 2. Pliny XXXVII. 103. Theophr. *L*. 16 ff. Strabo XVI. 1. 67, 69. *C.I.L*. II. 3386. Richter, lx. Bl. III. 233–6. Krause, 56, 180, 214. King, 144 ff. Watt, s.v. *Gem-stones*. Bauer, 269 ff., 274, 277–8. *Sk*. D. 11. Hl. 187

(garnet?). I have doubts about *Vienna*, Toreut. Arbeit. Pultk. 137, 147, 151, 198, 200; cp. *Marlb.* 352? King, 148, 404. *Jahr. d. D. Arch. Instit.* XII. *Anz.* 62 ; cp. *Anz.* 136. Tertull. *de Anim.* 9 (ceraunia). Mau, *Pomp.* 379. *Pauly,* s.v. *Schlange,* 550–1. Not common.

(**66**) Bl. III. 234, 236. Bauer, 278, 298. Watt, *Dict.* s.v. *Ruby.* Pliny id. 93 (? amethystizontes). King, 63–4, 119. O. M. Dalton, *Treasure of the Oxus,* xx. Smith, *Fine Art,* 356.

(**67**) Bl. III. 253. Bauer, 492, 302, 287. *Encycl. Brit.* s.v. *Cat's Eye.* Consult Pliny id. 149, 171, 131, 185. *Encycl. Brit.* s.v. *Chrysoprase, Chrysoberyl.* Bauer, 304–5, 317. Bl. III. 236. Pliny id. 113–114, cp. 76–7. Isid. XVI. 7, 6–7.

(**68**) Cosmas XI. 449 B. They would have to compete with Indian beryls. As Cosmas shews, the Blemmyes and the Axumites controlled that later trade.

(**69**) Pliny id. 62–5, esp. 65, 69, 71, 79. Clem. Alex. *Paed.* III. 4. 271. *Dig.* XXXIX. 4. 16. 7. 'Lucian,' *d. Syr. D.* 32 ; *Adv. Indoct.* 9. Strabo XVI. 1. 69. Sen. *Hippol.* 318. Isid. XIX. 32 etc. High prices, Pliny id. 67, cp. XXXIII. 2. Bauer, 310, 315. King, 311 ff. Walters, *B.M. Introd.* xiii. Was 'marakata' borrowed from the West?

(**70**) Pliny XXXVII. 76 ff. Krause, 37–8. Watt, s.v. *Gem-stones.* Bauer, 320–3. V. A. Smith, 461. Ptol. VII. 1. 86 ; VII. 4. 1. *Ind. Antiqu.* v. 237. Sewell, *J.R.A.S.* 1904, 595, 598 (Vaniyambadi about 150 miles E. of Padiyur).

(**71**) *C.I.L.* II. 2060, 3386; XIV. 2215, l. 8. Juv. II. 61; v. 37. Pliny id. 76–9. Sewell, id. *Ind. Antiqu.* v. 237–240. Thurston, *Madr. Gov. Mus. Coin-Cat.* II. 8. The vendors of pastes and precious stones in Kaviripaddinam (Pillai, 25) must have sold many false beryls.

(**72**) Richter, lix. Isid. XIX. 32. Macrob. *S.* II. 4. 12. Prop. IV. 7. 9. Compare also Diodor. II. 52. Strabo XV. 1. 69. *Louvre,* 714. 425–6. Chab. 2089 (= Furtw. XLVIII. 8), 2025, 2098, 1699. *B.M.* 1892 (fine blue), 1981? 2500. *Sk.* E. 1 and so on, cp. Furtw. XXXV. 18. XL. 3. 24 etc. Pliny id. 66. *Anth. Pal.* IX. 544. King, 130–2. Middleton, 80. Lucian, *Ver. Hist.* VII. 11. *Adv. Indoct.* 8, 9. Galen XIX. 735. Dionys. Per. 1011–13, 1119. *O.P.* XIV. 1679. 26. Masp. III. 67321, A. 8. B. 2. Joseph. *A.J.* xx. 183. Cp. Euseb. *E.H.* VI. 10. Pliny id. 64. *Dig., l.c.* Did Nero use a hollow aquamarine?

(**73**) *Peripl.* 39. *Dig., l.c.* Pliny id. 119–120. Dionys. Per. 1105. Theophr. *L.* 23. *Ind. Antiqu.* XIII. 235. Richter, lx. 168. Mask.

xviii. The 75 in *K.M.B.* are all later, cp. *B.M.* 3939, 3941 etc. Lucian, *Adv. Indoct.* 9. Fabrics coloured like lap. laz.—*SB.* 2251, *O.P.* 1739. 1, 7. Smith, *Fine Art*, 279 (in India).

(**74**) Marshall, *B.M. Jew. Introd.* lviii and Catalogues, passim.

(**75**) See Pliny id. 92–3, 95. 'Carbunculi' and 'lychnis' are ascribed partly to India—id. 92 ff., 103. For the modern names see Mask. xvii-xviii, Bauer, 253–4, Richter, lviii, *Encycl. Brit.* s.v. *Almandine.* Cosmas XI. 448 B, alabandenon of Caber; cp. alabanda in *Dig.*, *l.c.* The anthrax of Massalia (in Theophrastos) may be European pyrope, cp. Minns, 408 ff. Garnets and all brilliant red stones are included in the ceraunia of the *Dig.* list. J. Marshall, *Guide to Taxila*, 118.

(**76**) Cosmas XI. 448 B (Camara in the *Peripl.*). *Dig.*, *loc. cit.* Bauer, 353–4, 287. Watt, s.v. *Gem-stones*, cp. *Dict.* s.v. *Carnelian* and s.v. *Carbuncle.* *Peripl.* 48–9, 51, 56.

(**77**) *Marlb.* 270 = *Lewes*, 114 (dog Sirius on Syriam Garnet). *N.Y.* 252 (id.). *Lewes*, 97. Furtw. Pl. XXXI. 24. King, 54, 219. Rostowzew, *Ir. and Gr.* 135, 184–7, 77 etc. *Almandine*:—*B.M. Rings*, 563, 568. *Marlb.* 27, 144?, 229, 356?, 713?, 731. *N.Y.* 98, 252. *Sk.* C. 36, M. 8, P. 1, 2. Hl. 1315. Chab. 1806. Smith, *Fine Art*, 355–6. *Syriam*:—Rostowzew, *op. cit.* 177. Chab. 82. *K.M.B.* 1106–15, 1117–33 (small mixed Hellenistic). *Pyrope*:—*N.Y.* 139, 191, 287, 375. *Gall. Fir.* I. 17. 1? *B.M.* 4080? *Lond. P.* 77, 28? Pliny's Indian wine-red amethyst? *C.I.L.* XIV. 2215, l. 12?

(**78**) Pliny id. 95, 92, 94. Garnets perhaps in Galen XII. 207. Strabo XV. 1. 69. Athenae. XII. 539 D. *C.I.G.* 9536. *C.I.L.* II. 3386. Augustus ap. Macrob. II. 4. 12. Theophr. *L.* 8, 16 ff. esp. 18—very precious stone. King, 55.

(**79**) Bauer, 350–1, 287. *Marlb.* 215, 286. Pliny id. 127. King, 220.

(**80**) Dionys. Per. 1121. Steph. Byz. s.v. Τοπάζιος (where the Indian 'topaz' island is really in the Red Sea!). Chwostow, 89. Schoff and others think that topaz, not chrysolite, was meant, but see *Encycl. Brit.* s.v. *Topaz* and s.v. *Peridot.* Bl. 247–8. *J. E. Archaeol.* 1925, 143. King, 130, 137, 163, 165, 336 ff. Cp. Chab. 1626? *Louvre*, 638, 1669. *Gall. Fir.* I. 27. 2. *B.M.* 1881, 1986. Was the topaz known also?—*B.M.* 1835, 1967, 1969, 2531.

(**81**) *Encycl. Brit.* s.v. *Zircon*, s.v. *Hyacinth*, s.v. *Jargoon.* Bauer, 334, 287.

(**82**) *B.M.* has 19 jacinths, *K.M.B.* has 13, *Vienna* has 8; there are many others—examples in Furtw. vol. II. pp. 159–169, and 245, 196–7, 278 etc. Krause, 222–3. Bl. III. 236. Furtw. XXXI. 40 shews a gem that came from India (western work taken back there).

(83) Pliny id. 126, 128, 34, 52–3. Theophr. *L*. 28. King, 115–116, 216 ff.

(84) Pliny id. 173. King, 216–221, 283–4. Philostrat. *Apollon*. III. 46. Heliodor. *Aeth*. VIII. 11 etc. McCrindle, *Ctes*. 7–8. Pantarbes may be a corruption of an Indian word.

(85) Bauer, 369–370, 287. Watt, s.v. *Gem-stones*.

(86) Pliny id. 132, 181. Bauer, 427, 287. *Encycl. Brit*. s.v. *Moonstone*. Bl. III. 273. King, 91–2, 328–9. *K.M.B*. 2316.

(87) Bauer, 427. *Encycl. Brit*. s.v. *Sunstone*. Bl. III. 234. Pliny id. 132, 134–5. Possibly *Dig., loc. cit. C.I.L*. II. 3386. Isid. XVI. 13. 5. *Encycl. Brit*. s.v. *Amazon-stone*. Bauer, 426. King, 126. Pliny id. 74, 160. *J. E. Arch*. 1914, p. 186.

(88) *Encycl. Brit*. s.v. *Jadeite*. Watt, s.v. *Jade and Jadeite*; id. *Dict*. s.v. *Carnelian*, p. 167, s.v. *Jade*. Bauer, 461–8. Krause, 218. Bl. III. 277. Jade:—*Sk*. O. 14, N. 15, Qβ. 37, Qε. 6. *Louvre*, 736. Chab. 1045, 2180, 281. Nephrite:—Schliemann, *Ilios*, 238 ff. *K.M.B*. 2348(?). Cp. Pliny id. 118. Galen XII. 207. Jade in S. Russia and especially Panticapaeon—Rostowzew, *Ir. and Gr*. 204. See also V. A. Smith, *Hist. of Fine Art*, 354.

(89) Pliny XIX. 19. Steph. Byz. s.v. Βραχμᾶνες. Philostrat. *Apollon*. III. 15. Marco Polo I. 42. *Pauly*, s.v. *Amiantos*. Watt, s.v. *Asbestos*. *Encycl. Brit*. s.v. *Asbestos*. Strabo X. 1. 6. Sotac. ap. Apollon. Dysc. *H. Comm*. 36 etc. Daremb.-Sagl. s.v. *Asbestos*. Yates, *Textr. Antiqu*. vol. I. pp. 356–365. de Lacouperie, 187. Hirth, 41 etc. Chwostow, 146. ἄσβεστος also means quicklime.

(90) Bauer, 393. Pliny XXXVII. 110, 112, 147 (?angitis), 151, 163. Fabrics like turquoise:—*C.I.L*. XIV. 2215. *O.P*. 1449. 13. *Lond. P*. 193. 33. *O.P*. 1273. 15. *Tebt. P*. 421. 7. *O.P*. 1739, 3. 9; 1757, 10. *Lond. P*. 929, 30; 50. Mart. XIV. 139, 1–2. See Isid. XVI. 7. 10. *Peripl*. 39. Pliny id. 151. King, 136–7. *Dig., loc. cit*. Watt, s.v. *Gem-stones*. Richt. lx. *B.G.U*. 717, 6; 7. *B.M. Jew*. 2050, 2668–9. *Sk*. M. 3. *Vienna*, K. III. 1, 24, 34; K. IV. 1264. Blue:—*N.Y*. 329. *Marlb*. 532. Green:—id. 403 (Middleton, 150). *B.M*. 924?, 3945. Cp. *Jahr. des D. Arch. Inst*. Band XI. 1925, pp. 13–15, cp. XXI. *Anz*. 137. Sinai source (found in 1849) was unknown except in very early times—

Flinders Petrie, *Researches in Sinai*, 36, 41, 49, 51, 61, 69–70.
Turquoise used in S. Russia—Rostowzew, *Ir. and Gr.* 19, 135.
Minns, 230–2 etc. Achmet, *Onir.* 220—γαλαΐζειν, to be blue.

(91) Pliny id. 30 ff. esp. 46, 36, cp. 33 (Scythian), 39, 40 (shellac?).
Cp. Psell. *de Lap.* 9. King, 333.

(92) Pliny id. 147, 155, 160, 171, 177, 185, cp. XXXVI. 197.

(93) Athenae. v. 39 = 205 *e*. *Encycl. Brit.* s.v. *Marble*.

(94) Pliny XVI. 59–61.

(95) Probably many Indian stones with loads of glass imitations
were sent back across Indian seas from Egypt and Syria to China—
Hirth, 237, 245.

(96) *Anth. Pal.* VI. 261.

(97) *Peripl.* 36. Cosmas, 445 D. Copper-mines in India :—*J.R.A.S.*
1904, p. 612. Cp. Ptol. VII. 2. 20.

(98) Yet we know that the iron industry and trade of North
Chinese iron were very important in ancient times—Hirth, 226.
Iron of Yunnan—*Mem. of Geolog. Surv. Ind.* 47, pp. 82–97.

(99) Pliny XXXIV. 145. Oros. VI. 13. 2. Apulei. *Flor.* 6. *Dig., loc.
cit. Peripl.* 6, 39, 49, 56, 64. Ctes. *Ind.* 4. McCrindle, *Ctes.* p. 9.
Ezek. XXVII. 19 (perhaps). See also Clem. Alex. *Paed.* II. 3. 189 P.
Perhaps *O.P.* 520, and 84. Schoff, *J.A.O.S.* 35, 224 ff. (sepa-
rately as *Eastern Iron Trade of the R.E.* esp. pp. 8–9, 14, 16).
Kennedy, *J.R.A.S.* 1918, 594–5. Chera=Sera, Seram, Seri. Lassen
II. 570–1. *J.R.A.S.* 1839, 90. Chwostow, 127, 156. Watt, *Dict.* s.v.
Iron, 505 ff. *Man,* XXIV. 160; XXV. 15. J. Newton Friend, *Iron
in Antiquity,* 142 ff., 194 ff. Heeren, *As. Nat.* II. 63.

(100) Pliny XXXIII. 66; XI. 111. Schrader, *Prehist. Antiqu.* (trans.
Jevons), p. 173. McCr. *Anc. Ind.* p. 51. Strabo XV. 1. 44. *Ind.
Antiqu.* IV. pp. 225–232; XIII. 229–230, 232, 236. Pillai, 13, 27.

(101) *Peripl.* 36, cf. *Pauly,* s.v. *India,* 1301.

(102) I believe the ἀδάμας of Ptolemy to be the diamond, not, as
Renou would have it, steel. I should have added here the peculiar
arrangement by which the Greeks obtained Indian ebony, teak,
rosewood, and sandalwood only in the Persian Gulf, until at least
the 3rd century A.C., but always knew they were Indian. This was
an Arab-Parthian arrangement. I intend to deal elsewhere with
peculiarities of the Persian Gulf trade.

(103) Philostrat. *Apollon.* III. 4.

CHAPTER IV

(1) Philostrat. *Apollon.* III. 35. 1 ; VI. 16. 3. Cp. *Peripl.* 6 ff., 24, 28, 39, 49, 55–6, 57, 60 (cargoes from Egypt). Pers. v. 54–5.

(2) For St Thomas and India see *Apocryph. N.T.* trans. M. R. James, 365 ff. Cp. 203–4, 218, 468 (Bartholomew); see also Rawlinson, *Interc.* 47–8, 169. Hirth, 35–7, 169–170. *Ind. Antiqu.* XXXII. 1–15, 145–160 ; XXXIII. 12. See *Peripl.* 49. Strabo II. 3. 4. Needless doubts in *J.A.S.B.* XLIII. 246 ff.

(3) *Paddinappalai*, 185–191. Pillai, 27. Cosmas XI. 449 C.

(4) Pliny XXXII. 21–4. *Peripl.* 39, 49, 56. Dionys. Per. 1103. Pillai, 25. *Ind. Antiqu.* XXVIII. p. 29. Schoff, ad *Peripl.* 227, 168. J. Marshall, *Guide to Taxila*, 118. *Arch. Surv. Ind.* X. 428, 242 ff., 35.

(5) Hirth, 246. This coral is *Antipathes abies.* Modern coral-trade of India—Watt, s.v. *Coral.*

(6) *Peripl.* 36, 39, 49, 56. Pliny XIX. 7. Schoff, id. p. 190. *Arch. f. Pap.* v. 389. Philostr. *Apollon.* II. 20. 40. Pliny VIII. 196. Claudian. *in Eutrop.* I. 357.

(7) *Hist. Aug. 'Firm.'* 3.

(8) *Peripl.* 36, 39, 49, 56.

(9) Pillai, 37. Strabo v. 6. 13 ; XVI. 2. 9.

(10) *Peripl.* 28, 39, 49.

(11) Id. 49. Hirth, 41–2, 47, 263–6.

(12) Hirth, 268 ff. Schmidt, 130.

(13) *Peripl.* 49. Pliny XXI. 53, 150 ; XXII. 123 etc. Schoff, 191.

(14) *Peripl.* 36. Some may have come from N. Africa.

(15) Id. 39. Schoff, ad *Peripl.* p. 270. Hirth, 267.

(16) Pillai, 25.

(17) *Ind. Antiqu.* vol. LI. pp. 141–2. Sir W. Elliott, *Coins of S. India*, 22. Cosmas XI. 445 D. Ptol. VII. 2. 20. Pliny XXXIV. 2 ff. *Peripl.* 49, 56. Ancient copper articles very rare in India—Smith, *Fine Art*, 364.

(18) *Peripl., l.c.* R. Mitra, *Antiqu. of Orissa*, I. pp. 100–1.

(19) Pliny III. 30; XXXIV. 158, 164–5; XXXIII. 97; IV. 112 etc. *C.I.L.* VII. 1201, 1209; *Ephem. Epigr.* IX. 1264, 1266; VII. 1121. *C.I.L.* VII. 1204–5. *Ezek.* xxvii. 12. For commerce in lead see Besnier in *Rev. Arch.* 1920, 211 ; XIII. 1921, 36 ff. ; XIV. 98 ff.

(20) *Peripl.* 28, 36, 56, 49. Schoff, id. 151. Strabo XV. 1. 69 ; X. 1. 9.

E.E. IX. 1258–61. Pliny XXXIV. 2 ff. *C.I.L.* XIII. 4528, 2901. *Ind. Antiqu.* vol. XXX. 16–17.

(21) *Peripl.* 49, 56, 28. Mitra, *op. cit.* 101. Apparently European tin, like copper, coral, and storax, was sent to Cane and reshipped thence to India:—*Peripl.* 28, 27. Schoff, ad *Peripl.* 127.

(22) Borlase, *Tin Mining in Spain*, 15 ff. Pliny XXXIV. 156 ff., 163. III. 30. M. Cary, *J. Hellen. Stud.* 44, 1924, 167 ff. Cagn.-Laf. *I.G.R.* I. 26. *C.I.L.* II. 496; XIII. 625, 632, 4337, 6851, 2448, 1945, 5154; XII. 3072 etc.; III. 14148. 8. *E.E.* IX. 1262 (Cornwall). *Rev. Ét. Anc.* 1920, p. 50. Sulp. Sev. *Dial.* I. 3 (Gaul—Egypt in 30 days in merchant-ship). Pallad. *H.* I. 14. Sen. *Q.N.* Prol. 11. Lucian, *Hermotim.* 4. Leontius, *Vita J. E.* 3, 13, 15. Bronze remains in India:—*Archaeol. Surv. Ind.* XXXVIII. 1. 73 etc.

(23) Hirth, 249–252.

(24) *Peripl.* 49, 56. Smith, *Fine Art*, 279, 301.

(25) V. A. Smith, 463. Pillai, p. 38.

(26) *Peripl.* 39 (apparently for the king), 49; the silver ware would be made in Capua, Noricum, Rhaetia, Dalmatia, but above all Alexandria—Rostowzew, *Soc. and Econ.* 69, 71, 73.

(27) *Peripl.* 36.

(28) Pliny XXXVII. 30–51. Hirth, 73. Sten Konow thinks (*J.R.A.S.* 1912, 379–385) that epigraphic evidence suggests journeys of Goths: Baltic—Rome—India for amber-trade. *Arch. Surv. Ind.* XV. 20.

(29) *Peripl.* 39, 49, 56. Cosmas XI. 449 B. *Arch. Surv. Ind.* X. 428.

(30) Within the Empire and to the north of it Campanian glass (especially coloured glass) was in greater demand than Syrian and Alexandrian—Rostowzew, *Soc. and Econ.* 71.

(31) Charlesworth, 29, 51, 279. Hirth, 228–234. *Ind. Antiqu.* LII. 304. *Mém. concernant les Chinois*, II. 46. A. Williamson, *Journeys in N. China, etc.* I. 131. Rostowzew, *Ir. and Gr.* 233; id. *Soc. and Econ.* 513. *Burlington Magaz.* 1922, 235–7 (Pl. p. 250). R. Mitra, *Antiqu. of Orissa*, I. 101. Glass found in India: *Arch. Surv. Ind.* XXXVIII. 1, 73, cp. 1911–12, p. 94, 1914–15, 24. *Encycl. Brit.* s.v. *Glass*, fin. (quoted); *Khotan.*

(32) Strabo XVII. 1. 7. *C.I.L.* XIV. 102 (2nd cent. A.C.), 448 (Ostia). We must not exaggerate Italy's unproductivity—Rostowzew, *Soc. and Econ.* 69.

(33) Pliny XII. 84.

(34) Pliny VI. 101. Hirth, 42, 45, 226–8.

(35) Dio Chrys. *Or.* LXXIX. 5–6, Arnim. He does not include the Seres; so Pliny's Seres of XII. 84 may well be Cheras.

(36) Salvioli, 280. Trade with Arabia and Africa was largely by barter.

(37) Marquardt, *Röm. Staat.* II. 266. T. Yoshida, *Entwickelung des Seidenhandels*, 8–9. Nissen, *Verein*, H. 95, 1894, p. 19.—Ten or twelve times as much in 19th cent.—supplies of silver much greater. Friedländer II. 319; see also Beloch, *Jahr. f. Nationalök. u. Stat.* 1899, p. 631, n. 5.

(38) See Chwostow, 408–410. Hirth, 227–8. W. S. Davis, *Influence of Wealth in Imperial Rome*, 88. Beloch, *op. cit.* 631. Friedländer II. 319–320.

(39) Tac. *Ann.* XII. 53. 5; XIII. 42. Dio Cass. LX. 34, 4. Schol. ad Juv. IV. 81 (Crispus) etc.

(40) *Peripl.* 39, 49, 56.

(41) *Peripl.* 47.

(42) Philostrat. *Apollon.* II. 7 (trans. F. C. Conybeare).

(43) *Peripl.* 49.

(44) For a list of these coins see Sewell, *J.R.A.S.* 1904, pp. 623–637.

(45) Thurston, *Madras Gov. Centr. Mus. Cat.* 2, pp. 11–12; cp. 16. Slashed coins—*Num. Chron.* 1898, 304 ff., 320 (now in Brit. Mus.). They were probably cut to put them out of circulation after the decline of the Roman Empire in the third century.

(46) Thurston, *op. cit.* p. 7.

(47) Logan, *Malabar*, I. 269. d'Alviella, 59. The Greeks used δηνάριον as a name for both gold and silver; after the decline of Rome and Roman silver, the Indians found only Roman gold to be of any value and so 'dinar' in Indian records came to mean a gold coin.

(48) Thurston, *op. cit.* p. 22. *J.R.A.S.* 1904, p. 636.

(49) G. F. Hill, *R. Hist. Coins*, p. 171. *Numism. Chron.* 1898, p. 319. Momms.-Blac. III. 337–8. Eckhel VI. 171. In the Coimbatore district 131 of them have been noticed.

(50) Chwostow, 402, in Rostowzew, *Soc. and Econ.* 513. Denarii of Tiberius (apparently) in Ceylon—*J.R.A.S.* 1905, 156 ff.

(51) Sewell, *op. cit.* 633, 636–7, and pp. 121 and 123–4 of this book.

(52) Id. 590, 599–602.

(53) Sewell's theory implies the belief that Indian trade had to do with the city of Rome alone rather than with the urban and country populations of the whole Empire. It is true that silk, nard, pepper and perhaps all Indian wares went chiefly to Rome and Italy.

(**54**) Chwostow, 400–3.

(**55**) Smith, 225. Chwostow, 225–6.

(**56**) Hill, *op. cit.* 168–171.

(**57**) Chwostow, 402. Rostowzew, *op. cit.* 513.

(**58**) *Hist. Aug.* '*Firm.*' 3.

(**59**) Cosmas XI. 339.

(**60**) Momms.-Blac. III. 70–1.

(**61**) *Peripl.* 60.

(**62**) Paus. III. 12. 24. Should we read silver for bronze?

(**63**) Philostrat. *Apollon.* III. 35; VI. 16.

(**64**) Chwostow, 418, 420. *Hist. Aug.* '*Firm.*' 3.

(**65**) Cosmas XI. 338.

(**66**) See *Ann. of Archaeol. and Anthropol.* VII. 51–66, cp. *Numism. Chron.* 1910, p. 333.

(**67**) Milne, 25.

(**68**) *Camb. Hist. Ind.* I. 583–4, 702–3.

(**69**) See Smith, 270. Sewell, *op. cit.* 596, 620–1. *Ind. Antiqu.* XLVII. 74–5. *J.R.A.S.* 1908, 550, 551; 1912, 785–7; id. *Bomb. Br.* LXII. 1907, 223–244. Rapson, *Ind. Coins*, pp. 9, 16, 20, §15, §66, and Pl. II. No. 9. *J.R.A.S.* 1903, p. 30, n. 1, vol. XL. 179. Gardner, *Catal. of coins of Gk. and Scyth. Kings of Bactria and Ind. in B.M.* Pl. XXV. 1–5. *Ind. Antiqu.* XXXVII. 41; XXXIV. 252. *J.R.A.S.* 1907, 1029, 1042–4. *Peripl.* 38, 47. *Camb. Hist. Ind.* vol. I. 560–2, 583–4, 702–3. Every attempt at chronology must be uncertain.

(**70**) Smith, 270, cp. Rapson as cited, id. 70. Continued under the earlier Guptas—id. 91 (gold).

(**71**) Kennedy, *J.R.A.S.* 1912, 989 ff. Jevons, 40. Del Mar, *Prec. Met.* 17–20.

(**72**) *Peripl.* 36.

(**73**) *J.R.A.S.* 1912, 986. See also above, on Trajan. Smith, 271.

(**74**) Brought during the 'Second' Triumvirate, concludes Chwostow, pp. 220–1. Perhaps *via* Persian Gulf or by land—id. 222.

(**75**) Sewell, *op. cit.* 620–1. Smith, 270–1; id. *Fine Art*, 101.

(**76**) *Ind. Antiqu.* XXXIV. 252. d'Alviella, 56. *Peripl.* 47.

(**77**) Discoveries of Roman coins in Central Asia and China are very rare; see above, p. 134.

(**78**) Pliny XII. 59.

(**79**) Lanciani, *Anc. R.* 248–250. *Rev. St John* xviii. Tiber trade in pearls, linen, silks, cinnamons, and unguents—all eastern.

(**80**) Dio Cass. LXII. 24. Jer. *Chron.* Ol. 217 (A.D. 92).

(**81**) Mart. IX. 59; X. 80.

(**82**) Juv. VI. 153–7.

(**83**) *C.I.L.* VI. 9207, 9212, 9221, 9214, 9239, 9418 f., 9544–9, 9795, 9935, 641, 1925, 5972; X. 6492; II. 496. *Cod. Theodos.* XIII. 4. 2. Prop. III. 18 (II. 24), 14. Juv. VII. 133. Jordan, *Topogr.* I. 2. 287–8, 476; II. 553.

(**84**) *C.I.L.* VI. 9433–6, 9544–9, 33872 etc. T. Frank, *Econ. H. of R.* 2nd ed. 243–4. Sen. *Fr.* XIII. 52. Gummerus in *Klio,* XIV. 151–3; XV. 263–5.

(**85**) *C.I.L.* VI. 9397 etc., 33885, 9258, 7882, 10299, 1060, 9405. Cic. *Brut.* LIII. 157. Isid. *Orig.* XIX. 6. *Dig.* L. 16, 234. Dessau, 7214.

(**86**) Aristophanes, *Frogs,* 542 and Schol. *ad loc.*; *Lysistr.* 729. Cic. *Verr.* I. 34. Athenae. I. 21. 50. 28 *b*; cp. XI. 11. 72. 486 *e.* Pliny XXIII. 144. Isid. XX. 11. 3. 'Virgil.' *Cir.* 440. Beds and chairs of Miletos—Athenae. XI. 72 = 486 *e.*

(**87**) Diodor. V. 13.

(**88**) *Hist. Aug.* '*Ver.*' 5. 3; cp. '*Claud.*' 17. Mart. IX. 59; X. 80. Prop. IV. 5. 2. Juv. VII. 133; VI. 156, 155.

(**89**) Pliny XXXVI. 40.

(**90**) Taxation in kind (A. W. Persson, esp. 19, 36–7) was, I think, the rule even in luxury articles in Roman Egypt. Cf. authorities in next note and in Rostowzew, *Soc. and Econ.* 536, n. 31.

(**91**) Rostowzew in *Arch. f. Pap.* IV. 314. *Philolog. Woch.* 1924, 1305. *Fay. Pap.* 93. *Grundz. u. Chrest.* I. 1 (ii) (*Chrest.*), 360–1. *Arch.* III. 192; cp. II. 443, Nos. 63–4; V. p. 314. *Amh. Pap.* 92–3. Kenyon, *Gk. Pap.* II. No. 280, pp. 193–4. *Tebt. Pap.* 35. *Grundz.* etc. I. 1 (ii), 368–375; cp. 360–2. *Arch.* III. 185 ff.; IV. 311. *Grundz.* etc. 321–2 (No. 273). Chwostow, 444 (seals). A. Schmidt, 111 ff., 98–9.

(**92**) Athenae. XV. 38 = 688–9. Paus. IX. 41. 7; X. 32. 19. Pliny XIII. 20 ff. Galen X. 942; VI. 439, 440, 426; cp. XII. 429, 604; X. 79. 1 etc. Hirth, 74. Syria and unguents: West in *Amer. Philol.* 1924, 164–5, 179. Nard and casia oil in Syria: Duchesne, *Lib. Pont.* 177, 179.

(93) Dio Cass. LXVII. 14. Stat. *S.* IV. 3. Mart. I. 87. 2; III. 82. 6; XI. 15. 6. Juv. VIII. 86. Athenae. *l.c.*

(94) *C.I.L.* VI. 1974. Hor. *Ep.* II. 1. 269–270. Cp. Sat. II. 3. 228.

(95) Pseudo-Ascon. ad Cic. *Verr.* I. 154. Schol. ad Hor. *Sat.* II. 3. 228–9, cp. id. *Ep.* I. 20. 1; II. 1. 269. Jordan I. 2. 476; II. 553.

(96) Daremb.-Sagl. s.v. *Unguentum.* Dessau II. 7606–15.

(97) *C.I.L.* III. 5816; V. 324, 774 etc.; V. 6777, 7378?; VI. 1926, 9977–8, 6852, 9972, 7647, 9979 etc. Procop. *Hist. Arc.* 25. *Cod. Just.* X. 48. 7. *C.I.L.* III. S. I. 1949. 28, 17–30 etc. Silk of Syria, cp. Lucan X. 141. Antonin. Mart. 2; perhaps Dio Chrys. LXXIX. 1.

(98) Chwostow, 151. Hirth, 71, 80, 257–8.

(99) Forrer, *Röm. u. Byz. Seiden-Textil.* 11–12, 25 ff. *C.I.L.* VI. 9891–2, 9678; XIV. 371–2, 2793, 2812. *C.I.G.* 5834 (ignoring Boeckh's reading συριγγοποιός). Waddington, 1854. Sen. *Fr.* XIII. 52. Blattiarii dyed silk purple—*Cod. Theod.* XIII. 4. 2. (ed. Mommsen I. 2, p. 746).

(100) Transport was costly in Indian seas and even in Egypt, but much less so in the Mediterranean.

(101) Stat. *S.* III. 3. 86–98. Port-dues were generally less than they are now.

(102) Tac. *Ann.* XIII. 50.

(103) Chwostow, 375–7.

(104) Pliny VI. 84.

(105) *Dig.* XXXIX. 4. 16. 7. Dirksen, *Abh. d. K. Akad. d. W.* 1843, pp. 65–9.

(106) Schur in *Klio,* Beih. XV. 1923, pp. 46–8. Kennedy in *J.R.A.S.* 1916, 833.

(107) Rostowzew in *Arch.* IV. 310. Charlesworth, 63–4, 254.

(108) *Peripl.* 1. *C.I.G.* 5075. Levied also at other ports?

(109) *Peripl.* 4. Pliny VI. 172–4 (Adulis). *C.I.G.* id. Collectors at Syene—Wilck. *Ostr.* I. 276–8. *J. Rom. Stud.* 1917, 49–50.

(110) *Rev. Pap.* 52, 13 ff. (protective). *Peripl.* 19. Cp. Pliny XII. 64–5. Wilck. *Ostr.* No. 1363. See above. I hope to discuss the matter fully elsewhere.

(111) *Peripl.* 39, 44. *Camb. Hist. Ind.* I. 198 ff.

(112) See *Camb. Hist. Ind.* I. 210–211, 207 (*Ind. Antiqu.* XVI. 7–8, 50) (full details), 208, 215. Pillai, 16, 12, 24–6.

(113) Rostowzew, *Soc. and Econ.* 159–160.

(114) Chwostow, 358, 393, 397, 404–5. *Hist. Aug.* '*Firm.*' 3.

Reinaud, 242. Priaulx, 172–3. *J.R.A.S.* XX. 267. Epiphan. *Adv. Haer.*
42 = 66. 2.

(**115**) Chwostow, 405–7.

(**116**) Rostowzew, *op. cit.* x–xi. *C.I.L.* X. 1797, 1613.

(**117**) Pliny VI. 101. *Hou-han-shu*, 88; 28. *Chin-shu*, 16. Hirth,
42, 45.

(**118**) Cic. *ad Att.* V. 21. 12; *in Vat.* 12; *pro Fl.* 67.

(**119**) Momms. *Prov.* II. 86–7. B. Adams, *Law of Civ. and Decay*,
25–8.

(**120**) *Encycl. Brit.* s.v. *Money.* Cp. Friedländer IV. 574.

(**121**) Salvioli, 221, 31, 153.

(**122**) T. Frank, *Econ. H. of R.* 166 ff., 199 ff., 215–216.

(**123**) Different views:—Rodbertus, *Jahrb. f. Nationalök.* IV. 341.
Bücher, *Entsteh. d. Volkswirtsch.* 1904, 117. Salvioli, esp. 31, 153, 221.
E. Meyer, *Kl. Schriften*, 79 ff., 169 ff. Rostowzew, *op. cit.* 302–5.

(**124**) Salvioli, 229–230. Rostowzew, *op. cit.* 65.

(**125**) Id. 142 ff.

(**126**) Absence of capitalistic industry Rostowzew attributes to
lack of real competition. In the cities and country-districts of the
Empire (the real markets) the rich were few while the much larger
and poorer classes ever grew more numerous, id. 305.

(**127**) Id. 327 ff. The ruling classes in the cities, and the imperial
bureaucracy of the state dependent on them absorbed the state
resources.

(**128**) A. Del Mar, *Prec. Met.* 61 ff., 122.

(**129**) Id. 88–92.

(**130**) Jevons, 24.

(**131**) See Mattingly, *Coins of R.E. in B.M.* vol. I. xxii. n. 3.

(**132**) W. Jacob, *Prec. Met.* I. 225, 237. *Encycl. Brit.* s.v. *Money.*

(**133**) Chwostow, 411.

(**134**) Id. 434–5.

CONCLUSION

(**1**) King, *E.G.* 59–62, 64, 67. Mart. *Spect.* 6. Lassen III. 397–
412?; and see above.

(**2**) Chwostow, 145.

(**3**) Rawlinson, 177–8. Nothing is proved. For transmission of religious stories between India and the West see Kennedy, *J.R.A.S.* 1912, 209 ff. and 469 ff.

(4) *Encycl. Brit.* s.v. *Pantaenus.*

(5) Rawlinson, 169–171. A. B. Keith, *The Sanskrit Drama,* 57–68. *Pauly,* s.v. *India,* 1314–25.

(6) Smith, *Fine Art,* p. 101.

(7) For the Kushan coinage see above. *J.R.A.S.* .1904, 616; id. 1893, 717 ff. (astronomy); id. *Bombay Br.* I. 295–6. *J.A.S.B.* VI. 456. *Ind. Antiqu.* XXVIII. 109. A good summary of influences is in *Pauly,* s.v. *India,* 1314 ff. Cp. O. M. Dalton, *Byzantine Art and Archaeology,* 59 ff. G. N. Banerjee, *Hellenism in Ancient India. J.A.S.B.* 58, Pt. I, 107–197; 61, Pt. I, 50–76; 62, Pt. I, 84–7. d'Alviella, esp. pp. 32 ff. *Veröffentlich. d. Forschungsinst.* No. 5, 57 ff. Smith, *Fine Art,* 179, 275, 294, 352, 355, 360. *J.A.S.B.* 58. 1. 174etc. Fergusson, *Hist. of Ind. Architecture,* 181. Dahlmann, 90 ff.

(8) In Egypt the average load for a camel was not more than ten artabae of (for instance) wheat, and for an ass, three artabae. Neither animal could be hurried. Cf. Wilcken, *Ostr.* I. 355–7.

ADDITIONAL NOTES

P. 62. The more I study Rome's oriental trade the more am I convinced that references by Tamil poems to the Yavana, if not those of Muziris, at least those of Madura and Kaviripaddinam, and to the mart Saliyur, belong to the second rather than the first century.

P. 238. Since Pliny did not know that 'myrrhine' cups came from India, he probably alludes to crystal, not 'myrrhine,' cups when he speaks of drunkenness.

P. 274. Comparative scarcity of Roman coins on Arabian and E. African coasts is due to the permanent system of barter maintained, and to passing on of coins by Arabians and Africans to India.

P. 290. Melting down of Roman silver and perhaps gold in North India *only* may be reflected by finds, in North India *only,* of Indian gold and silver plate shewing Roman influence.

P. 293. The Tamil poem which speaks of the gold (not silver) brought by the Roman Greeks may reflect the cessation of the exportation of Roman silver and the continued maintenance of gold as the metal taken to India as coin.

P. 313. 'Roman industries, which were unable to compete with foreign luxuries brought from outside.' This statement does not give the whole case, because many of the luxuries from India were brought raw and were worked up within the Empire; so also with the exports from the Empire to India. But the statement is otherwise true.

APPENDIX

Page 15, line 30, *Periplus of the Erythraean Sea:* Suggestions have been made that this document belongs to the third century after Christ. J. A. B. Palmer, in *Classical Quarterly*, 1947, 137–40 thinks that political conditions in India indicated in the *Periplus* itself point to about A.D. 110–115. But convincing arguments for the first century are given by A. Dihle, *Umstrittene Daten: Untersuchungen zum Auftreten der Griechen am Roten Meer*. Wiss. Abh. d. Arbeits-Gemeinschaft f. Forschung d. Landes Nordrhein-Westfalen, 32 Opladen, 1965, chapter i, pp. 9–35.

Page 25, line 15, silk-traffic: Interruptions of international trade, with special reference to Chinese silk and the silk-routes, during the first century before Christ and several centuries after, may have been the ultimate cause of various upheavals extending from China to northern and western Europe. So argues F. J. Teggart in *Rome and China*, Univ. of California, 1939.

Page 27, line 29, shipwrecked "Indians": The alleged date was 67 B.C. The whole record, depending on Cornelius Nepos, is doubtful.

Page 37, lines 9 and 10, Seres in the meaning of Cheras [see index, s.v. Seres (meaning Cheras of India) for other references in this book]: This conjecture by Kennedy, (*J.R.A.S.*, 1904, 359 ff.) is frowned on but seems to me reasonable.

Page 37, line 29, Chinese (embassy): Even later alleged "Chinese" embassies to Rome are doubtful. M. P. Charlesworth, *Studies in Roman Economic and Social History* . . ., ed. P. R. Coleman-Norton, Princeton Univ., 1951, 140.

Page 39, line 25, basis of exchange: See below, note for page 279.

Page 43, line 24, freedman of Annius Plocamus: An inscription, a graffito, in Latin (the same is given in Greek) beside the road from Coptos to Berenice shows that, on the 5th July, A.D. 6, Lysa or Lysas, a slave of Publius Annius, came that way. This was thirty-five years before Claudius began to reign. If this Plocamus was the same man as the one recorded by Pliny, then he was engaged in oriental trade during many years. See D. Meredith, in *Journal of Roman Studies, XLIII*, 1953, 38.

Page 44, line 15, Hippalos: No conclusive evidence has been adduced for a really certain dating of Hippalos. Sir Mortimer Wheeler, in the light of his own discoveries at Arikamedu (see below, note for page 62) and of other considerations, gives good reasons for believing that Hippalus lived early in the first century after Christ and that full use of the monsoon winds came before the end of Augustus' reign in A.D. 14—Sir Mortimer Wheeler, *Rome Beyond the Imperial Frontiers*, London (Bell), 1954; Pelican Books, 1955, pp. 126 ff. = 153 ff.

Page 52, lines 29–30, *Periplus:* See above, note for page 15.

Page 56, lines 28 and 29, coin was exchanged: See below, note for page 279.

Page 56, line 32, Bombay: In an Andhra building at Kolhapur in Bombay province have been found a bronze Roman jug and a bronze statuette of a Greek or Roman god; a similar jug-handle was found at Akota (ancient Ankottaka), Baroda State; and a Graeco–Roman cameo at Karvan, Baroda. Cf. also discoveries at Nasik and Nevasa, below, note for page 112; Wheeler, *op. cit.* (Pelican Books) 180–181.

Page 56, last line; p. 57, line 6; p. 63, line 12, Andhra Kings: It is suspected that remains of many of the rouletted dishes found in India came from the West. Examples have been discovered on Andhra sites inland at Brahmagiri, Chandravalli, Maski, Kondapur and Amaravati, and at Sisupalgarh near Bhubaneswar (besides Arikamedu as described below). Cf. Wheeler, *op. cit.*, 150–153 = 179–182.

Page 57, line 6, Andhra King: See preceding note.

Page 58, line 25—page 62, Tamil poems: Besides V. Kanakasabhai Pillai, *The Tamils Eighteen Hundred Years Ago*, 1904, cf. also P. T. Srinivas Iyengar, *History of the Tamils . . . to 600 A.D.*, 1929; and *The Śilappadikaram* translated by V. R. Ramachandra Dikshitar, 1939.

Page 62, line 9, Poduce: About two miles south of Pondicherry is a tract on the east side of a lagoon caused by a former outlet of the river Gingee, a tract known locally as Arikamedu, near the village Virampatnam. After 1937 it was gradually revealed as an Indo–Roman trading-place partly by French and Indian investigators but mainly by Sir Mortimer Wheeler who in 1945 directed a careful excavation (by the Archaeological Survey of India) which was followed in 1947–1948 by further work conducted by J. M. Casal for the French authorities. The port began to rise about the end of the last century B.C. and reached its height about A.D. 50 and later. The Roman remains unearthed include many fragments of wine-jars (amphorae); many fragments of Italian mostly red-glazed ware made at Aretium or Arretium (Arezzo) and therefore called Aretine or Arretine (apparently first produced about 30 B.C. but not continued long after A.D. 45), some of them having the potters' stamps including one marked C. VIBI OF ("the workshop"— officina—"of Gaius Vibius") and another marked EVHOD (Euhodus); many fragments of rouletted dishes which look Western; some Roman glass; bits of two (and more?) Roman lamps; and one or two Graeco–Roman gems. Sir Mortimer Wheeler, in *Ancient India*, No. 2 (Delhi 1946) "Arikamedu with contributions by A. Ghosh and Krishna Deva", pp. 17 ff.; J. M. Casal, *Fouilles de Virampatnam-Arikamedu* (Paris, 1949), especially pp. 16 ff. Cf. also Sir Mortimer Wheeler, "Roman Contact with India, Pakistan, and Afghanistan", in *Aspects of Archaeology in Britain and Beyond:* Essays presented to O. G. S. Crawford, ed. W. F. Grimes (London 1951), pp. 345 ff.; and *Rome Beyond the*

Imperial Frontiers, 145 ff. = 173 ff.

Page 63, line 12, Andhra Kings: See above, note for page 56, last line.

Page 72, line 11, Mozambique: Doubtful relics of Graeco-Roman trade along east Africa are known. At Port Durnford, about 250 miles north east of Mombasa, have been found coins covering many centuries—one is Ptolemaic, one is of Nero, one of Trajan, two are of Hadrian, one is of Antoninus Pius, and about eighty are Roman coins of the fourth century after Christ. H. Mattingly, in *Numismatic Chronicle*, 5th series, XII, 1932, 175. This find may be significant; others are decidedly dubious. We can conclude nothing from a coin of Antoninus found at Zimbabwe, or from one of Constantine found in Madagascar.

Page 75, line 13, The *Milinda: The Questions of King Milinda* is a romance about Menander the famous Greek king of north-west India. The oldest extant version appears to belong to the early part of the first century A.D. T. W. Rhys Davids, *The Questions of Milinda*, II, 269. W. W. Tarn, *The Greeks in Bactria and India*, 1951, 414 ff. The latest translation into English is by I. B. Horner, *Milinda's Questions*, London, 1963. By Vanga is meant Bengal and by Alexandria presumably that in Egypt.

Page 82, line 26, A.D. 92: or earlier; H. J. Loane, *Industry and Commerce of the City of Rome*, 50; and in *Class. Phil.*, 1944, 10 ff.

Page 99, line 8, Maes Titianus: See M. Cary, in *Classical Quarterly*, XLIX = New Series VI, 1956, 130–134. He preferred to date Maes in the reign of Augustus, who died in A.D. 14.

Pages 99 and 100, Palmyra and trade with India: It may be that Palmyrene sculpture had an influence on Gandhara and Palmyrene textiles and jewellery on those of India.— A. C. Soper, "The Roman Style in Gandhara" in *Amer. Journal of Archaeology*, IV, 1951, 311; M. Rostovtzeff in *Revue des Arts Asiatiques*, VII, 1931-1932, 209; H. Seyrig,

"Ornamenta Palmyrena Antiquiora" in *Syria*, XXI, 1940, 305 ff. Some pieces of silk found at Palmyra may have been imported already woven from China, but this is not provable.

Page 107, line 13, Ptolemy; use of the word ἐμπόριον: On this point cf. Wheeler, *Rome beyond the Imperial Frontiers* pp. 124–125 = 151–152; J. A. B. Palmer in *Classical Quarterly*, 1951 (N.S., 1), 156 ff.

Page 110, lines 22 and 23, North and North-West India: (i) It must be remembered that the Indus and its tributaries, and Baluchistan and Makran, are now in Pakistan. In the northern part of this area, south-east of Peshawar, was Taxila (in Punjab) now known as Sirkap. It passed from Parthian to Kushan rulers, perhaps about A.D. 60–70. "Roman" things found there and nearby are naturally few but they have significance; they include two portrait heads and another head, all of stucco; a schist frieze; a bronze statuette (almost certainly made in Alexandria in Egypt) and probably others (to judge by their look), a decoration made of silver, bronze cooking vessels, a silver spoon, some gems and glass, a wine-jar, and a denarius of Vespasian. Sir John Marshall, *Excavations at Taxila*, 6 ff.; *Guide to Taxila*, 10 ff., 26 ff.; and his *Taxila*, 3 vols., 1951. In West Pakistan and Afghanistan examples of western art, or western influence, are frequent.

(ii) By the route from Bactra to India was a town now known as Begram, about forty-five miles north of Kabul. Here excavations made by the French Archaeological Mission to Afghanistan, 1936–1942, revealed a noteworthy quantity of things which apparently came from the Roman empire during the second century and the first half of the third A.D.: pieces of glass vessels from Syria or Egypt, bronze bowls, steelyard-weights, statuettes of bronze, jugs and other vessels of alabaster, medallions of plaster, and other objects. J. Hackin, *Recherches archéologiques à Bégram*, *Mémoires de la Délégation Archéologique Française en Afghanistan*, IX, 1939; R. Ghirshman, *Bégram*, Cairo, 1946.

On both Taxila and Begram cf. also Wheeler, *Rome Beyond the Imperial Frontiers*, 157 ff. = 187 ff.

Page 110, line 16, Ptolemy's account of Indian regions: See now J. O. Thomson, *History of Ancient Geography*, 1948, 301–306; E. A. Johnston, *Journ. of the Royal Asiatic Society*, 1941, 208–222.

Page 112, line 19, Nasik: Some red-glazed pottery of Mediterranean look has been found at Nevasa about a hundred miles from Bombay (and apparently at Nasik also) and also remains of several Graeco–Roman amphorae. Wheeler, *op. cit.* (Pelican Books), 180.

Page 114, lines 8 ff.; Coimbatore: See pp. 280–284 (coins) and note for pages 280–284.

Page 123, line 21, circulation; page 124, line 14, currency: This may not be right—see below, note for page 279.

Page 126, line 32, Cochin China; page 127, lines 4, 26 and 28, Gulf of Siam; and page 156 (foot) Indo-China: It must be remembered that this book was first published long before Siam, Annam, and Cochin China were transformed so that Siam became Thailand, and Annam became Vietnam (which includes Cochin China) and Laos. But the old names except Cochin China are still used as before. Traces of Graeco–Roman commerce with these distant regions have been found recently. (i) By the delta of the river Mekong, about fifteen miles from the coast of the Gulf of Siam, is the ancient site known as Oc-eo. Here, with copious eastern remains, have been found a gold coin of Antoninus Pius and one of Marcus Aurelius, and some gems which may be Roman. The excavations begun by M. L. Malleret in 1944 were hindered by war. *Bulletin de l'École Française d'Extrême-Orient*, XLV, fasc. 1 (Paris, 1951) 75 ff. (ii) About forty miles up the river Mekong a site near P'ong Tuk has yielded a rather fine Roman lamp of bronze. Cf. G. Coedès in *Journal of the Siam Society*, XXI, 3 (Bangkok, 1928) 204 ff. It may be of quite late date. Cf. Wheeler, *Aspects of Archaeology in Britain and beyond:* Essays presented to O. G. S. Crawford (London,

1951) ed. W. F. Grimes, 361. For Ptolemy on south-east Asia
see J. O. Thomson, *Hist. of Anc. Geography*, 313 ff.; A.
Berthelot, *L'Asie ancienne centrale et sud-orientale d'après
Ptolémée*, 1930.

Page 130, lines 10 and 11, Chinese annals: The passage
referred to here says that the Romans made coins of gold
and silver and traded honestly (there were "no double
prices"), with tenfold profit, with An-hsi (Parthia) and
T'ien-chu (India); that "their Kings always desired to send
embassies to China, but the An-hsi wished to carry on trade
with them in Chinese silks, and it is for this reason that they
were cut off from communication". Then follows the account
of the embassy from Marcus Aurelius in A.D. 166, which
brought ivory, rhinoceros-horns, and tortoiseshell. The
simplicity of these articles suggests a private trading-mission
rather than an official embassy; and their nature and the
approach of the "embassy" by way of Annam (now Vietnam
and Laos) argue strongly for a belief that the mission had
come by sea. F. Hirth, *China and the Roman Orient*, 39 ff.
174–178. F. J. Teggart, *Rome and China*, 145. It is suspected
that fragments of glass found in Korea and elsewhere came
from the West; and other objects likewise found in China
may be Graeco–Roman. But the matter is uncertain. C. G.
Seligman, "The Roman Orient and the Far East", in
Antiquity, XI, 1937, 5 ff.

Page 139, line 26, Axumites, and last line, Ethiopians:
Cf. A. Dihle, *Umstrittene Daten* as cited above in note for
page 15, Chapters 2 (Christianity and the Axumites) and 3
(the name *Aἰθίοψ*).

Page 143, Dish found at Lampsacos: I would like to point
out that my identification of the animals shown rather
dimly on the dish is not certain, as has been pointed out to
me by Indians whose familiarity with Indian mammals and
birds is naturally much greater than mine.

Very attractive is the ivory statuette, of the Indian
goddess of good fortune and prosperity, found at Pompeii

whither it was doubtless brought, perhaps from the Kushan territories and perhaps through Barygaza (Broach—see especially pages 55–56 of this book) before the destruction of Pompeii in A.D. 79. A. Maiuri, "Statuetta eburnea di arte indiana a Pompei", in *Le Arti*, Florence, 1938—1939, pp. 111 ff.

Pages 180 ff., Spices: An important contribution to our knowledge of ancient Indian commerce is made by J. I. Miller, *The Spice Trade of the Roman Empire*, 29 B.C.–A.D. 641, Oxford, 1969.

Page 235, lines 2 and 3, precious stones from India: For Indian sources of semi-precious stones and beryl, see Wheeler, *Ancient India*, 2, 121–124.

Page 250, line 20, beryl: See preceding note.

Page 272, line 19: To this account of articles exported from the Roman empire to India should now be added further details of discoveries noted in this Appendix:— besides a good deal more glass, there are the remains of Arretine ware, other red-glazed ware, rouletted dishes, wine-jars, pieces of alabaster; also bronze jugs, bronze bowls, bronze cooking-vessels, a bronze lamp, and ornaments, decorations and so on in stucco and in metal.

Page 274, lines 6 and 7, silver was essential for small currency, and line 12, to create a Roman currency there: See below, note for page 279.

Page 277, lines 1 and 2, were exchanged profitably with the local currency: See below, note for page 279.

Page 279, line 17, monetary circulation, and line 30, creating a Roman currency: I was probably not right in concluding that the importation of Roman gold coins and Roman silver coins had as an object the creation of a Roman currency in India. Of the twenty-nine finds of Roman coins of the first century A.D. in India at least twenty were "hoards"; all the coins are of gold or silver, those of Augustus and Tiberius predominating in numbers, and the gold coins were often either pierced through to make a hung ornament, or slashed with a cut across the obverse—the "heads" side. Only one silver coin has been found to be similarly slashed. Although there was no native currency of gold and hardly any of silver in all peninsular India, the natural explanation of the "hoards" before they were "banked" or lost in some way, is not the desire to create a Roman currency, but provision of bullion to be weighed against articles of commerce to be exchanged, each "hoard" being probably a unit or set of units, each unit being the sum paid for a set of articles. When the trusted coinage of Augustus and Tiberius gave way to less reliable issues after Nero's debasement of the coinage in A.D. 63, and when also perhaps the Romans curbed export of coinage, exchange by barter largely superseded exchange by bullion. The slashing of the coins in six or more of the "hoards" (the mutilated coins include coins of Claudius, Nero, Vespasian, and Hadrian) must have had as its object cancellations by Indians to put the coins out of any sort of circulation. Wheeler, *Rome Beyond the Imperial Frontiers*, 164 ff. = 137 ff.; *Ancient India*, 2, 116 ff. Similar considerations about bullion may apply to the coins, mainly of Arcadius and Honorius, found in Ceylon (see pp. 123–124 of this book).

Pages 280 ff., Roman coins in India (and Ceylon): Some more finds have occurred since this book was first published. See revised list in Wheeler, *Ancient India*, 2, 116–121.

Pages 280–284, coins found in and near Coimbatore: See p. 114. The finds of coins point (i) to active overland trade between the Malabar coast and the eastern coast at Arikamedu (see note for page 62) through the Coimbatore gap, thus avoiding, if such action was desired or necessary, the sea-voyage round Cape Comorin; and (ii) to a natural concentration of the trade of the three Tamil kingdoms Chera, Pandya and Chola in the district Coimbatore where, according to a Tamil tradition, the three kingdoms met.

Page 284, line 17; 285, line 14, currency; 286, line 8; 294, line 15, circulation: See above, note for page 279.

Page 289, line 4; 292, lines 18–19; 293, line 29, Andhra coinage: In central India, mainly in Andhra territory, have been found imitations of Roman coins. They are mostly of terracotta and may have been gilded when made. Most of them when lost were being used or had been used as hung decorations or as other ornaments. At the Andhra town of Kondapur (Andhra Pradesh) were found at least twenty imitations of gold and silver coins of Tiberius; and other imitations have been found at Chandravalli (Mysore), Kolhapur (Maharashtra), Ujjain (Ozene to Greeks and Romans), Sisupalgarh, and elsewhere. Wheeler, *op. cit.*, Pelican Books, 181–182.

Page 298, lines 18–21; 299, line 1, gold coinage of Kadphises II: The gold coinage of the Kushan empire was the only native gold coinage in India of the first and second centuries and was, it seems, not reinforced by Roman importations of bullion. But the adoption of the Roman standard by the Kushans points to some competition with Roman gold. I have stated on page 299 that Kadphises II did not get his gold from the Roman empire. I still believe this to be right; but it has been suggested that as much Roman gold as possible was taken in by the Kushans from other parts of India in the form of *aurei* which were reminted and restruck as Kushan. It must be noted that the chronology of the Kushans is still a matter of doubt. Cf. Grousset, *Histoire de l'extrême Orient*, I, 61; F. J. Teggart, *Rome and China*, 115; G. Adhya, *Early Indian Economics*, 179 ff.

Pages 299 (foot)—300, Roman coins in northern India and in Afghanistan: See list in Wheeler, *Ancient India*, 2, 118–121.

INDEX

In many cases, the first reference in the narrative to an ancient geographical name is followed by the known or supposed modern identification.